A Biography of ROBERT BALDWIN

The Morning-Star of Memory

MICHAEL S. CROSS

OXFORD

UNIVERSITY PRESS

OXFORD
UNIVERSITY PRESS

Oxford University Press is a department of the University of Oxford.
It furthers the University's objective of excellence in research, scholarship,
and education by publishing worldwide. Oxford is a registered trade mark of
Oxford University Press in the UK and in certain other countries.

Published in Canada by
Oxford University Press
8 Sampson Mews, Suite 204,
Don Mills, Ontario M3C 0H5 Canada

www.oupcanada.com

Library and Archives Canada Cataloguing in Publication

Cross, Michael S., 1938–
A biography of Robert Baldwin : the morning-star
of memory / Michael S. Cross.

Includes bibliographical references and index.
ISBN 978-0-19-544954-9
1. Baldwin, Robert, 1804–1858. 2. Baldwin, Robert,
1804–1858—Psychology. 3. Politicians—Canada—Biography.
4. Lawyers—Canada—Biography. 5. Canada—History—
1791–1841. 6. Canada—History—1841–. 7. Canada—History—
1841–1867. I. Title.

FC471.B36C76 2012   971.04092   C2012-902399-X

Cover image: John Wycliffe Lowes Forster, *Hon. Robert Baldwin, CB,* oil on canvas, ca. 1906, Archives
of Onatario, 693205.

Printed and bound in the United States of America
1 2 3 4 — 15 14 13 12

She was a form of life and light
That seen, became a part of sight,
And rose, where'er I turn'd mine eye,
The morning-star of memory!
Yes, love indeed is light from heaven;
A spark of that immortal fire
With angels shared, by Alla given,
To lift from earth our low desire.

—Byron, **The Giaour**

Contents

List of Illustrations

Preface

This is an account of the life and times of a very strange but courageous man. Robert Baldwin lived a public life that was marked by great accomplishments. He was the primary agent in establishing the fundamental principle of the Canadian parliamentary system, responsible government. Robert Baldwin also lived a private life marred by self-doubt, pain both physical and mental, and the early loss of his emotional anchor, his wife Eliza.

Robert's present was always clouded by the past and the future. It is necessary, in telling his story, to blend past, present, and future if we are to understand how he lived his life. This narrative attempts to do that.

The birthing of this account makes elephant gestation appear mercurial. It has been many decades in the making. Somehow life kept getting in the way. The project began as a joint effort with Robert L. Fraser to write the entry for Robert Baldwin in the *Dictionary of Canadian Biography*. We hoped to continue the partnership in writing a full-scale biography. Alas, Bob was not able to continue, and I only sporadically pecked at the work. It was the encouragement of John Ralston Saul and the pleasure of discussing Baldwin with him that finally stirred me to get the job done.

Robert Fraser is owed the greatest debt, and I hope he feels the final result is worth his contributions. Colleagues at Dalhousie University and family members have been reduced to stupefaction by stories of Baldwin, and I thank them for their patience. Library and archives staffs have been invariably helpful and pleasant. A special thanks goes to Tania Henley of the Baldwin Room at the Toronto Reference Library. She guided me through the still uncatalogued boxes of documents that were recently donated by the Baldwin family. At various stages, the work was supported by grants from the Dictionary of Canadian Biography, Dalhousie University, and the Social Sciences and Humanities Research Council of Canada. Jennie Rubio of Oxford University Press has been a pleasure to work with.

My wife, Patricia De Méo, has been encouraging and loving these many years. She is my own morning-star.

Timeline

1771	Margaret Phoebe Willcocks, Robert Baldwin's mother, is born in Cork, Ireland.
1775	William Warren Baldwin, Robert's father, is born at Knockmore, near Cork, Ireland.
1799	Baldwin family arrives in Upper Canada.
1802	William Warren Baldwin moves to York.
1804	Robert Baldwin is born in York, 12 May.
1812	Upper Canada is embroiled in war between Britain and the United States.
1813	York burned by Americans, the Baldwins flee to the countryside, 27 April.
1819	Robert is head boy at Archdeacon John Strachan's school.
1820	Robert's younger brother Henry dies.
1820	William Warren Baldwin wins election to the Upper Canada Assembly.
1820	Robert joins his father's law office as a clerk.
1825	Robert falls in love with his cousin, Augusta Elizabeth Sullivan, his Eliza.
1825	Robert is called to the bar, 20 June.
1825	The Sullivan family sends Eliza to New York to frustrate her romance with Robert.
1827	Robert marries Eliza in St. James Church, York, 31 May.
1828	William Warren and Robert Baldwin protest the dismissal of Judge John Walpole Willis.
1828	Robert stands for election for York County and is defeated.
1828	Robert defends newspaper editor Francis Collins in a libel case.
1828	Robert and Eliza's first child, Phoebe Maria, is born.
1829	Robert wins a by-election for the town of York, but the result is invalidated for irregularities in the writ.
1830	Robert wins a new by-election, but is defeated in a general election that year.
1830	Robert and Eliza's second child, William Willcocks, is born.
1831	Their third child, Augusta Elizabeth, is born.
1834	Their fourth child, Robert, is born by Caesarian section, leaving Eliza in delicate health.
1834	York is renamed Toronto.
1835	Eliza goes to New York to recover.
1836	Eliza dies, 11 January.
1836	Robert joins the executive council of Upper Canada, 20 February.
1836	Robert resigns from Executive, 12 March, writes to Francis Bond Head to explain on 16 March.
1836	Robert leaves Toronto, 30 April, to travel to England and Ireland.
1836	Robert is in London, 8 June to 24 August, fails to get hearing from the Colonial Office.

1836   Robert stays in Ireland, September to December.

1836   Robert leaves for Canada, 20 December.

1837   Robert visits family in New York, 27 January to 1 February.

1837   Robert is back in Toronto, 10 February.

1837   Robert and John Rolph carry a flag of truce to William Lyon Mackenzie and the rebels north of Toronto, 5 December.

1837   Rebels march on Toronto, but are defeated by loyalists, 7 December.

1838   Robert defends rebels charged with treason.

1838   William Warren and Robert Baldwin have brief meeting with Lord Durham.

1838   Robert's letter to Durham explains the concept of responsible government, 23 August.

1839   Lord Durham's Report on the state of the Canadas.

1839   Francis Hincks opens communications with Lower Canadian liberals, 12 April.

1839   Charles Poulett Thomson, later Lord Sydenham, appointed Governor General.

1840   Robert becomes Solicitor General for Upper Canada, 14 February.

1841   The Union of the Canadas is declared, 10 February.

1841   Robert is elected for both Fourth York and Hastings, March–April.

1841   Government mob forces Louis LaFontaine to drop out of election for Terrebonne, Lower Canada.

1841   Robert dismissed as Solicitor General by Sydenham, 12 June.

1841   First session of the legislature of the Province of Canada, 14 June.

1841   Robert introduces resolutions on responsible government in the House of Assembly, 3 September.

1841   Lord Sydenham dies, 19 September.

1841   LaFontaine elected in Fourth York, Upper Canada, 23 September.

1842   Robert and LaFontaine become vice-presidents of the International Anti-Slavery Society.

1842   Sir Charles Bagot arrives as the new Governor General, 10 January.

1842   Second session of the Canadian legislature opens, 8 September.

1842   Robert and LaFontaine sworn into executive council, 26 September.

1842   Bagot seriously ill, November.

1843   Robert elected in Rimouski, Lower Canada, 30 January.

1843   New Governor General, Sir Charles Metcalfe, arrives in Kingston, 29 March.

1843   Bagot dies, 19 May.

1843   New session of legislature, 28 September.

1843   House votes to move capital to Montreal, November.

1843   Tory-Orange mob burns Robert in effigy in Toronto, 7 November.

1843   Executive councillors resign over Metcalfe's patronage policies, 25 November.

1844	William Warren Baldwin dies, 8 January.
1844	Reform Association of Canada formed, 6 February.
1844	George Brown establishes Toronto *Globe* as Reform newspaper, March.
1844	Francil Hincks establishes Montreal *Pilot* as Reform newspaper.
1844	Robert reveals to family his wedding ritual in memory of Eliza, 31 May.
1844	Robert attacked by Orange mob at Bradford, Upper Canada, June.
1844	Metcalfe dissolves Assembly, calls election, 23 September.
1844	Reformers defeated in election, but Robert wins Fourth York, November.
1844	First session of legislature in Montreal, 28 November.
1845	Tories try to build alliance with French Canadians.
1845	Metcalfe leaves Canada, November.
1845	Earl Cathcart appointed administrator of the province, 26 November, becomes Governor General in April 1846.
1846	House votes to recognize French language, 31 January.
1846	Britain repeals the Corn Laws that gave preference to Canadian grain.
1846	Tories try again to woo French Canada, June.
1846	Robert's speech at Dundas, Upper Canada, spells out Reform policy, 11 November.
1847	Irish famine migrants swamp British North America.
1847	Lord Elgin arrives as new Governor General, 29 January.
1847	Last Tory attempt to ally with French-Canadian liberals, February.
1847	Last session of the second Parliament, June.
1847	Robert is treasurer of the Upper Canada Law Society.
1848	Reformers win majority in the election, Robert wins Fourth York, January.
1848	First session of the third Parliament, 25 February.
1848	LaFontaine called to form new government, 7 March.
1848	Hincks lays out program for economic development to Executive, 20 December.
1849	Second session of third Parliament, 10 January.
1849	House passes Rebellion Losses Bill, 9 March.
1849	Robert's home in Toronto attacked during riots against William Lyon Mackenzie, 22 March.
1849	Robert and William Hume Blake reform court system.
1849	Elgin signs the Rebellion Losses Act, Montreal riots begin, 25 April.
1849	Baldwin and LaFontaine residences attacked by mob, 26 April.
1849	Robert and LaFontaine deliver address to Lord Elgin, Governor General attacked by mob, 30 April.
1849	Robert's Municipal Act passes House, 15 May.
1849	Robert's University of Toronto Act passes House, 18 May.
1849	Legislature is prorogued, 30 May.

1849   Attack on LaFontaine's house, 15 August.

1849   Annexation Manifesto published, 11 October.

1849   Declaration of removal of capital from Montreal to Toronto,
        14 November.

1849   Radical Reformer Peter Perry elected, 4 December.

1850   Markham convention launches the Clear Grit movement, 12 March.

1850   First session of legislature in Toronto, 14 May.

1850   Robert is treasurer of Upper Canada Law Society, to 1858.

1850   J.H. Price's resolutions on clergy reserves introduced in House, 18 June.

1851   Robert's daughter Eliza marries John Ross, 4 February.

1851   William Lyon Mackenzie elected to the House, April.

1851   Canada assumes control of its post office, April.

1851   Robert's mother dies, 15 May.

1851   Fourth session of the third Parliament, 20 May.

1851   Hincks forces Robert to accept municipal debts for railways, May.

1851   A majority of Upper Canadian members vote against Robert's Chancery
        Court, 26 June.

1851   Robert presents his resignation to LaFontaine and Elgin, 27 June.

1851   Robert's resignation speech to the House, 30 June.

1851   Robert is defeated in York North, 19 December.

1852   Robert declines his election as chancellor of the University of Toronto.

1853   Robert declines a judgeship.

1853   Robert has near-fatal illness that spring.

1854   Robert's grandson Robby is born.

1854   Robert made a Companion of the Order of the Bath.

1855   Robert declines to become chief justice of the Court of Common Pleas.

1855   Robert's daughter-in-law, Eliza, dies.

1856   Robert is president of the Upper Canada Bible Society.

1856   Robert's grandson Robby dies.

1858   Robert agrees to stand for election to the Legislative Council, then
        withdraws.

1858   Robert dies, 9 December.

1858   Robert's funeral, 13 December.

1859   Senior male family members carry out Robert's postmortem
        instructions, January.

1866   Robert's son Willcocks sells the Spadina estate.

1874   Robert is reburied at St. James's cemetery.

Chapter 1

The Blessed Hour,
January 1859

It was twenty-three years since Eliza was taken. Robert had finally found his rest.

Robert Baldwin had lived in the shadows since his retirement from politics in 1851. Only rarely was he seen in the streets of Toronto, a ghost-like figure who shocked old acquaintances by the pallor of his face and the debility of his body. He was forty-seven at retirement, but he was already worn into premature old age by responsibility, illness, and his everlasting grief.[1]

His one preoccupation was with his long-dead wife. He sat in her room at Spadina, the family home, organizing his papers and reading, over and over, the thirty-year-old letters from Eliza. Below the window, cut into the hillside, was the family burial vault. Throughout the last years of his life Robert carried in his waistcoat pocket a two-page memorandum. This wrinkled, stained little note was his anguished plea to the benevolence of strangers. In it he begged:

> that in the case it be God's will that I should be taken away suddenly . . . I may not be interred without my last injunction as to the operation mentioned being scrupulously complied with. And I earnestly entreat of those who may be about me when I die, both Physicians and others, that for the love of God, as an act of Christian charity, and by the solemn recollection that they may one day have themselves a dying request to make to others, they will not on any account whatever permit my being enclosed in my coffin before the performance of this last solemn injunction. And that, if from this memorandum not having been found in time, or other accident I may have been interred

without this request having been attended to they will see that I am disinterred for the purpose of complying with it, so that under no circumstances may my body be finally left to its repose in the grave till such operation has been performed upon it. And may the blessing of God rest with those who shall make it their business to see [to] this my request.[2]

He had been dead for a month, lying in the crypt at Spadina. Four men gathered in the vault during a bitter Toronto January. They were senior male family members—his son Willcocks, his brother William Augustus Baldwin, and his brother-in-law Lawrence Heyden—along with the family physician, Dr. James Richardson. They were there to honour Robert Baldwin's last request. Dr. Richardson grasped a scalpel with his numb fingers, and made an incision into the corpse's abdomen, "extending through the upper two thirds of the Linea Alba." Robert Baldwin was now complete, gone to eternity bearing the same surgical wound as his beloved Eliza, the scar of a Caesarean section.[3]

It was the culmination he had longed for since six o'clock on the morning of 11 January 1836 when Eliza had died. He had written then, "I am left to pursue the remainder of my pilgrimage alone—And in the waste that lies before me I can expect to find joy only in the reflected happiness of our darling children, and in the looking forward, in humble hope, to that blessed hour which by God's permission shall for ever reunite me to my Eliza in the world of Spirits."[4] Now he was no longer alone.

Chapter 2

Living in Memory

The past of family and marriage flowed through him. The future of his country and his solutions for it animated him. There was little room for the present.

Robert Baldwin lived in memory of the far and recent past, and he lives on in parliamentary memory of his great idea—responsible government. The far past was his family heritage in Ireland where the Baldwins struggled to find a middle way for that troubled country. Responsible government was the logical result of the Baldwins' approach to Ireland's dilemma, as Robert Baldwins' bicultural Canada was the heir to the Anglo-Irish dream. Robert visited the old homeland in 1836 and hoped it made him a better Irishman. It certainly made him a better Canadian.

The recent past was his immediate family. His memory was fresh with his father's call to duty, the obligation to serve that came with wealth and privilege. It was no small thing to be a Baldwin. That was emphasized at the family dinner, at the law courts where father and son attended the legal muse of order and stability, and in politics where they still sought that middle way. The more recent past was his Eliza, his morning-star. She was the one person who made him come fully alive, the one who appreciated him as a person, not a symbol of the family purpose. Her death in 1836 was the decisive moment of his life. Her memory sustained him, helped him deal with the political trials of his present. Yet his present was always seen through a distorted lens of her memory, where the past seemed more real than today. It was enticingly easy to abandon the present and retreat into memory. He would resign office again and again in frustration with the real world of politics.

Robert thought he was defending British ideals in the colony. Those ideals were bound up in the role of his social class, the landowners who had always represented order and duty in the British system of governance and social hierarchy. In reality, by the time he achieved political power in the 1840s, that system was itself only a memory in Canada. A new economic order was emerging that would alter both the political and social balance of power. His great reform of responsible government would empower a new class and sweep away his own social order.

Whatever changed, Robert Baldwin's legacy remained fresh. Responsible government provided Canada with a simple and reliable way to maintain the balance between strong government and responsive government. The alliance of French and English that he created and maintained through the difficult early years of the Union of the Canadas was the essence of nationhood.

⸺◈⸺

Upper Canada was a vast but sparsely populated place. When Robert was born in the small provincial capital of York in 1804, the nascent city had a few hundred people. The colony as a whole was home to fewer than 70,000. During his lifetime, the agricultural lands flourished and the towns thrived. By his death in 1858, Upper Canada had grown to more than one million people, at least 40,000 of whom lived in York, renamed Toronto in 1834. The outlines for the future province of Ontario were now clear.

Robert and his father, William Warren Baldwin, were important actors in the legal and political life of the colony. Sometimes, however, Robert was simply swept along by the tides of events. His family had to flee their homes when, in 1813, the American army surged into York and put much of the capital to the torch. In 1837, Toronto was threatened by a domestic army. A brief and badly planned rebellion, led by Toronto's first mayor, William Lyon Mackenzie, was routed, but it permanently altered the politics of the province. Robert and his father deplored the resort to arms as much as they deplored the arbitrary rule that sparked the rebellion. They took no part in either the uprising or the loyalist suppression of it. Yet Robert would be the beneficiary of the events. His moderate liberalism would become an attractive middle ground between autocratic Tory government and radicalism. His creation of a bicultural political party in alliance with his Lower Canadian counterpart,

Louis-Hippolyte LaFontaine, assured that it would be Robert's ideas that triumphed when a new political entity, the Province of Canada, merged Upper and Lower Canada in 1841.

He did not need to uproot the basic institutions to accomplish the reforms he contemplated; indeed, the colonial political structure is still apparent in Canada's governance. The Governor General and provincial Lieutenant-Governors are recognizable descendants of the colonial administrator. The federal Senate, like its colonial predecessor, the Legislative Council, is an appointed body with legislative functions. The House of Commons mirrors the former House of Assembly. The structure remains, up to the head of state, the English monarch. What Robert Baldwin did in the 1840s was to fill the colonial vessels with new wine. Responsible government was his constant goal, a simple reform but difficult to achieve. In essence, responsible government stripped the governor and the Legislative Council of the power to manage colonial affairs and gave it to the House of Assembly and an executive council (today's Cabinet). The Executive was responsible to the Assembly in that it could be driven from office by a vote of the Assembly members. Implicit in Baldwin's scheme was the idea of party government. Elections would be fought by clearly defined political parties and executives would be formed by the leaders of the party that won the most seats in Parliament.

This was not democracy. Most of the population was still denied the vote, since the franchise was limited to landowners and those who paid substantial rent, and it excluded all women. Baldwin was opposed to democracy as an American innovation that would debase politics and betray British tradition. His reform was, all the same, the first step toward modern democratic government. Wise as he was, Robert could not foresee that once he had opened the floodgates, there was no stopping the rush of change.

For the last twenty-two years of his life, Robert dwelled in the past with his dead wife. He created, more than anyone else, Canada's political future of responsible government and biculturalism. It was the present in which it was difficult for him to exist. Robert was always shy and uncertain, uncomfortable in the public life that his father had decreed for him. After Eliza's death, he suffered from chronic depression, if not more serious mental issues. Nineteenth-century medicine had no cure for his illness, or even a diagnosis of it. Yet a remarkable vision emerged from his troubled mind.

Robert told his father that he was content that historical memory should judge his career.[1]

Let it be so.

Chapter 3

I Am Not So Certain of My Future as Others Seem to Be

Eliza had been dead for five years and five months. She was still his beacon to a happier day. She was still with him, helping and encouraging him. It was June 1841.

Resignation was Robert Baldwin's usual course when reality could not be shaped to his principles, when he and others could not achieve the perfection that his nature demanded. But it was a course lined with pain. That pain stabbed at him as he paced his plain room in Olcott's lodging house. The humid early summer night in Kingston was as stifling as his thoughts. Intractable reality wrestled him to his knees and he prayed for guidance.[1]

It was the night of 12 June 1841. Two days earlier Robert had suffered a humiliating interview with Governor General Sydenham. Robert had gone to Government House full of purpose and moral certainty to challenge Lord Sydenham, to compel the governor to accept unequivocally the principle of responsible government. Instead, Sydenham had seized the initiative. Baldwin could barely get in a word as Sydenham launched his attack. Baldwin's principles were self-serving cant, his honour had been compromised by his dealings with politicians of dubious loyalty. Sydenham struck at every Baldwinian sensitivity. Robert was left almost speechless and he fled Government House in confusion. During the long cab ride back to town, he thought about what to do, his doubts punctuated by every clop of the horse's hooves. Now, after agonizing over the implications for two days, he was left with only one course of action: to resign from office. Without a party to follow him, with the mercurial French Canadians as his only substantial allies, it was a dangerous and painful course.

The Union of Upper and Lower Canada had once seemed the solution to the political problems with which Baldwin wrestled. It was the instrument that would accomplish responsible government and bring peace and prosperity to the colony. Yet it had gone terribly wrong. Once again he had put his faith in institutions and overlooked the influence of men, which was not surprising for one who found it so much easier to understand institutions than to fathom men. He had thought of Lord Sydenham as an ally, the representative of the British institutions that Baldwin trusted implicitly. He was wrong. Those institutions were guided by real men with real ambitions, none more ambitious or more cunning than Lord Sydenham. To achieve his goals, Sydenham wove a web of power and deceit within the institutions imported from Britain. But Baldwin saw only the gleaming form of British government, not the enemy within it.

———•✦•———

To confront a British governor was painful, for it was to challenge in surrogate the Britain that was so truly the home country for Robert Baldwin. It was all the more difficult because there was so much in Lord Sydenham that reminded Robert of his own father—the flamboyance, the confidence, the wide-ranging talents. And as with his father, Sydenham's towering presence filled Robert with self-doubt. He was left wondering whether he should leave public life, a life he thought he was "not at all calculated for."[2]

Yet it was public life for which he had been raised. The Baldwins had a political history stretching back to Cork in Ireland where Robert's great-grandfather had risen from sheriff to mayor of the city between 1730 and 1737. In the 1780s the Baldwins were in the thick of the fight for parliamentary reform in Ireland. The defeat of prospects for reform, and the inexorable decline in the Irish economy, led Robert's grandfather— "Robert the Emigrant" as he was known in family history—to seek better economic and political prospects in Canada.[3]

The dream of political reform and the centrality of the family, these were the articles of the Baldwin faith. In October 1797, the family set off for British North America to make the faith real in the New World. The adventure began badly with three false starts thanks to storms, illness, and an unreliable captain. The caprices of nature and men were finally overcome and the packet ship *Grantham* carried them safely to New York in June 1799. From there they made their way by bateau up the Hudson and the Mohawk rivers and across Lake Ontario to York, Upper Canada, arriving on 13 July. The homely little town, its seventy-odd houses scattered over a plain on the shore of Lake Ontario, gave scant notice of its future as the city of Toronto and as the political arena where Robert Baldwin would triumph—and fail.

The family took up land some eighty kilometres east of York in Clarke Township, Durham County, to satisfy Robert the Emigrant's passion to be a farmer, albeit a gentleman farmer. The oldest of his sons, however, craved a more urbane environment. William Warren Baldwin was twenty-four when the family came to Canada, and a medical graduate of the University of Edinburgh. Family obligation bound him to the farm in Clarke, but the prospect of a medical practice, and a more exciting life, drew him to York. By 1802 the farm was well established and he was able to settle into the town and move among the provincial capital's elite. In this little world personal ties were all and the family was the most important instrument of advancement. Fortunately the Baldwins had come from Ireland armed with introductions to well-placed people in Upper Canada. Thanks to this entree, William was able to move into the Duke Street home of William Willcocks, cousin of one of the leading governmental figures, Peter Russell.[4]

"Muddy York," as it was derisively called, was no metropolis except in the political sense. For the ambitious, such as William Warren Baldwin, that was enough. He could look beyond the muddy ruts that passed for streets, beyond the drabness of unpainted and whitewashed buildings, look beyond them to the promise of the provincial capital. As the colony grew, the capital would grow with it and so would the influence and the wealth of the well-connected. Already there was emerging in the little town a provincial elite, an elite of power around the chief office holders of the government. This group, which would later be stigmatized as the "Family Compact," would gradually add wealth to power by rewarding itself and its coterie with land grants and well-paying offices. William Warren Baldwin could not become part of the Compact; his liberal political views were incompatible with the deep conservatism of the provincial elite. But his personal connections, in Ireland and in

Canada, his education, his aristocratic bearing, all combined to assure him a prominent place in the little society of York.

He looked the part he would play. He was both robust and elegant, a heavy-set but graceful figure. A receding hairline made the massive forehead even more prominent, emphasizing the impression of a man of ideas. The face was handsome and strong, but the pouting lips perhaps betrayed the self-importance that fuelled his sense of certainty in everything he undertook. He had talents to buttress that certainty. He had been a brilliant student at Edinburgh, achieving accolades along with his medical degree at age twenty-two. In Upper Canada he would succeed at several careers, first as a doctor, then as a teacher of the children of the elite at his own school in York, as a lawyer, even as an amateur architect. Swatting up the subject in his spare time, William became accomplished enough at architecture to design York's jail and courthouse, and its most striking building, Osgoode Hall, headquarters of the Law Society. His talents were prodigious and so was his ego. Much of his importance in provincial politics flowed from his self-confident assurance in the correctness of his ideas and, even more, in the special destiny of the Baldwins. Those who did not accept the rightness and importance of William and his family could expect scorn or ridicule, or sometimes deadly fury. It was no surprise to find him, in 1812, taking offence at some real or imagined slight delivered him in court by the acting Attorney General of the province, John McDonell. William challenged McDonell to a duel on Toronto Island, an affair which fortunately passed off bloodlessly. There clearly was nothing bloodless about William Warren Baldwin, however. He was larger than life and he would loom over his children, even after death.[5]

William quickly consolidated his position in York. In 1803 he married William Willcocks's daughter, Margaret Phoebe. Like William, Phoebe was Irish born, some four years older than her new husband. She was intelligent, strong-minded, and inclined to be severe in her dealings with others. She was also heiress to the social position, political power, and wealth of the Willcocks-Russell clan. The marriage helped to consolidate William's position. He had already found a more lucrative profession than pioneer medicine when he was called to the bar of Upper Canada earlier that year. More lucrative yet were the bonds of family.

In 1806 Peter Russell, executive councillor and great landholder, made provision for his property to pass first to his sister, Elizabeth, and then to William Warren Baldwin's eldest son. Russell died in 1808 and Elizabeth had use of the estate, the value of whose land was steadily increasing, until her death in 1822. The Russell fortune then fell to the Baldwins. A contemporary estimate was that the Baldwins inherited some 20,000 hectares of prime Upper Canadian land.[6]

The heir to this largesse was born in his father's house at Palace (later Front) and Frederick Streets on 12 May 1804. Robert Baldwin inherited a place in the provincial elite and, more important, in his family. From birth to death he lived in an extended family of Russells and Baldwins. Often living within the same household and almost always within a short walking distance of each other, his family supplied the emotional support, the political counsel that Robert needed, but also the unrelenting obligation to be a Baldwin. This small world into which he was born was a closed circle; with few exceptions he would not become close to anyone outside the bounds of the family. It was, nevertheless, often a nourishing circle. His mother lavished attention on him and marked his psychology indelibly. He would later refer to her as "the master mind of the Family." When he was small, his grandfather and his Aunt Maria doted on him. Elizabeth described a visit from the four-year-old Robert: "He is very noisy and unruly. His grandfather and Maria spoil him by humouring him."[7]

Elizabeth Russell's home was the hub of this small elite. She spent much of her day entertaining at tea, at dinner, in the evening. Her visitors were the cream of this very sparse crop. Peter Hunter and Alexander Grant, the men who administered the province in the absence of governors, were regulars as was Lieutenant-Governor Francis Gore. Among her most frequent guests was her nephew William Warren Baldwin, who was also both friend and family doctor. Elizabeth was generous to the Baldwins, seeing to young Robert when his parents were absent or when the boy's mother, Phoebe, was ill as she was for an extended period in the early months of 1806. The toddler began his involvement with the Upper Canadian elite there in Russell Abbey on the eastern end of town, where the government and legal structures gathered near the harbour. Not yet two years old, he was shy when introduced by Miss Russell to leading figures in the government. He was far from shy in exploring the house and grounds, however, and had the usual scrapes associated with curious children. Elizabeth found him too much for her in April 1806, fearing he would take another tumble while in her care. She was probably relieved when Phoebe was well enough to resume supervision of the boy. A year later he was still alarming her with his penchant for injury. He was sporting a cut under his eye from a fall when she saw him in May 1807.[8]

Even a small child was affected by the harshness of early nineteenth-century existence. Robert had the common childhood afflictions, but his mother was often ill and his younger brother suffered greatly. Augustus William was born in 1805 with poor prospects from the beginning. He was sickly and deformed with a very large head and protruding eyes. William Warren Baldwin had dropped in to see Elizabeth on the evening of Saturday, 26 April 1806 when a breathless servant arrived to call him home. Little William, just short of six months old, was desperately ill. He died the next day.[9]

Still, Robert was an active and happy boy. He was good natured and playful, an ordinary child in all apparent ways. The boisterous and happy four year old gave little evidence of the dour, self-contained adult Robert was to become. The realities of nineteenth-century life made their contributions to the change from boy to man. One of those realities was death. There were five brothers. Augustus William died as an infant in 1806. Henry died at thirteen in 1820. Quetton St. George died at nineteen in 1829. Elizabeth Russell commented on the death of Robert's grandmother Phoebe Willcocks in 1807 that, even then, the Willcocks-Baldwin clan seemed fated to tragedies with five deaths in the immediate family within three years. Of the Baldwin children, only Robert and William Augustus, four years his junior, lived to adulthood. Although these were the calamities that all families endured, they cast permanent shadows over domestic existence. Robert felt the tragedies more than most. His father was struck by the intensity of Robert's emotions, and the shallowness of his own, when a relative died in 1834. "Robert grieves heavily—indeed I seem amongst them [the family] not to feel as much—as much as I ought . . . and yet I seem to myself quite hard—when I witness the distress around me—what strange comportment is Mine—I really know nothing of myself—I wish a friend could tell me—and yet I would shrink from his candour."[10]

The father's insensitivity shaped his son. As Robert matured, William Warren treated him more as an heir to property and ideas than as a child to be comforted and loved. He set Robert's life course and life goals without considering Robert's wishes or needs. Yet, certainly, William Warren took great pride in the little boy. Robert trailed after his father to the law office, to court, to political meetings, for William Warren loved to display his heir and to educate him in the responsibilities of a Baldwin. Robert was sent to the best school in the province: the Home District Grammar School. Operated by the Anglican rector of York, John Strachan, the school was the training ground for the provincial elite. While Robert studied there, the school moved from its humble rented premises to a large blue wooden building on College Square, between Richmond and Newgate (now Adelaide) Streets in the heart of the town, a building and location that better proclaimed the importance of the academy. William Warren followed Robert's education closely and was delighted to boast in 1818 that his son was the best classics scholar, indeed "the most advanced boy in the school." But he looked far beyond Robert's education in the classics. The boy's future was laid out for him. "I shall keep him yet two more years at school with Doctor Strachan." William Warren Baldwin told his brother, "I intend please God to bring him up to the bar." What Robert might want probably never occurred to either of them.[11]

It was a warm and close-knit family despite the father's aloofness. Three generations lived together in a house at Front and Bay Streets, where the family had moved in 1807. The grandfather, Robert the Emigrant, had been a widower since 1791 and when he grew too frail for life on the farm in Clarke township in 1809, he joined his son in York. The house on Front Street was full of family and usually overflowed with friends. A French émigré, Baron de Hoen, was a frequent visitor. At Christmas dinner in 1809, the baron reminded William Warren Baldwin that it was his twelfth Noel meal with the Baldwin family. On that occasion, another refugee from revolutionary France and close friend, Quetton St. George, was absent but not forgotten. Young Robert and his Uncle Henry led a chorus of song as a toast was drunk to the absent St. George. The house full of friends and family, ringing with song, was more than years removed from the silent solitude of Robert's tortured retirement in the 1850s.[12]

The tranquillity of home and school was only occasionally disrupted. The most dramatic intrusion was the War of 1812, that indecisive conflict with the United States. In April 1813 an American fleet attacked York. Robert and his family, except for his father who stayed to tend the wounded, were evacuated to Baron de Hoen's farm 6.4 kilometres north. Robert's grandfather joined them reluctantly, anxious as the old man was to smite the Yankees. The rest of the family was more than willing to leave the threat behind. It was a considerable coterie of Baldwins and kin that hiked north—the sole vehicle was Elizabeth Russell's phaeton that she crowded with so many necessities there was no room for people. Phoebe Baldwin shepherded her four boys, who needed varying degrees of attention. Robert was almost nine, but Quetton was only a toddler. They also had to bring along an invalid, Major Fuller, who had been under Dr. Baldwin's care. Add Phoebe's sister Maria and her Aunt Elizabeth, and the expedition was large. The wisdom of the effort was soon evident. Halfway to the farm, they were startled by a great crash from the south. The magazine at the York garrison had exploded. William Baldwin, tending the wounded at an improvised hospital back in town, was showered with debris from that explosion.[13]

It was far enough away to be safe but close enough to see the smoke from the public buildings as the Americans ransacked the town. Even after the invaders departed, leaving the legislature and other buildings in ruins, the Baldwins remained in the countryside until they were certain all threats had passed. They moved onto a farm near Millbrook, twenty-nine kilometres northeast of York, a few days later. There young Robert resumed his studies, his mother taking Rev. Strachan's place as teacher. The period at Millbrook may have been one of emotional distancing for the boy. For the first time he was out of his father's long shadow, which, curiously, allowed William to be more open and affectionate with his son. He would write to the boy, "When I folded my letter to you, I did not anticipate the warm emotion I felt when writing 'My dear Robert.'" When Robert himself became a father, he too would find it easier to express his love for his children in letters than in person.[14]

When the family came home at war's end and took up their normal lives, it was in a society and a province deeply altered by the hostilities. As with many other Upper Canadians, the Baldwins had friends and relatives in the United States, they read American books, they received their British mail after it had passed through the United States. Yet the trauma of the war and the destruction of York would cast new light on the United States, and make its menace more apparent. Robert would always remain deeply suspicious of American influences and American values. Somewhere in his mind's eye, for the rest of his life, he would forever see the curling smoke of burning York.

Neither war nor peace could stay Robert's destiny, or at least his father's plans for it. As prescribed he finished school in 1820, when he was sixteen, and entered his father's office as a law student. He was called to the bar on 20 June 1825, just a month past his twenty-first birthday, and three days later his proud father, himself then treasurer of the Law Society of Upper Canada, presented him to the court. Robert had taken the first step along the road his father had paved for him. It would never be an easy road. Unlike William Warren Baldwin, Robert was never comfortable performing; he found an audience—whether in a courtroom or a political meeting—to be terrifying. He was, nevertheless, an effective lawyer. A young lawyer had to travel extensively, following the court circuit and legal business, around the province. It was a pleasant enough time for a young man who enjoyed solitude. The long hours after court in strange towns allowed him to immerse himself in reading Goldsmith's histories of Greece and Rome, Homer's *Iliad*, and the novels of Smollett to retreat into worlds less threatening than his own. To his surprise, he was often successful in court and he enjoyed those triumphs as much as the vicarious ones in literature.[15]

When he had to measure himself against other, more urbane men, the legal life became less pleasant. In the late summer of 1825 John Rolph asked Robert to assist in his legal practice. Rolph, like Robert's father, was both a doctor and a lawyer and, since 1824, a liberal member of the provincial House of Assembly. And, again like the elder Baldwin, he was a talented, confident, outgoing man. Robert was naturally intimidated. On his second day in Rolph's practice he lost a case. It left him "very low spirited" and "terrified," his new-found confidence shattered. Soon after he went to court with Rolph for a case in which Rolph would oppose the distinguished Tory lawyer and member of the executive council, James Buchanan Macaulay. To Robert's horror,

Rolph unexpectedly ordered him to address the jury. Robert rose in utter confusion. "I felt such an intolerable weight on my heart that I absolutely despaired." He gradually recovered his poise and gave such an effective address that Macaulay praised the young lawyer in his summary to the court. From that point Robert gained confidence in himself and completed his first court circuit in triumph. There was always a dark cloud behind every silver lining, however. His friends judged him a success and believed his performance "affords a prospect of my one day not being altogether undistinguished in my profession—I have a horror of not rising above mediocrity—I am not however by any means so certain of my future as others seem to be." How could he be? He had been raised to the belief that he would be measured by what family he came from and what victories he won in the world, not by who he was as a person.[16]

His father was certain. Once established in his profession, Robert's next step was to enter into public life. William Warren Baldwin had become a leading spokesman for the Reform Party in the province, which emerged in the 1820s to combat the Tories in elections for the Assembly and to contest the dominance of the Family Compact over Upper Canada. It was, to most eyes, a peculiar role for one of Upper Canada's wealthiest and best-placed professional men. Yet it was entirely consistent with the tradition of the Irish Baldwins. Espousing reform meant increasingly bitter conflict with the administration of Lieutenant-Governor Sir Peregrine Maitland, who managed the province between 1818 and 1828, a regime that made an art form out of petty tyranny. The matter that placed the Baldwins in open opposition to the governor was the dismissal of Mr. Justice John Walpole Willis.[17]

Willis had come out from England in 1827 to sit as a justice in the Court of King's Bench. His haughty manner and his sympathy for liberal ideas soon won him the enmity of the provincial elite. The enmity degenerated into full-scale political warfare in February 1828. Willis dismissed charges against Reform journalist Francis Collins, who had been accused of libelling the government. Willis then compounded the insult for Tories by acting on a complaint from Collins and ordering the trial of provincial Solicitor General Henry John Boulton for acting as a second during a fatal duel more than a decade before. The case was purest spite; the duel was not only long in the past but the winning duellist, Samuel Jarvis, had been exonerated in 1817. Prosecution of this hopeless case fell to Robert Baldwin. Not only was this matter ancient history, juries rarely convicted anyone for duelling, no matter a simple second. Robert did the best he could with a poor hand, but of course lost the verdict. Judge Willis, meanwhile, was not finished with his political gestures from the bench.

On 17 June 1828 Willis shocked a sitting of the Court of King's Bench by declaring the court was incompetent to hear cases in the absence of the chief justice who was in England on sick leave. Willis then withdrew from the bench, paralyzing the system of justice. Nine days later Maitland dismissed Willis from his judgeship. The Baldwins rallied behind Willis and helped organize lawyers to protest against the legality of the court and refuse to argue before it. When Willis returned to England to argue his case, Robert became Lady Mary Willis's solicitor to protect her interests in Canada. And the two Baldwins led the creation of a Constitutional Committee to petition the British government.[18]

Willis and his legal niceties were excuses to challenge the arbitrary government of Maitland and the Compact, to rally the voting public behind the emerging Reform political bloc. Robert rose to the call of duty in the crisis and agreed to stand for York County in the provincial election of July 1828. The sturdy yeomen of the county were unimpressed by his stodgy lawyerly style and he finished a distant last among four candidates. His cousin, Robert Baldwin Sullivan, confirmed to Robert that his reserved manner had been the cause for his defeat. Robert's father, however, was returned for Norfolk County. Ironically, the winning candidates in York were two Reformers: businessman Jesse Ketchum and the radical publisher of the York newspaper, the *Colonial Advocate*, William Lyon Mackenzie. This fight among the Reformers demonstrated that, if the Baldwins were seen as traitors by much of the gentry, they were still considered elitists by some liberals. Mackenzie, when asked if he knew Robert, replied, "I know nothing about him—but I will oppose him because I do not like the family."[19]

The election campaign and the petitions on behalf of Willis provided opportunities for the Baldwins to publicize their reform agenda. They believed there must be reconstitution of the Legislative Council, the appointed upper house of the provincial Parliament, which had persistently blocked good legislation passed by the elected lower house, the Assembly. They called for cheaper government and especially for curbing the extravagant salaries and privileges of government officials. Most important, they advanced their peculiar solution to the political problems of the colony. William Warren Baldwin spelled it out in a petition to the British prime minister, the Duke of Wellington, in 1829:

> I am desired by the Committee particularly to [direct] Your Graces thoughts to that principle of the British Constitution in the actual use of which the Colonies alone hope for <u>peace</u> <u>Good Government</u> and <u>Prosperity</u> . . . the principle alluded to is this, the presence of a provincial ministry (if I may be allowed to use the term) responsible to the provincial Parliament, and removable from office by his Majesty's representative at his pleasure and especially when they lose the confidence of the people as expressed by the Voice of their representatives in the Assembly; and that all acts of the King's representative should have the character of local responsibility by the signature of some member of this ministry.[20]

This was the essence of the reform that John Baldwin and Robert the Emigrant had proposed for the Irish parliament fifty years before. This "responsible government" was premised on the need to check the exercise of arbitrary power by the Crown or by irresponsible executives. It was an eminently moderate reform, as might be expected from upper-middle-class liberals such as the Baldwins. Responsible government did not require any social or economic changes; it did not even require an extension of the franchise. It simply meant that executive misrule could be stemmed by the representatives of the "people," or at any rate that portion of the people who had enough property to qualify for the vote. The executive would be required to muster the support of a majority of the members of the Assembly on votes of confidence, and the governor would have to act, on matters of local concern, with the advice of that responsible executive. It was a simple and moderate mechanism and one hallowed by its acceptance as a basic principle of government at home in Britain.[21]

The petition marked both Baldwins, father and son, as enemies of the colonial administration. Lieutenant-Governor Maitland was angry that the Colonial Office should even receive such rabble-rousing demands. He warned the undersecretary in London that the petitioners were in league with the Scottish agitator Joseph Hume and English radicals. The Reformers' committee was no more than a gaggle of envious men. William Warren Baldwin stood out among them for "with the exception of his son, he is the only person throughout the Province, in the character of a gentleman, who has associated with the promoters of Mr. Hume's projects." And the Baldwins were poor examples of gentlemen, at that. According to Maitland they were both liars, who spun falsehoods about Judge Willis's treatment and about alleged Tory election fraud.[22]

Robert clung to his reputation for honour, despite Maitland's aspersions, and to the logic of responsible government. Politics were rarely so simple and rational, however, a fact that Robert always had difficulty grasping. If the Baldwins understood responsible government, few others in Canada did. Nor was the principle so transparently obvious to British politicians as Robert and William Warren Baldwin believed. It would not be until after 1841, when there was a parliamentary crisis over the extent of the royal prerogative, that responsible government was clarified in Britain. Nevertheless, the Baldwins' persistence in pushing their reform at every opportunity, their unshakeable confidence in its efficacy, won over their liberal colleagues. By 1835 the Baldwins had elevated responsible government to something like the official platform of Reformers, even though it was apparent that various Reformers had widely diverse interpretations of what responsible government meant. The liberals in the Assembly made responsible government the centrepiece in their petitions to Britain, although radicals such as William Lyon Mackenzie would have preferred to agitate for more concrete reforms such as an elective Legislative Council. Through a desire for a united front, even the Patriotes, or reformers, in Lower Canada were convinced to adopt responsible government as their basic demand.[23]

Both Mackenzie and the Baldwins were correct in their analyses of responsible government. Mackenzie was right in suspecting that responsible government was a profoundly conservative reform. It would do nothing to alter the balance of economic power between elites and ordinary Upper Canadians. Indeed, any shift of political power it would engender would be slight. An emerging professional and commercial bourgeoisie would replace colonial governors and Tory compacts in the seats of colonial power, but for lower-class people the change would signify little. The Baldwins were correct, however, in believing that responsible government was an idea that would have a resonance in the voting public, a public that would invest the concept with much more capacity for change than it really contained. Historian Paul Romney, writing about the significance of responsible government in the 1840s, sees it as an agency that papered over the natural division of interests between the bourgeoisie, on one hand, and farmers on the other, thus allowing the creation of a Reform Party, which allied these unlikely confederates:

> this class feeling was dampened by the logic of the Baldwinite position, which defined colonial politics as a struggle between the Upper Canadian community and an oligarchic elite whose preeminence depended ultimately on external (i.e. imperial) backing. Aspirations that were basically social and economic were subsumed in the quest for an institutional panacea: colonial internal sovereignty and responsible government.[24]

The Baldwins, themselves firmly planted in the social elite, did not set out to make the colonial world safe for capitalists. Their rank in society was very different from that of the new bourgeoisie. It was their reform, responsible government, however, that would allow the commercial and industrial middle class to seize power. In the process, not only would farmers fail to gain influence but the Baldwinian gentry itself would be swept aside.

For the moment, the implications of power were not immediate concerns. A Reformer had to grow wearingly used to defeat, as Robert discovered. The year 1828 seemed one defeat after another. First the failed prosecution of H.J. Boulton. Then the election loss. Then the failure to save Justice Willis, who never returned to Upper Canada. Finally, in October, Francis Collins was put on trial again for libel, with Robert and John Rolph as his defence counsels. The case created a sensation in the little world of York, involving as it did the popular newspaper editor as defendant, Attorney General John Beverley Robinson as the injured party, and the scion of the Baldwin family as attorney. The courtroom was crowded that October Saturday when Collins was brought before the York assizes. Leading government figures crowded one side of the room, Reform notables such as Mackenzie, John Carey of the liberal newspaper the York *Observer*, and William Warren Baldwin, the other. Rolph and Baldwin were eloquent, but it was another failure. The jury retired in considerable perplexity, unable to understand the legal definition of libel. It asked for the use of a legal dictionary, but Mr. Justice Christopher Hagerman denied the request. Left to flounder in their confusion, the jury members deliberated for five hours before finding Collins guilty. To Robert and Collins's astonishment, the editor was sentenced to a year in prison, a savage and unprecedented punishment.[25]

The Collins trial and verdict underscored the bitter, personal nature of politics in York. Politics were entangled in private antagonisms, in family ambitions, in the endless elbowing for place and favour that marked this still-forming society. Men were made to seem larger, or smaller, than life in such an overheated environment. So it was with Robert Baldwin. Francis Collins was fawningly grateful for Robert's assistance in his two legal travails that year and he raised the young man to heroic stature. Collins had urged the Reformers to nominate Robert as their candidate for York town in the summer election. According to Collins, "the temper of the town cried out for Baldwin," because he "was the only man in York that could put out the Attorney General," J.B. Robinson. Collins continued to blame Mackenzie for not nominating Baldwin and therefore losing the town seat. The picture of Baldwin drawn by the Tories was rather different. After the Collins' trial in October 1828 the capital was flooded with copies of a scurrilous broadside attacking Robert for his defence of the newspaperman. "My name is Robert, On the Gallows Hill / My father hatches treason," the placard began. It claimed that Robert defended the villain because he was a republican and because of personal ambition; Robert, it contended, wanted to bring down the Attorney General so he could take the position himself. Thus:

> I took this cause,
> and Hell-directed came this day to do
> The shameless deed which blasts my rebel name.[26]

Robert was neither Collins's hero nor the Tories' villain but he did have the opportunity to demonstrate something of what he really was. A by-election was held in the town of York in 1829 to replace the former member, John Beverley Robinson, who had been appointed chief justice. Robert declared as a candidate against a moderate supporter of the government, James Edward Small. Even Mackenzie rallied behind Baldwin because of the symbolic importance of a Reform win in the capital. In the November election, Robert won handily, 92 votes to 52. Speaking to his cheering supporters, he pronounced himself "a whig in principle, and opposed to the present administration." Alas, the election writ had been improperly issued and Robert's election was voided. In a new run-off in January 1830 he faced a more difficult opponent, district sheriff William Botsford Jarvis. Robert eked out a victory of 109 votes to 100. The slim margin made the triumph all the sweeter, and defeat all the more bitter. Robert was chaired through the town by the joyous Reformers, while the disconsolate Tory Jarvis trailed along the street behind the procession, silent and alone. The next day William Warren Baldwin proudly presented his son to the House of Assembly.[27]

Robert was an active member of the House but hardly a leader. His faltering speeches and bland personality left him overshadowed by flamboyant Reformers such as his father and Mackenzie. His parliamentary career was short lived at any rate. King George IV died on 25 June 1830. By the practice of the time, the death of the monarch was automatically followed by dissolution of Parliament and a new general election. The province, which had swung sharply to Reform in 1828, swung as dramatically Tory in the October 1830 elections. Robert lost to Jarvis by some thirty votes, while William Warren Baldwin was also defeated in Norfolk. Robert was victim of a general shift to the Tories, but some radical Reformers blamed his defeat on his performance in the House.

His old friend Francis Collins of the *Canadian Freeman* now charged that Baldwin had been too moderate, too easy on the government, and had associated too closely with "a certain low, hypocritical and corrupt faction" of centrists.[28]

Robert was probably relieved to be free from politics for he was uncomfortable in the limelight and recognized his shortcomings as a public man. He did consider standing again in the next election, which was held in 1834. He made gentlemanly inquiries to possible supporters, enough to alarm the member for York, William Botsford Jarvis, who complained to his sister that "Baldwin is making great efforts to throw me out at the next election & I fancy it will be a pretty hard go for us both." As it developed, Robert did not run. Personal obligations, for a time, seemed to outweigh public ones. On 31 May 1827 he had married his cousin, Augusta Elizabeth Sullivan. The union was rapidly blessed. Their daughter Phoebe Maria was born on 27 February 1828, and three other children would follow: William Willcocks, born in 1830; Augusta Elizabeth in 1831; and Robert in 1834. Baldwin was preoccupied with a growing family and a burgeoning law practice. His happy domestic life made him him more open emotionally with his children than he could ever be after Eliza died. Sometimes his two loves, family and law, converged delightfully. When his wife was absent on a trip in 1833, the doting father was elated by the increased attachment of the children to him. Two-year-old Eliza refused to be left with relatives "so I have been obliged to choose between the alternative of putting a constraint upon that will at the expence of a hullabloo or of taking her to Court with me." Little Eliza's will apparently won out.[29]

Legal business still required him to leave the family and travel across the province. The law was a duty and honour, as well as a business, and Robert assumed willingly his obligations to it. When he rode the court circuit he also served as an examiner for aspiring law students. In 1832 he read law exams at Brockville in eastern Upper Canada. He was especially impressed by the work of one sixteen–year-old aspirant and invited the young man for a personal interview to encourage him, and offered to pay the boy's articling expenses in Belleville. The student was John Ross who, nineteen years later, would become Robert's son-in-law. At home, the practice flourished. Robert worked with his cousin R.B. Sullivan and, while they did not rival the premier law practice in York, that of Robert's former senior colleague John Rolph, they were successful. This was so even though Sullivan, something of a dilettante and a good deal of a drinker, was often sloppy in his work, mistakes Robert had to repair. In 1835, for example, the firm lost the ability to discount notes at the Bank of Upper Canada because of Sullivan's errors in handling money until Robert was able to sort out the matter.[30]

To the family and the law was added the burden of ill health. Robert suffered periodically from abdominal pains and inflammation of the lungs, while his wife's health was always delicate. She was acutely ill after their son Robert was delivered by Caesarian section on 17 April 1834. In 1835 she travelled to New York to recuperate while Robert spent their eighth wedding anniversary at home, longing to be with her. Characteristically, he wrote to her how much he wished to join her, but concluded that he could not do so because "it would be inconsistent with duty."[31]

The sense of duty had been bred into him. It was an overpowering obligation, one to be served even at the cost of wracking pain. The cost was high, the pain searing, in 1836. Eliza came home, but she came home to die.

> On Monday, the eleventh day of January in the year of our Lord one thousand eight hundred and thirty-six, at six o'clock in the forenoon, at the family residence in Front Street in the City of Toronto, died my beloved wife Augusta Elizabeth Baldwin . . . She died of an attack of water on the brain, in which the general derangement of her system consequent on the extensive hemmorage attendant on her last confinement (to me at least most unexpectedly) terminated. During our short married life we were blessed with the most perfect and unbounded mutual confidence and affection. She was all a husbands love could wish her.[32]

The loss of Eliza completed Robert's evolution from the lively child to the melancholy adult. He already had a funereal bearing, hunched shoulders, a pronounced stoop, a heavy, fleshy body. His complexion was pallid, made all the more pasty by the dull, expressionless Baldwin eyes. The inner man mirrored the outer. Nagging insecurity and lack of self-confidence, an oppressive shyness and discomfort in the glare of public performance, his family-wrought peculiarities had made him an aloof, cold man. Eliza had died "to me at least most unexpectedly," a death unexpected despite the evidence of her symptoms, because Robert could not allow himself to admit that his one strong link to life was dissolving. Her death was a shock, then, and it pushed him beyond peculiarities to the purgatory of melancholia, depression, and hysteria. Increasingly he would suffer from sleeplessness, and when sleep came it was frequently filled with troubled, frightening dreams. He often found it difficult to stir himself to carry out his daily tasks. Not surprisingly, given the torments of his nights, he could be overpowered by weariness during the day. The afternoon of Thursday, 27 March 1847 saw a not uncommon scene of hilarity in the Canadian Assembly. The House was debating a motion about sessional indemnities for members. Baldwin was slumped over his desk, fast asleep. His bench mate poked him as his turn came to vote and, a newspaper reported, Baldwin "rose in a state of happy ignorance of the question" to cast his vote, while his fellow parliamentarians cheered and clapped at his confusion.[33]

Perceptive colleagues might have read much into his performance in the House. He was the bane of parliamentary reporters who had enormous difficulty catching what he said. Indeed, one visitor to the gallery of the House in 1850 claimed that it was only because Baldwin was standing that he was aware that the politician was speaking, so faint was Baldwin's voice. The loss of voice, or aphonia, was a classic symptom of the Victorian catch-all disease, hysteria. So too were parapraxes (slips of the tongue) and unexplained forgetfulness. At his most troubled, Robert would write, as he did to a compatriot in January 1848: "As respects respects . . . popular opinion in in U.C." Or he would forget. In February 1850 he wrote a note to the provincial secretary recommending an appointment to the Court of Common Pleas, but he misspelled the name of the applicant—a long-time associate—and referred to the court, with which he dealt daily as Attorney General, as "Common Plies." From that day in January 1836 he was spiralling down to the crypt at Spadina.[34]

Chapter 4

A Better Irishman

It had been a scant few months since she was gone. Immersion in the
past, in the land of family legend, was a kind of balm for his wounds.
It was the summer of 1836.

Governor General Sydenham was one of a long line of British admin-
istrators who Robert Baldwin worked with, catered to, and confronted.
It was never anything but fear-provoking to do so. A governor represented
the majesty of the Britain that Robert truly loved and a social system that
he treasured. Sydenham, snide and intimidating, was more terrifying than
other governors. Yet, that spring of 1841, Robert was driven by something
greater than fear or respect: duty.[1]

The sense of duty had been bred into him. It was an overpowering
obligation, one to be served even at the great personal cost such as when
Eliza died in 1836.

Yet when duty called he responded, then as later. In 1836 Upper
Canada had a new Lieutenant-Governor, Francis Bond Head, who
came with instructions from Britain to calm the political unrest in
the province. The atmosphere had become poisoned with relations
between Reformers and the Tories dangerously heated; in Lower
Canada there was already ample evidence that violence would ensue
unless solutions were found to the political conflicts. Head's chosen
method of reconciliation was to reconstitute the executive council. He
consulted a number of political figures about who should be added to
the Council. He even interviewed the radical William Lyon Mackenzie
who recommended the moderate John Henry Dunn; the Reform
speaker of the Assembly, Marshall Spring Bidwell; and William
Warren Baldwin. Instead, Head decided on Robert Baldwin, whom
Head considered more moderate than his father. In early February,
less than a month after Eliza's death, Robert had his first face-to-face
confrontation with a governor. Head had summoned Robert to call

on the evening of 8 February. In a panelled office in Elmsley House, the King Street residence of the Lieutenant-Governor, Robert was offered a place in the Council and, in return, presented his demands to Head. The executive council must be made responsible to the Assembly, Baldwin insisted, and the old irresponsible members of the Council must be ousted. Head was no less brash and overbearing than Sydenham would be, and he was no less outraged at the idea of a truly responsible colonial regime. But Head needed Baldwin to give a gloss of reform to his new government, he needed him desperately. So Head remained inviting despite their lack of agreement. They agreed to meet again. This time Head offered to appoint Dunn and Reform notable Dr. John Rolph, along with Baldwin. Robert still declined, believing nothing short of responsible government as he understood it was acceptable. His father and Rolph prevailed upon him, however, arguing that they must seize the gains they could. Reluctantly, perhaps with foreboding, Robert agreed. On 20 February 1836 he, Dunn, and Rolph were sworn in as executive councillors.[2]

However reluctant his acceptance, Robert's willingness to serve was astonishing evidence of the pull of duty. He had been emotionally devastated by Eliza's death, left with only the consolation that his own death would reunite them. Yet, when duty called, and his father urged, he responded. It was an act of the rawest courage. But it was more. Duty had been drummed into him by his father, he had been forced to accept the burden of the Baldwin mission. Now duty was not simply a burden, it was an assuagement of guilt. Classical psychological theory saw three kinds of palliative measures that enable us to live with the harshness of life. Deflections permit us to forget our disappointments as we turn to, say, cultivating our gardens. Substitutive satisfactions, such as art, diminish the pain. And intoxicants numb us to life. For Robert Baldwin, the duty of office was all three. Entering provincial politics deflected pain into reformist fervour. His father's pleasure substituted for Eliza's love. The excitement of the inevitable confrontation with Francis Head was itself intoxicating for a man so naturally retiring. Somewhere, too, was the guilt—the guilt of the Robert Baldwin whose final and greatest need would be to bear the scar of Eliza's birthing pain. The loving husband and doting father was also William Warren Baldwin's son, a self-labelled failure because he could not achieve perfection. Duty was his penance for his imagined culpability in his wife's death.[3]

So he entered the arena. But not for long. Against his better judgment Robert joined a council that included three veteran placemen: Peter Robinson, the provincial commissioner of Crown lands; George Markland, inspector general of accounts; and Joseph Wells, bursar of the elite educational academy, King's College. None, on the face of it, were promising material with which to build a new political system. Of the new members, Dunn was not much better, an essentially apolitical bureaucrat who had been receiver general of accounts since 1820. Only Dr. John Rolph shared Robert's reformist bent. Yet to everyone's surprise, especially that of Governor Head, reform soon captured them all. The council met on 22 February to consider a legal issue concerning land. It did not reconvene until 3 March when, to Head's shock, it insisted on discussing constitutional matters. The next day the council adopted a representation to the governor. Colonial affairs were in crisis, the councillors said, because of "the hitherto unconstitutional abridgement of the duties of the Executive Council." They were wasting their time meeting once a week about petty land matters "while the affairs of the Country are withheld from their consideration and advice." The governor had the right to reject the advice of his council, but he must receive it on all important matters of local government. Head was outraged by the temerity of the message and he was perfectly sensible where they were leading. To concede the council's right to be consulted, he wrote to the Colonial Secretary in Britain, was to concede "the error of responsibility."[4]

Head was a bully and if he had stayed with it, bullying might have succeeded. His sternness cowed Markland, Robinson, Wells, and Dunn, and they were prepared to recant; however, Head also saw himself as a master tactician and insisted on playing out an elaborate scheme. If he accepted the councillors' apology and dismissed Baldwin and Rolph, he would have to explain the basis of the controversy and thus open up discussion of responsible government in the Assembly. Therefore, he insisted that the representation must disappear. It must be withdrawn by the same council that produced it, that is, Baldwin and Rolph also must agree. The result of this stratagem was not only to make the representation disappear but also to make the executive council disappear. The councillors met on 12 March and all six resigned.[5]

Upper Canada was plunged into a political crisis. The Reform-dominated Assembly rallied to the late councillors and on 15 April voted to withhold supply and cut off the government's funds. Head retaliated by dissolving the House and calling new elections. It began a sequence of events that would result, a year and a half later, in rebellion.

It has been widely believed that Robert Baldwin was the prime mover in this whole affair. He had outmanoeuvred Head and skilfully won over the Tory councillors. Indeed, Head's successor as Lieutenant-Governor, Sir George Arthur, contended that the "ultimate consequence" of Baldwin's appointment to the executive council was the rebellion of 1837. Yet Robert's career would show that he was unskilled in smooth intrigue at the best of times, and the late winter of 1836 was far from the best of times. Robert was sunk in depression after Eliza's death, a condition which militated against careful, cunning plotting. It is much more likely that Rolph and Bidwell planned the steps which led to the confrontation; indeed, the Council's representation to the governor probably flowed from Dr. Rolph's pen, not Robert Baldwin's. Nevertheless, Robert was centrally important to the plot. He had a reputation for honesty and a sense of duty. His presence among the councillors gave them credibility and acceptability. And if he did not plan the mass resignation of 12 March, he readily went along with it; resignation, retreat into unsullied principle, was so often his response to the world's imperfections. It was also his heritage. Principles were inflexible, he had been taught. As he wrote in a letter read to the House of Assembly by Peter Perry, "these opinions were not hastily formed . . . they were, on the contrary, those which I had imbibed from my father."[6]

Robert did not wait for the denouement. On 30 April he left Toronto for New York; the first time he'd left the province since a childhood visit to relatives in 1816. He was not present in Upper Canada for the disastrous July 1836 election that saw the Reformers snowed under. Head personally took the stump against them and bought votes, used patronage, and hired violent gangs to buttress his appeals to loyalty. Nor was Robert present to watch Head take revenge on those who opposed him. In July, as part of a general purge of Reformers from public offices, William

Warren Baldwin was ousted from his post as judge of the Surrogate Court of the Home District, and long-time friend George Ridout lost his judgeship in the Niagara District Court. William Warren's sin had been to chair a meeting of Toronto Reformers, which issued a statement charging Head with "a Disregard of Constitutional Government and of Candour and Truth." As Robert wrote when he heard of the dismissals, such petty tyrannies only hurried along the coming crisis.[7]

Robert himself was seeking escape from present grief by plunging into the warming past of the family. In early May he boarded a passenger vessel in New York and set off for Britain to search out his roots in Ireland. It was a rough voyage and Robert, unused to ocean travel, was sick almost constantly. All that was forgotten as the ship first sighted land, which to Robert's delight, proved to be the eastern point of the family home turf, County Cork. Then he travelled to modern England. For a colonial and especially one so "antediluvian," as Robert sometimes mockingly referred to his own conservatism, the noise and dirt and tumult of industrial England was both fascinating and repelling. His first glimpse was in the bustling port of Liverpool, where his ship docked on 5 June. The city was the receipient of much of the wheat and timber that Upper Canada shipped to Britain, and the source of much of the wine that graced the Baldwin table and the books housed in the family's library. Antediluvian he may have been, but Robert did not deny himself the heady delight of sampling the finest of modern technology. He took his first train ride from Liverpool to Manchester and from there returned via technology more familiar to an Upper Canadian: a stage coach to London.[8]

Even during the search for healing in family history, duty still called. Before pursuing his own needs, Robert went to London to present the case of the Upper Canadian Reformers and plead for the governmental changes necessary to save his province from disaster. It was a frustrating and humiliating experience, some of which he brought upon himself. He had no personal ties in England and knew no one in authority. He did have a letter of introduction from his old teacher—and current political opponent—Archdeacon John Strachan to the Colonial Secretary, Lord Glenelg. But instead of exploiting that entree, Robert chose to go through Reform political channels. Since Mackenzie visited England in 1832, the principal champion in Britain of the colonial cause had been Joseph Hume, a liberal member of the House of Commons. Robert asked Hume to transmit his representation, and a request for an interview, to Lord Glenelg. It was not an auspicious choice. Hume was known as a flaming radical, who often hinted at colonial independence. His recommendation would open few doors for Robert Baldwin.[9]

The closest Robert came to official acceptance was the outside of those doors. As he filled in his time with sightseeing and visiting those who would see him (Joseph Hume and his circle), he passed the Colonial Office often enough. This modest centre of the sprawling empire comprised two seventeenth-century houses at numbers 13 and 14 Downing Street. The buildings were visibly shabby and smelled of the medieval drainage ditch that ran nearby. Three years after Baldwin's trip a parliamentary committee would condemn them as beyond repair. Their condition would not endanger Robert, though, who did get as far as the main-floor waiting room. On 20 June he wrote to Lord Glenelg to explain why he had resigned from the executive council and to request an interview. The reply, eight days later, was frosty. Glenelg's permanent undersecretary, James Stephen, wrote that while he was always pleased to receive information he was "yet inclined to think that under the existing circumstances, it would be more advisable that such communications be made in writing than in conversation."[10]

Robert hoped for a change of heart and had ample time to play tourist while he waited. He visited some literary figures whom he admired, carrying introductory letters from John Strachan. One was Thomas Campbell, author of the epic poem *Pleasures of Hope*, a vastly popular and drippingly romantic verse. Another was John Gibson Lockhart, editor of the eclectic literary and political magazine, *The Quarterly*. It was a revealing choice for it was a journal with a mix of liberal and conservative editorial positions, not unlike Baldwin himself. More conventionally, Robert visited Windsor, Richmond, and Hampton Court, and collected facsimiles of the signatures of Mary Queen of Scots and King Charles I, curiously despotic choices for a liberal. He was true to his melancholic nature when he visited the church in London where an old school friend, Horace Ridout, was buried. Robert had the bemused sexton open the vault to view Ridout's coffin.[11]

Closer to current reality, he was able to gain an interview with the rising Whig political star, Lord John Russell. Their talk was amiable but it did nothing toward easing the contemporary political crisis or even to enlighten Russell's views when the lord became Colonial Secretary three years later. Sights, graves, and Lord John Russell did not fill up Robert's time and he had ample opportunity for reflection as he rested in his lodgings at 4 Trinity Court, Charing Cross. In fact, he poured out his reflections in a seventy-page letter to Lord Glenelg, warning the Colonial Secretary of the crisis that would determine whether Upper Canada would remain British. Unless the home country wished to hold the colony by force, it would have to reform the colonial constitution in fundamental ways. The answer, of course, was responsible government. As Baldwin told Glenelg, responsible government was essentially a conservative reform, one which required "no sacrifice of any Constitutional principle, no sacrifice of Royal Prerogative, no diminution of the primacy of Britain."[12]

Baldwin's suggestions and warnings fell on deaf ears. Glenelg was not prepared to debate the constitution with him. The Colonial Secretary shared Head's view that responsible government was incompatible with imperial rule. So Baldwin's letter, as with the other missives he continued to shower on the Colonial Office, was ignored. Finally he gave up. On 24 August he left London and journeyed to Liverpool to attend a meeting of the British Association for the Advancement of Science. From these intellectual heights he descended to his roots. Taking a steamer to Dublin, he immersed himself in the rediscovery of his family's past. The contrast was sharp in his own mind: from the careful crafting of his constitutional arguments to Glenelg and the erudition of modern scientists, to the pure emotionalism of his return home. Ireland was "this dear land of my parents and of my own Eliza and if it makes me a worse philosopher I shall be satisfied if it makes me a better Irishman."[13]

Robert tried to walk every sod connected to the Baldwin family. In a letter to his daughter Maria, intended as much as a geography test as personal information, he mentioned some forty-seven towns that he had visited, often more than once. Some of the visits were to carry out commissions from his mother who wanted news of old friends. So he trekked to places such as Woodside, northwest of Cork city, to deliver a letter from Phoebe to Mrs. Castleton. John William Baldwin of Cork helped him to find his grandmother's grave, and nearby in Bandon Robert found Grandmother Sullivan's resting place.[14]

The children were not forgotten. Robert wrote affectionate, if lecturing, letters to them for—as he reminded the eldest, eight-year-old Maria—her father "has now you know nothing to look for happiness here but from seeing his dear children grow up worthy of that dear excellent Mother." Even young Bob, barely two years old, was not spared that odd mixture of love and duty that always figured Robert's letters to the children. Robert assured the toddler that he was in his father's thoughts. Maria would read the letter to Bob, but it was Bob's responsibility, along with his six-year-old brother, to be a young man. "You and Willy must take care of your two Sisters because you know girls are not able to take care of themselves as boys are." It was a heavy obligation for a two year old, but he was, after all, a Baldwin. The children had other priorities. Maria's great news to her absent father was that Grandpa had taken her, Willy, and Bobby to the circus.[15]

He spent two months in Cork, visiting family acquaintances, arranging for a headstone for his grandmother's grave, and collecting sods from the family cemeteries to be packed carefully and sent back to Upper Canada. Increasingly he felt more comfortable with the dead than with the living. Yet the living family still pulled at him. The children were back in Toronto, being cared for by female relatives and by Francis Hincks's wife, Martha Anne. It was his duty to return to them. In late November he crossed over to Liverpool. After the delays that were inevitable so late in the shipping season, he sailed for New York on the *United States* on 20 December. It took five rough, cold weeks to reach America. A few days were spent with relatives, then on to Albany and more reunions with kin. Finally, at five o'clock on the afternoon of Friday, 10 February 1837, he was home.[16]

———◆———

Robert's political mission in Britain had failed, even if his sentimental one had succeeded. Although thirteen months had passed since Eliza's death, his grief was still deep, and when it allied with his disappointment over the Colonial Office's intransigence, he was left with little stomach for politics. Achilles-like he took to his tent, absorbing himself with family and the law while the political milieu around him declined into disaster. There seemed no hope of reform and an economic depression dogged the land. Mackenzie and the radicals moved closer to rebellion. Baldwin remained isolated from it all, safeguarded from the economic crisis by the family wealth, protected from the political crisis by his refusal to become involved. His first inkling of the true seriousness of the situation came at the beginning of December when news arrived in Toronto that armed rebels were gathering north of the city. Governor Head had sent the troops to Lower Canada, where rebellion had broken out in late November. Toronto was defenceless. Head had to play for time while militiamen could be mustered from surrounding communities. On 5 December he decided to send a flag of truce to Mackenzie and the rebels, ostensibly to learn if negotiations could be opened and to offer amnesty to those who had taken up arms against the government. Among his intermediaries he chose Robert Baldwin. Robert accepted the duty with enormous reluctance, loath to stir from his grief-filled lethargy. He would have been even more reluctant had he known that he was a pawn for both sides. Head had no real intention of negotiating; rather, he was simply buying time. Robert's companion in the mission, Dr. John Rolph, was playing a double game. Only Robert thought that a genuine attempt to stave off an armed clash was underway.

Baldwin and Rolph rode out from the city and reached the rebel camp at about one o'clock that afternoon. They delivered their message from the governor to Mackenzie. What, they asked, would satisfy the rebel chief? Grinning broadly, he replied, "Independence." More seriously he insisted that he could give no answer until he received Head's message in writing. Then Rolph and Baldwin rode back into Toronto. Head had recovered his usual blustering confidence by this time and, rather than supplying a written memorandum, he told his envoys that he was breaking off negotiations. The weary emissaries had to remount their horses and ride out to the rebels again to convey this news. When they returned to Toronto, they parted at the city limits. Robert went home, deeply discouraged.[17]

The rebels marched—or, more accurately, straggled—toward Toronto, but were met by armed militiamen. A brief exchange of fire sent the radicals fleeing and ended any hope for the rebellion. Robert stood neutral in his disgust with both sides, hunkering down at home with the family while the brief war was waged. However much he hoped to do so, though, he could not entirely escape the sordid affair. Reformers called on him for assistance in the Tory reaction that followed the abortive coup. A few days after the attack on Toronto, Robert was in court on routine legal business when he was handed a hastily scribbled note. It was from the leader of the moderate Reformers, Marshall Spring Bidwell, former speaker of the Assembly. Although, as Bidwell wrote, "I have been as ignorant of this lamentable affair as yourself was," Governor Head had taken revenge on a political opponent. Bidwell was ordered to leave the province or face arrest. As he hastily packed to flee to the United States, he begged Robert to assist in the disposal of his goods and real estate, and to help his sister in this difficult time. Others came to Robert as well. He defended John Montgomery, former owner of the tavern north of Toronto where the rebels had gathered, and Dr. Thomas Morrison, a prominent radical Reformer. In trials in the spring of 1838 Robert won acquittal for Morrison, but was not so successful for Montgomery, who was convicted of high treason and sentenced to death, a sentence later commuted to transportation for life.[18]

Some lives were lost, many others were blighted by prison or exile. The province's economy was even more impoverished amid the threat of invasion from expatriate rebels and their American sympathizers, a threat that hung like a pall for some three years. Yet something did come from it all. The crisis in the Canadas shook the British government awake to the reality that colonial problems must be addressed. The man charged with resolving the situation was John George Lambton, Earl of Durham, who was appointed as Governor General of British North America and high commissioner to investigate the Canadian situation. An advanced liberal in British politics, "Radical Jack" Durham seemed the ideal man for the job in the eyes of Canadian Reformers. With his arrival at Quebec in May 1838 some of the gloom began to lift for the Baldwins and other moderate Reformers who had survived the reaction after the rebellion. They did not have the opportunity to make their case to him for some time, however. Durham was preoccupied with establishing order in Lower Canada, where the rebellion had been larger and more serious.

He did not visit Upper Canada until July. As with most British travellers to Canada, he made the obligatory stop at Niagara Falls, British North America's most famous attraction, on 13 July. He was suitably impressed by its grandeur, but the next day, on a side trip to Fort Erie, he fell ill, struck by the migraine headaches that so often tormented him. He was still suffering on 18 July when he travelled by steamer to Toronto. His arrival had to be delayed while he took treatment for his illness. Still groggy, he arrived in the city, which had declared a public holiday in his honour. The cacophony of a military band and the bells of the fire companies did little to ease his suffering, but Durham did his duty. He spoke to the crowd at the dock and spoke again that evening at a gala dinner, doing his best to ease minds with his repeated assurances that all would be well. Although he was too ill to venture out the next day, he received a steady stream of visitors to his rooms at Government House. Among them were the Baldwins, father and son.[19]

Durham could spare them only twenty minutes. They were momentous minutes. The passion with which William Warren and Robert Baldwin made their brief for responsible government impressed his lordship enough that he asked them to write to him at length when he returned to Quebec. The Baldwins spent the next weeks polishing their ideas and produced documents that amply reflected their personalities. William Warren's letter of 1 August was a characteristically political and practical presentation. After providing a long list of the grievances of the Upper Canadian people, he laid out four solutions: a responsible executive; the addition of some "more popular men" to the Legislative Council, or even making that body elective; the prevention of judicial interference in elections; and the protection of the electoral process from "undue influence" by governor and executive.[20]

Robert worked over his memorandum much longer and, also characteristically, took loftier ground than had his father, soaring off on general political philosophy. He had vowed, he wrote Durham on 23 August, to avoid "any further interference in the politics of the Province," but duty required him to point out the path toward the resolution of the Canadian problem. Some of the ideas Durham might be contemplating would only make matters worse, Robert contended. A general legislative union of the British North American colonies, for example, would be the first step toward independence. So too would be that departure from British tradition, the elective legislative council that his father was prepared to consider. The one and only answer, of course, was an eminently British and soundly conservative remedy: responsible government.

> To conclude My Lord with all the deference which becomes me when addressing your Lordship yet with all the firmness which I owe to my children and my country as a Canadian subject of her Majesty[,] I object first to the alteration of the Constitution in the minutest particular and secondly to the sacrifice of any single branch of the Royal Prerogative—Both of them are my birthright and I claim from your Lordship the preservation of them in all their integrity—And I lastly claim to have applied to that Constitution and to have used in the exercise of that Prerogative the same principle of responsibility to the people through their representatives which is daily practiced in the Executive Government of that mighty Empire of which it is yet my pride to be a subject.[21]

Robert never saw Lord Durham again after that brief discussion in July. The governor's political enemies in Britain would bring him down over some of his actions in Lower Canada. Durham returned home angry and disillusioned, but he would also return home with the germ of the idea that Robert Baldwin had given him: responsible government. It would grow into the central recommendation of Durham's famous report on Canada, which appeared in January 1839. Although the British government was not ready to accept responsible government at that time, Durham's endorsement gave the idea power and credibility. It would continue to grow until Robert Baldwin harvested it in the 1840s. Robert's letter to Durham helped to rescue Canadian Reform from the disaster of the rebellion and defeat the seemingly triumphant Toryism of 1838. Francis Bond Head had once explained to Lord Glenelg his "weasel strategy" for victory over the Reformers. "Do you happen to know why a little weasel always kills a rat? . . . The rat is the strongest animal of the two, and his teeth are the longest, but he bites his enemy everywhere, whereas the weasel always waits for an opportunity to fix his teeth in the rat's jugular vein and when he has done so, he never changes his place or lets go till the rat is dead." But it was Robert Baldwin who proved to be the successful weasel, fastening on to the Tory constitutional jugular and never letting go until responsible government was accomplished.[22]

The coming of Durham had revivified the Reform movement. With Mackenzie and other radicals driven into exile or tried and shipped off to Australia, the field was left open to the Baldwinian moderates. That summer of 1838 they began to think about how their ideas might actually flourish in the fluid atmosphere of post-rebellion Canada. Robert and William Warren were joined by a recent Irish immigrant, Francis Hincks, and the three would play the central roles in recreating Reform. When he came to York in 1832, Hincks rented a warehouse on Yonge Street from the Baldwins to carry on a wholesale business. He soon became a close friend and a strong political ally. When Robert travelled to Britain in 1836, it was Martha Hincks who helped out with his children. Robert turned to Hincks again in 1838 when he was planning to revive the party. Together they decided on the need for a new liberal newspaper in Toronto to preach the gospel of the Baldwin solution; when the *Examiner* first appeared under Hincks's editorship on 4 July 1838, "Responsible Government" appeared on the masthead. Baldwin and Hincks also carried the message beyond the city. They travelled the hinterland that summer, stirring the embers of Reform, creating a network of men committed to responsibility. The two men were determined that theirs would be the answer to Canada's problems, and they shrugged aside other responses to the crisis. There was an attempt to create a bipartisan group to map a political future, a group led by Tory W.B. Jarvis and James Small, who had articled as a lawyer in the office of Baldwin and Son. They tried to recruit Robert to their cause. He wanted no compromise, however. His eye was steadily on the prize of responsible government.[23]

The appearance of Lord Durham's report in 1839 gave the Reformers' efforts sharper focus. That summer the Baldwins and Hincks began to hold meetings to express support for the report and to petition for its adoption by the British government. In the rough-and-tumble politics of the early nineteenth century, that could be dangerous work, as they discovered on 15 October 1839. They had called another in their series of

"Durham meetings." Runners were sent out into the countryside around Toronto summoning Reformers to gather at Finch's Tavern on Yonge Street, north of the city, at 11 that Tuesday morning. As the liberals arrived they found a band of Tories already in the meeting field. Led by Sheriff Jarvis, Robert's erstwhile electoral opponent, they had come out from the city in wagons, well armed with jugs of whiskey and, Reformers would later allege, with muskets and heavy sticks of hickory. Although the gathering Reformers heavily outnumbered their opponents, the latter included some thirty or forty experienced street fighters, hired at two dollars each.[24]

Dr. Baldwin tried to take the platform to begin the meeting, but Jarvis shoved him back and seized control of the gathering himself. As the Tories held their own anti-Durham meeting, the Reformers retreated some 137 metres and gathered around a wagon. William Warren jumped up on the back of the farm vehicle to address his compatriots, but his speech was a short one. He was drowned out by blood curdling yells as the Tories rushed the Reformers, delaying only long enough to smash down a fence to use its boards as weapons. The conservatives overwhelmed the liberals with the sheer ferocity of their attack. They were all over the wagon, shattering it into pieces, as Dr. Baldwin leaped for his life. He and Hincks dashed off through the surrounding fields, fortunate to outdistance the furious Tories. Not all the Reformers were so lucky. A boy named Leppard was struck down in the attack on the wagon and left to die in that farmer's field.

Tory violence could not stem the tide of reform. If the radical Reformers had been crushed in their failed rebellion, the high Tories had also been discredited, widely blamed for creating the conditions that led to rebellion. The conditions were favourable for the re-emergence of liberalism, and for Robert Baldwin to assume its leadership. His rise as leader was to be explained partly because of his early advocacy of responsible government. As that reform was buoyed by Durham's support and seized upon by liberals in Britain, Canada, and Nova Scotia as a solution to the colonial problem, the stock of its pioneer advocate quite naturally soared. There was, as well, a vacuum of leadership, with Mackenzie and Bidwell and Rolph and so many others driven from politics. Robert Baldwin, that most reluctant of politicians, that most private of public men, was sucked into the vacuum. It had fallen to him to lead his province into a new constitutional, and indeed a new social and economic, era.

———◆———

In the immediate prospect, Robert's assumption of leadership led directly to his humiliation by Lord Sydenham in June 1841. It had all begun promisingly enough. Lord Durham's report had recommended that Upper and Lower Canada be united into a single colony. There would be one legislature with equal representation from each of the old colonies in its lower house. In large measure this recommendation was made by Durham, and adopted by Britain, as a way of controlling the French Canadians of Lower Canada. Although more numerous than the English, they would be underrepresented in the new Union Parliament where, as well, their language would be proscribed. Despite the injustice which lay at the base of the proposed union, it had become clear to Baldwin and Hincks that in that union lay their great opportunity. If liberals could steal a march on conservatives by creating a united, cross-province Reform Party, they could dominate the politics of United Canada. The arrival in October 1839 of a new Governor General, Charles Poulett Thomson—who soon would receive the title of Baron Sydenham and Toronto—confirmed the imminence of union and gave urgency to the party building.

Their chosen ally in constructing the party was Louis LaFontaine. LaFontaine was thirty-one in the spring of 1839 and the bright light among Lower Canadian liberals. Though young, he had served in the provincial Assembly before the rebellion. His political success was supported by a brilliant legal career and a considerable personal fortune, a fortune which flowed from his wealthy father-in-law, Amable Berthelot. Like Baldwin, LaFontaine had remained on the fence during the rebellion. He was arrested during the second Lower Canadian uprising of 1838, but was released without charges and with his reputation unsullied. LaFontaine was a handsome and charming man, but he could be irritatingly pretentious. He moved among the people, one advanced liberal scoffed, like an aristocrat of the *ancien régime*. It was characteristic that he had changed his name from the bourgeois "Menard dit

LaFontaine" to the aristocratic "LaFontaine." He delighted in his striking physical resemblance to the great Napoleon Bonaparte and carefully coiffed his hair in the Napoleonic style. As well as the emperor's hairline, he had much of the Bonaparte strut. But he was engaging, politically astute, and most important, he held the correct political opinions.[25]

LaFontaine believed that French Canadians must make the best of their situation and make the British constitution work for them. This pragmatism lacked the romance of the isolationist nationalism which had been defeated in the rebellion and which was still espoused by major political leaders such as John Neilson, editor of the *Quebec Gazette*. But LaFontaine's approach fitted the facts. French Canada was British and likely to remain so. The real issue was how best to protect the French language and culture within that reality.[26]

LaFontaine's moderation attracted Baldwin and Hincks. The latter initiated correspondence with the Lower Canadian in April 1839, inviting him to join in an alliance of French and English Reformers in the future United Canada. LaFontaine was interested, and flattered, but he recognized that the gamble was a big one for both sides. Could Hincks and Baldwin trust the French to trade nationalism for constitutionalism? Could LaFontaine trust the English to give justice in a Union whose guiding purpose was the assimilation of the French? They felt their way toward an understanding in an extended correspondence between LaFontaine and Hincks. There were direct contacts as well. In August, William Woodruff, a Reform politician from the Niagara region, met with LaFontaine and Jacob DeWitt, a Montreal businessman and liberal notable. They exchanged information and discussed future election strategy. The key was the correspondence, however. Ideology, tough-minded practical politics, hopes and fears, and simple attempts to become comfortable with each other, all blended in their letters. What was needed, for the Lower Canadians, was some gage, some guarantee of the good will and the reliability of the Upper Canadian Reformers. That assurance came from the character of Robert Baldwin, and it became the basis for the trust that developed between the Reform leaders of the two provinces. His reputation for integrity was as familiar in Lower as in Upper Canada, thanks to the existing links between individual liberals. Hincks could assure LaFontaine that Baldwin's leadership of the Reform party was itself a promise of justice. Baldwin the "incorruptible," as Hincks referred to him, would stand by his friends in Lower Canada even if "he was sure of being deserted by the Whole of Upper Canada." It was salesmanship on Hincks's part to create this idealized image of Baldwin but the image, in fact, proved to be remarkably accurate in the political practice of the Union of the Canadas.[27]

Baldwin's character could also produce strains on the relationship. He had never met the new Governor General, Charles Thomson, but he responded with reflex loyalty to a vice-regal summons. Thomson asked Baldwin to enter the Tory-dominated ministry as Solicitor General for Upper Canada and, to the his colleagues' astonishment, Baldwin agreed to do so on 14 February 1840. LaFontaine angrily rejected the parallel post for Lower Canada. The French leader recognized that Thomson was a deceitful, hard-edged, even dictatorial politician who masqueraded as a friendly liberal. Luring Reformers into his government was a ploy to give the ministry credibility and to stave off demands for political reform. LaFontaine knew this and was puzzled that Baldwin apparently did not. Yet the deal made sense to the two principals. Thomson crowed to the Colonial Secretary, Lord John Russell, that he had accomplished a brilliant coup. Baldwin's presence in the government would reduce the influence of the Family Compact, on whom Thomson had had to rely in Upper Canada, and at the same time buy the silence of the radical Reformers.[28]

Baldwin's reasoning, typically, was more complicated. Robert knew that his decision to accept the offer would surprise and alarm his allies. To reassure them he set out his thinking in letters to prominent Reformers across Upper Canada. He had taken office, he said, "under a sense of public duty and with a Sincere desire of aiding the Governor General in carrying into effect the Commands of Her Majesty to administer the Government of these Provinces in accordance with the well understood wishes and interests of the people," as Lord John Russell had instructed Thomson to do in a dispatch the previous autumn. He recognized that entering a ministry filled with political opponents put him in "an anomalous position," but he wished it understood that he had not joined a coalition. He served only the governor and had confidence only in him. This somewhat naive explanation was good enough for most Upper

Canadian liberals who had a compulsion to trust and support a British governor. Few questioned the assumption that was implicit in Baldwin's letter—the assumption that administering the provinces "in accordance with the well understood wishes and interests of the people" meant the introduction of responsible government.[29]

Baldwin revealed much of himself in the letter. There was his exaggerated sense of duty that compelled him to aid Thomson in easing the transition to Union, despite the obvious political risks. There was his invincible innocence—or, to the less charitable, credulity—which led him to trust the honeyed words of others. These were dangerous attributes when dealing with Thomson. The danger was compounded by Robert's tendency to believe what he wanted to believe, even when there was compelling evidence to the contrary. For the next year Robert would believe that he had received firm assurances from the governor that responsible government (as Robert understood it) would be established in Canada. That belief sprang from a confusing meeting between Baldwin and Thomson on 13 February 1840.[30]

Thomson gave his version of events in a letter to Lord John Russell. He was visiting Toronto and summoned Baldwin to Government House to offer him the Solicitor Generalship. Maybe Baldwin was now seen as more radical, thanks to the agitation over the Durham Report, so, Thomson reported, "I thought it right to administer your Dispatch of the 14th Oct . . . to him, with every word of which he concurred." Robert's concurrence was an act of massive self-delusion, one which would have appalled his allies. The dispatch from Russell to Thomson of 14 October 1839 was, in fact, an attack on colonial responsible government. It was impossible for a governor to serve two masters, the Crown of England and a colonial executive council, Russell insisted. The campaign for responsibility was "the cause of embarrassment and danger." Small wonder Thomson considered it a triumph to gain Baldwin's acquiescence to the terms of the 14 October dispatch.[31]

But there is another perspective to the meeting: Baldwin's. Shift the scene. Nervously, Robert enters the Lieutenant-Governor's office at Government House where C.P. Thomson is waiting. After an amiable conversation about the great work they will do together, Thomson "administers" Robert the Russell dispatch of 16 October 1839, not the dispatch of 14 October. Robert has many voices echoing in his ears as he listens to Thomson read. One is the voice of Lord Durham speaking through the conciliatory words of the 16 October dispatch, promising responsible government in all its essentials. Another voice is that of Lord John Russell, assuring that true reform will come to the colonies. Yet another is that of Robert's father, urging that they grasp this token of progress toward the promised land of responsibility. And there is the voice of Thomson himself, cajoling and confusing. Small wonder that Robert should lose the underlying meaning of Thomson's words amid this cacophony.

If it was the dispatch of 16 October that Thomson read, Robert's agreement is much more explicable. That document had a very different tone than the harsh attack on colonial responsibility of two days earlier. The 16 October dispatch was a circular letter to colonial governors about the tenure of public officers. Such officials were no longer to have lifetime tenure, but could be called on to retire "as often as any sufficient motives of public policy may suggest." Russell intended to strengthen the governors' hands by permitting them to adjust their ministries to both imperial and political needs. Yet it is understandable that Baldwin might see this as a concession to responsible government; others, including Nova Scotian liberal leader Joseph Howe, saw it that way as well. Such a policy, after all, meant the destruction of permanent oligarchies such as the Family Compact and the wishful might well assume that the "motives of public policy" would be to satisfy the growing demand for responsibility. Such an interpretation was reinforced by Thomson's artful muddying of the waters. When the Upper Canadian Assembly asked him to provide copies of the two Russell dispatches, he declined to do so. Instead he sent the Assembly a message on 14 January 1840, which gave his own ambiguous version of the two documents. The queen had commanded him, he said, "to administer the Government of these Provinces in accordance with the well understood wishes of the people." What else could this mean, to the ears of a true believer such as Robert Baldwin, but the concession of responsible government?[32]

How should we interpret these different scenarios? Thomson may have willfully lied about which dispatch he read as part of his elaborate scheme to scuttle the Reformers. Baldwin may have thought he heard what he wanted to hear rather than the governor's actual words. Whatever the truth about the meeting, the result was the same. Baldwin was trapped and he soon would realize it. Thomson did not share Baldwin's constitutional opinions and by the summer of 1840 he was openly denouncing discussion of responsible government as "fruitless." Robert found himself in a terrible tangle. As an officer of the government he could not criticize publicly the policies of Thomson (or, rather, Lord Sydenham, as he became in August 1840). This imposed silence strained relations with LaFontaine and Hincks, who had no such limitation. As Sydenham unmasked, as he made evident his intention to operate government according to his own lights, not those of his ministry, as responsibility remained a distant flicker, advanced liberals grew impatient. The French, and some Upper Canadians, wanted Baldwin to resign in protest against Sydenham's arbitrary style of government. Most western Reformers, however, were still prepared to trust a British governor and urged Baldwin to stay in the ministry. Robert was attempting to bind the Reformers into a party and therefore had to listen to the moderate majority in Upper Canada. The party, after all, was the keystone for any successful political reform. As he would tell the Assembly in June 1841, he was "a party man, and he should continue as such. Parties were incidental to all popular governments and it was only through the instrumentality of party, that such governments could be successfully worked." To build the party that would make responsible government possible, he needed to stay in office and avoid conflict with the governor. Yet the governor himself might be the major barrier to responsible government and Baldwin's retention of office strengthened the governor. Doing one's duty was straightforward enough for a man of integrity. The problem was in knowing where duty lay.[33]

It was not made easier by the character of the governor. Robert was fortunate to be serving in Toronto while Sydenham was domiciled in Montreal, minimizing their personal contacts. Even so, he heard the rumours. Robert was nothing if not proper and he never revealed his private opinions about Sydenham, but he must have found the vain and flamboyant governor distasteful. For Sydenham the government, if not the state, was himself. All triumphs were personal ones. "I have put matters right for you in Nova Scotia," he crowed to Russell;

"I have succeeded in Lower Canada"; "I" always "I". Even Robert Baldwin eventually realized that it was unlikely that Sydenham was going to transmute into a constitutional sovereign. Nor was his egotism his only troubling characteristic. A friendly observer, Charles Greville, chronicler of English public life at the time, called Sydenham "very good humoured, pleasing and intelligent, but the greatest coxcomb I ever saw, and the vainest dog." A coxcomb he was and a rake to boot. The goings-on at Government House were widely reported, especially in the French press. *Le Fantasque*, a satiric Quebec journal, delighted in stories about Sydenham's harem and his "maids of honour." After the governor's death the novelist John Richardson was emboldened to discuss Sydenham's "sacrifices to Venus [and] to Bacchus" and his philanderings with ladies both married and unmarried. If politics had not divided Baldwin and Sydenham, morality would. Baldwin, after all, was a man who, when he was in power in 1848, would vet candidates for public office on the basis of their moral characters.[34]

Sydenham also had prejudices that would infuriate Baldwin. A deeply dyed English chauvinist, Sydenham was contemptuous of the French who, he believed, would be better off under "a despotism for ten years or more; for, in truth, the people are not yet fit for the higher class of self-government—scarcely indeed, at present, for any description of it." LaFontaine and the other French leaders were "a little clique of Lawyers and Doctors" who told absurd lies to their illiterate and gullible followers. Nor was Sydenham above petty spite in his desire to keep the French in their place. That was part of the motivation behind his choice of 10 February 1841 as the date for the proclamation of the Union of the Canadas. "To the lovers of coincidence," he mused, "the 10th has many charms." It was the anniversary of Queen Victoria's marriage and of the christening of her infant daughter. More intriguing was that it was also the anniversary of the cession of Canada by France in 1763 and of the suspension of representative government in Lower Canada in 1838. There was pleasure in some gentle twisting of the knife.[35]

Chapter 5

This Struggle between Good Government and Evil Government

She lay in the family crypt, in the hillside below his window. That was calming in this time of decision. She had been there for five years and one month. It was February, 1841.

The Re-Union Act was adopted by the British Parliament in July 1840 although it did not take effect until February 1841. It created one province out of two, but the structure of the new government was familiar enough: a legislature made up of an appointed Legislative Council and an elected assembly; a governor exercising the prerogatives of the Crown whose independence from the legislature was buttressed by the provision of a civil list to pay the salaries of officials; an executive council comprising the heads of major government departments who would now be expected to hold seats in the legislature.[1]

The province over which this government would prevail was still recovering from the turmoil of the rebellions, still threatened by rebel military threats from the United States and by civil disorder at home. So uncertain was the prospect that one government officer, the inspector-general for Upper Canada, John Macaulay, was reluctant to build a house at the new capital of Kingston. "It would hardly be worth our while to build a comfortable House for the Yankees or our own people to batter down." The province was also in poor shape financially. Sydenham estimated the provincial debt to be £1,226,000 sterling, almost all of it accumulated by Upper Canada in building canals and other public works.[2]

Still, it was a place of promise. There was a vast sweep of territory from the Gaspé Peninsula in the east to the Hudson's Bay Company lands in the north and west. Population was concentrated in the Great Lakes–St. Lawrence Lowlands where the bulk of the 1.1 million people lived. Despite the Union these people continued to think in terms of the two old provinces and continued to use the old names. Lower Canada had the larger population, about 650,000 to Upper Canada's 450,000, and the preponderance of French Canadians gave it a unity that was lacking in polyglot Upper Canada. Lower Canada also had the major commercial centres: the timber port of Quebec with its 35,000 people and Montreal, the chief transshipping and financial entrepot, then a city of more than 40,000. Upper Canada lacked developed urban centres; Toronto, the largest, had only 14,000 people. Upper Canada's strength was its great agricultural frontier full of potential for economic progress and population growth. It would outstrip Lower Canada in population and wealth over the next decade and Toronto would emerge to rival Montreal. The rich future of this new Canada, however, was far from obvious to all in the troubled present of 1841.

There were mixed feelings in Baldwin's Toronto. Lord Sydenham chose the small city of Kingston, at the east end of Lake Ontario, as the capital rather than Toronto. As with other prominent Torontonians, the Baldwins had expected their city to win the prize and were chagrined at the choice of Kingston. Yet Robert would come to see the wisdom of the decision. Had Toronto been chosen, Montreal would have been enraged. More, a neutral location such as Kingston was symbolic of the new start that the Union represented. And Robert was delighted that Sydenham was making a clear statement that the power of the Toronto Family Compact was smashed beyond repair.[3]

Torontonians made the best of it. The initiation of the Union was marked on 10 February by a reception at Government House in Toronto with entertainment by celebrated magician Signor Blitz and a banquet at the Ontario House hotel in honour of the retiring Lieutenant-Governor, Sir George Arthur. The proclamation ceremony had taken place the previous day in the executive council chambers. Robert Baldwin and the other government officers joined the judges, municipal councillors, and other prominent citizens of the city in the soon to be redundant Upper Canadian parliament building on Front Street. It was the last convocation of the ruling elite of Upper Canada, who would see its political and social primacy diluted in the larger society of United Canada. Robert knew them all; he moved socially with many of them. Across the room, all in ecclesiastical black and purple, was his old teacher and now political foe, John Strachan. Raised to the dignity of Bishop of Toronto in the Church of England in 1839, Strachan was the very image of the stout and hearty Anglican pastor, though his face was showing his sixty-two years and his manner reflected something of the passing of his once overreaching power in Upper Canadian politics. Near Sir George Arthur as he read the proclamation of the Union were the executive councillors whose terms were expiring along with the independent life of Upper Canada. There was old William Allan, the business genius of the Family Compact, alongside the bland bureaucrat, Provincial Secretary R.A. Tucker. Two of the councillors were Baldwin relatives. Captain Augustus Warren Baldwin, a retired naval officer, was Robert's uncle and neighbour, a man as self-satisfied and complacent as Robert was uncertain and nervous. Robert Baldwin Sullivan, cousin, brother-in-law, and law partner, was as gregarious and charming as ever, looking always as if he was about to down a stirrup cup and ride off to the hounds. The relatives had greeted each other warmly, as usual. Yet it was indicative of this family's unique place in Upper Canadian society that its members should be so prominent on both sides of provincial politics, that Augustus Baldwin and R.B. Sullivan should be as stoutly opposed to Robert as were Bishop Strachan and the other Tory notables present. It was also indicative of the intimate scale of Upper Canadian society, and the impermeability of its elite, that the gentry politicians—Tory or Reform—had studied at the same schools, frolicked at the same skating parties, and enjoyed the same benefits of patronage and land grants. It had seemed the natural order of things for so long but here, in the council chamber on this late afternoon of 9 February 1841, it was passing away.[4]

The reorganization of the government completed the establishment of the Union. On 13 February Robert received a summons from the Governor General to join the new executive council. While the other seven new councillors promptly assumed their seats, Robert pondered. He did not go to Montreal to take the oath of office, but he also did not write Sydenham to decline. He went about his daily business, handling routine matters at the Solicitor General's office, giving his usual rather absent-minded attention to the law practice. Much of his time, however, was consumed by consultations with Hincks and other Reform leaders in Toronto and even more by solitary contemplation in his office at Spadina. There, with his view out over the family estate and over the crypt where Eliza lay waiting, he weighed the risks. If his retention of the Solicitor General's post had been controversial, how much more would be a seat on the executive council? There he would have to advise the governor daily, and work beside the Tory enemies who dominated the council. So he waited and thought.

Even so he was in a compromising position. In theory the Solicitor General was a non-political law officer, preparing and prosecuting cases on behalf of the Crown. It was the Attorney General, now the conservative leader William Henry Draper, who was supposed to carry out the more political functions of advising the government on points of law and drafting legislation. In practice, with the law departments very small and in a primitive stage of development, both senior officers became embroiled in political-legal responsibilities. Robert could not avoid being involved in the political planning of an administration in which he had no confidence. But his own partisan zeal also contributed to the problem. He could not resist the chance to assist the Reform cause. Pressing his recommendations for patronage appointments and political tactics could assist Reformers in the upcoming elections. On 15 February 1841, for instance, he wrote to Sydenham with a list of suitable returning officers for Toronto-area ridings and suggested locations for polling places. The polls should be convenient for voters, he wrote, "but above all they [should be] as far as possible removed from the neighbourhood of any orange clique." The Orange Order, the ultra-Protestant fraternal order, had an established record of violent intervention in elections on behalf of Tories. The information about suitable poll locations, he noted, had been obtained while he was on the court circuit carrying out his supposedly non-political functions as Solicitor General.[5]

Robert attempted to ease his mind about his anomalous position, but his awkwardness led only to humiliation. The first attempt was verbal when he confronted William Henry Draper. Draper, the new Attorney General West, was the most amiable of Tories, a cheerful, chubby little man. He was on good terms with political friend and foe, including the

Baldwins. Indeed, he was a tenant in one of Robert's Yonge Street houses. He was among the first to drop by to congratulate Robert on joining the Union government. Ushered into the parlour of the Front Street house, Draper was astonished to find a polite exchange of pleasantries quickly turning into a ponderous Baldwin lecture. He was accepting office, Robert explained patiently, but it should be understood that he was not accepting the political principles of his fellow government officials. Draper excused himself as soon as he could, but they parted amicably enough since Draper put little weight on Baldwin's reiteration of the obvious. Robert's next attempt at clarification created a greater stir, however.

On 18 February he wrote to Sydenham. He acknowledged the summons to the executive council, but emphasized the terms on which he would serve in the ministry. He had "an entire want of political confidence" in all of the ministers except receiver general J.H. Dunn, provincial secretary west S.-B. Harrison, and provincial secretary east Dominick Daly. If it became apparent that the political principles of the other ministers were to be the basis for the government, he would have to decline office. In a revealing phrase, he indicated his "almost nervous anxiety" over being misunderstood on this crucial issue. To avoid misinterpretation he intended to communicate to the ministers "his sentiments in regard to them politically." On 22 February he did so in individual letters to each. He advised the unsound ones of his lack of confidence in them and his continued adherence to the principles of responsible government. He had done all he could to end the ambivalence of his position.[6]

Draper professed to be puzzled by all the stir, and probably was. There was enough work for the government officers in achieving peace and prosperity for their fellow citizens, he replied to Baldwin, without picking quarrels over impractical principles. Draper stood by Russell's dispatch of October 1839 and as long as the ministry accepted its broad truths and got on with their jobs, "it was a matter of secondary consideration whether we agreed or not." Most of the ministers, and most of the public, would have endorsed Draper's commonsensical approach and would have been equally perplexed by Baldwin's harping on abstractions. But, then, Draper's unwillingness, or inability, to grasp the ultimate importance of such abstractions would be the final difference between him and Baldwin; despite his good sense and his charm, Draper would be dumped on the scrap heap of history in the next decade.[7]

Sydenham was less accommodating than Draper. He wrote to Baldwin on 1 March, striking his usual lordly tone. He had seen the Solicitor General's letters and thought them presumptuous. It was not Baldwin's place to judge his colleagues. Sydenham would ask for advice when he wanted it and he would judge its merits if his councillors disagreed. Until such a time there would be no "general & sweeping declaration of confidence in one man & want of confidence in another." Whatever he had hoped to accomplish, Robert had failed and he beat a hasty retreat in the face of vice-regal displeasure. He humbly retracted. Writing in his usual stilted third person, Baldwin declared that he had no difference from the governor on the principles that underlay the ministry, the principles of the ubiquitous Russell dispatch. He did not even comment on Sydenham's autocratic view of advice from the cabinet or the governor's tacit rejection of the concept of cabinet solidarity. The teapot tempest was over, and Robert could only accept defeat.[8]

There were more immediate concerns than the principles of government, at any rate. Baldwin could see Sydenham applying pressure to political moderates, both conservative and liberal, building something like a political party that owed allegiance only to Sydenham himself. Even close associates in the Reform ranks were draining off to Sydenham, wooed by promises of progress and by loaves and fishes—government jobs, public works for their constituencies. To make matters worse, Robert himself did not have a seat for the forthcoming elections to the Union Assembly. He had announced as a candidate for Toronto as early as February 1840, but his hopes there had been dashed. The Baldwinites had tested the waters by running candidates in the municipal elections in the fall of 1840. All of them were routed by the power of the "Corporation," as the local Tory power brokers were known. The entrails were easily read and Robert withdrew as a candidate for Toronto in January 1841. He compounded the humiliation by issuing a public broadside attacking the corruption of the Corporation. In reply, Toronto city council passed a motion demanding that Baldwin explain his part in the rebellion and hinting darkly about his loyalty. The sordid public quarrel made Sydenham wonder whether it was worth the trouble to keep Baldwin in the ministry. Baldwin's decision to withdraw from Toronto was foolish, Sydenham complained to Harrison, and "His address is mere stuff, and will deceive nobody."[9]

Robert's political clumsiness was turning the promise of the Union into ashes. The fiasco in Toronto undermined confidence in him and increased the desertions of Reformers to the governor's party. Waverers were not reassured by the spectacle of the liberal leader shopping about for a safe seat. In the Toronto region he was rebuffed in Halton and Fourth York, where Reform candidates refused to stand aside for him; in eastern Upper Canada, the Reform committee for Lennox and Addington demanded a pledge of support for the government, which Robert declined to provide. Finally, in early March, the reluctant altruist in Fourth York, John McIntosh, agreed to retire and Baldwin was elected without opposition. He also was nominated for Hastings County, east of Toronto, and decided to run there as well in the hopes of securing another Reform victory. Hastings proved to be a hotly contested, and peculiar, election. The conservative candidate was Robert's cousin, Edmund Murney, but little familial affection was apparent. When the polls closed on Saturday, 3 April, Baldwin had a narrow victory of 626 votes to 590. He also had a crop of charges by the Tories of intimidation and corruption on the part of the returning officer, who was alleged to have received illegal votes for Baldwin.[10]

The general election was no more pleasant an experience. Sydenham had cajoled moderate English-speaking candidates to pledge themselves to him, rather than to Baldwin or the Tories. Then he took off the gloves to assure election of his candidates. He created ridings where he could control the results, urban seats for Cornwall, Niagara, Bytown, and Sherbrooke in which, he boasted, he could choose members from his own "drawing room." He intimidated government employees into voting for official candidates. The cities of Montreal and Quebec were ruthlessly gerrymandered. The suburbs were divided off into separate ridings so that the cities proper would elect anglophone candidates. Those were the benign tactics. To reinforce them Sydenham imported from England · an expert in election chicanery, Nicholas Fullam, to manage the planned violence. In many constituencies hustings were located in areas most favourable to government candidates and thugs were recruited to control these polls. Polling then was still open, by public voice vote, and took place over several days. As a result, threats of physical violence could be highly effective in intimidating voters. Fullam and his lieutenants hired canal workers, road crews, and militia units to secure the polls in key ridings, especially in the Montreal region. They made good use of the weapon that would be a decisive implement in electioneering for the next decade: the "life preserver," a whale-bone club weighted with lead at each end. Armed with life preservers Sydenham's hirelings carried the day. Sometimes opponents were too frightened even to attempt to vote. Elsewhere the message was conveyed by a few examples. Resistance often collapsed after a freeholder, who stepped up on the voting platform to declare for an opposition candidate, was hauled down and beaten with clubs. Such violence played a decisive role in at least seventeen of the eighty-four ridings. In eight of the seventeen (four in Lower Canada and four in Upper Canada), people were killed.[11]

Sydenham enjoyed the election from his vantage point in Montreal's Government House, far from the bloodshed. He kept a running count of the results and estimated that he had elected twenty-four government members and twenty moderate reformers who would work with the government. There were eight other elected members who were uncertain, but might be won over. Despite his violence he had been unable to prevent the election of thirty-two oppositionists—twenty from the French Party of Lower Canada, five Upper Canadian Ultra Reformers, and seven Compact Tories. The surprising independence and courage of French Canada was a disappointment, but at least he had rid himself of Louis LaFontaine. When LaFontaine and his supporters marched to the polls in Terrebonne on 22 March 1841, they found the hustings surrounded by an army of Orangemen, tannery workers, quarrymen from Montreal, and a militia company hired in Glengarry, Upper Canada, by Fullam. Rather than lead his people to slaughter, LaFontaine withdrew from the contest. He was in no doubt where the responsibility lay, as he told a Montreal newspaper: "Lord Sydenham, est descendu dans l'aréne pour combattre corps à corps avec un simple individu."[12]

In Toronto Robert Baldwin did not share Lord Sydenham's delight in the election results. Robert had campaigned as a party leader, making sorties by carriage and on horseback into nearby ridings to support friendly candidates. Although he secured his own return in Fourth York and Hastings he saw his party disappearing before his eyes. Most moderate Reformers who were elected owed their success and their allegiance to Sydenham, not to Baldwin. As Robert waited in Toronto for the receipt of election results, he also received letters and visits from Reformers who urged him to make his peace with Sydenham and stay in the ministry. The messages from Lower Canada were very different.

After LaFontaine's defeat, the de facto leadership of the French Party passed to John Neilson, an elderly political veteran who was deeply embittered by the election fraud. Neilson rejected responsible government as a naive delusion and insisted the only protection for French Canada lay in dissolution of the Union. It was a dismal prospect. The "Reform Party" of Upper Canada had largely been captured by Sydenham. The French Party was drifting away into isolationism. Baldwin, the party man, found himself without one.[13]

Ironically, while the party dissipated, Baldwin carried the burdens of a party leader. Tory hostility toward him remained strong in the mistaken belief that he still commanded the Reformers, the "Movement Section" as Draper called them. As soon as the election was completed there was a flurry of letters exchanged among Draper and his allies, trying to create a bloc that could keep Baldwin out of the speakership of the Assembly. In the assemblies of both Upper and Lower Canada, the leader of the majority in the House had traditionally served as speaker. In the new political structures, Draper's concern was based on a complete misreading of the situation. Baldwin did not command the Reform and liberal groups. Nor did he seek the speakership. In a parliament evolving toward responsibility, the majority leader would no longer sit as speaker. Instead a party leader had to be in the parliamentary trenches, guiding and, often, disciplining his troops.[14]

Draper's hostility was expected and unthreatening. More serious was the disenchantment of radical Reformers. Robert's maneuvring for a seat had alienated many, especially in the radical stronghold of Fourth York. Baldwin had pushed and pushed for the Reform nomination there until a popular local liberal, Robert McIntosh, was finally shunted aside in his favour. Supporters were naturally angered when Robert, after all this, chose to desert them to sit for his other seat, Hastings. The key organizer in Fourth York was David Willson, patriarch of the breakaway Quaker sect, the Children of Peace. He tried to be understanding, but warned Baldwin that "the way things are agitated is rather injurious to your reputation." That was an understatement. Although Robert would win election there in 1844 and 1848, he never re-established the trust of the radicals. Fourth York would become the centre of secessionist agitation within Reform, the centre of the Clear Grit radical revolt in the late 1840s, and Robert would suffer a humiliating personal defeat there at the hands of the Grits in 1851.[15]

Of course, it was not only his choice of riding that alienated radicals. His attempt to hold the moderates by retaining office also made him suspect. Many in Fourth York would have agreed with William Lyon Mackenzie's assessment that "Mr. Robert Baldwin took office, on the principle that if he did not approve of the measures of the government he must retire. Gracious Heavens! What a mass of crime he has had to approve of, and we find him in office still, and beating about for a rotten borough to shunt his head in when even Toronto rejects him." The post in Sydenham's government, the undignified shopping for a seat, the choice of Hastings over Fourth York: all were decisions made in the interests of building a broad Reform Party. But all cost him trust among his potentially most reliable allies, the radicals. Those decisions would contribute to Baldwin's ultimate destruction in 1851.[16]

Baldwin had mishandled the election, misread the political situation, and now found himself politically isolated. He had done much to justify the opinion that Sydenham had expressed after the want-of-confidence fiasco: "was there ever such an ass!"[17]

———◆———

On a sunny morning in the first week of May, Robert Baldwin boarded the steamer for Montreal and began a journey to a clearer future. Viewed from the deck that morning, the future might have taken several forms. Robert's ostensible purpose was to take up his seat on the executive council. The more important underlying reason for the trip, however, was to assess relations with the French Party and, he hoped, to patch them—the shape of the future depended on that. There was also a more dramatic possibility. Robert felt it was time to challenge Sydenham on the issue of French Canada, to force the governor to be more tolerant. It was possible that he might so irritate Sydenham that he would have to resign from the ministry. Robert at least knew that some of the ambiguity of his position would soon be resolved, but he could not even guess how. It was an uncertain, even frightening, prospect. Yet, like the lake wind blowing through his hair, the familiar Baldwin sense of destiny refreshed and encouraged him. The family had seen him off, full of assurances that he would win through. Strengthening him in Montreal would be a letter from his father, reminding him of the divine guidance that directed the journey toward responsible government. Act "by the dictates of your own heart & conscience & God will direct you therefore you cannot err."[18]

The journey had many rough patches, nevertheless. No sooner had Robert settled into his room at Rosco's Hotel in Montreal than he received word that a fire in Toronto had razed a section of Yonge Street including several of his properties. Among them was William Draper's home. Their common loss did nothing to warm relations between them, for Baldwin had decided to push Sydenham and Draper. He went to Government House to take the long-delayed oath of office, and to begin to shove. Ushering Robert into the governor's lavish office, Sydenham was all cordiality, suppressing his well-justified impatience. He handed Robert a sheaf of papers, the oaths of office required of an executive councillor, and asked him to read and swear to them. Sydenham's aplomb was shattered when Robert looked up from the papers and declared that he could not swear to one, the oath of supremacy, which affirmed that "no foreign prince, prelate or person" had authority in Canada. That was a false oath. The pope had authority that was legally recognized by the British Crown. He could not and would not take a false oath. His anger rising, Sydenham tried to argue Robert into recognizing the purely formal nature of the oath, but to no avail. The oath was false, Robert insisted, and offensive to the Catholic citizens of Canada, and he would not swear to it. They parted with Robert resolute in his position and Sydenham, slumped behind his desk, mumbling his exasperation. Over the next several days Sydenham consulted the law officers of the

Crown—who, ironically, included Robert Baldwin—and learned the oath of supremacy could be foregone. The issue clearly was not worth a political crisis. Robert was summoned again, took the inoffensive oaths, and assumed his seat at the executive council table on 17 May, over three months after his first summons. Puzzled and irritated by the confrontation, Sydenham poured out his anger in a letter to Lord John Russell. Baldwin, he complained, was "the most crotchety, impracticable enthusiast I ever had to deal with."[19]

Crotchety he may have been, but Robert was in fact playing a double game and playing it with greater skill than he had previously. He joined his fellow councillors in routine committee work, but attempted to drive wedges between them at the same time. Even before taking his seat he had written to his father about tactics. Tell Hincks, Robert advised, to have the *Examiner* describe certain of the executive councillors—the moderates Dunn, Harrison, and Daly—as worthy of public confidence while denigrating the others. But it should be done carefully, in such a way as to make it clear that Baldwin remained the leader of liberal opinion. Dunn, Harrison, and Daly should be described "as men who are looked to with some considerable amount of confidence if not as much as I am." The strategy took him closer to the edge of honourable behaviour. Some days he would leave the council chamber and go directly to a meeting with the opposition to the council, at the home of LaFontaine or Augustin-Norbert Morin. In these secret talks Robert attempted to rebuild his rapport with the French, always harping on the evidence of his sensitivity to the concerns of French Canada, his refusal to take the anti-Catholic oath of supremacy.[20]

The journey had begun well. But Robert knew that the Reform Party was still as wracked as the countryside he passed on the steamer back to Toronto. The Union had been born amid the alternating rain and heavy snow of a exceptionally harsh winter. As the politicians jockeyed in the aftermath of the elections, Upper Canada suffered through a dreary spring and farmers turned from thoughts of politics to worries about getting their crops in the ground. Like the political situation the year would get worse. The wet and cold spring that forced Robert to bundle in a greatcoat as he mused by the ship's rail became a June drought. Now farmers foresaw a shortage of hay and a parched potato crop. But that lay ahead. By the time Robert reached Toronto the cold rain had ended and a spring of success seemed possible.[21]

That was certainly the case for his native city. Despite the disappointment over losing the capital to Kingston, Toronto was in the first flush of the dramatic growth that would mark the initial decade of the Union. Arriving at the busy steamer dock at the east end of the harbour Robert could see the three-storey commercial buildings that were mushrooming throughout the downtown core. Along the major business thoroughfare of King Street—still a dirt path, but now proudly lined with street lamps—were the most important firms, some of them standing on Baldwin-owned land. Looking north he could see a blackened scar where the fire of 8 May had burned more than forty buildings along Yonge Street, including his two rental houses. And, to the west, was home.[22]

At the northeast corner of Front and Bay Streets was the austere townhouse where the family lived for most of the year, except for the brief respites when they escaped the city's increasing bustle for the quiet of Spadina, 4.4 kilometres to the north. Robert perhaps thought, as he enjoyed the familiar cityscape, that the Front Street house suited him better than it did its flamboyant master, his father. It was plain, like Robert, an oblong brick two-storey, its only ornamentation the four Greek columns that flanked the porch and supported the overhanging roof. It was a large and comfortable place, but far from the ostentatious mansions enjoyed by other members of the elite, such as Bishop Strachan's palace further west on Front Street or the Boulton's elegant Grange at the head of John Street. Yes, it fit him well, a homely house for a homely man.

There were pressing political issues to be confronted on the return home. A way had to be found to build bridges to the political moderates, to those liberals seduced by Sydenham. The speakership of the Assembly provided one small span. Hincks and Baldwin were able to convince the French Party not to nominate a radical such as Morin but to support Austin Cuvillier, member for Huntingdon in Lower Canada, who was suitably moderate but also suitably French. Cuvillier's choice was an olive branch to strayed liberals and it had effect. A representative sample of Upper Canadian Reformers was willing to attend a strategy session at the Front Street house on the evening of 28 May. John Henry Dunn was there, the inspector general in Sydenham's ministry who also could speak for the other two liberal executive councillors, Harrison and Daly. Thomas Parke, member for Middlesex County, was a wavering moderate, uncertain whether his future lay with Reform principles or Sydenhamite patronage. Francis Hincks and Dr. Baldwin were identified with the "ultra" wing of liberalism. James Hervey Price and James Edward Small were loyal Robert Baldwin men. All of the six were at least prepared to discuss legislative strategy with Robert, but finding common ground was difficult. Dunn, Parke, and Small all advocated sticking with the existing government as long as it could be pressed into advancing progressive legislation. The others all leaned, with varying degrees of enthusiasm, toward bringing the government down as soon as possible. It was not surprising that the evening ended with no agreement on strategy.[23]

The Ultras' confidence that they could smash the government had been raised by news of Lord Sydenham's critical illness. The political world was buzzing with the word that the governor might be near death. Yet, even confined to his bed, Sydenham was more than a match for Baldwin and Hincks. He was aware that the Ultras were wooing the moderates and "colloquing" with the French, but he was not alarmed. "[T]the Members [of the legislature]," he wrote Arthur, "shall choose between idle discussions upon the terms of Union, or Responsible Govt. and improvement. If they like the first, they shall not have the last." He guessed correctly that few would join Baldwin in choosing principles over loaves and fishes.[24]

———◆———

Shortly after noon on Friday, 28 May 1841 two steamers, the *Brockville* and the *Traveller*, put into the commercial wharf at the foot of Store Street in Kingston. They were bringing Governor General Sydenham and his entourage to take up residence at the new capital of United Canada. The mayor, the presidents of the local national societies, and other notables were at dockside to greet Sydenham as the Royal Artillery fired a viceregal salute. Sydenham and his suite rode on horseback up tree-lined Store Street and under a flag-bedecked arch. Even the houses along the route were dressed out in evergreen boughs and flags, and elegantly attired ladies waved from upper windows, to be appraised in turn by the bachelor governor. The town was, in some ways, a perfect selection as capital. Rich in the heritage of empire, Kingston had been a fortress city of first the French and then the British empire. In rather more ways, however, it was a peculiar choice. Kingston was now a merchant town of barely 5000 people who subsisted on lake shipping, the spending of the garrison, and the new penitentiary. It had few of the facilities or amenities expected in a capital and owed its dignity only to the fact that Montreal and Toronto had cancelled each other out in the contest for the seat of government.[25]

Even Government House was makeshift. Sydenham's procession proceeded beyond the town liberties to reach the new governor's residence, a journey of some 4.8 kilometres from the city centre. Alwington House had been rented from a private citizen, Baron Grant, and hastily renovated. The workers were perhaps too hasty, for a fire broke out during the renovations. With this setback, the work was hardly finished when Sydenham arrived. The facilities for Parliament were also improvised although they would prove more satisfactory than Government House. A new building designed as a hospital, halfway between the town and Alwington House, was converted for the legislature. It was a commodious stone building with some touches of luxury—the hallways featured heavy stuffed armchairs, covered with embossed green moreen, for the comfort of lounging politicians. Still, it had not been built for parliamentary sessions and would always have the air of the temporary.

There were more serious problems than the shortcomings of the official buildings. The town was an unhealthy place, in part because the drinking water was drawn from an inlet of Lake Ontario into which the filth of the city was deposited. There had been an outbreak of hydrophobia (a symptom of rabies) in March which was checked by orders from the town council that all dogs running loose be destroyed. Kingston was also desperately crowded. Housing was scarce and rents high. Even before the government departments began to arrive, military and civilian officials stationed at Kingston were agitating for increased allowance money to meet rising costs. Loss of some buildings in a major fire had combined with profiteering by the citizenry to double rents since the announcement of the choice of capital. Indeed, little accommodation was to be found at any rent. A longtime resident, Ann Macaulay, commented that as early as March, "it puts me to mind of war times with the Billets."[26]

Robert Baldwin was among those who arrived in Kingston in early June, travelling down on the noon steamer, the *City of Toronto*. He moved into a comfortable room at Olcott's lodging house, but his mind was far from at ease. He still could not decide whether to stay in office or move into open opposition to the governor. While pondering his options, he spent his first days in Kingston organizing a province-wide Reform Party. He did so with the delicate sensibilities that only he could have understood. He attended a caucus of members from both sections where the new Reform Party was formally established. Yet he refused to take part in a subsequent meeting where a vote of confidence in the ministry would be discussed, on the grounds that it would be dishonourable to do so while still a member of the government. Since the whole point of the United Reform Party was to bring down the administration, this was a singularly fine point, one too subtle for many of his colleagues to grasp. It was, in fact, a razor-thin point because Robert was now only technically a member of the ministry. While he was writing to Morin on 14 June with his refusal to attend the strategy meeting, another letter was on its way to him, a letter from Lord Sydenham dismissing him as Solicitor General.[27]

Robert had gone to Alwington House on 10 June to tell Sydenham of his dissatisfaction with the government and to announce that he had joined the United Reform Party. It was hopeless to attempt to govern without French-Canadian representation in the ministry, he advised the governor. Draper, Sullivan, Ogden, and Day should be dropped from the Executive and replaced by French leaders. As things stood, Baldwin would have to vote against the government on any question of confidence. That, of course, would require him to leave the ministry. All of this was said, he was careful to insist, "in the faithful discharge of the sacred duty imposed on him by his oath of office . . . to tender good advice."[28]

The result became a cornerstone myth of the Reform Party. Baldwin had bravely resigned in the cause of responsible government. The reality was less heroic. He had merely warned the governor that he might leave unless the ministry was reconstructed. He was still teetering over what course to follow, which ended only when Sydenham pushed. On 13 June Sydenham wrote to accept the resignation that Baldwin had not yet tendered. The governor's letter was a scathing indictment, full of charges that struck close to the bone. Baldwin had expressed no dissent from the executive council's plans for the coming parliamentary session. Indeed, he had largely remained silent. Instead of debating policy the Solicitor General had engaged in "plotting measures with persons out of the Government for [the] ejection from office" of his council colleagues. Sydenham, he wrote, had put up with all this only in the hope of a peaceful opening of Parliament but now his patience was exhausted. He had no regret at being deprived of Baldwin's services.[29]

Not only did he have no regrets, Sydenham was delighted. He could blacken Baldwin before the moderates and, he was sure, finish him forever as a public figure. The leading moderates were already firmly under control. Dunn, Harrison, Daly, and a new reformist minister, H.H. Killaly, all snubbed Baldwin and stayed snugly in office. Further, Parliament had yet to meet, so Baldwin's demand for reconstruction of the cabinet was, even by a strict interpretation of responsibility, premature and probably improper. Baldwin could be shown to be acting only "from factious motives and with a view entirely to embarrass the Government in its actions at this critical time."[30]

The charges hit home. Circumstances had forced Robert to play a double game and he could not help but wonder whether it had been proper to do so. His personal dilemma was confused together with the country's constitutional dilemma. But the personal could also make the conundrum bearable. His family gave him their warm support. For them there was no dilemma, Robert had acted in the cause of honour and duty and British liberty. His mother rejoiced at his resignation. His father offered "Thanks to the God who gave you the strength to resist the temptation of worldly honours thrown in your way to seduce you." The cause was transcendent, and Robert its agent, his father was sure: "God almighty directs us all in the way he would have us go in this important struggle between good Govt. and evil Govt." Their certainty about Robert's destiny, and his inability to do wrong, was unshakeable. In 1843, when they believed that responsible government had at last been achieved, William Warren wrote to his son that "my dear Robert, you are the man—the only man under Gods providence that was fitted for these struggles—and God so ordered you." And his brother, William Augustus, told Robert that "your magic influence is the only thing that can save society." This certainty flowed from their sense of the Baldwinian duty, and the Baldwinian rightness. Robert, however, had a special responsibility and a special talent because of his place in the family. He was the eldest son in a family that placed enormous emphasis upon primogeniture. As with the aristocratic families of the past, the Baldwins believed in the sanctity of property, and in the necessity to maintain and expand the family estates. In this belief the eldest son had a peculiar role, for to him was passed the undivided estate and the keeping of the family's tradition.[31]

As William Warren Baldwin explained, when drawing his will in 1842:

> one child only can be born first—and this in all times and societies barbarian as well as polished has been received as the appointment of Providence . . . this is a motive of the human heart so general that we must hold it natural and therefore just and also useful—it tends to preserve a reverence for the institutions of our ancestors, which though always tending to change, for by nature all human affairs must change, yet resist innovations but those only which are gradual and temperate.

As always, Robert was his father's son. Opposition to primogeniture was an article of faith for North American liberals who hated Old-World traditions of landed power. Yet Robert sailed against his party's position and held doggedly to primogeniture until its eventual abolition in 1851. In his own first will, drafted in 1840, Robert urged his own first son, Willcocks, to "never forget the duties which devolve upon him as the head of a family" and "not merely to use without impairing the property which he inherits from his Ancestors but by diligence industry & economy to increase the same so as to be able besides providing property for the rest of his children to transmit the family Estates to his heir enlarged as well as improved according as God has prospered him."[32]

Chapter 6

The Apple of Discord

It was barely fourteen years since his happiest day, the day of their wedding, and five-and-a-half years since his saddest, the day of her death. Her strength was needed now more than ever. It was June 1841.

At two o'clock on the afternoon of Tuesday, 15 June 1841 Lord Sydenham arrived at the hospital building to open the first Parliament of United Canada. Some of the drama, if not the grandeur, of the occasion had been undercut because the unopened Parliament had already had an afternoon of political excitement. The members met on Monday at noon to take their oaths and choose a speaker. The nomination of Austin Cuvillier was proceeding quietly until Hincks rose and, as one member complained, threw "the apple of discord into the Assembly." He would support Cuvillier, Hincks said, because the nominee opposed the terms of Union and the present ministry. This intrusion of politics into the pleasantries caused a great stir. But the general desire to avoid confrontation in an uncertain political situation led to a rapid smoothing of the waters Hincks had roiled. Cuvillier was elected without opposition.[1]

The excitement was not quite over. Thomas Aylwin, a mercurial French Party member for Portneuf, gave another mighty toss of Hincks's apple of discord. He insisted that the governor ought to have come to meet them that day. Since he had not, Parliament had not opened and therefore the meeting could not adjourn. Aylwin and some of his colleagues intended to sit there until Sydenham did come. It was the first example of Thomas Aylwin's delight in creating trouble for trouble's sake. His intransigence set off a long and uninformed debate about correct parliamentary procedures. Finally the Tory leader, Sir Allan MacNab, called on Baldwin for an opinion. Baldwin sat in stony silence, as he had all afternoon. He explained the next day that he felt constrained from speaking because his resignation was not yet formally announced, a characteristically Baldwinian fine point. More practical were the concerns of the independent member for Essex, Colonel John Prince. He "objected particularly to continuing their sitting, as it had arrived at that hour when they might be better employed in discussing their dinners." The alimentary triumphed over the parliamentary, and Aylwin permitted the confused house to adjourn.[2]

The official opening was more decorous on 15 June. The legislative council chamber, where the speech from the Throne was read, was well disguised in rich velvet curtains to hide its hospital origins. Sydenham was regal in an ornate court suit, enthroned on the speaker's dais and surrounded by a staff glittering in military uniforms. Such state occasions were among the few political events when women were welcome. The historic significance of this day drew a large assemblage of genteel ladies. Many were decked out in that year's fashion features, pins and bracelets in exotic design known as "algeriens," peignoirs in muted colours and, despite the heat, velvet bonnets. It was all flash and colour, a brilliant beginning for the new Union Parliament. There was perhaps a portent in the fact that it was also a stiflingly uncomfortable occasion. So many spectators had crowded in that there barely was room for the members of the Assembly. They were jammed together at the bar of the chamber, sweating and squirming in the mid-June afternoon. The members were grateful when the ceremony was over and they could retire to their own chamber and get down to business.[3]

Robert had a good view of the first Assembly. He was seated in a roost to the far left of Speaker Cuvillier, a position that was as isolated as Sydenham could arrange. As Robert looked down, many of the faces were familiar, some painfully so. Along the ministerial benches across the floor were many men who claimed membership in Baldwin's United Reform Party, but who owed their seats and their votes in the House to Sydenham. Among them were close friends such as James Edward Small, member for the Third Riding of York, a long-time associate who had studied law with Robert's father. Near him was William Hamilton Merritt with whom, until a few days previously, Robert had been corresponding about party strategy. Not that Robert should have been surprised to see how comfortably Merritt nestled into the government benches. Merritt was a prototypical Sydenhamite, nearly as elegant and as arrogant as the governor himself. Merritt also shared Sydenham's view of what was important: rapid economic expansion. The member for Lincoln had won a lasting reputation as a business genius for initiating the Welland Canal in Upper Canada; the fact that he had run it into bankruptcy did nothing to dull the sheen of that reputation. Merritt sat contentedly on the government benches alongside a grab bag of business-minded liberals and conservatives, a leaven of Upper Canadian farmers uncomfortable in their parliamentary clothes, and a few unclassifiable eccentrics such as John Prince, he of the growling stomach during the adjournment debate. The people who Baldwin watched most closely on that side, however, were the members of the ministry ranged along the first bench.

The man who would emerge as the government's most effective spokesman was Robert's erstwhile tenant, William Henry Draper, Attorney General for Upper Canada. Samuel Bealy Harrison was titular head of the ministry and provincial secretary for Upper Canada, but he never matched Draper's influence in the House. Harrison's earnest and ponderous speeches, delivered in an accent that betrayed his Manchester origins, sounded more important than they were. Once one scratched the surface of Harrison, one found only more surface. Beside Draper and Harrison were the lesser lights. John Henry Dunn of Toronto was another old associate of Baldwin. His open and cheerful manner made him popular, but it was already clear that he was an unreliable trimmer who cravenly spanieled after power. Worse, his morality was suspect. As receiver general he safeguarded government funds. It would turn out that he safeguarded them in his own bank account where they earned him handsome interest. Two of the other frontbenchers were avowedly apolitical bureaucrats. Dominick Daly, whom the Baldwinites curiously had thought of as a liberal, was to be known as the "perpetual secretary" as he continued his role as provincial secretary for Lower Canada as if the Union had never happened. His Upper Canadian counterpart was Hamilton Hartley Killaly, an engineer who served as head of the Board of Works. Killaly stood out more because of his appearance than his talent. He was a great bear of a man who strutted about Kingston in a costume that gave witness to his dual role. The bottom half was the bureaucrat in tight satin breeches and patent leather pumps, the top half the canal engineer in much dented hat and rough outdoors shirt, open to expose his hairy chest. Finally, hardly visible from Baldwin's perch, or from any-where else throughout the session, were the other two ministers: the Solicitor General East, C.D. Day, and the colourless Attorney General, C.R. Ogden. What Baldwin did not see at all, of course, were French Canadians—there were none.

There was probably more talent, and certainly more colour, on Baldwin's side of the House. In LaFontaine's absence, leadership of the French Party belonged to Morin and Neilson. A.-N. Morin was a cultured Quebec lawyer. Unhappily, he spoke little English and was by nature very reserved so that he rarely took a prominent role in debates. Nothing inhibited the crusty old editor of the *Quebec Gazette*, John Neilson, who could spout fire in both languages. Neilson, enemy of the Union and proponent of French-Canadian isolationism, was one whom Baldwin would watch closely. So too was Neilson's desk mate, Denis-Benjamin Viger, a veteran of the Lower Canadian Assembly since 1808. Age had not diminished Viger's good looks or his courtly manners, but the little man was as idiosyncratic in his views as Neilson. Both cared little for constitutional principles and, ultimately, both would seek the best protection they could find for French-Canadian culture, wherever that might be on the political spectrum. Yet these two veterans were anchors of stability compared to their colleague Thomas Cushing Aylwin. Baldwin had already had a glimpse of Aylwin's style in the mischievous adjournment ploy the previous day. Aylwin was a tiny man with a perpetual squint, a product of his extreme shortsightedness. But there was nothing foreshortened about his advanced liberal opinions, his warm sympathy for the concerns of working people, or his soaring rhetoric. He was probably the best debater in the House. His reputation in Parliament, though, would be chiefly that of stormy petrel. He had a bizarre sense of humour that was usually fuelled by alcohol. He was given to outrageous and unfair attacks on opponents, flamboyant rhetoric, filibusters full of bad jokes, and the use of obscure parliamentary procedures to thwart the government. Aylwin was not someone with whom Baldwin felt comfortable, but he often was an effective ally in opposition.

At Robert's side were his trusted followers, the little group of Ultras. The trust was not always well placed since two of them, Hopkins and

Durand, were listening to the blandishments of Sydenham. Caleb Hopkins was a Yankee farmer from East Halton, a veteran of the Upper Canadian Assembly, but never a leading light. Now, in his mid-fifties, he was a quiet, bucolic parliamentarian, but one who always had an uneasy relationship with his leader. James Durand, who represented the adjoining riding of Halton West, was cut from a different cloth. He was a smooth Anglican merchant who had politics in his blood. His father had been a member of the Upper Canadian Assembly and his father-in-law was the prominent radical, Dr. John Rolph. Like Hopkins, Durand had his ears open to the governor's siren call. There was no worry about the man at Robert's right hand, however. James Hervey Price of First York was a Baldwinite first, last, and always, a devoted friend and political acolyte. Nor, as the session opened, did Robert have any doubts about the final Ultra, Francis Hincks.

Although only three years younger than Baldwin, Hincks was from another generation. He certainly looked it. Where Baldwin was heavy and middle-aged, Hincks was handsome and youthful. His hair was carefully arranged, his dress elegant. Dramatic flowing sideburns framed a clean-shaven face and reduced the impact of his prominent nose and pinched mouth. Baldwin was deliberate, even ponderous, but Hincks was dartingly quick in motions and in mind, a clever and witty speaker, a powerful polemicist in his newspaper, the *Examiner*. It was in ways a curious friendship, although a warm one. More than different in appearance and style, they diverged widely on many points of ideology, especially economic. Hincks was a modern man, entranced by advanced capitalist ideas and enticed by thoughts of personal wealth. Their closeness through the turmoil of the past few years made Robert feel a strong and uncritical affection for Hincks, forgiving his friend's strayings. In 1841, however, Robert was fortunate that he did not have to sit with his back turned to Francis Hincks.[4]

The small Ultra group was isolated in more than seating. The link of moderate Reformers to Sydenham was strengthened by the throne speech, which promised extensive public works and rapid economic development. Most of the Reformers even refused Baldwin's invitation to meet to discuss a legislative program. The rift was widened when Hincks attacked Thomas Parke of Middlesex for accepting the post of surveyor general. Fifteen Reform members of the legislature drew up a petition supporting Parke and chastising Baldwin for resigning from a progressive ministry. In these early days of the session Robert was left to cast about for a way to build an opposition to Sydenham, even briefly considering overtures from the Compact leader, Sir Allan MacNab, for a Tory–Ultra alliance against the government.[5]

There was little opportunity to launch an offensive at any rate because Robert was busy with defence. Between 15 June and 21 July he faced a series of challenges to his right to sit in the House. First there were charges that his election was corrupt, then claims that he should have had to seek re-election because he took an executive council post after being returned for Hastings. Baldwin was successful in turning back the challenges, but they distracted him from more important business. Even more distracting were the troubles within the Ultra ranks. Francis Hincks had described himself to Merritt in April as "a good party man." That meant, in June, advising Baldwin to resign from the government and counselling open war with the Executive. Yet by early July, Hincks was writing in the *Examiner* that the government should be given latitude because some of the ministers were good liberals. As the session wore on Hincks more often voted with the Sydenhamite majority. By the end of the year he would openly call for all Reformers to join the administration. Hincks's movement had begun immediately after the Thomas Parke affair when he saw how badly he had misinterpreted Reform opinion. And the more he saw of Sydenham's pro-capitalist program, the more he liked it. Hincks was also flattered by attention from the government, praise both inside and outside the House by ministerialists, and his nomination to the chair of the important House committee on currency and banking. Equally influential in his shift was his growing dislike of many of the Ultras' French allies. Familiarity truly bred contempt as Hincks began to see the French as politically and economically backward and illiberal.[6]

There was no United Reform Party, Hincks came to believe, because there was no program that could unite English and French reformers. There was much truth in his analysis. Many in the French Party were indeed conservative and all were preoccupied more with French-Canadian survival than progressive reform. Few felt a bond with their

Upper Canadian colleagues who were, Aylwin wrote to LaFontaine, an ignoble lot. As for the Upper Canadians, they were individualistic, more interested in doing well for their constituencies and themselves than in toeing any party line. And most, as with Hincks, felt that Sydenham had conceded the basics of responsible government by the time the first session had ended.[7]

The central question remained: had responsible government been conceded? Hincks and most other Reformers believed it had been, Baldwin did not. Hincks had had a clear understanding of the matter in February when he had written in the *Examiner* that there were two parts to the principle. One was that British authorities should not interfere in local matters. The other was that the province should be managed by a provincial ministry, chosen from the party that had a majority in the assembly; a ministry that changed when the majority changed. Had Hincks and the others not been bedazzled by Sydenham they would have seen that only part of the second proposition had been conceded. Certainly Sydenham was prepared to change his ministers to keep peace with the parliamentary majority. But he was not about to cease interfering in local affairs, to allow provincials to determine provincial priorities, or to permit party government. Baldwin, unlike Hincks, could see all this and see how far they still had to go to win responsible government.[8]

Part of what had to be done was to keep responsible government in the forefront, to sharpen the contradictions. Robert remembered his father's injunction that "God almighty directs us all in the way he would have us go in this important struggle between good Govt. and evil Govt." God laid out the broad path, but Robert had to steer. He managed to provoke two major debates on the issue: the first on Friday, 18 June and the second at the end of the session in September. In June the House was droning through an insipid debate in reply to the Speech from the Throne. A ministerial newspaper, the *Kingston Chronicle & Gazette*, was impressed by the "courtesy and intelligence" that marked the discussion. A less sympathetic observer might have characterized it as boring and self-serving. Members praised the virtues of their districts and constituents, congratulated the governor for his wisdom, and avoided anything smacking of controversy. Baldwin broke through this polite facade. William Henry Draper was delivering one of those genial addresses which had won him the sobriquet of "Sweet William." He was explaining the present position of the government. The Governor General was responsible to Britain and with that responsibility went the right to exercise wide powers within Canada as royal prerogative. The major function of the provincial ministry was to maintain harmony between the government and the people and to advise the governor about colonial concerns. This was his version of responsible government, or at least his public version. His private views were deeply conservative, as he had confided to his friend J.S. Cartwright in April 1841.

> I half suspect that the advocates of responsible government will not give us that question in its true shape—They will most likely profess themselves satisfied with the [Russell] despatches—& the assurance that the Government is to be administered in accordance with the well understood wishes of the people & and those other generalities which I understand to mean no more than that the Government will endeavour to propose such measures & pursue such a policy as they will be able to carry out with the representatives of the people. But Lord Sydenham no more intends to administer the Government "with the advice and assistance of the Executive Council acting as a Provincial Cabinet"—or to render the Executive Council directly responsible to the representatives of the people, as the ministry at home are to the Imperial Parliament than Sir Francis Head did— [9]

Baldwin was aware of Draper's real views and would not let him escape with sweet platitudes. Robert began mildly enough. Heaving himself to his feet, his movements as ponderous as his speech, Robert intoned that he was happy to note that there appeared to be little difference between Draper and himself. Certainly the governor was responsible to the home government. But he was still unclear where Draper stood on the role of the Canadian domestic government: "if I understood the Hon. gentleman right . . . the Council of his Excellency are to offer their advice only when it is demanded of them, and on all other occasions remain mere passive observers of the measures adopted by the Government, I would beg leave from such a system as this entirely." Councillors, he insisted, were bound by their oaths to bring all matters connected with the public good before the governor and, if their advice was rejected, to resign.

Draper saw the shadow of the trap Baldwin was laying and tried to sidestep by reading the portion of Russell's dispatch of 14 October 1839, which stressed that instructions from the Crown took precedence over local advice for governors. Baldwin was interested, but not diverted. He had one question for Draper. "In the event of such instructions coming from the Home Government, as he could not coincide with, in what manner would he then act?" The trap was sprung, Draper was bagged. If he wished to hold Reform support for his ministry, there was only one answer he could give. Draper rose wearily to his feet. He would, he said, immediately resign.[10]

Baldwin would doggedly test the government's words and actions to force it to commit itself publicly, piece by piece, to the basics of responsible government. It was not easy. It was hard to keep the minds of members on the constitution when they were constantly straying to roads and canals. That was one reason why Hincks's defection was so serious. He shared common ground on economics with many Reformers and could have helped bridge the gap to them. Baldwin, himself, was isolated from most English-speaking members during a session that Sydenham kept focused on issues of development. Reformers might sympathize with Baldwin's political liberalism, but many were repelled by his economic conservatism.[11]

Robert summed up his economic philosophy late in the session, in September 1841. He was opposing the removal of limits on the interest rate charged on loans. He objected "to all new experiments, of which . . . we have had enough this session." As indeed he might, given his station in life. Propertied gentlemen needed no experiments. Their future success did not depend on large public expenditures, on banks or on financial institutions. Both their financial and social fortunes rested on the most conservative of bases, landed property. They might support economic development that was perceived to be good for the country because the wealth and prestige they enjoyed also imposed social responsibility for the general good. But inflation and instability were threats to their place. Hard money was safe; paper money that fuelled capitalist investment was dangerous and fraudulent. Hincks, on the other hand, spoke for a different group: the rising capitalists. For them easy money was a necessity; interest rates should be determined by the market, not by morality. That summer, Sydenham's economic program compelled Baldwin and Hincks to confront their fundamental differences.

Their first major clash was over the "bank of issue." On 11 July Sydenham informed the House that he intended to introduce legislation that would create a state-controlled institution with a monopoly over the issuance of paper currency. With a secure basis for paper currency, the money supply could be increased to support public-works development. As well, the government would turn a handy profit on discounting notes. As chairman of the committee on banking and currency, Hincks was the chief proponent of the bank of issue. Baldwin was vehemently opposed. He was concerned not only about the expansion of soft money, but about the proposed bank's profits that would expand government revenues and therefore the potential for government patronage and influence. As debate dragged on over the measure, Baldwin gathered a loose and curious coalition of bank opponents. Some were rural Upper Canadians who, as with Baldwin, were suspicious of big government and financial chicanery. Most French Canadians joined the opposition, uneasily allied with supporters of private banks, which would lose their ability to issue paper notes. On 31 August they were able to defeat the bank of issue. The humiliation, as much as the financial implications, of the defeat would drive Francis Hincks further away from Baldwin.[12]

Robert found few English-speaking allies for his most dogmatic opposition to big government. He stood against the development projects such as canals and roads that most Upper Canadians believed were necessary to bring the province out of its economic doldrums. He even argued against expenditures to finish the paving of the major highways in the Toronto area, damaging his popularity in his own backyard. How heretical his views were in development-minded Upper Canada was captured in a debate on 2 September:

> Mr. Baldwin said that he thought we ought to stop where we were; and not to vote any more taxes.
>
> A great sensation was produced in the House by this declaration of Mr. Baldwin.[13]

He had hardly more support for his consistent championing of the cause of French Canada. Most of his English-speaking colleagues would have been quite content to see Durham's vision realized, to see French Canada assimilated. Robert, however, recognized the pivotal political position of the French and knew that the English politician who won their trust could control United Canada. He also had an instinctive appreciation of French sensitivities and of the injustices to which they had been subjected, easy enough to understand for an Irishman. Most important, he understood that the Union had set Canada on a difficult but rewarding road toward biculturalism. Robert had few dealings with French Canada before the Union; he spoke no French. Yet he was prepared to stake everything on an accommodation with the French, to run great risks to achieve justice for the French. And he attempted to assure that his children would have a place in the bicultural Canada he visualized. He sent them to schools in Quebec to assure they would not suffer the same embarrassment he felt over his unilingualism.[14]

When leaders of the French Party moved a resolution on 23 June, charging that portions of the Union Act violated the rights of franco-phone subjects, Robert supported them, but could only muster the votes of five other Upper Canadians. It was a measure of his isolation in his advocacy of French-Canadian interests. Even fewer of his compatriots joined him in his demand for complete equality of French and English. When a bill was introduced promising improved municipal institutions for Upper Canada, Baldwin refused to accept it unless Lower Canada also received the reforms. "I would rather have a worse bill [for Upper Canada] which would be precisely similar to that which our fellow subjects enjoy, than a better bill which would be different."[15]

If Robert was often conservative on fiscal matters, he could also be so on social ones. His most emotional outburst in the first session was over a marriage bill. It was a measure to provide simple justice to those who belonged to no religious denomination. At present they were compelled to solemnize marriage before a clergyman, but the new legislation would permit them to "contract" for marriage before a justice of the peace. Baldwin lectured a bemused and largely unsympathetic House on the evils of such a practice. "The sacredness of the obligation" of marriage would be "reduced to a common-place bargain," he warned. Few members were impressed or convinced by his outrage; few probably understood it. He was concerned for the institution of marriage, not for the privileges of religion. Indeed, earlier in the session he had led the fight against the attempt to use the Bible as a text in schools because religion in the schools was a violation of the rights of non-believers. But marriage, strengthened by sanctification, was the foundation of social stability. It was also a very poignant personal concern for the widower Baldwin.[16]

———◆———

Robert and Eliza stood before the altar of St. James Church on 31 May 1827. As Rev. Thomas Phillips led them through the sacrament of marriage, their families looked on. Many of their joint relatives were silently disapproving. Eliza was still very young, not quite eighteen. Robert had just turned twenty-three. Worse, the two were first cousins. Some of the relatives, including Eliza's mother, Barbara Baldwin Sullivan—sister of William Warren Baldwin—had attempted to prevent this day from coming. The family had discovered early in 1825 that Robert and the sixteen-year-old Eliza had fallen in love. To nip the relationship in the bud, Eliza was bundled off to stay with mutual relatives, the Morgans, who lived at 4 Bond Street, New York City. John Jordan Morgan was married to William Warren Baldwin's sister, Elizabeth, so the New Yorkers were considered safe custodians of the young lover. The city's distractions were expected to cool ardour and dampen unhealthy thoughts. The enforced separation, however, only romanticized and deepened the forbidden love.[17]

Robert, so controlled and sensible on the surface, had always been deeply romantic. His correspondence with friends had revealed an almost obsessive interest in women and love. To the dismay of his boyhood companion James Hunter Samson, who would be his groomsman in 1827, Robert exalted love between man and woman over friendship between men. In 1819 Robert had written Samson, who was living in Kingston, to tell him about his interest in a young woman. When several months passed without further correspondence from Baldwin, the disconsolate Samson wrote wondering if Robert was in love and pleading, "but believe me she cannot love or esteem you more than I do."

Robert's capacity to invest his entire being in a romantic relationship both puzzled and alarmed his friend. Baldwin was in despair because his "fair one" seemed to trifle with other young men, cast into depression by his fancied loss of affection. Not yet fifteen, Robert was already prey to his powerful and secret passions.[18]

The two young men had been schoolmates at Dr. Strachan's academy. Their friendship there had deepened into something more, at least on Samson's part. He was happy to believe that Robert's relations with young women were but meaningless and fleeting excesses. He claimed that Robert had given himself over to passion at least ten times, a remarkable total for a fifteen year old in a small town. Yet each time, Samson reminded his friend, he had been cured. Their relationship, on the other hand, was genuine and lasting. It was also a constant source of stress for young James. Robert was anything but faithful in correspondence, leaving Samson "tortured by anxiety and suspence" as he walked to the post office each day, only to be disappointed when, once again, there was no letter from Baldwin.[19]

Robert did confide in Samson in a way that he did with no one else. It was James who read of his friend's awkwardness, his inability to ask the object of his affection to dance; James approved of Robert's decision to assuage his awkwardness by taking dancing lessons. It was James who learned of Robert's new commitment to church attendance, although Samson suspected that Baldwin paid little attention to the sermons and much to a certain "Gallery Goddess." And it was James who acted the acolyte, enthusing over Robert's boyish scribblings at poetry and agreeing to act as editor when the missives were gathered into a slim volume. He must have ached at the recognition that his apparent passion for Robert was unrequited, for most of the verses were dedicated to the charms of individual women or women in general.[20]

Robert's notion of love was exalted and he and Samson had deplored the casual sexuality of the young squires of York. Samson echoed Baldwin's own views when he warned in 1820 that, "There are many very immoral young men there. . . . They talk of virtue as a mere bye word, long since obsolete, the arts of seduction as necessary accomplishments, and the feelings of parents as matters of ridicule." Another school friend, James Givens, was typical of the young blades. When Givens visted

Kingston in 1819, he stayed at Moor's Coffee House. It was a delightful place, he told Baldwin, for it was full of "fine girls."[21]

This was not Robert's way. When he fell in love, truly in love, in 1825 it was deep and all-embracing, an emotion that encompassed everything he was and could be. Eliza became, as he wrote in one of his poems,

> The loved companion of my way
> My hope—my joy—my more than pride
> My beacon to a happier day—

To most observers, Eliza was in no way out of the ordinary. She was plain in appearance with the ample family nose and the rather disturbing, expressionless Baldwin eyes. Even with her dark hair piled high on her head in the current fashion and her long neck graced by a jeweled choker, she was a duckling, not a swan. Her correspondence, too, was plain; if anything marked it, it was juvenile, kittenish, and self-conscious. For Robert, however, she was indeed a swan and her writing filled him with admiration. The style impressed him: "I admire your letter because it is written in that easy style of sprightliness which forms the greatest beauty of epistolary writing which few can attain." And the thoughts and opinions influenced him powerfully: "Oh Eliza your's is indeed a <u>valuable</u> heart there was more prudence & delicacy in that silence than (I fear) I should have shewn—I will profit by your example the time will come when I shall not only be able to profit by your example, but to have the benefit of your immediate advice."[22]

When their families separated them, the correspondence between York and New York often had the style and tone of a bad novel. On 15 May 1825, for example, Robert was agonizing because an expected letter had not arrived:

> I left the house & came down to the Abbey [Russell Abbey, a
> home owned by the Baldwins] where I entered the little Study
> I threw myself into the chair that stands opposite the window
> and gave myself up to the most exquisitely painful train of
> reflections the window was open & the perfume of the blossoms
> of the fruit trees & the buds of the Lylacks just opposite the

window was blown in by the breeze those were the very lylacks from which I used formerly to pluck bouquets for you they brought to my recollection a thousand little instances of your preference and can the thought have deceived me can she have pretended an injury I had done to your delicacy (will you forgive me). Was it possible that the gaities & fashionable frivolity of the City had so soon blotted me from your recollection I could not believe it I would have given the world for a flood of tears to relieve me but they would not come though my head was in dreadful pain—[23]

This could have come from the pages of Robert's favourite novel, *Camilla* by Fanny Burney, which he read each spring from 1824 to 1826. It was a popular romantic novel of love consummated by marriage. Robert himself recognized that some of his melancholic dreams probably resulted from reading *Camilla*. That was true of a dream in May 1826, one which "diffused over my mind a tender yet not altogether agreeable melancholy." He dreamed he saw Eliza at his uncle's home, although she was in fact still in New York:

there was a sadness in her countenance that struck me to the heart it was accompanied with a paleness that startled me. . . . I turned around and saw my Eliza leaning against the pillar that supports the portico on the side nearest the shop with a countenance so deeply impressed with suffering a frame so weak from its ravages & eyes full of tears that I was rushing to support to console but the agony of my feelings awoke me.[24]

Yet if the conventions were those of romance fiction, the sensibilities were authentically Robert Baldwin's. He knew himself. "I am a strange being Eliza I frequently bear pain without a tear but joy always overcomes me." That was because joy was such a liberating emotion, and his whole life was devoted to restraint, to duty, to doing what others thought necessary. And it was also because he had so little experience with joy, outside of the relationship with Eliza who only wanted him to be happy. Robert believed, all too presciently, that his experience with joy would be short lived. On the evening of 14 May 1826 he sat down alone to review his life and think about the future. Those thoughts led to images of the deaths of his parents, his childhood friends "sunk into the grave" and finally even Eliza gone. "I was left there alone the spot on which I stood a waste." Melodramatic, but a vividly accurate portrait of his life a few years hence.[25]

For the moment there was the joy. After more than a year of separation the family recognized that the young couple's love was not to be denied. Eliza was permitted to return home and plans began for the wedding. Even James Samson came around. Samson had been hurt when Robert told him in 1825 that he planned to marry Eliza. "It seemed to me as if I were losing some portion of that, to which I had prior claim . . . I love and esteem you with my whole soul; but can you tell me why your letter has made me so low spirited?" How Samson worked through his confusing emotions he kept to himself. But on 31 May 1827 he stood beside his beloved Robert at the altar of St. James Church.

It was not the grand affair that the Baldwins' social standing might have justified. Rev. Thomas Phillips, not Archdeacon Strachan, performed the ceremony. Quietly disapproving relatives were joined by some close friends. It was an inauspicious beginning to a great romance.[26]

Marriage was all Robert had hoped it would be. Barely ten months after the wedding their first child, Phoebe Maria, arrived. Robert and Eliza were doting and loving parents to all four of their children, in ways more unselfish and undemanding than any parental love Robert himself had experienced. Eliza spoke for both of them when she lilted, "I wish every one was as happy as I am." It was rich, this happiness, but it was short. Less than nine years later Eliza was dead, and emotionally, in many ways, so was Robert.[27]

———◦◦◦———

The lonely struggle against the Sydenham system in the summer of 1841 roused both the energies and the moribund emotions of Robert Baldwin. Again and again, the problem was to force principles ahead of economics. The municipal bill, where Baldwin had advanced his extreme form of equality between the two Canadas, was a good example. Upper Canada lacked municipal institutions that could satisfy even the most basic needs of the population. Hincks and other Reformers recognized that Sydenham's municipal bill was less than perfect, but they were prepared to settle for a measure that made real improvements in local government. Baldwin, frozen in his principles, fought a bitter and futile opposition to the entire bill. During one sitting, on 18 August, Baldwin and his disciple Price moved twelve consecutive amendments and lost them all. The basis of Robert's opposition was, of course, responsible government. He insisted upon the complete application of the elective principle to local government, to make it responsible in parallel to a responsible provincial government. This enthusiasm for local democracy would fade with the years and his own municipal act of 1849 would sharply limit the elective principle. In 1841, however, he was still flushed with the possibilities of responsible government at all levels of administration. Fiscal conservatism was also part of his agenda. He tried to prevent the new municipalities from having the power to borrow money. They were to be models of democracy, but not have the right to make up their own minds on financial matters.[28]

Robert's attacks became ever more extreme as his frustration increased. The municipal legislation was this "abominable bill, this monstrous abortion." His fevered rhetoric and obdurate obstruction produced the first highly public conflict with Hincks. It was 19 August and the municipal bill came forward for third reading. Hincks, smooth and pragmatic, held the floor, patiently explaining the bill's merits. Like some bloated cork, Baldwin popped up from his seat to denounce "the political hallucination of the Member for Oxford" and to level thinly veiled charges of betrayal of principle against Hincks. Hincks's business-like manner dissolved and he gave his old friend equal measure in return. It was Baldwin, he shouted, who had betrayed principle and become an ally of the mossback Tories. This was too much for the faithful J.H. Price, who leaped to Baldwin's defence. The stilted language of debate did not disguise his cold fury at Hincks's betrayal of Reform and of their leader. Baldwin, he reminded Hincks, was "leader of the <u>opposition</u>, to which the hon. member from Oxford once belonged; and the harmony and peace of which he had, by his violence, destroyed and then deserted." Speaker Cuvillier was on his feet, calling Price to order, but the angry Reformer got in one last shot before sitting down. "Our present Governor will not leave this, his truckling government, without testifying his gratitude in no unequivocal way for the assistance rendered to the treasury benches by the hon. member for Oxford." It was an unparliamentary, but an accurate, insult.

Price was red-faced with anger, but Baldwin had cooled to sorrow. This was the Baldwin more familiar to the House, ponderously pulling to his feet, to speak in the low monotone that members strained to hear. The flatness of the delivery, however, did not disguise the drama of the message. Turning to Hincks, Robert delivered an epitaph on their long political partnership: "if the time should come when the political tie which bound them to each other, was to be severed forever, it would be to me by far the most painful [event] which had occurred in the course of my political life." Robert, as always, was better at being a friend than an enemy, a quality of little political value it was true. Francis Hincks, who understood when to be friend and when to be enemy, sat silent as the House voted to pass the municipal bill.[29]

As the session wore down some of the outlines of United Canada's politics were filling in. The issues were more complicated and there were more of them than had been the case in the smaller provinces of Upper and Lower Canada. The difficulty of bringing English and French together added to the complication. As Sydenham remarked to Lord John Russell, French and English in Canada were as unacquainted with each other's views, customs, and histories as if they had grown up on different continents. Learning about each other often did not produce greater understanding. Looking back over the session, John Neilson remained convinced that French Canada was being oppressed by an alien, free-spending Upper Canadian minority who wanted to live on the backs of French Canadians.[30]

Kingstonians, at least, could enjoy being in the capital of the new bicultural colony. The sleepy garrison town was revitalized. A single week in late July and early August saw a large regatta in the harbour, well-attended horse races and a grand ball at Daley's Hotel, with the governor himself charming ladies around the floor. Kingston also became a regular stop for travelling shows. The talk of the town that August was not the municipal bill but a giraffe from "the Southern deserts of Africa," the only one in captivity Kingstonians were assured, which could be seen for an admission fee of one shilling three pence.[31]

Robert Baldwin had bigger, if less exotic, prey in sight. At the tag end of the session, on 3 September, he finally forced a full airing of responsible government. The resolutions passed by the Assembly that day became the basis of Reform legend, the cornerstone justification for the Baldwinite constitutional position in years to come. The legend, embroidered by Reform politicians and codified by historians, ran like this. Baldwin introduced a series of resolutions on responsible government. Recognizing that Baldwin's motions were widely popular, the government drew up propositions of its own that were introduced by S.B. Harrison. The Harrison resolutions, to win support, had to embrace most of Baldwin's view of responsible government. Their passage therefore committed all future governments to the essence of that doctrine. In future, whenever governors strayed from the truth, Reformers could point triumphantly to the resolutions of September 1841. Such was the stuff of political legend.[32]

The reality was a less ambiguous triumph for Baldwin, and less a demonstration of his virtue. He had carefully drafted a set of resolutions on responsibility, which he thought would win majority support in the House and commit the government. The ministry, hearing rumours of his plan, decided to pre-empt him. Resolutions were prepared, probably by Sydenham himself, and entrusted to Harrison for political management. Harrison showed the resolutions to Baldwin who accepted them and, so Harrison understood, agreed to introduce them as bipartisan motions. But in his passion for principle Baldwin had second thoughts, which he did not share with Harrison. Perhaps he wanted to be certain that the precisely correct version of the doctrine was put on the record. Or perhaps his vanity required that his views, the correct views, be aired independently. At any rate he broke his agreement with Harrison.[33]

On the afternoon of 3 September, government members took their seats to the right of the Speaker, content that the session would embody another triumph for the Sydenhamite strategy of smooth management. Instead they were shocked when Baldwin rose and began to drone out his own resolutions, not Harrison's. That Baldwin expressed agreement with the substance of the Harrison proposals was cold comfort. Some of them perhaps did recognize that it was a measure of the supreme importance of responsible government to him that Baldwin would compromise his honour by breaking his word. Government leaders could not afford to be generous in their assessment of Baldwin's motives, however, and there was much anxious whispering as they put heads together to sort out a strategy for dealing with the surprising turn of events.[34]

The circumstances were not the unvarnished demonstration of integrity that lived on in legend. Nor was the victory of Baldwinite responsibility so total. The ministers decided that Harrison should introduce his resolutions himself. They passed easily, and they really captured the gist of only two of Baldwin's six motions. Harrison upheld the right of the provincial parliament to legislate upon local matters, although Baldwin had gone further to limit Britain's jurisdiction to matters which, "on the grounds of absolute necessity," were imperial. Harrison also confirmed that the administration must have the confidence of the Assembly, a point Baldwin made in stronger language.

There were equally important differences between the Harrison and Baldwin versions, especially on the question of relations between governor and ministry. Harrison offered a mild reminder that, while the governor was ultimately responsible to Britain, on local matters he should exercise his authority with the assistance and counsel of his colonial ministers. Baldwin, in contrast, had insisted that the governor "is not constitutionally responsible to any other than the authorities of the empire." That is, responsibility for local governance rested only with the colonial ministers; the governor was totally removed from the party government of the colony. Again, Harrison was vague when he urged provincial ministers to make "their best endeavours" to assure that the imperial authority was exercised in a manner consistent with the wishes and interests of the people in the colony. Baldwin was clear and concise. "[T]his House has the constitutional right of holding such advisers politically responsible for every act of the provincial government, of a local character," and for assuring that the imperial authorities exercised *their* authority in the interests of the Canadian people. Nor could the ministers evade their responsibility by hiding behind the governor; Baldwin's resolutions obliged the governor to make use of the advice of his ministers.

The significance of it all was in the eye of the beholder. For the conservative newspaper, the *Kingston Chronicle & Gazette*, there was no real difference between the two versions and they were all nonsense anyway.

> Mr. Baldwin rose to move certain unintelligible Resolutions.
>
> Mr. Harrison moved in amendment some which we might call counter Resolutions, though they were precisely the same, except that the Grammar was corrected . . . Every body perceived it was a farce and nobody interrupted the performers by any observation. The Magna Charta of Responsible Government is therefore now on the Journals of the House, understand it who may. The public at large seems to be coming into [Tory member] Dr. Dunlop's opinion . . . "that responsible Government was a trap set by knaves to catch fools."[35]

It certainly caught most Reformers. The scene and its results became coloured in glory as Reformers reflected on the resolutions. Robert Baldwin Sullivan, by then in the Reform ranks, contended in a campaign polemic for the election of 1844 that:

> If the resolution of 1841, assented to by the Crown, produced any change in the mode of administering the Royal Prerogative in this colony . . . that change makes the people of Canada judges of the acts of the advisers to the Crown to the same extent that the people of England are judges of the conduct of the ministers of the Crown there . . . . When Canadians obtained Responsible Government, they got the life and soul of the constitution with it.[36]

The truth lay somewhere between the *Chronicle*'s farce and Sullivan's constitutional triumph. Baldwin had won some ground by forcing the government to spell out the limited kind of responsibility that Sydenham was prepared to concede. But he could not gain commitment to key elements of the doctrine. His had introduced a resolution compelling the governor to receive the advice of his ministers and another making the provincial ministers responsible for imperial actions. They were not adopted by Harrison and were defeated on division by the House. If in the long run Reformers could find considerable propaganda value in the resolutions, in the short run Sydenham had once again dammed up the current of constitutional change.

Sydenham did not have long to enjoy his triumph. The day after the debate on responsible government the governor was riding in the countryside near his home. The horse stumbled and Sydenham was thrown. He suffered a badly broken leg and deep gashes in his shin. His body, already ravaged by venereal disease, could not recover. The incompetence of his doctors sealed his fate. They set the fracture incorrectly and Sydenham was soon suffering the agony of crepitus as the broken bones ground on each other. Infection spread and throat spasms left him unable to swallow. Death was always close and familiar in nineteenth century society; bad doctors made it intimate. Their blistering and other heroic remedies only hastened on the result. On the morning of 17 September 1841 Sydenham began to heave and sweat with violent spasms in his abdomen. A few hours later his jaw locked. Finally, at 7:05 on the morning of Sunday, 19 September, Charles Poulett Thomson, Lord Sydenham and Toronto, was declared dead.[37]

The grief which was expressed by the press and at the state funeral on 24 September was not universally felt. On 8 September, while Sydenham was still suffering at the hands of his doctors, a motion of condolence to him had been introduced into the House. To the shock and outrage of many, four members refused to stand to vote for the motion. The four were three Lower Canadians—John Neilson, Joseph-Guillaume Barthe, and D.-B. Viger—and Robert Baldwin. The House was an uproar of angry denunciations as the four recalcitrants tried to explain that their objection was procedural, that the condolence motion took a form inconsistent with parliamentary precedent. It is unlikely their real reason was so legalistic. It was rancour, not rules, that motivated them. In the seven months since the proclamation of the Union, Baldwin had lost some of his naïveté. He had come to recognize at least one of his enemies and he could muster little sorrow over that enemy's discomfort.[38]

Because the governor still lay in the throes of his critical injury, the first Union Parliament was prorogued on 18 September without the pomp that had accompanied its opening. The deputy governor, Major-General John Clitherow, came to the legislative council chamber that Saturday at noon, dressed in a plain military uniform and accompanied only by an aide-de-camp and the governor's personal secretary. The session thus ended in a hush, but it had been productive and eventful. Now, like his colleagues, Robert Baldwin could go home. As he was gathering his papers and belongings at Olcott's boarding house the next morning, he heard of Sydenham's death. This session was over, but Robert would return for another. Sydenham would not. There was comfort in that reflection. Robert thought back on his confrontation with the governor in June and Sydenham's assessment of it. "I have got rid of Baldwin and finished him as a public man." Sydenham would not be the last governor to underestimate the durability of Robert Baldwin.[39]

Chapter 7

Home—My Own Dear Home

Eliza was always there, at the dinner table, in his study in the evening, when he talked to the children—always there. She had been dead for five years and eight months. It was September 1841.

He could feel the tension easing, flowing from his body, as the steamer neared Toronto, bearing him home. Robert was pleased enough with the first session of Parliament, but more pleased to be escaping back into the security of family. His contentment was increased by the knowledge that, even as he sailed, family members were successfully completing the last piece of business from the parliamentary session. They were electing LaFontaine as member for the Fourth Riding of York.

The Fourth Riding had been vacant all summer. Robert had won it in the general election, but chose to sit for Hastings instead. When a by-election was announced in early August the local Reformers selected William Warren Baldwin as their candidate. Robert saw a great opportunity, however. He could secure a safe seat for LaFontaine and consolidate his alliance with French Canada by inserting the Montrealer into Fourth York. It was a political master stroke, but one carried out with Baldwin's usual bluntness and insensitivity. He asked his father to withdraw, without even consulting LaFontaine or the local Reformers. And once the decision was made Robert turned his attention to other things, leaving his father and brother to worry about the details of securing LaFontaine's election. Robert never visited the riding to introduce LaFontaine or to bid farewell to his erstwhile supporters.[1]

William Warren Baldwin dutifully withdrew and arranged for LaFontaine's nomination by the Reformers on 21 August. A few days later, LaFontaine arrived to canvass the riding, accompanied by Étienne Parent, editor of the Quebec newspaper *Le Canadien*. He stayed at the Baldwin home and made a good impression on Robert's daughter Maria.

She wrote to her father in Kingston that, "The more I see of Mr LaFontaine the more I think him like you in his manners and indeed so everyone in the household says." Not all Upper Canadians were so smitten with the friendly French Canadian. LaFontaine was subject to attack both because he was a French interloper and because of Baldwin's legislative record. The Tory press was outraged that the Baldwins, who already had disrupted the political process because of "their querulous, discontented and bilious habit of mind, and a love of fault finding," should now try to foist off a foreigner on Upper Canadians. The *Kingston Chronicle & Gazette* could not believe that the people of Fourth York would "elect a *Frenchman* opposed to progressive improvement of our colony. If they will oppose the Governor General's policy, let them at least choose a representative of whom they know something. And let him be at least an Upper Canadian, an Englishman, Irishman, or Scot." An anonymous broadside placarded around the riding was more concerned with the failings of Robert Baldwin. He had voted to spend public funds on canals in Lower Canada to the disadvantage of roads in his own neighbourhood. Fourth York should elect someone who would do right by the district. The complaints could not change the fact that LaFontaine was a certain winner in this, the strongest Reform riding in the province. No opposing candidate came forward. Nevertheless, the grumblings about Baldwin and about an alien candidate left many Reformers disgruntled. The chief Reform organizer in the riding, David Willson, complained to Baldwin that LaFontaine's "Election cost us more grief than Any heretofore on account of that foolish—and sinful opposition."[2]

William Warren Baldwin and Robert's brother William Augustus organized a series of meetings for LaFontaine at the main centres of the riding during the week of 6 September. This was LaFontaine's introduction to the heart of radical Reform, the rich farmland north and northeast of Toronto, from Stouffville to Lake Simcoe. It was an area entrapped in the economic influence of Toronto but one suspicious of the city and of modernization. Travelling there the would-be aristocrat LaFontaine had to rub shoulders with the rough radicals who were the shock troops of Reform. The French leader may even have quailed at the name of the organization that was sponsoring him. The local Reform association called itself "the Committee of Vigilance of the County of York," a title that echoed of the area's support for the 1837 rebellion. Indeed Willson had been arrested for his activities in 1837 and subsequently pardoned.

LaFontaine was Willson's guest at the village of Sharon on 6 September. There he was polite but puzzled as he was shown Willson's strange and beautiful temple. It was the central symbol of the Children of Peace, the schismatic Quaker sect that Willson had led for some thirty years. The mysterious frame structure gleamed white in the summer sun, twenty-one metres high in its reach for heaven. The first storey was eighteen square metres, the second eight square metres, the third three square metres, the wooden ziggurat topped by a huge gilt ball. Had LaFontaine been there the previous week he would have seen the farm folk streaming into the temple for the annual love feast, which was held on the first Friday of September. This harvest festival and the June seeding feast were the only occasions during the year when the austere temple was used by the congregation of the Children of Peace. For the rest it stood as a peculiar monument in the green countryside of York County, lighting the rural darkness with the large square lanterns that hung on the corners of each storey, and with the passions of David Willson and his people.[3]

The same impulses that made the Children of Peace religiously rebellious and communalist in their social life also made them Reformers. Yet if this rural Reform world seemed strange to LaFontaine it was equally alien to Baldwin. He would work closely with the radicals of Fourth York, both the Willsonites and their more earthbound allies, and represent them in Parliament from 1844 to 1851, but he would never be one with them. The great social gulf between a wealthy, urban patrician and the yeomen farmers was mirrored in fundamental differences in political program. That was already apparent in 1841. Less than three weeks before LaFontaine's nomination, the local Reform leaders had adopted a set of resolutions that set out political demands far in advance of Baldwin's ideas, including voting by ballot and abolition of the court of requests.[4]

The political differences between Baldwin and the Fourth York Reformers would blossom into the Clear Grit revolt after 1849, when radicals would turn on Baldwin and the Reform government he led. By then he would be utterly alienated from his constituents, their insistence on democratic reforms, and their nativist distrust of French Canada.

Their alliance had always been a curious one, of course. Relations were warm enough during Baldwin's campaigns in Fourth York for the 1844 and 1848 elections. Baldwin and Willson corresponded regularly, Baldwin curried favour by donating instruments and sheet music for the brass band that was the pride of the Children of Peace. Even then, however, Robert would not go so far as to accept Willson's invitation to stay at "my humble dwelling." Was it amusement or embarrassment with which Baldwin read Willson's scrawled correspondence? What did he make of Willson's attack in 1843 on the activities of Governor General Metcalfe "which has disquieted a happy and tranquillized Country"? Robert felt both at the rough social occasions he had to attend among the local Reformers, occasions that violated the most basic social conventions of Baldwin's caste. Willson warned his leader of the group's peculiarities when he was arranging a dinner for Baldwin in 1848. There would be none of the toasts that were the mainstays of ordinary political banquets because toasts were "not agreeable to us and a number of [Reform members were] teetotalers and Quakers." There was an even more unorthodox arrangement to draw to Baldwin's attention. "NB our reform women are anxious to attend on these occasions and to hear and partake with our representatives and it is with difficulty that we could close the house or exclude them from the table in some way that is agreeable both to you and them. They have a strong hand in reformation."[5]

Such common ground as Baldwin and the radicals found in the struggle for responsible government was eroded once responsibility had been achieved. That would prove a tragedy for both because it would allow politics to be dominated by Francis Hincks and the men of business, the real enemies of the radicals as much as of Baldwin. Again Robert's inability to recognize the real enemy would have serious results. But that all lay far ahead. For the moment there was unity against the Sydenham system. Louis LaFontaine was returned for Fourth York on 23 September 1841.

He was home with the children. The three months in Kingston had been Robert's first extended absence from them since his trip to Britain in 1836. But his new political career would mean many more months apart and fundamental changes in their relationship. The time had come for change, at any rate. Maria, the eldest, was now thirteen and ready for a broader educational experience than she could receive at home. Robert wrote LaFontaine about the possibility of a French education for Maria, and LaFontaine recommended a convent in Montreal. That November LaFontaine sent Maria the curriculum of the convent and a French novel, accompanied by a jocular and encouraging letter about the adventure that awaited her in French Canada. Despite his colleague's advice, Robert decided against Montreal and instead sent Maria to the Ursuline Convent in Quebec in 1842, apparently unconcerned that a French education meant a Catholic education. The convent was a dreary, sprawling complex of buildings above St. Louis Street in the Upper Town of Quebec, but Maria was happy enough there. By 1843 she was sufficiently accomplished in French to translate letters for her father, and in 1844 when Francis Hincks visited her at the convent, he claimed that "[s]he speaks English quite with a French accent." That year she was joined at the convent by her younger sister Eliza while the two boys, Willcocks and Robert, were sent to the so-called Minor Seminary which was only a few blocks away, near the ramparts overlooking the St. Lawrence. Maria continued to be the most adept at the new language. When she went to Washington in 1845 to visit cousins General John Adams Dix and his wife Catherine, she impressed the Americans with her linguistic skills. The Dixes called on the Belgian ambassador, whose wife spoke no English. Potential embarrassment was avoided because Maria comfortably translated the conversation.[6]

Education in Quebec had its rewards but also its travails. The separations were lengthy and stressful for a family that emphasized its closeness, at least physical if not emotional. Robert, who was never comfortable travelling, was required to make trips to Quebec to see the children and to attend important events such as their formal examinations, the public displays of learning that were *de rigueur* at good schools. When he could not go to Quebec to accompany them home, an elaborate network of associates was established to assure they had proper escort—perhaps as much to ease their grandmother's anxious mind as to see to their safe passage. In 1843, for example, Maria travelled to Kington to visit her father. When she left the convent she stayed at the Quebec home of Louis Massue, a wealthy liberal supporter, while John Neilson made her travel arrangements and Dominick Daly, the provincial secretary, kept her father informed of her progress. She left Quebec with Étienne Parent, clerk of the executive council, who accompanied her to Kingston. All this for a fleeting visit during which, Robert told Neilson, "She will have just time to get tired of Kingston by the time she will have to resume her studies at the Convent."[7]

The price was worth paying to assure that the children did not suffer from their father's linguistic disability. When considering young Willcocks's future in the summer of 1844, Robert told LaFontaine that the boy must go either to France or to a Lower Canadian college. "I must not expose him to the miserable embarrassment that I labour under myself from a want of French." Baldwin struggled to gain at least a reading knowledge of French, urged on by LaFontaine who advised him to take lessons from the children; that was unlikely advice for someone as stiffly formal and conscious of appropriate roles, in the family and without, as Baldwin. His struggles were in vain; Robert never learned even the basics of French. Yet there is no doubt about the seriousness of his concern. He was convinced that the future of Canada was a bicultural one, a nation in which French and English worked together on a footing of complete equality. To play a role in that future nation young people, such as his children, needed to be bilingual. This was a firm and consistent belief, one he held from his first contact with Lower Canadian liberals in 1840. Given his own unilingualism and his lack of previous experience with French Canada, his rapid conversion to bilingualism might seem inexplicable. There were, however, three bases for the belief. One was his quick assessment of the political realities in a United Canada. To build a party that could govern, and achieve responsible government, it was obviously necessary to build an alliance with the French. Conceding them respect, equality, and language rights was essential to cement that alliance. His belief was also rooted in his nationalism. He wished to see Canada evolve within the loose framework of the British Empire as a unique nation, measurably different from both the United States and Britain itself. Biculturalism, the partnership of English and French, would help to mark Canada off. And he understood, in his soul, the lessons learned at the knees of his grandfather and father. Their tales of the troubled Irish homeland rang true, and he determined the ethnic and religious differences there must not torment his Canada.[8]

Robert's approaches to his children's education were not always so well considered. All too often his major educational tool was criticism. Typical were his letters from Kingston to twelve-year-old Willcocks in the spring of 1843: On 17 April he lectured the boy about taking care to write properly. Admittedly, Robert himself wrote poorly but that, he warned, sprang from bad habits when young. Willcocks requested the right to use his father's books. Yes, he could do so, "provided you say you do not soil them—but I am like your grandfather in this point very particular—It gives me pain to see a book ill used." A month later, in a letter intended to arrive for Willcocks's thirteenth birthday, Robert praised his son's improved writing in his last letter, but could not resist drawing attention to a spelling error. He also deplored the boy's reference to pleasure reading. "Don't let your amusements interfere with your business. You see I dont do so. And you know your Lessons are your business." Even on birthdays, one must be a Baldwin.[9]

Robert was a notoriously poor correspondent, but he did not accept the same failing in the children. In May 1845 he was angry that the youngest, Bob, had not written from Quebec. The father's letter was accusatory and unsympathetic. He had heard that Bob and Willy were dissatisfied with the food at the seminary. That was "nonsense" as far as Robert was concerned. Perhaps Bob had not written because of an earlier exchange that year when Robert lectured the boy at length about the need to write well and spell carefully. As an afterthought, he noted that Bob had been ill. It was surely confusing for the children for Robert could, at times, be chatty and loving. In the letter previous to his hectoring Bob about his writing, Robert had shared with his son insights about the House of Assembly and weather in Montreal. When Willy, Bob, and Eliza sent him birthday letters in 1846, he expressed his delight and complimented Bob on his ability to compose poetry in French. It was not lack of affection, then, that made Robert an epistolary taskmaster. It was the family sense of duty, the obligation to be a good Baldwin. It was an onus that was quickly recognized by the young. Maria, the eldest, sounded like her father when she wrote to Bob about the need to apply himself to his studies. "[R]emember that our own Dear Father now looks to us for all his comfort and what can ever give more pleasure to an affectionate parent particularly to such a one as ours, than the efforts of his children to improve and profit by the advantage they enjoy."[10]

Robert sought for the same perfection in his children that he expected of himself. And he had the same difficulty in expressing his unalloyed affection for them that he had in opening himself to his friends and associates. His granddaughter, Mary Jones, remembered him as a man who was fond of his children but not close to them. He was as much feared as loved by them; he was as much a schoolmaster as a father. These personal failings were compounded in the 1840s by his absences at the seat of government. The rearing of the children was left to nuns and priests at school and to his mother at home. She was a strong, even domineering woman. She, too, taught by criticism rather than praise. As she aged, Phoebe became ever more set in her ways. She usually stayed in her room until four in the afternoon when she came to the parlour for tea, esconsced in front of the fire. She had strict rules. She never went to the kitchen, nor were the children permitted to do so. The second daughter, Eliza, in particular, suffered from this stern upbringing. Constantly reminded that she was neither clever nor good-looking, she grew into a woman wracked by lack of self-confidence.[11]

Robert remained suspended between his stern demands of the children and his love for them. He often wrote to them of his sorrow that the duty of public life kept him away from home, "my own dear home ... which brings tears into my eyes when ever I think of it." He felt great bitterness, he told Maria on her twentieth birthday in 1848, that he could not be home for such an important occasion. Well he might, for the family was central to all he was and all he believed in. That was so in a personal sense. He trusted implicitly in the wise advice of his mother, the "master-mind of the family," and his father. Sydenham, for one, had believed that Robert was completely under the influence of William Warren Baldwin. After their first confrontation in March 1841, Sydenham still thought that Robert could be salvaged: "I really believe that when away from that mischievous old ass, his Father, good may be made of him." It was more than his father's advice that made Robert what he was, however. Family was also a political institution, the cornerstone of society, and a living organism that grew with its members and sheltered them. It is common for people to use metaphors drawn from the family experience when discussing politics and public life. Yet for few is family not just a metaphor but the reason for political activity as it was for Robert Baldwin.[12]

Robert projected his intimate experience into politics. Family duty became public duty, even at the cost of personal comfort, at the cost of separation from his own dear home. "That God may bless you my dear Boy," he wrote to Willcocks, "and keep you & my other dear Children in the path of duty is the constant prayer of your affectionate father." Duty meant public service in the pursuit of the liberal values that motivated the family: the spread of English liberty, the establishment of a rational system of government, the protection of property. His intimate experience was also of testing and proving oneself, responding to the goad of parental criticism. This was extended into public life as an unrealistic expectation of how a political party, the analogue of the family, could be expected to function. Baldwin was always surprised that others expected praise and rewards, and that others would settle for something less than perfection. And his intimate experience was that those who enjoyed wealth and position had to justify their privileges by a paternalistic interest in the common weal. Much of this was captured in his first will, drawn in March 1840, in which he lectured his children on the nature of family and the responsibilities of the head of a family.

> And such Head by God's blessing will (I trust) never forget the duties which devolve upon him as the head of a family, which (as well as their ancestors) have always been distinguished for their unbending integrity, and for the warmth of their family affection. Moreover I look upon it as the duty of the head of a Family like ours not merely to use, without impairing the property which he inherits from his Ancestors, but by diligence[,] industry and economy to increase the same, so as to be able, besides providing properly for the rest of his children to transmit the family Estates to his heir enlarged as well as improved according as God has prospered him. That as the Family increases in each succeeding Generation, (if such should

be God's blessed will) the means of Good in the hands of their head may be increased likewise. And that the exertion to fulfil such obligation may ever preserve in activity that mental energy which can alone preserve any family from falling to decay.[13]

The sense of duty and the reverence for property were characteristic of the English as well as the Canadian landed elite. In another metaphor from the family, it fostered in them a paternalism toward the rest of society. For Baldwin, as for others of his station, moral duty intertwined with an urge to enhance prestige and, especially, to protect property. All this required paternalistic public service. The gentleman must justify his place in society by making society better for the rest of the population. That improvement had the not incidental benefit of reducing the likelihood that the masses would rise up against the propertied, a consideration that was probably not central for Baldwin. Robert was not as fearful of the masses, or as absolute in his belief in the sanctity of property, as some of the gentry. John Macaulay, Tory public servant and land speculator, was worried in the summer of 1841 when Parliament was debating Sydenham's municipal bill. He warned a friend that "[t]he District Councils will be established beyond a doubt with power to tax to an immense extent. Landless men will have no mercy on other folk's acres." In contrast, during that debate, Robert tried unsuccessfully to have "wild land," land that lay undeveloped for speculative purposes, assessed and taxed on the same basis as developed land. The absolute rights of property were, for him, tempered by liberal concern for justice and equity.[14]

Robert nevertheless believed that property was the basis for social stability. That required him to break from the evolving liberal orthodoxy, for instance on the franchise. He remained adamantly opposed to granting the vote to the unpropertied. He equally opposed measures that would facilitate turning property into capital. One was the persistent attempts by Reformers to abolish the law of primogeniture under which estates of those who died without a will passed to the eldest sons. Almost all liberals favoured dividing estates among surviving children, but not Baldwin. Again, many liberals supported the abolition of dower rights, which gave widows the capacity to retain their husbands' estates, but not Baldwin. On these and other issues he would be in sharp conflict with men such as Francis Hincks, who wanted rapid turnover and sale of land so as to produce capital for economic expansion. The great economic crisis that confronted Canada after 1846, when Britain revolutionized economic relationships by adopting free trade, would bring these differences to the fore. The political struggle over property and capital would only end in 1851 when Francis Hincks won an unconditional victory over Robert Baldwin.

Even without ideological concerns Baldwin had much to defend in his advocacy of traditional property rights. The family estates were an important part of his income, but only a part. He had several sources. The least important was the salary he drew from the public purse. When he was Attorney General in 1842–1843, his initial salary was £1200 or $4800, later reduced by the legislature to £1100 per annum. He regained that salary in 1848 although the legislature again reduced it to £1000 or $4000 in 1850. This was generous compensation at a time when a labourer might hope to earn £40 to £50 per year. It was, however, the smaller part of his income. His two law practices of Baldwin and Son as well as that with his cousin, Baldwin and Sullivan, were usually lucrative. How lucrative they were is impossible to determine with any precision since the records of the firms have not survived. One extant report on the billings by Baldwin and Sullivan for the last quarter of 1840 totalled £1750 or $7000, but there is no way of knowing how typical this was.[15]

Robert's law income was earned without great personal effort. Even by 1840 the practice took a distant second place to politics, and he gave it less and less attention over the years. This often hurt the business. For example, Robert received a letter from an angry client, Saundy Scott, in January 1848. Scott wrote that he had come to the firm because of Robert's reputation only to find himself foisted off on another lawyer— presumably Adam Wilson, who had assumed the burden of the practice in the 1840s. That lawyer, Scott sputtered, gossiped about his clients' business; "his *tongue* is too long for his body," and "he thinks himself no sheep shanks." Unless Baldwin personally saw to his legal problems, Scott would take his business elsewhere. What the client, in fact, did about his legal matters is unknown, but it was Baldwin who took his business elsewhere, ending any active participation in the practice by 1848 although he continued to draw an income from the firm. It was not the difficulty of combining law with politics that led to his retirement; he simply did not find the work compellingly interesting. He loved the law as an institution, but was not gripped by it in practice so it was natural enough that he should spend the last decade of his life administering the institution of the law, as a bencher and treasurer of the Law Society, rather than in working at its details.[16]

How good a practicing lawyer he had been is a matter of doubt at any rate. The record of his cases is ambiguous. As a young lawyer, he was one of a small number of attorneys who argued cases in the superior court, the Court of King's Bench. He became wearily familiar with the men he contested in the upper court, the solicitors and attornies general J.B. Robinson and H.J. Boulton, and lawyers such as J.B. Macaulay and Daniel Washburn. Robert was a working attorney and took a wide variety of cases. He defended debtors and creditors, widows seeking their dower rights as well as large landowners protecting their privileges. There is no philosophy of law or society to be found in the cases, just an earnest young man arguing the best interests of his clients. If there was something to distinguish his practice it was a delight in finding obscure precedents and procedures. At times he prevailed, as when he defended the heir of an estate against debt claims by a Montreal company, a case that turned on whether the company had both residence in the province and a timely order for payment. At other times the court was unimpressed with his cleverness. In 1830 Robert argued for a client against the powerful monopoly, the Canada Land Company, that controlled vast acreage in western Upper Canada. The provincial Solicitor General had tried to have set aside a writ of *distringras* that ordered the sheriff to seize certain property on the grounds that it had not properly been preceded by a writ of summons. Initially Robert prevailed by raising a technicality. Since there was no court of chancery, as in England, there was no appropriate agency to issue a writ of summons and therefore *distringas* was indeed the proper form. The justices ruled in Baldwin's favour. However, he was eventually undone by another technicality that he had overlooked. The Court of King's Bench reconsidered the case in 1831 and found that, since the Canada Company was legally a foreign organization, chartered in England, Robert's writ of *distringas* had no force. He was a busy young lawyer who took many cases, lost as often as he won, and applied no large view of the law.[17]

There were trials with clear political implications and, again, Robert's record was mixed. Barely two years an attorney, he joined with his father in 1827 in a matter that was ostensibly about the continued incarceration of a prisoner in the Kingston jail. In fact, as the Baldwins were openly opposing the government and supporting the maverick Justice John Walpole Willis, their confrontation with Attorney General Robinson had clear political overtones. They attempted to argue a novel theory of "voluntary escape" since the prisoner had been taken out of the prison for a hearing by a magistrate without a writ of habeas corpus or other legal justification. Their application for release of the prisoner was summarily dismissed.[18]

Politics figured larger in some matters. Despite their political differences Robert defended Hincks in 1842 against a suit brought by the Laird of McNab, who controlled a feudal domain in the Ottawa valley. The suit charged that Hincks had libelled the laird in the *Examiner*. Robert's eloquent defence of press freedom was effective and McNab won only token damages for a clear legal libel. The case was not only significant for civil rights but for the Reform Party, as it helped keep the channels of communication open between Robert and the errant Hincks. He had been less successful in the charged atmosphere of the rebellion trials in Toronto in 1838. His legal assistance had not saved Samuel Lount and Peter Matthews from the gallows or prevented John Montgomery from receiving a death sentence, later commuted, during the rebellion trials of 1838.

The few recorded glimpses of his later legal practice suggest he was sometimes more confident in his knowledge of the law than was justified and that he still was bewitched by unusual precedents. In 1845 he submitted a writ, which he described as "a writ of Error Coram Nobis," to Provincial Secretary Daly. It was, he proudly told Daly, a virtually unprecedented procedure. The only previous example in Upper Canada was in the case of *Boulton v. Randall* some twenty years before. Condescendingly, he gave Daly detailed instructions about where the documents were to be filed and which should be returned to Baldwin. With considerable pleasure Baldwin's old nemesis, Attorney General William Henry Draper, intervened to point out that Robert had the precedent wrong—it was *Boulton v. Fitzgerald*—and was wrong about where the papers were to be filed. Perhaps scholar Baldwin's motto ought to have been "less flash and more care."[19]

Much of the time that Robert spent at the law offices, in the plain wooden building on King Street, was preoccupied with real estate rather than the law. The family lands were held in the names of various members of the clan, but they were managed jointly by William Warren and Robert. After William Warren Baldwin died in January 1844 the two sons, Robert and William Augustus, were joint trustees of the estate until it was legally partitioned in July 1848 when Robert, as the eldest son, gained the lion's share of the property. Through inheritance from Elizabeth Russell, government grants, and purchases, the Baldwins had accumulated land across Upper Canada from the London District in the west to the Johnstown District in the east. The heaviest concentration of lots was close at hand, in the Home District surrounding Toronto and in the city itself. Much had been sold off, but by the end of the 1830s they still held more than 8,910 hectares in rural areas. In Toronto they owned eighty-two lots, along with eight hectares of land on the city commons, eight-and-a-half hectares surrounding the family home, Spadina, and the twenty-four-hectare Spadina farm. As well, they managed properties for others, including the small estates of Nathan Clarke and J.S. Thomas, the 486-hectare estate of Captain De Hoen and the Upper Canadian lands of political colleague John Neilson.[20]

The most valuable properties were in and around the city, their prices steadily driven up by Toronto's expansion. The Baldwin presence was everywhere: offices on King Street, the chief commercial thoroughfare; a lumber yard on Queen Street; a warehouse on Yonge; the Spadina farm south of Davenport Road, which was rented out; and the Spadina estate sprawling across the suburban village of Yorkville. To the west and north of the city's commercial district was a patrimony of vacant lots, awaiting the city's growth. There the family would be immortalized in the street names—Baldwin, Eliza, Robert, St. George, Willcocks, Russell. Rich farmlands lay in the outskirts. In the township of Whitby, east of Toronto, Robert conveyed by outright sale some 790 hectares between 1838 and 1855, had taken back mortgages on another 324 hectares, leased out 101 more hectares, and retained

81 hectares. To the north he had held 810 hectares in York township, 810 in King Township, and smaller parcels in three other townships.

In the mid-1840s much of the Toronto property was either vacant or in family use. Rents for the rest returned a modest £300 to £400 per year. Land sales produced a larger, if fluctuating, income. One property on King Street, sold to Dr. Christopher Widmer in 1833, was valued at £2000. Robert took back a mortgage for the whole sum, which was not retired until 1854. Other properties on King Street sold in the 1850s for £3100. Robert's return from sales and mortgages in Toronto averaged about £1200 per year. Sales, mortgages, and rentals outside Toronto produced at least another £1200 annually. At a conservative estimate, land income totalled about £2400 per year. This compared very favourably with the income derived by other large landholders. Some fifteen years after Baldwin's death another prominent politician, George-Étienne Cartier, earned the equivalent of £790 per year from his extensive rental properties in Montreal. In total, from the law and land, Robert's income was on the order of £5000, supplemented when he held office by honoraria from £1000 to £1200. In comparison, a wealthy and successful Toronto lawyer of the 1850s, Larratt Smith, boasted of earning £1500 per year.[21]

Yet Robert could have earned much more had he pursued more aggressive sales and development policies. That was illustrated dramatically when long after Robert's death parts of the Baldwin estate were finally subdivided in 1883–1884. The improved portion was two blocks deep, from Bloor Street to Lowther Avenue, and two blocks wide, from Huron Street to Bedford Road. It was a subdivision Robert could have undertaken in his lifetime at great profit. Nineteen of the 48 lots were sold at the time of the subdivision at an average price of $2587 or £647. At Robert's death, the estate still held land outside Toronto that had mortgages for some £7000, in addition to houses, offices, warehouses, and the hectares of the Spadina block along that street and what was known as Crescent Gardens, from Spadina to Huron Street and from College Street to the Boulton Grange along Dundas Street. But, of course, it was no surprise that Robert's land management was conservative. He wished to secure an estate for the family in the future, even if that limited income in the present. The sad irony was that his caution was wasted. His son, William Willcocks, was a profligate. He mortgaged the Spadina property only five months after his father's death and continued to have financial problems. Driven to the wall by debt, in February 1866 he sold the house and thirty-two hectares of land to James Austin for the fire sale price of £3550.[22]

As with the law, the idea of property was more compelling for Baldwin than the practice of property management. After his father's death in 1844 the land business became a burden. Robert hired a manager for the properties and, typically, he kept it within the family. In 1845 he took on Lawrence Heyden who was married to his sister-in-law, Barbara Sullivan. Lawrence and Robert had known each other since childhood; Heyden was only five days older than Robert. Their careers had gone in very different directions, however. While Robert went on to wealth and fame, Lawrence had succeeded at nothing. By 1845 he had fallen on very hard times because of poor health that left him too frail for farming. Robert was aware of Heyden's failings as a businessman. In his 1840 will, Robert left money to Barbara Heyden with the stipulation that it was "for her own use, exclusive of her husband," for fear that the debt-ridden Lawrence would squander it. Lawrence was family, nevertheless, and required help, so Robert hired him and at a generous salary. The going rate for work of the kind Heyden would do was £150 per year, but Lawrence said he needed £200, so that was what he was paid. It was cheap at the price, at any rate, since Robert was happy to shuck off the day-to-day details of the business. He did insist on being kept informed about developments and retained the right to make final decisions on unusual cases. Such cases included especially important properties such as the Spadina farm, on which Robert made decisions about leasing; and politically sensitive relationships such as the renting of lots to J.H. Dunn, H.J. Boulton, and other political figures.[23]

In the evenings he sat in his study catching up with correspondence and dealing with small but troubling business matters. One subject that furrowed his brow was money lending. Financial dealings were always, at root, moral exchanges. Unfortunately, a fortune as large as Robert's entailed ambiguities. He had powerful doubts about the morality of usury, especially in an undeveloped country such as Canada. He would fight strenuously in the Assembly to limit the negative impact of debt by retaining the traditional 6 percent limit on loan interest. He refused to become involved himself in commercial lending. When such a proposal was made to him in 1846 he declined on the grounds that "any agency of that kind in a country where there are so many borrowers and so few lenders may be made a political engine." Robert attempted to avoid using his wealth as a political engine, but he could not avoid becoming a lender, through extending mortgages and outright cash loans. Even the prominent were often at his door seeking loans in this society where cash was short, but pretensions were not. In such cases Robert often provided the loans while maintaining his moral image of finance. Prominent men had a particular responsibility to be upright in their dealings, and Robert pursued them like a nemesis when they failed to do so. In 1847, for example, he was outraged to discover that a member of the elite Ridout family had failed to pay off a debt. Robert dictated to Heyden the steps to be taken in hounding the delinquent debtor and snapped, "[T]hese are my final instructions and I shall expect they will be punctualy obeyed."[24]

Many of his loans were more philanthropic than business. He received scores of importuning letters each year, filled with sad stories of misfortune and hardship. He responded to many of them with money. Some never repaid him, but others scrimped to retire their debts. On Boxing Day 1849 Patrick Brennon wrote to Baldwin from Warwick, a village in Lambton County, Upper Canada. He was repaying an interest-free loan of $10. Brennon was one of the subsistence farmers who eked out a living, almost day to day, and who needed the generosity of someone like Robert Baldwin to survive when a particular setback occurred. Brennon had cobbled together the sum over a period of time and from a variety of sources, as evidenced by the rainbow of currencies he sent to Baldwin—a $4 bill from the Bank of Upper Canada, a $2 bill from the Bank of Montreal, two $2 bills from the Farmers' Joint Stock bank. He was not alone in receiving open-handed treatment from Baldwin. Louisa Rolph was the sister of the prominent radical Dr. John Rolph, the same John Rolph who had deceived Robert during the "flag of truce" episode in 1837. Louisa had been abused and cast from the family home in 1845 by another brother, George, and was alone and penniless. She begged Baldwin for help, and that July he sent her £10, to be repaid with nominal interest. The next May Louisa wrote that she was still financially troubled. Would Baldwin accept only the interest on the loan until she could obtain a teaching job? She could "take her own time re interest," Baldwin replied. There is no indication he ever received his £10.[25]

Louisa was not the only Rolph who proved to be an expensive associate. John betrayed Robert in 1837 and he intrigued against his leadership of the Reform Party in the 1840s. Yet Robert, as usual, was not vindictive. Rolph had an old debt with the firm of Baldwin and Son. When that business was wrapped up the debt was transferred, along with others, to the estate of William Warren Baldwin and to Robert personally. In 1847 Robert was attempting to clear up accounts and came across the record of Rolph's debt. He wrote to Rolph releasing him in full from the encumbrance. It was an act of generosity that Rolph would soon forget.[26]

Robert was most content at home among the family and dealing with outsiders at the safe distance of the mails. But wealth and position carried social responsibilities that drew him out into the world. He was not a community leader in the active sense as had been the paternalistic members of the Family Compact. He was too reserved for that. There were, though, some especially compelling institutions that lured him from the safety of his home. One was the church. His religious feelings were deep, if simplistic. He had been a sceptic as a young man, a scepticism that was part of the general uncertainty he felt about life and about himself, faced as he was with the smug certainty of his father and the expectations of his family. All religious doubt dissipated when he discovered Eliza and love. Indeed, his fondest hope for his children was that they too would enjoy "the *thorough conviction* which after having been when a young man a sceptic—may God forgive me though I hope not wholly an unbeliever, I arrived at of the *absolute truth* of the Religion of the blessed Redeeemer." It was like his love for Eliza, his love for God, a secret and bubbling passion hidden below his placid exterior. He carried with him a small bundle of prayers, a set of invocations he had composed and worked over, along with favourite Biblical homilies. His prayers made it clear that the benchmarks of his worldly life—family and duty—were aspects of his devotion to God. He knelt by his bed with Eliza at his side or alone after she died to pray "that I may enter upon this duty with the deepest reverence, & sincerest purpose of devoting my whole heart to thee."[27]

Robert's religious convictions were those of the established Church of England, but they could verge on the evangelical at times. His admonitions to the children to love God and shun doubters could have come from a Methodist circuit rider. In April 1847, Bob had written to his father about his sister Eliza's illness. It was an opportunity for the elder Baldwin to reflect on mortality:

> Thus it is my dear Boy that none of us young or old know the moment when we may be called unto the presence of our Maker. How necessary then is it to try and be prepared for so awful a change. This can only be by a thorough conviction that we are of ourselves wholly unable to deserve the Almighty Mercy and that it is only through the merits of our blessed Saviour that we can hope to attain it. The pretenders to human wisdom either will not or harden their hearts so that they cannot embrace this doctrine. Never my dear child let anything induce you to listen to these fallacies. That we cannot fully comprehend all that we are taught to believe is no reason for disbelieving it—[28]

Religious devotion could create awkwardness in a world where not everyone was so devoted. The political imperatives sometimes intruded on the sabbath, for example. In December 1840 Baldwin and Hincks had been busy wooing politicians of all stripes in anticipation of the coming Union. Stewart Derbishire from Montreal made a fleeting visit to Toronto, and Hincks thought it essential that Baldwin dine with him, even though it was a Sunday. Robert wrestled with his conscience before finding a compromise: "It is as you know only on particular occasions that I feel justified in accepting invitations for Sunday—I will have dinner with you tomorrow—stipulating your permission to return in time for an Evng Sermon."[29]

The church itself took him into the world. Religious issues were always at the forefront of politics and he debated them ardently in the House. His firm belief that religion should not be entwined with the state kept him in persistent conflict with the hierarchy of his own Anglican church. It did not deter him from dedicating his energies to religious causes, however. In 1843 he joined the board of management of the Church Society in Toronto, which was presided over by Bishop Strachan. Board meetings were frosty that fall when Baldwin introduced into the legislature a bill to create a secular university that Strachan considered a pagan assault on true religion. Things were more comfortable for Robert at the mission-oriented Canada Bible Society where he was vice-president and his cabinet colleague, John Henry Dunn, was president. In 1846 Robert moved up to the presidency. Religion, both institutional and personal, remained central throughout his life. He considered himself a strict High Anglican despite his apostasy on issues of church–state relations and believed his work for the church was as important as his political responsibilities. In the loneliness of his bedroom he still repeated that prayer he had written twenty years before, reaffirming his "sincerest purpose of devoting my whole heart to thee."[30]

His nationality also could occasionally draw him out into the community. The St. Patrick's Benevolent Society was one of his philanthropies, and he served as its president in 1846. When famine struck Ireland Robert led Toronto's relief effort. This was an emotional response to a disaster in his ancestral homeland since his rational position was one of Ricardian liberalism. In the assembly in 1843 he had attacked the previous government's encouragement of large-scale immigration and made clear he thought there was no room in Canada for pauper migrants. In 1847, however, he helped to organize the Migrant Settlement Society to aid arrivals from Ireland in finding jobs and land. He was at the rostrum for a large public meeting at Toronto city hall in April 1847 where the mighty of the city rubbed shoulders with artisans and shopkeepers, all united by shared concern for the Irish catastrophe. Robert proposed the motion to establish the society and was elected to its management committee. He had also taken the lead in soliciting direct relief for the troubled country as chairman of the Committee for the Relief of the Destitute in Ireland, organized earlier in 1847. Robert and the management committee reached out across the province to urge sympathetic people to hold public meetings, canvass for funds and remit cash and food to the committee rooms in Toronto. He even swallowed his distaste for the Corporation, and his pride, to solicit a donation from the Toronto city council.[31]

There were other good works. Orphans especially drew his sympathy. In 1846 he was part of an unsuccessful attempt to establish an industrial school in Toronto that would teach trades to orphans and neglected children. A decade later he donated a large lot on Sullivan Street east of Spadina Avenue, for a new Orphans' Home and Female Aid Society. Perhaps it was the thought of his own motherless children that led to his involvement in such projects. Or perhaps it was that he too had been a kind of waif since Eliza's death. Whatever the reason, the cause of orphans was an unusual public passion. Robert shared neither the aristocratic paternalism of the old gentry nor the modern belief in institutional solutions to social problems of the new business elite. He was too private a man for either.[32]

His personal life was lived in homes that belied his considerable wealth. They were substantial, but not ostentatious. The house on Front Street where they spent most of the year had amenities suitable to a large gentry family including three parlours and a library and, in the basement, a large kitchen, a roomy wine cellar, and a meat room. To move about the city Robert had a gig and horses, as well as two sleighs. His mother and father kept another horse, a cow, two carriages, and a sleigh. The children had two dogs to keep them company. Front Street, then, was a well-equipped and comfortable town house, but it did not turn heads. The Baldwin house was plain and undistinguished compared to the grand homes of the neighbourhood—the estates of the Macaulays and Sherwoods, the graceful Boulton villa, and Bishop Strachan's regal palace. It was, nevertheless, a good deal grander than the summer place at Spadina. The most imposing thing about Spadina was the location, on an elevation high above the city, surrounded by the eight odd hectares. The house itself was a rustic, one-storey villa. The hectares around the house included a small working farm where apples, pears, and grapes were cultivated for sale at the city market. The bulk of the grounds, though, were a romantic delight, which carefully cultivated pretense of wilderness that thrilled the early Victorian gentry. There was a gurgling brook running through the property from the northwest to the southeast near Bloor Street, on its way to the Don River. A "goose walk" ambled down from the farmyard to the stream, enclosed for easy walking with fences of split rails. The path had originally been cut to allow Aunt Maria Willcocks to drive her ducks and geese to the water. Now it was a romantic strolling place for family and visitors amid Spadina's lush woods. Visitors could stop halfway down the path at a tiny log cottage where they made entries, usually of poetry, in a book kept there.[33]

It was a comfortable existence shared between the large town house and the bucolic Spadina retreat. The accoutrements of a genteel lifestyle were always at hand. Robert could consult the extensive and well-selected library accumulated by his father, which included a good collection of maps and two big world globes. At dinner he drank wine chosen from the ample wine cellar and served from an Irish silver decanter. The gentry lifestyle was not left behind when he went into the city. The family's status was confirmed on Sunday by their large double pew on the west aisle of the Cathedral Church of St. James. The Baldwin prominence was visible even in the city's streetscapes. Toronto's widest thoroughfare, Spadina Avenue, was named for their property. It had been laid out by William Warren Baldwin in the 1820s through Maria Willcocks's park lot 15. The avenue swept up to the Baldwin estate at Bloor Street but did not cross their property—the estate was entered from Yonge Street along Davenport Road. From the house there was a grand vista, looking down Spadina Avenue to the ornamental circle above College Street and beyond to the ships in the bay, the avenue lined for its length with double rows of chestnut trees on either side. Twice the normal road allowance, Spadina Avenue was a symbol of Baldwin prestige.[34]

Despite his propertied status, Robert did not live the life of the landed gentry; that had been his father's style—a duelist, party-giver, and hail-fellow-well-met. It had long since leeched out of Robert, however. The gaiety that had sometimes been there in his youth had been overburdened in adulthood with extra pounds, a surfeit of dignity and gloomy reflections. It was now perhaps as hard for him as it was for others to imagine him gliding across a dance floor. Yet he had been a part of York's social scene as a young man. He greatly enjoyed the family entertainments that enlivened the Front Street house, especially the plays performed by family members and guests, which were such a staple of early nineteenth-century recreation. Dancing parties at the homes of the gentry brightened the winter, and Robert was an enthusiastic if not a graceful dancer. There was a rakish cut to Regency social life that he never accepted, however. When Eliza was in her family-imposed exile in New York in 1826, Robert wrote to tell her about his embarrassment at a party. He had to flee from the embrace of a partner who "dances too much from her hips instead of with her legs & feet—do you understand what I mean?"[35]

That flight from worldliness became his way of life after Eliza's death. Robert never mentions attending dances or the theatre or musicales, no matter the cricket matches and horse races that were popular among the Toronto elite. It was a rare indulgence in February 1851 when he permitted Willy and Maria to arrange a ball at their home, a ball raised to a great event by the presence of the governor, Lord Elgin, and his wife. Usually, Robert lived more like an earnest bourgeois than a country squire. But those gentry values remained. They defined his place in society even if he never explicitly characterized it. He rarely spoke about his social station beyond the sort of generalities found in his will and spoke not at all about social class. *Class* he used as a pejorative term. In reforming the provincial university in 1849, for example, he said he was concerned to avoid it becoming "a mere class corporation." *Class* was a modern word that came more easily to the tongues of the rising business-minded men. It was one such, Francis Hincks, who proposed in 1843 that the Reform Party make its rallying cry, "We are now fighting the battle of the *Middle Class* against the aristocracy." Robert might have been more comfortable with the older usage in which pre-industrial society was separated into "ranks," "orders," or "degrees." They implied a society that was more integrated with "gentle slopes of gradation" formed by what the English ruralist William Cobbett called "the chain of connection" between the mighty and the humble. At least ideally, in such a society gradations were defined by the duty appropriate to rank, the privilege of property carrying with it the responsibility to serve society. That was a social order that Robert Baldwin could understand.[36]

Robert was ambitious to serve his family and the institutions of his society. Ambition had personal roots, as well, in the need to live up to his family's tradition of prominence. He remembered how that had been personified in Eliza. He told her in 1825 that "there is a certain indescribable transport in the prospect of success" in a legal career "since

I have looked forward to you as the partner of it." He confessed "that I have a horror of not rising above mediocrity.... Oh Eliza you can scarcely know how trembling anxious I am on this head—without commanding respect from my profession I never would be worthy of you[.] I never could make you happy—And if I cannot rise with you into consideration I will never drag you down with me into insignificance—"[37]

The most powerful check on ambition, if the most difficult to employ with precision, was honour. Ambition must always be tempered by the dictates of honour. As political brokering went on after the collapse of the Sydenham system, Robert assured LaFontaine that he would sacrifice personal ambition to the common good. If an administration could be formed that rendered justice to French Canada he would enter it or, if that were not politically useful, he would support it without enjoying office personally. "For myself while I do not profess to be wholly indifferent as to the possession of power I will never either on the one hand make a sacrifice of principle to obtain it or on the other make myself an impediment to any arrangements that may be beneficial to the interests of my Country." Honour, ambition, and duty were the stuff of dinner-table conversation at the Baldwin home and of the epistolary letters that Robert wrote to the children from the capital. When he took office in September 1842 it had to be the occasion for another homily on the subject. His new responsibilities would keep him from home even more, but duty required him to accept them. "You will see then that being Attorney General is not so desirable a thing as you might have supposed it to be. And therefore not a thing to be boastful of. And I hope my dear children will therefore not boast of it—I do not mean that they should not feel pleased of it because <u>as it was honourably obtained</u> it is natural that they should feel pleased at their father's promotion—"[38]

However, the family was all at home that winter of 1841–1842. The long table in the panelled dining room of the Front Street house was surrounded each night by three generations of Baldwins. The conversation was dominated by the patriarch, William Warren, still hale and voluble in his mid-sixties, still full of teasing jokes and *ex cathedra* political judgments, all delivered in his booming squire's voice. Decorum was maintained by mother Phoebe, now seventy years old, her caustic remonstrances as pinched as her face. Often the second son, William Augustus, and his wife Isabella were there. He was a cheerful young man of thirty-three who lived at Spadina with Isabella and a growing brood of children—they would have five sons and two daughters before Isabella died in 1850. And, of course, Robert and his children were there. Robert listened quietly to his father for the most part, occasionally offering an opinion in his hoarse whisper of a voice. At dinner, as always, he betrayed little of his feelings, but he was happy to be there in the bosom of the family.

Robert and the children had little opportunity to be out and about in the fall of 1841 because of the unseasonably cold weather that gripped Toronto from the time of his return until late October. He filled his days with the law practice and land dealings, and spent long hours on correspondence with Reformers across the province. There was sunshine there, at least. Sydenham's coalition began to collapse after the governor died. The lacklustre Draper and Harrison had neither the political acumen nor the amoral ruthlessness of their dead mentor. Reformers were drifting back to Baldwin. And then came a remarkable Indian summer, a golden November of sun and breeze and warmth. Robert and the children were able to enjoy walks around Spadina, the boys whooping after ducks and squirrels while Robert and the girls chatted in the little lodge on Aunt Maria's goose walk. By Christmas it was cold again with heavy snow, good weather for outings in the sleighs and for warm evenings around the family fire. They might as well as have been in some small town for all that the city and its life impinged on them. With the society of theatres and parties and dancing as far behind him as Eliza's embrace, Robert found a kind of happiness in quiet, perhaps in resignation. It was a good enough life, at least until quiet and resignation curdled into something more damaging.[39]

——◆——

On the afternoon of 11 April 1842 Robert walked from his law office at King and Yonge Streets to the cramped council chambers of Toronto's city hall, which was crowded onto a second floor above the noise and smells of the market hall at the corner of King and Jarvis Streets. He had been called to join the notables of the city who would adopt an address to the new Governor General on the occasion of his first visit to Toronto. Robert was called to take the chair at the end of the meeting in the place of Mayor Henry Sherwood so that the usual vote of thanks to the mayor could be made. He did so with a glow of pleasure because a new governor meant a new opportunity to right politics in United Canada.

There had been a great sea change in politics since the last session of the legislature. Even before Sydenham's death British officials had been nursing doubts about the viability of his system. The prime minister, Sir Robert Peel, believed that Sydenham had created a tangled web of deceits and impossible promises to build his "party." His death, Peel contended, had relieved the governor, and Britain, from potential embarrassment since "it is evident that his policy was on the eve of exposure." That official discontent may have sprung as much from concern that Sydenham had conceded too much in the Harrison resolutions as from any moral scruples about Sydenham's corruption. At any rate, the Sydenham game was up and another, more subtle, game was about to begin.[40]

The choice as Sydenham's successor was Sir Charles Bagot. He was named in September 1841, but would not arrive to take up his duties until January 1842. He was an experienced diplomat, a former ambassador to the United States. More, he was, according to Peel, "a perfect Gentleman in manner and feelings" who might be expected to charm Canadians and smooth troubled waters. The change Peel had in mind was one more of style than of substance. Bagot would present a more honest and kindly image while still seeking the same goal of containing Canadian tendencies toward autonomy. His instructions from the new Colonial Secretary, Lord Stanley, were to carry on the "great experiment . . . affecting the constitution and internal arrangements" of Canada. Bagot was instructed not to thwart the Assembly by gubernatorial veto or by action of the Legislative Council, but he also should not concede ground to political parties or constitutional theorists. "[Y]ou will endeavour to avail yourself of the advice & services of the ablest men, without reference to party distinctions, which, upon every occasion, you will do your utmost to discourage." This was to be a regime of harmony, avoiding Sydenham's ruthlessness and deceit, but it was nevertheless to be a non-party regime firmly under British control.[41]

A kind of regime of harmony did settle on Canada. While awaiting Bagot's arrival, the government fell to a caretaker administrator, Sir Richard Downes Jackson, commander of the troops in British North America. He was a pleasant man and a benign ruler, and politics slumbered. Or so it seemed. Hincks continued to attack Baldwin and the Ultras and by December was urging all true Reformers to support the present ministry to gain progressive reforms. For once, however, Hincks was trimming his sails to the wrong wind. Throughout that winter there was a drift in Reform sentiment. Without the bracing influence of Sydenham's personality and bribery his coalition dissolved. When Bagot arrived in January, despite his confidence—born of innocent ignorance of Canada and its politics—that no-party government was secure, it was already too late to reverse the drift. The only hope for the ministry was a commitment of support from the Upper Canadian Tories whose natural adherence, after all, was to the Crown and to Attorney General Draper. However, the Tory leader Sir Allan MacNab distrusted and envied Draper and attacked him at every opportunity as a toady to rebels and radicals. That gave Baldwin the chance to do some mischief. He wrote to leading Tories, offering to throw in Reform votes in any attempt to bring down Draper and the ministry at the next session of Parliament. These most unlikely of bedmates, Baldwin and MacNab, had very different but equally compelling reasons for wanting to shatter the harmony of no-party government.[42]

On Thursday, 21 April 1842 Bagot, some three months into his rule in Canada, made his first visit to Toronto. Robert Baldwin was at the dock, along with other prominent citizens, as the steamer *Traveller* arrived from Kingston. The weather was brilliantly sunny as the vessel put in to the Yonge Street wharf to the loud cheers of the loyal. Bagot stepped into a carriage for the procession through the city to Government House. First came the band of the 93rd Highlanders. The fire companies, resplendent in colourful uniforms; the national societies of English, Scots, and Irish; the officers of the Mechanics Institute; the city fathers and Bishop Strachan—all these preceded the carriage with the beaming little governor. Robert walked behind with the provincial judges, members of the learned professions, and the council of King's College, all undignifiably sweaty in the early afternoon sun. Behind them came a straggle of other prominent citizens, the whole procession completed by the high bailiff, sporting his cocked hat. Robert joined in other festivities. He met Bagot at a governor's levee the next afternoon and stayed up for the grand Government House ball that evening which commenced at 10:00 p.m. and lasted long past the lavish midnight supper. Robert may even have savoured the irony of his attendance at the ceremony in Queen's Park on Saturday afternoon. Before a throng of 15,000 Sir Charles laid the cornerstone of King's College, the Anglican university that Baldwin eventually would destroy. Robert then could withdraw from the unaccustomed social whirl. Bagot remained in the city for a few more days. On Monday, 25 April he attended the steeplechase at Boulton's race course, an event enlivened by a great spill in which Charles Boulton's horse was killed and the young aristocrat himself badly shaken. Finally, at 6:00 p.m. that evening, Sir Charles boarded the *Traveller* again, his chief minister Draper at his side, to return to Kingston.[43]

Robert had much to think about. His chats with Sir Charles had been amiable enough. But the two men were quietly positioning themselves for a political struggle, a struggle on which hung the fate of responsible government.

Chapter 8

A New Definition of Loyalty

Eliza had been dead for six years and eight months. She would be proud about her husband's promotion as it was honourably attained. It was September 1842.

"Have you heard the new definition of Loyalty?" the young Tory John Hillyard Cameron asked his fiancée in September 1842. "[C]alling a rebel to put him into office." Cameron was working in Kingston on the revision of the Upper Canadian statutes and he was content to spend his time with the documents because he found it depressing to be out among public men that September. Their entire conversation, he complained, "is upon the political issues of the day, repeating in parrot fashion the same things over and over again, exhibiting no new ideas, and only awakening up one's conservative feelings to an uncomfortable degree of sensitiveness, as not much good can be done by their being awakened at all." The rebels had been called to office, that traitor to his people, Robert Baldwin, was now the chief adviser to his Excellency Sir Charles Bagot.[1]

———◆———

It had seemed straightforward and manageable when Sir Charles first arrived in Kingston on 10 January 1842. He had reason to believe the worst was over after his ordeal in getting to Canada, what with his ship colliding with another, ice preventing him coming up the St. Lawrence, and an arduous overland journey from Boston to Kingston. Kingston was warming, however. The citizenry was welcoming, Alwington House was comfortable if not viceregal, and the province, Bagot assured Colonial Secretary Stanley, was "in a state of perfect tranquillity." Bagot intended to keep it that way. Although he sought to maintain a higher tone for government than Sydenham had, he followed the previous governor's tactic of winning hearts with loaves and fishes. He lavished jobs and let big contracts to continue work on the Welland and St. Lawrence canals. He set out to win over the French Canadians to support of his government. The French, he thought, were "still sulky and will always be troublesome," a people full of "unreasonable pretentions," but they had to be conciliated. He appointed a number of French Canadians to judgeships, named others as Queen's Counsels and made a flag-showing tour of Montreal and Quebec in June. And he acted promptly and favourably on petitions for amnesty for rebels of 1837.[2]

Even Bagot's political foes were impressed by his energy and popularity. Robert Baldwin certainly was. He cautioned LaFontaine to avoid offending the governor because Bagot was both popular and open-minded. "The present Gr Gl is the first Gr we have ever had who from his assumption of his Government has been in a position to act as the Head of the whole people without reference to parties to classes to races." The liberals' policy should be to attempt to win Sir Charles's good heart while at the same time applying pressure to him by weaning Reformers away from the ministry.[3]

Bagot was an optimist, but as the months wore on even he came to realize that Baldwin was steadily gaining ground. Sooner or later the legislature would have to be recalled, and it was becoming doubtful whether the government could survive a session. Bagot tried to shore up the ministry by finding a French Canadian willing to join it, but he was rebuffed at every attempt. On Lord Stanley's advice he approached Tories who were, Stanley still believed, "the Class of men to fall back upon." That failed, too. Tory John S. Cartwright declined a post because he believed the government could never be effective without French-Canadian support. Only the wobbling Reformers were left. Bagot even considered appointing William Warren Baldwin to the legislative council as a gesture of good will—an idea he abandoned after the predictable explosion by Lord Stanley. His one success was with Francis Hincks. They had begun to talk in early February. Although Hincks was "at heart radicalissmus," Bagot saw many virtues in him, above all that he had quarreled with Robert Baldwin. Bagot was worried about Hincks's reputation and tried to balance him with a Tory but found none who could stomach sitting at the same council table as radicalissmus Hincks.

Bagot could wait no longer and Hincks was appointed inspector general for finance on 9 June 1842.[4]

It was not nearly enough to save the crumbling government. Finally adding a Tory, Henry Sherwood as Solicitor General west in July, also failed to reverse the decline. Early that month S.B. Harrison and W.H. Draper met in Kingston to discuss the prospects for their administration. They agreed that Baldwin would certainly defeat them in the Assembly, but they disagreed about the remedy for their situation. Harrison presented his view to Bagot in a memorandum on 11 July. The only hope was to win French-Canadian support. But no French Canadian would join the cabinet without the French Party's ally, Robert Baldwin. So Baldwin must be offered a cabinet post. Draper gave somewhat different advice in his memorandum of 16 July. Bagot should appeal to Baldwin's patriotism and urge him to agree to French Canadians entering the ministry without him. To make the deal more palatable to Baldwin, Draper was prepared to resign. Draper did realize that it was possible that the French would reject any arrangement that excluded Baldwin from the government. "I do not feel well able to give an unbiassed opinion on the course to be pursued in that event . . . You cannot get on without the French while it is necessary for me at the same time to declare frankly that I cannot sit at the Council board with Mr Baldwin[.] My resignation will be immediate on my becoming aware of his appointment."[5]

Draper and Bagot had swallowed Hincks as a minister, but Baldwin, the symbol of the defeat of the old order, was too much. Bagot wrote to Stanley that "there is hardly any extremity to which I should not be disposed to submit, or hazard which I might not think it even prudent to incur, rather than see Mr. Baldwin again introduced into the Council"— yet there was little Bagot could do but squirm. Sitting in his study in Toronto, his lines of correspondence stretching across Upper Canada, Robert Baldwin could feel power oozing toward him. Bagot's desperate thrashings could not affect that. Nor could the flood of gratuitous advice that Bagot received from Britain. Stanley and Peel insisted on no concessions to Baldwin, no dealings with traitors such as LaFontaine or Viger. They urged that he must do what he had already failed to accomplish: split off individual French Canadians and Tories while making no accommodations with the parties. "It is a fine opportunity,"

Stanley wrote, in the best playing fields of Eton style, "for playing the game of Divide et impere." By the time this dispatch arrived in late September, the time for games had passed.[6]

＊＊＊

The executive council chamber in Kingston was as makeshift as the rest of the hospital-turned-legislature; however, the glow of great events bestowed it a certain grandeur on the afternoon of Friday, 16 September 1842. The men around the council table were sober, somewhat crestfallen, aware that their political world had taken a great lurch.

At the head of the table was Sir Charles Bagot, his pudgy face for once lacking its sunny smile. He opened the meeting by announcing what his councillors already knew: Louis-Hippolyte LaFontaine and the Honourable Robert Baldwin had agreed to join the executive council. Two councillors, C.R. Ogden and W.H. Draper, had resigned. The clerk was dispatched to fetch the two new members who were waiting nervously in an antechamber. They entered the silent council room. Sir Charles administered the oaths of office, first as executive councillors, then as attornies general. LaFontaine and Baldwin sat down where Ogden and Draper had sat twenty-four hours earlier. With a shuffle of papers Sir Charles plunged the Council into its first item of business, arrangements concerning the provincial debt, as if nothing untoward had happened. Yet his mind must have been focused more on Britain's reaction to his sitting down with seditionists than with the details of exchange warrants.[7]

It had been a bewildering few days, perhaps especially for Bagot. The business of the province could wait no longer, and he had called the legislature to meet on 8 September, only two weeks short of a year since its last session ended. The prospect for him was bleak. His government was clearly in a minority and growing weaker by the day. Baldwin came down on the steamer from Toronto before the session and he was the centre of attention. He closeted himself with Sir Allan MacNab at the Tory leader's rooming house, searching for the terms of an alliance to vote down the government. Bagot did not feel it worthwhile to make a counter-offer to MacNab, remembering Sydenham's comment about

Sir Allan that there was no use trying to buy someone "whom he would have to purchase every Monday morning."

As it turned out, Baldwin did not need to purchase MacNab either. When the Assembly convened on 8 September it was clear the ministry could not survive even briefly. On Saturday, 10 September Bagot began his retreat, hoping to save something of the old order. He sent for LaFontaine to discuss terms for French-Canadian support of the government. The governor still thought he could follow the no-party strategy. He had approached the French, he told Stanley, "as a Race, and a people rather than as a Party." LaFontaine, however, was selling a party, not a race. He insisted on four council seats, one of which had to go to Baldwin. That destroyed any chance of an agreement. With barely concealed anger, Bagot dismissed LaFontaine and went off in search of an alternative that did not include the wretched Baldwin. There was no shortage of rumours to be heard that weekend, nor of kingmakers anxious to offer Bagot their solutions. But neither rumours nor kingmakers provided the governor any safe and realistic path around the looming obstacle of Baldwin. The game was up on Monday when Bagot came under pressure from a surprising source. His ministers held an informal meeting and drafted a memorandum to the governor. It was "indispensably necessary" to bring the French into the Council, they wrote. To do so, LaFontaine should be offered four cabinet posts plus the clerkship of the executive council; a fifth council seat—that of the Solicitor General west—should be open for negotiation when its incumbent, Henry Sherwood, arrived from Toronto. Among those prepared to go to make way for the Reformers was the government leader, William Henry Draper. As he wrote to a friend a few days later, Draper was convinced that Baldwin had to enter the ministry as part of any deal. And, "taking the view I do of his conduct when we were last in council together I feel I should dishonor myself by being in that body if he were there also." So Draper and the other Tories would go. If Bagot could not accept this advice, the entire Council would have to resign in face of the political difficulties confronting them.[8]

The next morning Bagot made a new offer to LaFontaine. The two attorneys general, Ogden and Draper, would resign. John Davidson, commissioner of Crown lands, would also leave. And LaFontaine could fill the vacant post of Solicitor General east and the clerkship of the council. In return, pensions would be provided to Ogden and Davidson in recognition of their long service in Lower Canada. To Bagot's shock, LaFontaine refused the deal. As the governor had feared, it was Baldwin who precipitated the rupture in the negotiations. Bagot had hoped to bypass Baldwin by declining to include him in the discussions. "By these means, if I succeed," Bagot told Stanley, "I should dethrone Mr. Baldwin from his post as leader of the French party, and make him in my council, and in the eyes of the public, but a subordinate member of the arrangement." Bagot imagined the terms he was offering LaFontaine were too juicy to resist, even if it meant jettisoning Baldwin. It was a foolish miscalculation, given Baldwin's influence over LaFontaine. Robert had set minimum terms for an accommodation and would not budge from them. And LaFontaine would not budge from Baldwin. The Reformers insisted that Sherwood also must go and that the new arrangement be described as a "reconstruction" of the government rather than Bagot's euphemism that the existing council was being "added to." And Baldwin must be a member.[9]

Bagot had one card left to play. When Parliament convened that afternoon, Sullivan rose in the Legislative Council at the same time that Draper was standing in the Assembly. They each revealed the governor's offer to LaFontaine. The intention was to stampede Reform back benchers who, on hearing Bagot's generous terms, would force their leaders to accept. As members spilled into the lobbies, buzzing about the news, some clearly were impressed while others agreed with Baldwin's hard line. The informal debate was cut short, and members rushed back into the House; LaFontaine was about to reply. He needed to be at his polished best. Draper had been conciliatory, and many Reformers were wavering. Hardly had LaFontaine begun, carefully choosing his words in French, when nervous thoughtlessness on the government benches gave him his theme and steeled the resolve of Reformers. LaFontaine was cut off by a shrill cry. "Speak in English," shouted John Henry Dunn, the receiver general. Through the shocked silence of the House, LaFontaine replied, icily and devastatingly. "Je regrette de ne pouvoir me rendre aujourd'hui . . . la demande de l'honorable membre." He would not speak English on demand, but he welcomed Dunn's insult as another argument for voting no confidence in the ministry.[10]

This day, if LaFontaine was ice, Baldwin was fire. His had been a role of enforced passivity in the affair, compelled to wait and worry while others wrangled over the fate of the country, and his fate. Now the initiative was his. Taking the floor after his colleague, he poured scorn on Draper. While he was delighted that Draper was now prepared to resign in the interest of doing justice to French Canada, he wondered why the Attorney General had clung so tenaciously to office over the last year. The issue of French Canada had been just as pressing when Baldwin resigned in 1841, but Draper had smugly stayed in the council. The learned gentleman and his colleagues "were, to be sure, quite friendly to the poor, oppressed Lower Canadians, but they could not think of deserting a government that opposed them!" While Baldwin shook his fist at Draper, swept away by an anger the House had never seen before, Reformers roared "Hear, hear!" and hooted in laughter at the government's discomfort.[11]

Even in his anger, Robert developed a closely reasoned case for a change in government. At its base were the twin principles of justice and patriotism. The Union of the Canadas was worthy of support but "Not a union forced down the throats of the people by bayonets, but a union the voluntary choice of a free people." He loved Britain and wished to maintain the connection with it. That connection could best be secured by the conciliation of French Canada. Yet, if he loved Britain, he loved Canada more.

> I am a Canadian born, son of a Canadian; the grandson of a man who made Canada his home when it was a howling wilderness. I am proud of my birth, proud of the independence and industry of my fore-fathers, who placed me in the position in which I stand. And I wish to see that national feeling more generally appreciated from Sandwich to Gaspe.

The country needed a government that understood all this, that would give justice to all its people and stir in them a healthy patriotism.[12]

On this crest of nationalistic rhetoric, he moved a motion of non-confidence in the ministry and followed with a set of resolutions that reiterated the Harrison resolutions of September 1841. The House voted to send the resolutions to committee and adjourned in a state of confusion and excitement. For the first time since responsible government had been thrust to the forefront of Canadian politics by Baldwin, the capacity of an Assembly majority to oust a government on a vote of confidence was about to be tested. Small wonder members were confused and excited.

For the next three days Robert was at the centre of anxious activity, as Reform leaders met to agonize over their decision and assess the swirling rumours, which seemed to be Kingston's only topic of conversation. Bagot, too, was busy meeting with advisers, finding the limits of his own nerve. Could he capitulate to Reform demands and risk the wrath of the Colonial Office? Would it be worse to let events play themselves out and perhaps set an unhappy precedent of responsibility should the government be forced out on a confidence vote? While he dithered, the Reformers decided to act. On Friday, 16 September LaFontaine delivered an ultimatum to the governor. The Reformers would enter the government, but Sherwood must go, and the question of pensions for Ogden and Davidson would remain open. A weary Bagot gave in. He invited LaFontaine and Baldwin to the council chambers that afternoon to be sworn in.[13]

It was a humiliating defeat but, wily diplomat that he was, Bagot immediately began to put the best face on it. He created a new mythology in which he was the gracious architect of a new system of government, a mythology so powerful that historians down the ages would echo his self-serving phrases. He began to spin it while carrying out what would otherwise have been an ignoble task. He had to write to Ogden in England and Sherwood in Toronto to advise that he had jettisoned them in their absence. In the letter to Sherwood, however, Bagot coined the grandiose phrase that in future would turn his humiliation into a triumph of statesmanship. The change of government and the conciliation of French Canada became "this great measure." Sherwood, sulking over his loss of place, probably was unconvinced, but generations of historians have repeated Bagot's boast about his "great measure," which may—or may not—have given Canada the essence of responsible government.[14]

The "great measure" was actually a compromise whose implications were murky. It would be some time before even the cabinet shuffle was completed. One reason was LaFontaine's poor health, which left him confined to bed a few days after joining the executive council. Baldwin could not press on into controversies involving French Canada without LaFontaine to speak his lines. And of controversy there was plenty. For the first but not the last time Robert would find his plan complicated by a troublesome meddler, Edward Gibbon Wakefield. Back on 12 September Bagot had been astounded when his then incumbent councillors had recommended that Jean-Joseph Girouard be added to the ministry to placate French Canada, and to avoid adding LaFontaine and Baldwin. Girouard was a notary and scholar who was widely popular in Lower Canada. He was also, however, a leading figure among the rebels of 1837. The astonishing idea of adding the rebel Girouard to a conservative cabinet came from Wakefield. He had been an adviser to Durham in 1838 and had returned to Canada in 1841 to build a canal at Beauharnois on the St. Lawrence River. He imagined himself capable of constructing more than canals and became an inveterate manipulator in political back rooms. His current project was the reconciliation of French and English. Such reconciliation would stabilize the government, confirm Wakefield's influence, and protect the interests of his Lower Canadian canal.

His chosen instrument was Jean-Joseph Girouard. Wakefield opened a correspondence with Girouard in August 1842 with an offer to create a bi-national government of two largely autonomous sections, "[Y]ou taking the East and we the West." He was undisturbed by the fact that neither he nor Girouard was in government or even held a seat in Parliament. Scheming on, Wakefield used his undeniable charm and persuasiveness to convince the desperate executive councillors to support the addition of Girouard. However improbable their alliance with the rebel, it might be the only hope of undermining the leadership of LaFontaine and Baldwin in the French Party.[15]

The idea soon had a life of its own. Bagot had not been enthused by Wakefield's ploy, but the movement to draft Girouard did not die with the old council. Many Lower Canadians, including LaFontaine's brother-in-law Joseph-Amable Berthelot, urged Girouard to join the new LaFontaine–Baldwin administration, and twelve Lower Canadian members of the Assembly presented him a petition to that effect. Baldwin had to face the demand and, given the delicate health of his political support, yield to it. He knew the Colonial Office would be furious and that appointing Girouard to the cabinet would revitalize the Tory opposition, but Lower Canada was adamant. And, indeed, the conservative reaction was predictable, if rather inconsistent. The Tory lawyer, J.H. Cameron, gave a clever twist of the knife when he suggested that Girouard's salary be docked to repay the reward laid out for his capture in 1837. Cameron did not, however, comment on why Girouard was the noble symbol of reconciliation when conservatives offered him a job but an unregenerate rebel when Reformers did. In London, Lord Stanley was near apoplectic. How could he present the name of a traitor like Girouard to the queen, he demanded of Bagot?[16]

As it turned out, the excitement was wasted. Long before Lord Stanley received notice of Girouard's nomination, no matter before he had to present it to the queen, Girouard declined office. The affair had its price, however. The completion of the cabinet was delayed for a month until Girouard's replacement, Augustin-Norbert Morin, joined the executive council on 14 October. More important was that the controversy reinforced the image of the LaFontaine–Baldwin ministry as one of rebels and seditionists, an image that earned it continuing hostility at the Colonial Office. And Wakefield, who had started it all, would still hover in the wings, eager to create further mischief.[17]

Robert had enough trouble with the cabinet without the Girouard contretemps. It was an unstable mix of disparate elements. The new ministers—Baldwin, LaFontaine, Aylwin, Small, and Morin—were co-hesive. Unfortunately they joined six incumbents who were anything but. Samuel B. Harrison and J.H. Dunn were moderate Sydenhamite Reformers. Dominick Daly and H.H. Killaly were apolitical bureaucrats. Francis Hincks was the great betrayer of Reform. And R.B. Sullivan was the ultimate trimmer. Many of the Reform faithful were aghast that Baldwin would sit at the council table with this gang of rogues, and especially the great satan Hincks. William Buell of Brockville summed up the feelings about Hincks in a letter to Robert. He was "a man ambitiously desiring office and power, and seeing them within his grasp, in an evil moment, reached out his hand for the apple which looked sound and delicious without, but which proved corrupt and bitter within." Even Robert's most faithful acolyte, James Hervey Price, let his leader know how difficult it was to support an administration "polluted" by Hincks.[18]

It was not only the personnel that was difficult. There had been no prior agreement about policy, no understanding that the old ministers would agree to the program of the new. Further, the change had been accomplished without a vote of non-confidence in the old government and, therefore, it was unclear what precedents had been established. All this must have troubled such a stickler for propriety as Robert. That eternal enthusiast, William Warren Baldwin, had no doubts, though, that the creation of the new administration had enshrined the principle of responsible government once and for all. The divine mission had been completed under the providential leadership of his son. If this was so, God was speaking through something less obvious than a burning bush or a stone tablet. Responsible government was still widely misunderstood and would remain so until several preconditions were met: a full party administration was formed; a change of government was accomplished on a vote of non-confidence in the Assembly; and a ministry was in office that had a full and unequivocal commitment to the principle. All of these preconditions were only met in 1848.[19]

There was another precondition as well: acceptance of the principle by Britain. The home government was far from ready to do so in 1842. The condemnation in Britain of Bagot's "great measure" was vehement. The general opinion among politicians of both major parties was that Bagot had been "undignified" in yielding to pressure from colonials. His uncle, the aging hero the Duke of Wellington, was more forthright. "What a fool the man must have been, to act as he has done!" Wellington complained to Prime Minister Peel, "and what stuff and nonsense he has written! and what a bother he makes about his policy and measures, when there are no measures but rolling himself and his country in the mire!" At the Colonial Office, Lord Stanley was more measured but no less angry, especially about the way in which the Canadian government had been changed. "[I]t was done, in the face, and almost at the bidding, of the Assembly [which] seems to me to invest that body with a dangerous power of delimiting the choice of the Crown in reference to Individuals." Given the situation in Canada, the British government had little choice but to accept the *fait accompli*. Stanley made clear, however, that this did not imply acceptance of the principle which Reformers thought lay behind it. Baldwin and LaFontaine were not privy to the confidential dispatches sent by Lord Stanley to Bagot, no matter to the private exchanges of British politicians, but they would soon learn that the struggle for responsible government was far from over.[20]

For the moment all that could be overlooked. Robert and LaFontaine were immediately accepted as leaders of the ministry, virtually co-premiers although that term was not yet used. At the council table, Robert was clearly the dominant figure and he watched with pleasure as the old ministers quickly fell into line. Hincks, with his keen nose for power, went through another transformation on his political road to Damascus and was once again a loyal party man, affable, co-operative, bubbling with ideas for legislation. Even more miraculous was the birth of Robert Baldwin Sullivan, Reformer. As late as 13 September, cousin Sullivan was asking the legislative council, "Are we to carry on the government fairly and upon liberal principles or *by dint of miserable majorities*?" Once the new ministry was formed, however, Sullivan quickly joined the miserable majority and paraded as a strong Reform supporter. With this somewhat artificial unity in place, Robert kept the ministers hard at it developing a program for the brief legislative session he planned.[21]

Given the magnitude of the changes, it was no surprise that the session began with anger and confusion. The House met on the afternoon of Monday, 19 September, the galleries packed with excited spectators. They were not disappointed. The first item of business was a motion expressing confidence in the new ministry. The Tories were predictably furious, both about the new government and about this attempt to create a precedent for responsible government. The spectators murmured in anticipation of a good show when William "Tiger" Dunlop rose on behalf of the Tories. The member for Huron, Upper Canada, was a rogue elephant, even in his party of eccentrics. A great hulking man, over six feet tall and nearly as broad, Dunlop was always disheveled, always loud and vulgar, and often drunk. It was no shock that he found a government based on French Catholic support to be an abomination: "I am asked to thank His Excellency for doing an act he was driven to; he took these men to his council as the Devil does Holy Water."

Tory John S. Cartwright continued the attack, reminding the House that there often had been "suspicions" about Hincks's loyalty to the Crown. When the Speaker called on Cartwright to withdraw this unparliamentary remark, the Tory refused. The donnybrook was on. Members on both sides were on their feet shouting and threatening, some starting across the floor for direct confrontation. The spectators joined in the tumult until the Speaker had the galleries cleared. While shouted threats still echoed around the chamber, order had been restored sufficiently to pass a motion expressing satisfaction in the governmental changes. At the conclusion of the vote, Sir Allan MacNab and John Cartwright led the defiant Tories out of the House, screaming taunts at the members who remained.[22]

This purging of emotions seemed to leave the House exhausted and prepared to see the government's legislative program adopted with little opposition. The first bill passed was very much Robert Baldwin's. It was an electoral reform designed to curb violence at the polls such as had been epidemic in the election of 1841. Polling places were to be located in townships, parishes, or wards rather than following the old practice of a single polling place for a constituency, a practice that had made it so easy for polls to be controlled by thugs. The time for polling was reduced to two days, and provisions were made for policing the polls. Party colours, flags, and labels were banned in the vicinity of the hustings. Robert's well-conceived reform would pay dividends in future elections. Freed of some of the intimidation, people were encouraged to exercise their franchise and the number of votes cast increased by 40 percent between 1841 and 1844. This success was followed by an impressive, if short, list of reforms in land registry, courts, and other areas before the brief session ended on 12 October.[23]

Not everyone was delighted with the new government's accomplishments. The conservative Montreal *Gazette* believed that "a FRENCH mob" was in power "and the heel falls, each time, with insulting ingenuity, on the necks of the BRITISH." In Toronto and Brockville, constitutional societies were forming that fall, and extremist groups pledged to protect English rights and to resist the government. Robert had at least been spared Tory abuse in the House because he, as with all new ministers, was required by practice to seek re-election. He was not spared on the hustings, however. He returned to Hastings for the by-election when the polls opened at the town of Belleville on Tuesday, 3 October—polls held under the old election law since his own legislation was not yet in effect. The opponent was once again his cousin, Edmund Murney. And, again, familial ties did not discourage election violence. Both sides feigned innocence. The Murney supporters insisted they were attacked by "a gang of roman Catholics from the backwoods" while the Baldwinites claimed it was

Tory thugs who started the trouble. Robert described the scene for LaFontaine in letters on 6 and 7 October.

> 6 October: The troops are here and I really believe if they had not come we should have had bad work here tonight. Murneys men however had complete possession of the Hustings as they had taken it without resistance in the early part of the day. I insisted on its being cleared or at least half of it being cleared so that my Friends might have an equal opportunity of polling. This the Returning Officer did not do but adjourned till tomorrow at 6 oclock—Murneys friends are however still round the Hustings and avow their determination of remaining there all night—
>
> 7 October: The day passed off pretty well as to peace but there was some breaking of windows tonight and the troops are now (1/4 to 10 PM) drawn up in the middle of the main street.[24]

Mr. Baldwin's matter-of-fact tone suggested how common, almost normal, violence at the polls was at the time. Equally common was the ineffectiveness of the troops. Their passivity at Belleville assured victory for Murney and his bully boys. Once again Robert was shopping for a seat. The Second Riding of York, in the Toronto area, had just been declared vacant because of irregularities in the last election, so he shifted his campaign there. But Second York was Hastings revisited. There was widescale violence and intimidation, and Robert lost again. The triumph of the new government was tarnishing quickly as its leader became a subject of ridicule. "[T]hey have been calling you the rejected member for Upper Canada," lamented one supporter.[25]

Fortunately, there was an attractive alternative. While watching the street violence in Belleville and realizing Hastings was lost, Robert had written to LaFontaine suggesting the possibility of standing for a Lower Canadian riding. It would be a gesture of unity to parallel LaFontaine's election in Fourth York, as well as a safe haven from Upper Canadian Tory mobs. LaFontaine moved slowly and it was not until January 1843 that Michel Borne, the member for Rimouski, Lower Canada, was convinced to resign his seat. Baldwin tarnished the noble gesture somewhat by staying at his desk in Kingston rather than campaigning in Rimouski. A disappointed Borne lamented the lost opportunity to give his leader "a true Jean Baptiste reception." Nevertheless, the absent Upper Canadian was returned unopposed for Rimouski on 30 January. When the next session of Parliament convened, Baldwin would be able to take his rightful place alongside LaFontaine on the government benches.[26]

——◆——

The triumph would have been complete were Eliza there to share it. She had been entwined with his hopes for success, she was much of the reason why it was important. "I almost tremble with anxiety," he had told her when he feared that he would fail her, for he knew "how much of your happiness depends upon my success in my profession." So, too, would it have been with politics. She was the person to whom he could reveal himself in times of difficulty for, as he told her in 1825, "[T]hough I am surrounded by the best and kindest of friends there is not one to whom I can open my bosom as I could to my Eliza." She was both an emotional and an intellectual companion. He valued her intelligence so much that he even compared her to his revered mother. As he insisted to his father, "my dear departed one . . . if she had not a mind of fully the same force and power as my dear Mother was far from being deficient in either of these qualities— And had assuredly all others others which make a husband happy."[27]

Distance could not break the bond. When the family had sent Eliza to New York in 1825 hoping to end the romance, the lovers had arranged to have "ideal" meetings on the first day of each month. They would gaze at the heavens at the same time, "indulging in a thousand delightful recollections and anticipations." These meetings were a great comfort to Robert for there was "something so soothing in the certainty that we were mutually occupied with the image of each other at the same moment."[28]

If distance could not break the bond, neither could death. When he was at home, and when the bustle of the family had subsided late at night, he shared his life with her. Even when he was at Kingston, busied with the stuff of politics, he could reach into an inner pocket, where he carried letters from her, and keep alive her words and her thoughts. Before his death he made copies of all his correspondence with Eliza and passed them on to his daughter Maria with an explanation of how the letters had comforted him.

> Often and often when you and the rest of the family have been in your beds, have I for hours together held sweet converse with my departed E, and pouring over these hoarded treasures recalled many of the sensations chastened and subdued but still delightful, with which I first beheld them fresh from the beloved hand that wrote them; with a thousand other mournfully happy recollections of the past which have become associated with these precious relics. I have never left home for any time without taking one or more of them with me for I never wish to die without one of them near me.[29]

Those "mournfully happy recollections" were more important, and more real, than the political triumphs of the present. His thoughts were still of death and the completion it would bring.

Life went on, nevertheless, including political life. The Reform government was a success, but it was not without its vicissitudes. Robert found the court-related functions of the Attorney Generalship to be more taxing than he had anticipated. He was expected to represent the Crown in both civil and criminal cases. However, the Attorney General did not control the scheduling of court sessions, nor did the civil and criminal courts have coordinated schedules. This made it exhausting for Robert to attempt to fulfill his court responsibilities and carry on his administrative duties as well. A partial solution was to forego some of the income of his office. The Attorney General, in addition to a salary of £1200, was entitled to collect fees for certain services. Robert found he had no time for fee-earning services, such as drafting patents for Crown land grants, and instead referred applicants to private solicitors. That sacrifice did little to ease the burdens, especially the burden of time stolen from his family as he plodded on horseback or bounced in stage coaches following the court circuits of Upper Canada.[30]

Sometimes the muddy roads of the court circuits seemed preferable to dealing with his colleagues at Kingston. Inside the cabinet, Francis Hincks and John Henry Dunn were at each other's throats. Dunn, he of the ethnic slur against LaFontaine, was never the soul of discretion. He went too far even for him, however, when he gossiped about Hincks's possible involvement in the rebellion of 1837 in front of Tory leader Sir Allan MacNab. The story naturally showed up in various Tory newspapers. Hincks was furious and struck back by raising doubts about Dunn's honesty in handling government funds in his capacity as receiver general of accounts. Dunn was continuing the old practice of keeping government money in a private account and using it for personal financial speculation. Robert managed to keep the two ministers from a public break and, before the government's term had run out, to secure public funds in a bank, safe from peculation.[31]

Cabinet ministers were a minor irritation compared to the governor. Baldwin and Bagot inevitably irritated each other over responsible government. Robert was anxious to establish the triumph of responsibility on the public record. Sir Charles wanted to maintain as much ambiguity as possible. Robert's persistence in raising the issue at every opportunity became too much for Bagot in late October 1842. The governor summoned the co-premiers to his office. Bagot was not playing the smooth diplomat this day. Anger flashed from his eyes as he waved a document in front of the two Reformers. It was a legal opinion prepared by the Attorney General West to which Mr. Baldwin had gratuitously attached a long dissertation on responsible government. He would not have this sort of thing, Bagot lectured; he would not have ministers attempting to intrude their political theories on the apolitical business of the Crown. It was humiliating for Robert, being reprimanded in front of LaFontaine, being charged with bad faith. Yet his instinctive deference to the queen's representative made him bite his tongue and swallow the humiliation.[32]

A direct challenge to responsible government, however, forced Robert to overcome his habit of deference. As with previous governors, Bagot continued to make appointments to some government positions without consulting his ministers. For Robert, this was a fundamental violation of the principles of responsibility and he steeled himself to fight it out with

Sir Charles. LaFontaine, as always, was much less concerned about the principle, less willing to confront the governor. Badgered by Baldwin, however, LaFontaine agreed to make an appointment with Bagot during the last week in November when they would call the governor to task. Robert was full of anxiety awaiting the meeting, perhaps with images of his unhappy clashes with Sydenham playing across his mind. All of the nervous energy was wasted. Sir Charles came down sick and was confined to bed at Alwington House, unable to see his ministers. Robert went home to Toronto, still agitated by the patronage issue. LaFontaine, the cynical realist, wrote him from Kingston that it was better to let the matter rest at any rate; a British governor would always try to undermine the influence of a Reform government and this inevitable interference was not worth a crisis.[33]

Bagot's illness solved the problem, although not in a way anyone would have wished. Sydenham's death was still fresh in everyone's mind, so news that Sir Charles was seriously ill became the major topic of discussion in Kingston. Among the most popular explanations bandied about was the story that he had broken down because his daughter was embroiled in a scandal back home in England. The truth was more prosaic. Bagot's troubles were physical, not emotional, and he would be bedridden for the rest of his governorship. However tragic Sir Charles's fate, it was the opportunity for Robert to exercise the full scope of responsibility. As Bagot grew weaker, Baldwin and LaFontaine became the real heads of government, developing policy and distributing patronage with a free hand. They had truly passed over into the promised land. Quite naturally, they developed the warmest sympathy for Sir Charles who had paved their way. Forgotten were the quarrels of the autumn. The dying governor was now invested with saintly qualities. And he played out his role in this little drama. His last injunction to the executive councillors was a message in which he said that he left his reputation in their hands. "I know you will protect it. I am too exhausted to say more." When Sir Charles died at Alwington House on 19 May 1843, Baldwin and LaFontaine were pledged to honour that last request. And his reputation was indeed in good hands as the legend of Sir Charles Bagot and his "great measure" joined the Harrison-Baldwin resolutions of September 1841 in the Reform canon of creation myths.[34]

Chapter 9

An Enthusiast—Almost a Fanatic

It had been seven years, with only his principles to warm him. He pored over her letters, seeking her help in an uncertain time. It was the spring of 1843.

Sir Charles Metcalfe was still settling in to Alwington House, his servants unpacking his clothes and books and dispatches from the Home Government. He had seen enough of his new colony and its leaders to form strong impressions, though. Once having formed them, Sir Charles was not the man to ever change them. His opinion of the Attorney General West was scathing. Robert Baldwin was his father's son and the elder Baldwin had become an ultra radical because of personal quarrels with members of the Family Compact, not because of principles. The son was "an enthusiast—almost a fanatic," driven by his uncompromising ideas. He seemed "to delight in strife" and there was "a sort of sublime egotism about him" that allowed him to pretend to be acting out of duty when he was really only serving his own vanity. With such a man, Sir Charles knew, conflict was inevitable.[1]

Conflict was far from Robert Baldwin's mind. When news came in February 1843 that Metcalfe had been appointed to succeed the dying Charles Bagot, Robert had been delighted. Reports from England described Metcalfe as an advanced liberal with a brilliant record of administration in difficult situations—as acting governor in India and governor in Jamaica. Robert was not in Kingston on 29 March when Metcalfe arrived after an arduous journey across the winter-tossed Atlantic and by train and sleigh from Boston. But he shared the enthusiasm of the crowd who cheered the new viceroy at the capital. His enthusiasm, at least, was misplaced. Sir Charles had not been sent to confirm responsible government but to keep it in check. Authorities in Britain had never been reconciled to Bagot's cowering before a miserable majority and the fury was especially intense at the highest level of authority. Queen Victoria and her husband, Prince Albert, had studied the dispatches from Canada with growing discomfort. In May 1843 Albert wrote to Lord Stanley at the Colonial Office, "I dont think, the Crown of England could allow the establishment of a responsible government in Canada as that would be tantamount to a declaration of separation from the mother country." Stanley and Metcalfe did not need much prodding. Metcalfe's liberalism had been much exaggerated in reports. Robert should have remembered that Francis Bond Head, too, had been described as a liberal before he descended on Upper Canada like a reactionary plague. Metcalfe left England with powerful prejudices against the Reformers and let nothing influence his biases. Within a month of taking up his office, he told Stanley that only the Tories were truly loyal and that his cabinet was full of "men of extreme opinions." Robert's naive goodwill in the face of yet another imperial governor would, again, cost him dearly.[2]

The power of paternal influence was so great that it took enormous provocation to move him to resistance. As yet, there seemed no need. Metcalfe's views were not immediately apparent and routine business proceeded without friction. The Executive had been summoned to Kingston and were kept occupied by the new governor. However, it was spring and in the absence of political crisis Robert could turn his thoughts to home and to his own parental responsibilities. He made time to supervise the homefront by letter. His daughter Eliza was a faithful correspondent but not a polished one, and Robert was punctilious in correcting her spelling in his return letters. He also chided the family, through her, for not keeping him informed about the progress of his geraniums and lemon trees.[3]

It was a short spring. Some Reformers were quickly disillusioned with Metcalfe, especially the acerbic Solicitor General East, Thomas Aylwin. By mid-April he anticipated that they would have trouble with Metcalfe over patronage. The governor liked to take arbitrary actions, to play "*le roi Sultan des Indes*" (Sultan of the Indies), Aylwin warned LaFontaine. He would have to be controlled. Robert did not share Aylwin's suspicions and he accepted Metcalfe's much more activist interpretation of the governor's role. He could hardly do otherwise. Metcalfe played the stern father to his ministers, keeping all important matters in his own hands. As he described the process to Stanley,

> The business of the Government is carried on by myself in communication with the secretaries, no orders are issued without my personal direction or sanction, and only those matters are referred to the Council which the law or established practice require to be so dealt with, or on which I really wish to have the benefit of their local knowledge and advice.

When the executive council met, they sat at a long table in a small and makeshift council chamber, with Sir Charles ensconced paternally at the head of the table. He initiated most of the proposals brought to the Council and initialled his approval of every report presented by committees of the Council. To challenge this system of gubernatorial leadership, which Sir Charles had initiated without discussion or advice, would have demanded that Robert confront paternal authority directly. Sir Charles may have thought that Robert delighted in strife but, in fact, he would compromise even his own sense of what constituted good government to avoid conflict with Metcalfe.[4]

There were other compromises. When Hincks returned to the Reform fold, Robert embraced the black sheep as if he had never strayed. He welcomed Hincks's political advice, the blinkers of friendship and loyalty blinding him to the realities of Hincks's recent behaviour. One area where Hincks's views prevailed was on patronage. He and Samuel Harrison agreed that the ministry must not be too partisan on patronage. They would be criticized as corrupt if they appointed only Reformers to office and, more serious, they would offend Metcalfe who, Hincks contended, "is really acting very well." Hincks recommended appointing equal numbers of Tories and Reformers as magistrates in Toronto and at least twenty-five Tories in the Home District outside Toronto. As usual, Hincks had a cunning and elaborate explanation for his scheme. "I feel quite satisfied that our friends cannot complain & I see that great political good will result. We are now fighting the battle of the *Middle Classes* against the aristocracy. Our commissions will be attacked on the score of unfit people that is not *gentlemen*. Now I would select Tories from the *same class* that we take our friends from so that when the cry is raised by the Tories they will *hit their own* friends." The defensive tactic in this was less important than the larger strategy. For Hincks, class interests overrode political ones; he was indeed fighting the battle of the new middle class, his class.[5]

The Hincks approach clashed with Baldwin's own instincts on patronage. He told an aspirant for office in February that his personal preferences in appointments must always give way before the political interests of the Reform Party. "I always have been in the strictest sense of the word *a party man* . . . were it my father or brother who stood in the same relative party position I should give them the same answer— whatever influence I possess is not *mine* to be used for my benefit or for the gratification of my own feelings but a trust to be accounted for to my Country and my party." Yet he accepted Hincks's judgment and permitted Tories to continue in office and new Tory appointments to be made. Baldwin's friend and cabinet colleague J.E. Small was among those who were outraged by the rewarding of political enemies. As with other Reformers, Small's anger was ignited by more than old grievances against Tories. He recognized, as Baldwin did when he was not under the sway of Hincks, that every office was needed to bind together the loose Reform alliance. "Patronage is power," James Hervey Price had also reminded Baldwin. "Men like Hopkins, Steele, Cameron, Parke etc will support your administration or the administration of a Nero provided you allow them patronage and power."[6]

Robert heard from Reformers great and small who were bewildered by the government's patronage policy. An old friend, Andrew Buell of Brockville, warned of the consequences. "A General of an Army would be thought imprudent if not *mad* to select from the ranks of the enemy captains and officers . . . and defeat & disgrace would be the inevitable result." Rank-and-file Reformers, who for years had been at the mercy of local officials who were Tories and Orange bullies, could not understand why a liberal administration would leave the same villains in place. In Barrie, north of Toronto, for example, local Reformers had trudged through snow drifts in late March to express their appreciation to outgoing governor Sir Charles Bagot. But armed Orangemen took over the meeting, led by men who were on the commission of magistrates just issued by the Reform government. It was a similar situation in Adjala township. Local liberals protested the appointment of a prominent Orangeman and Tory partisan as clerk of the district court. The offensive appointee, they told Baldwin, had led a party of Tories who seized all the guns belonging to area Reformers during the rebellion of 1837. They, like their compatriots in Barrie and elsewhere, saw their faith in the ministry, their belief that it represented real change, ebbing away thanks to the ill-considered patronage policy initiated by Hincks and naively accepted by Baldwin. Even Robert's father wrote about how bitter Reformers were over some of the appointments.[7]

As the summer wore on, Robert was stung by the criticism, increasingly defensive over his tolerance of Metcalfe's domineering, and alarmed by the rifts in the party. He took his solace where he could find it. One sunny day he climbed into a Kingston cab, driven by a garrulous Irishman. The cabman was delighted to serve the Reform leader and asked if he could name one of his carriages *Spadina*. Robert was pleased at the recognition and the by now rare expression of support. But with his usual exaggerated sense of propriety he told the driver that it would be necessary to obtain the approval of his father, who after all was the owner of Spadina. Robert may have lost another Reformer supporter, as he seemed to be alienating so many. Some of the key Reformers were restless about the governor and bewildered that their government seemed to be doing so little; why was there not a session of the legislature? There was not a session because Metcalfe did not wish one until he had built his own power base. And Baldwin, deferential to a fault, allowed the drift to continue. Despite Metcalfe's aspersion, Robert would go to enormous lengths to avoid personal conflict. And despite his appearance of controlled competence, he would defer again and again to the breezy self-confidence of Francis Hincks.[8]

Robert still had no inkling of Metcalfe's real views and as a result he put the best construction on the governor's actions. Metcalfe felt that the issue on which to fight his ministers in the inevitable confrontation was patronage, where he could argue the initiative of the Crown. To assure they would dispute on the ground he chose, Metcalfe tried to neutralize other, more uncertain, issues. One was amnesty for the rebels of 1837, a highly emotional matter for many Reformers. Stanley would not agree to a general amnesty so Metcalfe dealt sympathetically with individual cases brought to him. Baldwin, for instance, was happy with Metcalfe's amnesty for the old Reform leader, Marshall Spring Bidwell.

Other prominent figures, including Dr. John Rolph, were also pardoned. Robert was pleased, but LaFontaine was furious. He was angry that there was not a general amnesty and even angrier that Upper Canadian pardons were being expedited while French Canadians languished in exile. LaFontaine met with his francophone cabinet colleagues, without Robert's knowledge, and they agreed to resign unless Metcalfe did justice to French Canada. The governor yielded, even pardoning the notorious Louis-Joseph Papineau, the man Britain had vowed never to absolve. LaFontaine's tough-minded approach was in the sharpest contrast to Baldwin's polite deference. One result was that there was a de facto general amnesty for French Canadians while the Upper Canadian rebel leader, William Lyon Mackenzie, was frozen in exile for another six years. Mackenzie would not forget that Baldwin had refused to confront Metcalfe over his pardon.[9]

Metcalfe's concession to LaFontaine reflected his more general attempt to placate French Canada, to remove the "race" issue from the political agenda. He showed a consistently generous spirit to French Canadians and advanced them in government office at every opportunity. But he was much less generous to his own ministers. During the summer of 1843 Metcalfe was plotting against the Reformers. He met secretly with leaders of the opposition, including Ogle Gowan, chieftain of the Orange Order. Gowan came away from Alwington House exultant after hearing from Metcalfe about the governor's differences with his councillors. Gowan sat down at his rooming house and, as Metcalfe had requested, carefully laid out on paper his strategy for precipitating a crisis with the ministry. He could not resist sharing his triumph with a friend, William Harris. He wrote to Harris, "Don't be surprised if Baldwin, Hincks, & Harrison, *walk*, or that Cartwright [a Tory] succeeds the latter." This plotting between a governor and a bitter enemy of the Executive did not come to light until the following May when Andrew Buell obtained a copy of the letter and sent it on to Baldwin. Even then Robert was seized by his exaggerated sense of correctness. He withdrew to his study in Toronto and agonized over whether the incriminating letter could be used. LaFontaine, always more earthy and pragmatic, was puzzled by the lengthy correspondence in which Robert struggled with his conscience. The letter involved the governor and it was marked "expressly confidential." As a result, Robert could not bring himself to publish it although he did compromise enough to agree "to make use of this letter confidentially among my friends." Metcalfe was never troubled by such compunctions. That may help to explain his victory over Baldwin.[10]

This uneasy government finally met in Parliament on 28 September 1843. For the first time Robert was a participant in the pomp and ceremony of a parliamentary opening, in his capacity as an executive councillor, rather than as a distant spectator. For him, as for others there, the glitter of the occasion only heightened the horror as Sir Charles Metcalfe entered the Legislative Council chamber to greet his parliamentarians. Under the viceregal cocked hat, his face was terribly disfigured. In the middle of his left cheek was a grotesque fleshy tumor, now the size of an acorn and seemingly larger every day. Soon the cancer would eat through his cheek. It was hard to concentrate on the governor's words as attention was constantly drawn to the insidious lump on his face. Robert's mind wandered, contemplating the peculiar curse that seemed to fall on governors of this province. First there had been Lord Durham, called home in disgrace and barely outliving the publication of his monumental report. Then Lord Sydenham, dying in agony in Kingston, and Sir Charles Bagot lingering on for months until death gave him relief. And now the fourth, Governor Metcalfe, being eaten away before their eyes.[11]

Metcalfe's losing struggle with cancer became entwined with Robert Baldwin's fate. For the moment that fate seemed very promising. With an overwhelming majority in the House, Robert was able to rush through a spate of legislation, much of it very important. He did not mind that the dominant figure in the Assembly was Hincks, not himself. As Hincks's old paper the *Examiner*, which he had left in other hands, commented, "The Inspector General, Mr. Hincks, is decidedly *the* man of the House." Hincks was in his glory with power and prestige finally his, lolling confidently on the front benches, rising to instruct the members on the fine points of finance or to dress down bumptious oppositionists. He shepherded through a long list of important bills, establishing import duties on agricultural products, reforming the Upper Canadian school system, and establishing a new assessment regime in Upper Canada.

The assessment bill was perhaps the most controversial legislation, but it produced the unusual sight of Hincks and Baldwin passionately united on an economic issue. The bill repealed existing local taxes in Upper

Canada and applied a new tax on property according to its "rent value." Wild and developed land, personal property, and income were all subject to assessment at their real value. Hincks drew inspiration from American examples and saw the tax as a progressive one that would stimulate economic activity. Baldwin was attracted by its equity. Although a large land owner, he had never approved of the speculative trading in land that had been encouraged by the old system's exemption of undeveloped land from taxation. Whatever the bill's merits, it brought down on their heads a storm of protest. Land owners were outraged but so too were ordinary folk who feared the "inquisitorial" nature of the legislation. Just as Prime Minister Sir Robert Peel had discovered in England when introducing assessment for an income tax, the cliché that a man's home is his castle was taken very literally. A Canadian Tory paper charged that assessors would be sent out each year "to pry into everyman's private business and domestic arrangements" and a Reform supporter warned Baldwin, "[T]here will be a rebellion in the Country if it goes into effect." Hincks and Baldwin had to retreat and exempt personal effects from assessment, but they fought out the basics of the bill in a House that was in tumult throughout the debate. They would pay heavily for their victory in the next election as the assessment act hung around their necks like a particularly ugly albatross. Upper Canada, no matter Lower Canada, was still far from a modern place, a fact that Baldwin above all ought to have appreciated.[12]

The Reform leaders were rarely in such agreement on economics. The difference between them was that Robert expressed his disagreement in cabinet while Hincks often publicly embarrassed his leader. It was easy enough for Tories to exploit the rift. On 24 October Tory Henry Sherwood moved for the creation of a select committee to study the effects of the usury laws. The cat was among the Reform pigeons. Robert leaped to his feet to announce the ministry's opposition to the proposal and Morin confirmed that the French Party would not have the usury laws disturbed. For traditionalists such as Baldwin and Morin, the 6 percent limit on interest rates protected against the evil of unearned profit, of money made by exploitation and manipulation instead of honest effort. The capitalist modernizers, however, wished to remove any barriers to the flow and employment of capital. The positions were well known, but Hincks refused to maintain a discreet silence. To roars of approval from the opposition, he declared his support for an end to the usury laws. It became a free fight with other bourgeois Reformers, including S.B. Harrison, joining Hincks in his dissent. To Robert's anger and humiliation, Sherwood's motion was only narrowly rejected by four votes. It was a clear indication of how tenuous was the balance in the party between conflicting economic philosophies, a balance that could shift with the relative influence of the two leaders: Baldwin and Hincks.[13]

The ministry was revealing its divisions and showing its wounds. They were flesh wounds to this point. Two other controversies would fatally injure the government. One was the emotional question of the capital of United Canada. Kingston was hardly the favourite of anyone, except Kingstonians, but it had been chosen because larger rivals cancelled each other out. That shaky compromise collapsed in 1843. Robert found himself under powerful pressure from his French-Canadian colleagues to move the capital east of the Ottawa river. It was, they insisted, the needed symbol of justice to French Canada, the final gesture that the French were full partners in the Union. Robert knew that he would face the fury of Upper Canada if he did so, but he became convinced the gesture must be made. As with so many other issues involving French Canada, Robert assumed a curious personal sense of guilt about the injustices done to the French and he therefore could not resist their cries for redress. So, in October, he asked the executive council to approve moving the capital to Montreal. The action cost him Harrison who, as member for Kingston, felt he must resign from the ministry. It was no great loss in terms of administrative ability or personal loyalty, but it hurt politically. The ministry was already stung, then, when Baldwin and LaFontaine moved a motion in the House on 2 November to authorize the change of capital. While the motion carried comfortably Robert ought to have seen the danger signs. The debate was acrimonious, filled with innuendo about undue French influence. And some important Reformers voted against the ministry, including that weather vane William Hamilton Merritt and the aging veterans Malcolm Cameron and Caleb Hopkins. Both Cameron and Hopkins would be disaffected for years to come and both were capable of hurting Baldwin badly.[14]

The other controversy was Robert's creation alone: legislation against the Orange Order. The Order was deeply abhorrent to him. Its religious bigotry, political conservatism, anti-French biases, and ready resort to violence all were insults to his most basic values. And there was the purely practical consideration that Orange bully boys were the shock troops of Tory electioneering in many parts of the province. Robert's father had led a group of citizens who in 1841 had petitioned the legislature, unsuccessfully, for suppression of the Orange Order. Once in power, Robert could act against the ultra-Protestants. He established a de facto policy of excluding Orangemen from public office but it was events in the summer of 1843 that drove him to more sweeping measures. The major Orange annual holiday was 12 July, which celebrated the Protestant victory over Catholics in Ireland at the Battle of the Boyne in 1689. All too often the Orange parades turned into melees with disapproving Catholics, as was the case in Kingston on 12 July 1843. Robert heard the noise of the Orange demonstration turn into something more ominous—the sharp crackle of gun fire. He joined a crowd running to the site of a new Catholic church under construction. To his horror he saw a party of Catholics barricaded in the excavations for the church, exchanging fire with hundreds of Orangemen who swarmed about the site. By the time the fury was spent a sixteen-year-old apprentice, Robert Morrison, was lying dead in the summer sun and both sides were taking their wounded off to safe houses for treatment.[15]

The Orange Order must be reined in; it must be stripped of its capacity to commit more outrages like the Kingston riot. The answer was the package of three bills that Robert introduced to the House on 9 October. One, to regulate the calling and conducting of public meetings, passed with little opposition. He found the resistance stiffening over the other two: a bill to restrain partisan processions and a bill for the discouragement of secret societies. Opponents organized against him across Upper Canada, and the Orange Order was capable of powerful organization. It had tens of thousands of faithful adherents, attracted not just by its loud loyalty to the Crown and its anti-Catholic credentials, but by the support the Order provided for Protestant immigrants. It was an immigrants' aid society that offered help to the sick, buried the indigent dead, and embraced the lonely in fellowship. It was a formidable foe.[16]

It was ironic that Robert faced so much trouble over his legislation because he had not wanted to introduce legislation in the first place. He was impressed by the British precedent of adopting an address to the Crown for royal action to discourage Orangeism. Metcalfe disagreed with that approach and advised Baldwin to proceed by legislation. Whether by design or good fortune, Metcalfe had laid a clever trap for his despised Attorney General. With his introduction of the party processions and secret societies bills, Baldwin promptly proceeded to fall in.[17]

Robert's disgust for the Orange Order produced draconian bills, too harsh for even some Reformers. On the party processions bill, few openly opposed legislation to stop parades that generated hatred in the community. However, many bridled at the provision for summary conviction by magistrates, with a penalty of four months imprisonment and no appeal. After an angry debate, Robert was forced to retreat, to reduce the period of summary incarceration to twenty-four hours and provide for appeals. This was enough to win House approval for the bill on 27 October.

The main event was the secret societies bill. Baldwin believed that membership in the Orange Order was fundamentally incompatible with citizenship. The Order fostered hatred between people on the basis of religion and ethnicity, whereas the foundation of a successful Canadian state was the capacity for people of differing religions and ethnic groups to live and work together. His own struggle to hold together a bi-national party, his decision to have his children educated in French, indicated the strength of his belief in a tolerant Canada. The Orange Order was also a secret organization, an offence to Baldwin's liberal vision of a society based on open, honest dealings between individuals.

Beginning from these premises, Baldwin was prepared to strip Orangemen of some of the privileges of citizenship. Under the secret-societies bill, members of such organizations were banned from holding civil office or serving on juries. Innkeepers who permitted meetings of secret societies on their premises would have their licenses revoked. Robert knew this was harsh medicine and that he could expect stiff opposition, although the ferocity of that opposition still surprised him. The Tories were prepared to go to almost any length to protect their fighting arm, the Orange Order. The House was in chaos for days. Sir Allan MacNab hurled abuse and charges of rebel sympathies at the government until reined in by the Speaker. Orangemen in the galleries showered the Reform benches with threats of retribution, forcing the Speaker to close the galleries to spectators. Members on both sides shouted across the floor, shook their fists at their opponents, and generally provided graphic evidence why legislation against political violence was needed. The Tories were badly outnumbered in the House and they could not prevent the bill passing on 4 November with a substantial majority of Protestant members supporting it.[18]

The legislation still faced difficult hurdles. It had to pass the legislative council, but that house was in utter confusion. A dozen members were on strike, refusing to attend sessions because of their opposition to the way in which the seat of government address had been pushed through the chamber. The secret-societies bill was passed by the remaining members, but the absence of so many councillors provided Metcalfe with an excuse to reserve the bill for consideration by the British government. Robert was angered and astonished when Metcalfe reserved the very legislation that he had urged the Attorney General to introduce. And Robert knew the bill's likely fate. Indeed, it disappeared into the Colonial Office until Lord Stanley announced on 27 March 1844 that the secret-societies bill had been disallowed because it violated the rights of British subjects. The disallowance came in time to free Orangemen to rampage during the 1844 election.[19]

What made all this worse was the heavy price Robert paid for trying to legislate against violence. There was a dramatic increase in the number of Orange lodges and in their membership in 1843 and 1844, perhaps in reaction against the secret-societies bill. Orangemen, in the fall of 1843, had openly warned of violence if the bill was passed. A notorious gang of Orangemen in one Upper Canadian township, the Cavan Blazers, promised a reign of terror against all Reformers. What was hardest for Robert was that his family bore the brunt of Orange fury. On the evening of 7 November 1843 Orangemen in Toronto held a immense parade to show their displeasure at the passage of the bill in the Assembly. They massed on Yonge Street, thousands of torches glittering on Orange banners and ribbons, and illuminating a huge four-sided transparency whose inscriptions denounced the traitors Hincks and Baldwin. The procession marched through the city, stopping at Dr. John Rolph's home to give three groans of disapproval before heading along Front Street to the Baldwin house. There effigies of Hincks and Baldwin were strung up and burned.[20]

Robert's daughter Eliza showed remarkable sang-froid for an eleven-year-old. She reported to her father that the effigies, soaked in tar, were placed in front of their door and set ablaze. "Mr Hincks burnt up very quickly but they could not get you to burn at all at last they succeeded and then they gave a groan for you when you were burnt up." Her matter-of-fact account of the outrage was a harsh reminder of the dangers of mid-nineteenth-century life when the children of the premier might find it natural enough to watch a mob rage about their house, to spend the night guarded by armed relatives. And, indeed, it was not an isolated event. In June 1844 Robert himself faced an Orange mob. During a meeting at Bradford in the Fourth Riding of York, Orangemen stormed the platform during a speech by J.E. Small. The platform guests, including Baldwin, had to flee across the fields with the stone-throwing Orangemen in hot pursuit. Baldwin assured LaFontaine that he "would have been severely beaten to say the least of it had we been overtaken."[21]

<hr/>

The abuse of his family and his own travails made him all the more ambivalent about his life in politics. There was much to do and it was important work. His father's assurance that he was the one man able to set things right always resonated in his mind. Even more, as a religious man, Robert understood the world in terms of providential dispensation. With God's assistance he would live virtuously and fulfill his duty honourably. In one of the prayers that he had shared with Eliza in the early days of their happiness, Robert asked for guidance "in the discharge of those important political duties" to do "what shall be the best for the good of my King & my native country & for the establishment upon a sure foundation of its wealth happiness and tranquility." And yet he also had prayed, "O Lord God, so soon as thou seest that I can be no longer useful in a public capacity restore me, I most humbly beseech thee, to the walks of private life." He could repeat that prayer with even greater fervour in the winter of 1843–1844.[22]

The strength to accept what God had dispensed, to struggle down the road of public life, came as always from Eliza. Their common bond in religion helped to keep her with him. As Robert told his father after her death, he found her in the chapters of scripture he read every day.

> We had previously always read them through consecutively from Genesis forwards—Many & many a time since have I in my solitary chamber recalled the pleasure and profit of those our daily exercises—And yet much as I enjoyed them formerly it is now that they seem to come still more home to my heart— my desolate heart—& when I again meet some passage which she had pointed out either as confirmatory of our faith or consolatory to our hopes I can scarcely believe but that I hold communion with her blessed spirit—I am indeed rich in these treasures and blessed—oh how blessed in every recollection connected with her memory—Should the Almighty in his wisdom see fit to call me hence instead of restoring me to my poor children above all things let them know the <u>comfort</u>—the <u>consolation</u>—the <u>happiness</u> which both their parents derived from that blessed religion which the Son of God came into the world to reveal and offered up himself to establish.[23]

However buffetted by the opposition in the streets and in the House, the government continued to be a productive one. Hincks was primarily responsible for the most important piece of legislation, the Upper Canadian School Act of 1843. It created the basic structure for all educational legislation that would follow: funding of schools jointly by the province and the municipalities; popularly elected school trustees; and the creation of Catholic separate schools.[24]

Baldwin himself took on the issue of higher education. Although not a university man himself, he had long been concerned with the question. That interest was widely shared by Upper Canadians. In 1827 Archdeacon John Strachan had gained a charter for an Anglican university, King's College, and with it an endowment of 91,507 hectares acres of land to support the university. King's, as an Anglican "missionary college," was a hated symbol of religious exclusiveness and a political storm centre.

As such, it became a major issue between the Assembly and Legislative Council in Upper Canada. The resulting political deadlock meant the charter remained moribund. Sir Charles Bagot, himself an Oxford graduate, created a storm by deciding to proceed with the Anglican university. He laid the foundation stone for King's College in Toronto on 23 April 1842 and teaching began in 1843.[25]

King's was a tiny school, serving the elite of Upper Canada. Its symbolic importance was much greater than its size, however. It was an icon of the religious and political favouritism that responsible government was intended to eradicate. Robert was determined to smash the icon. The key question, he told Metcalfe, was that of divinity. If the teaching of divinity, Anglican divinity, were abolished at King's, the university could become "a Provincial Establishment" in which all could feel comfortable. Should that be impossible the best course was to make its divinity degrees open to all by having the university certify degrees from theological seminaries of all denominations. Some such solution was necessary, he warned the governor, or there would be endless and widespread agitation in the province. The principle of Baldwin's university bill was contained in this memorandum of March 1843, even to the new name which would be applied; the memorandum referred to the "University of Toronto" as the title of the provincial establishment. Such was the power of the Anglican elite, however, that it would be another six years before Baldwin's vision became reality.[26]

Baldwin attempted to exert pressure on Metcalfe over the university question. He and Hincks encouraged the trustees of Queen's College, the Presbyterian school at Kingston, to petition the governor. Baldwin kept busy meeting with opponents of King's, a campaign that culminated in a public rally at Toronto's Wesleyan Methodist Church on 2 October. The ground was prepared for legislative action. The first class at King's College—some twenty-six students, twenty-two of them Anglican—had barely settled into their studies when Baldwin introduced his university bill into the House on 12 October.[27]

The bill created a highly centralized University of Toronto. This appeared to be at odds with his usual view that centralized power was dangerous. It was a reflection of the strength of his opposition to sectarian higher education that he was prepared to put aside his normal repugnance for consolidation of power. In his view, sectarianism was the enemy of an efficient university and of dispassionate learning. Sectarianism could be avoided only be creating a single secular college for the province. Therefore the University of Toronto must control all the educational functions, and the existing religious colleges must shrink to mere divinity halls, affiliated with the university. There would be no professors of divinity at the provincial university and no religious tests for teachers or students. In his prescription to cure sectarianism, Baldwin was laying out the basic pattern for higher education in Upper Canada and Ontario for generations to come.[28]

The counterattack was swift and furious. In the House, the assault on Baldwin's bill was led by Tories Henry Sherwood and W.H. Draper. Outside, Bishop Strachan rallied his troops with florid rhetoric. The university bill, he charged in a petition, would "place all forms of error upon an equality with truth." It was worse than the worst excesses of the French revolution, indeed it was unparalleled in the history of the world "unless . . . some resemblance to it can be found in Pagan Rome." Nor was Strachan alone in his exercise of hyperbole. An enraged clergyman wrote to Baldwin, denouncing the Attorney General as a "fallen" member of the church who was perpetrating "a monstrous system of rampant and Hydra headed Error." Baldwin was stealing the property of King's for a "mixum-gatherum Hotbed of Error, Infidelity and Republicanism." The churchman contemptuously returned the money Baldwin had donated for the enlargement of his church.[29]

However fantastical the metaphors, these charges stung. Robert was a devout Anglican, he considered himself a High Church man. His religion was one of his few comforts in a world of despotic duty and crushing loneliness. To challenge the basic beliefs of his church was to risk that comfort. That Bishop Strachan had once been his teacher, a figure of authority of the kind that Robert found it so difficult to confront, made it all the more unsettling. Yet, perversely, Robert's personal discomfort was a political advantage. As an Anglican, he could not be dismissed as some fanatical evangelical out to spoliate the Church of England. Unfortunately, Robert's discomfort was not immediately compensated by victory in the university affair. There was strong support in the House, and the bill undoubtedly would have passed. However, as with other legislation, the university bill had not been adopted when the government resigned in December 1843 and the measure died. Baldwin would have to repeat his work in 1849, when his dream of a University of Toronto became reality.

It had been a productive session but an unruly one. Even Baldwin's celebrated aplomb was tested beyond endurance at times. The Tories returned again and again to their insinuations that the new executive councillors were a pack of rebels. When Sir Allan MacNab repeated the charge on 3 October, Robert rose from the government benches, visibly angry. MacNab's standard of government, he shouted, was that of Sir John Colborne after the rebellion, "who carried fire and sword in to the dwellings of the people." As for Robert himself, "I thank God that I have a reputation, and I am perfectly willing to rest that reputation upon the verdict my country would pass upon these passages of my career." The magic of his reputation was enough to silence his critics.[30]

The tumult was not always so easily controlled. Baldwin introduced a municipal bill for Upper Canada, incorporating municipalities and regulating their elections. A second bill divided the province into counties. These measures struck at the cozy cronyism that had allowed Tories to control municipal government in many parts of Upper Canada. The Tories determined to defeat them by paralyzing the House with parliamentary manoeuvres and the intimidation of noise and threats. To make matters worse, Baldwin's cousin and conqueror, Edmund Murney, was at the forefront of the Tory attack. No argument was too petty to be employed. "Tiger" Dunlop charged that the municipal bill was fatally flawed because elections were set for on, or near, New Year's Day, and everyone would be too drunk to make a sensible decision. Even Reformers had to admit that Dunlop spoke from vast experience.

By the time the bill creating counties was in committee in early December, the floor of the House was a riot, members shouting and threatening, throwing paper about the chamber, "a general scramble" as one reporter described it. Above it all could be heard the high, piping voice of Thomas Aylwin, drunkenly heaping invective on the opposition.[31]

The municipal bills, too, expired with the government. Still, much was accomplished, some of it especially gratifying. In October Robert's father was appointed to the Legislative Council. It was an honour the son had lobbied for, but one granted only grudgingly by Sir Charles. Metcalfe had first offered seats in the Council to five French Canadians who had all refused. Then he tried J.H. Price and another Lower Canadian, Desalles Laterrière, who also declined. Only then did he agree to William Warren Baldwin. Nevertheless, Robert felt joy at the recognition of his father's contributions, and at the prospect of having that wise political head in the upper house.[32]

However successful, the government still struggled with the realities of the Province of Canada. One was the difficulty of keeping French and English pulling in the same direction. There were mutterings on the back benches, and open dissension in Reform ranks outside the House, over "French domination." That was the catch phrase for undue French-Canadian influence over the government, a catch phrase that encompassed all the Upper Canadian suspicions and fears about their francophone neighbours. Since 1841 there had been concern about Baldwin's pro-French sympathies. The parliamentary session of 1842–1843 gave new cause for chauvinist anxiety. The assessment bill, which applied only to Upper Canada, was passed by French votes against a majority of Upper Canadian members. So too was the resolution to move the capital to Lower Canada. It was French domination, indeed, when matters of vital and exclusive Upper Canadian concern were being carried by the votes of French aliens.[33]

Baldwin might have allayed some of the discontent had he distributed the largesse of politics more skillfully. His instincts about patronage were sound. He believed that the basis of party government was the use of patronage to reward the faithful and to assure those holding public offices were loyal to the administration. At the same time, Robert disliked the actual practice of patronage, dealing with the wheedling, self-serving importunings of job seekers. So he readily enough sloughed it off to the willing, like Francis Hincks. However, as was so often the case, Hincks was too clever by half. His attempts to win over moderate conservatives by sharing the spoils with them served only to damage the Reform Party. The faithful were infuriated to see Tories being confirmed in government jobs. John Carey's complaints were not untypical. He wrote to Price that Orange violence was rampant in the Streetsville area, near Toronto. The problem was Tory magistrates who did nothing to stop the outrages. "But, who is to blame for this? A poor, torpid, milk-and-water administration, who are sanctioning a corrupt bench of magistrates."[34]

Even more serious were the problems with Metcalfe over patronage. Thomas Aylwin's comment the previous spring about Metcalfe playing "Sultan of the Indies" on patronage was all too accurate. The governor was never shaken in his beliefs about the basics of the constitutional situation: the head of government consulted with his ministers only when he chose to do so, and appointments to office were firmly within the royal prerogative. These convictions were reinforced by instructions from home. On 1 November 1843 Lord Stanley advised Metcalfe:

> On one point I am sure it is necessary that you should be firm I mean in the disposal of Patronage: this is an instrument, effective in all governments, but peculiarly so in Colonial ones; as long as you keep it in your own hands, and refuse to apply it exclusively to party purposes, it will be felt that you have really substantial power, and I think the Province will support you: but if you let your Council take this out of your hands, they will at once strengthen a party already too compact & too powerful, & tend to reduce your authority, as I doubt not they would desire, to a nullity.[35]

Again, Stanley was making clear that he accepted only the most narrow definition of responsible government; that ministers needed to maintain a majority in the Assembly. Cabinet government, genuine responsibility for government actions and, even more, party administration, were still rejected.

Robert and LaFontaine learned the full dimensions of the problem that November. The post of Speaker of the Legislative Council fell vacant when Robert Jameson resigned in protest over the seat-of-government issue. Robert and LaFontaine felt it was important to make a symbolic gesture by appointing a French Canadian. The choices they offered to Metcalfe were D.-B. Viger and René-Édouard Caron. Hardly had they done so when the Kingston rumour mill informed them that the governor, without consulting his ministers, was already shopping the position around. He offered it first to a high Tory, Livius Peter Sherwood, then to John Neilson. Only when they rejected the Speakership did he turn to Caron.[36]

Even more irritating was Metcalfe's appointment of a Tory Orangeman, Francis Powell, as clerk of the peace in the Dalhousie District of eastern Upper Canada. The Reformers heard of the appointment from an opposition member who was boasting that he made the nomination. This was the final straw. For many months Baldwin and LaFontaine had been biting their tongues over Metcalfe's arbitrary exercise of patronage, but they could be silent no more. It was a measure of their frustration that they confronted the governor over the Powell case, because it was not the ideal issue on which to establish their constitutional principles. John Powell, the previous clerk of the peace, had died leaving his family in straitened financial circumstances. His widow had come to the governor and begged the appointment for her son, Francis. Metcalfe, who had a well-earned reputation as a philanthropist, obliged. With its grieving widow and loyal son, the issue was hardly the clear-cut instance of responsibility on which the Reformers ought to have fought.[37]

However muddy, the ground had been chosen. Robert and LaFontaine went to see Sir Charles on Friday, 24 November. Robert was controlling himself, reining in the anxiety of yet another confrontation with a British governor. Yet the flatness of his tone, the near-whisper in which he spoke, could not disguise either his seriousness or his trepidation. The ministers, he told Metcalfe, found themselves in a humiliating position. They were being sneered at by opposition members who had more access to the governor than did the ministers themselves. Yet the cabinet officers had to take responsibility for actions of which they were not even informed. Metcalfe cut him off. Of course he knew there was antagonism between the council and himself over patronage, but he could not compromise his principles. But some resolution must be achieved, Baldwin insisted. The antagonism was public knowledge and it was weakening the administration. However, Sir Charles held out no olive branches, and Robert left as troubled as he had arrived.

Again, shift scene. Sir Charles greeted his Attorneys General cordially, only to be met with stiff-necked defiance. Baldwin peremptorily demanded that no appointments be made without the prior advice of the Council. Even more presumptuous was the Reformers' insistence that the governor was not to make "any appointments prejudicial to their influence . . . In other words, that the patronage of the Crown should be surrendered to the Council for the purchase of Parliamentary support." To this, Sir Charles thundered, he could never agree. He dismissed his ministers and immediately began to prepare for the crisis that would soon break.[38]

Whichever version of the scene was accurate—Baldwin's or Metcalfe's—the crisis was now inevitable. The next day, Saturday, 25 November, the executive councillors met to thrash it out. Baldwin and LaFontaine reported on their meeting with the governor and asked for advice. Much of the day the ministers sat around the table, desperately searching for a solution that would repair relations with Metcalfe while still protecting the principle of responsible government. Much as they argued out every possibility, no one could offer a satisfactory compromise. They recessed for a few hours, scattering to their rooming houses to freshen themselves and snatch a hasty meal, before meeting again that evening. Wearily, they all agreed there was nothing to be done but resign—all, that is, but the "perpetual secretary" Dominick Daly, who did not see why petty principles should interfere with his tenure in office. For Baldwin, at least, it was the natural thing to do, to flee from the imperfections of politics and the world.

The House reconvened on Monday, 27 November. It was Louis LaFontaine's responsibility to rise from his bench and announce the resignation of nine ministers. The House was left to flounder in confusion as the ex-councillors plotted how to put the best face on the situation. That did not come until Wednesday when Baldwin explained the situation. The House was unusually quiet, as members responded to the unprecedented nature of the crisis and struggled to hear Robert's near whisper. He was subdued, his low, droning voice, his heavy body stooped over the sheaf of papers in his hand, belying the drama of the occasion. But he was precise and lawyerly as he carefully laid out the case.

There were three major motifs. The governor had made arbitrary appointments without seeking the advice of those responsible for them, his ministers. The governor had chosen to reserve one of the ministry's major pieces of legislation, the secret-societies bill, again acting in an arbitrary fashion. Both of these sets of actions had cut at the very heart of responsible government. Finally, the governor had shown hostility toward his ministers from the very beginning and had favoured their political opponents.[39]

It was a clear statement of principle, but it was also an act of political positioning, an attempt to stake out the high ground in the battle to come. As was usual in his conflicts with governors, however, Robert was a step behind. Metcalfe was already well advanced with his battle plan, and his first regiment was embodied in the diminutive form of the venerable Denis-Benjamin Viger. The veteran Lower Canadian Reformer bounced up to interrupt Baldwin. Did Mr. Baldwin have "la permission positive ou spéciale de Son Excellence" to offer this explanation? Startled, Robert assured his erstwhile colleague that he did. He could not say what he really wanted to: Why was Viger—the old Lower Canadian nationalist, the plotter behind the rebellion of 1837—of all people, so concerned about the governor's prerogative? Robert must have had a foreboding of the answer to the unspoken question. Metcalfe was hard at work wooing prospective replacements for his old ministers.[40]

Viger's concern for confidentiality was ironic. As soon as Baldwin sat down the ministry—that is, Dominick Daly—read two documents to the House. One was a confidential memorandum on the events of the last week that LaFontaine had prepared at the governor's request. The second was Metcalfe's "correction" to it, his version of the discussions. In it Metcalfe offered two lines of defence. One was that the attempt by Baldwin and LaFontaine to make the quarrel one over responsible government was specious. Sir Charles claimed that he had always upheld the resolutions of 1841 and the principles of responsibility understood since then. The second defence was on the grounds prepared by Viger, that of the royal prerogative. Metcalfe could not allow the prerogative to be sullied for the profit of a mere political party. The secret-societies bill was a good example. The old ministers expected him to surrender his responsibility to make independent judgments so that they could pass "an arbitrary and unwise measure," one unprecedented in British legislation.[41]

Many Reformers considered the introduction of private correspondence to be "an arbitrary and unwise measure." The House collapsed into the chaos of shouting and threats that now seemed its normal condition. Amid all the confusion of the next four days, the Assembly was able to carry on the semblance of a debate on a resolution of confidence in the resigned ministers. The Reformers argued that the crisis was a simple contest between honesty and dishonesty. The symbol of good was, of course, Robert Baldwin. Hear Mr. Baldwin's most faithful disciple, J.H. Price:

> I can tell the House that no man in Upper Canada has one-tenth the influence his honorable friend had in Western Canada that influence he has secured by his moral rectitude his political consistency his firmness of purpose and his unblemished reputation and the dignified, honest, constitutional and manly course he has on this occasion taken, will endear him to every friend of civil and religious liberty in this Province.[42]

Contrast that, Price went on, with the "secret power at work . . . a power behind the Throne stronger than the House itself—constantly, insidiously, unconstitutionally, exerting influence over the mind of the Head of Government." There was a cabal, a conspiracy, working to undermine the constitution and Metcalfe, Price implied, was its tool.[43]

There was no doubt whom Reformers suspected as the chief plotter. It was the member for Beauharnois, Edward Gibbon Wakefield. They remembered how Wakefield had attempted to shore up the conservative ministry in 1842 with his wooing of Girouard and they saw how welcome he was at Alwington House since entering the legislature in a by-election. It was no surprise, then, that Wakefield summed up the case for the governor on 2 December. Nor was it a surprise that Wakefield aimed his guns squarely at Baldwin since Baldwin's integrity was the surety that the Reform position was an honourable one. The member for Rimouski, Wakefield thundered, was "an ambitious party man—and had taken this step to the prejudice of the Governor, and to increase his own influence in the Province." Baldwin was prepared to wreck the peace of Canada over abstract theories because he was desperate for power, desperate because he was no more than a tail of the French, with no following of his own. The House was unimpressed and expressed its confidence in the former ministers by a vote of forty-six to twenty-three. Still, Robert could not help but find it ominous that two old associates, Viger and Neilson, had voted nay.[44]

It was over, the first bold experiment with Reform government. For Robert it was, on the surface, a straightforward and honourable act to resign; the only possible resolution of the constitutional issue. Beneath the surface, it was his familiar reflex, the retreat from imperfection. What he did not know was that some of his colleagues had more elaborate motives. LaFontaine had written to his brother-in-law, J.-A. Berthelot, on 27 November, the day LaFontaine made his announcement in the House. LaFontaine said he had reason to believe that Metcalfe would be compelled to recall the ministry and that Sir Charles himself would leave Canada within six months. Perhaps LaFontaine thought Britain would not support Metcalfe; at any rate, the Lower Canadian was supremely confident. Indeed, he may have seen the resignation as a mere ploy to force Metcalfe's retreat. That apparently was Francis Hincks's scheme. The following summer Hincks attended a dinner party at Trois-Rivières and, his tongue loosened by too much wine, confided to his fellow revellers that, "We did not believe our resignation would have been accepted."[45]

The "we," however, did not include Baldwin, who thought the constitutional issue was the basis for resignation. Caught up in his righteous fervor, he did not stop to wonder why LaFontaine and Hincks had reversed their positions. In 1842, he had wanted to confront Bagot on the patronage issue, even expressing his willingness to resign over it. But LaFontaine had urged caution. Now, a year later, LaFontaine was the firebrand. Why was patronage so much more important now than then? Robert did not ask and as a result he was borne along into a situation that compromised both his principles and his integrity. Yet it said as much about him as it did about his scheming colleagues. If he was misled about their intentions over the resignation, he had gone willingly into the administration in the first place, and that too had endangered principles and integrity. The mixed membership of the government and its formation without a vote in the House, had made it at best a blurry precedent for responsible government, rather than the triumphant symbol that Baldwin had hoped for. The circumstances surrounding the resignation again blurred the issues. His senior colleagues were engaged in a bold power play designed to do exactly what Metcalfe accused the Reformers of seeking, to reduce the governor to a tool in the hands of his ministers. Robert, of course, could not see it that way, but a majority of the Canadian electorate would. Even in his time of apparent moral victory, he was in fact compromised. He would need Eliza now more than ever.

Chapter 10

Leave Those Confounded Politics Alone

The triumph that the first Reform government had seemed to represent was melting away. He was beset on all sides as death had again reached out and into the family. Only in memory could he find relief. Eliza had been dead for eight years. It was April 1844.

Even an old acquaintance could believe the worst. Robert sat at his desk, in his familiar office in the Front Street house, reading the letter again. There was no signature, but there did not need to be. The writer addressed Robert familiarly, greeting him as a "person whom I have known so long." There was no friendship here, however. Echoing political opponents and much of the press, the correspondent charged Baldwin with fomenting another rebellion. He was ready for Baldwin and his rebels, he said: "[W]hy my dear Sir the soldiers alone would defeat you . . . if surrounded this very moment by five hundred Reformers I would sooner die than give up my arms . . . As you are a man of property I know if I were in your situation I would retire from Public life and leave those confounded Politics alone for they never do a man any [good]." The words were insulting but the advice had its appeal that spring of 1844. Politics did not seem to be doing Robert any good.[1]

The fall of the Reform government had been greeted by Tory celebrations in the streets of Toronto and a great bonfire lit at the gates of King's College. There were no celebrations in Parliament, just confusion in a House without a government. The session mercifully was ended on 9 December 1843 and the members fanned out across the country to deliver their versions of the events to the people. For Robert, however, politics were not his major preoccupation. His revered father was ill, gravely ill. Robert's return from Kingston seemed to give the old man new life, but on Christmas Eve he began to fail. He was unable to eat and he was very weak.

Christmas night, William Warren Baldwin sat about a fire with his family. He "seemed to linger with us in the evening," Robert wrote to LaFontaine, "remaining a full hour beyond his usual time of retiring as if he had a presentiment of its being the last he was to spend with us here." Servants had to carry him upstairs to his room and the presentiment proved correct. He never left the room again. Political channels were activated to get the news of their grandfather's decline to the children in Quebec. John Neilson went to the convent to tell Maria, and she in turn advised the other children. It was hard that they could not be there at the end. At one o'clock on the morning of 8 January 1844, William Warren Baldwin died.[2]

———————

The partnership of Baldwin and son had been a law firm, a political bloc, and a moral crusade. At the dark moments of Robert's public career, his father had supported him and sanctified him. The resignation in June 1841 had been, in William Warren's understanding, not just the right thing to do, the correct political decision. It was "the virtuous religious course." The father's moral certainty had raised his son's politics above the earthbound politics of ordinary men. Robert might often doubt himself and his abilities but he never could doubt the political ideals he had been bequeathed.[3]

The self-doubt was an equally important part of the heritage. William Warren heaped his son with praise, at least when Robert was faithfully carrying out the family mission. The words could not honey over Robert's feelings of inadequacy, his conviction that he was less than his father in most respects. He was reminded of that at home, as he listened to his witty, opinionated father hold forth. He was reminded of it as he walked the streets of his native city and saw its best building, Osgoode Hall, or the jail and courthouse that clustered about the city's most pleasant public space, Court House Square: they were all the products of his father's eclectic genius.[4]

Now life would be struggled through without the two most important people in his life: his father and Eliza.

———————

Robert had watched him fade, spending every possible moment in the sick room. The gradual slipping away did nothing to ease the pain of the moment of death. He confided in LaFontaine:

> [W]hen he was gone, when he who had been the protector of my childhood the guide of my youth & the Counsellor of my manhood was no more and I felt in all its weight the truth that I was indeed for the first time without a father I was more overwhelmed than I had expected ... when ... all I had to dwell in was the past that past which brings him back to my memory as one of the kindest of parents & best of men it seemed as if I could scarcely realize it myself that all was indeed past—And you my dear friend will not I am sure be surprised at my feeling little able to return at once to other subjects and least of all to that of politics from which if I could with honour I would fly for ever.[5]

Honour would not permit that. While his father was still in his sickbed, Robert had been drawn into attempts to strengthen the Reform Party and prepare it for the election that everyone anticipated would soon be upon the province. The first step was a grand dinner for the former ministers, held in Toronto at the new year. The highlight of the evening was a long speech by Baldwin, rationalizing the position of the late government in its quarrel with Sir Charles Metcalfe. More than speeches were needed, he realized, and the next step was the creation of a more efficient party structure. The Reform Association of Canada was established at a meeting in Toronto on 6 February 1844. It was carefully designed to create the image of a broadly based movement, rather than a creature of the party leadership. Baldwin rejected an offer of the presidency of the new association. Indeed, he counselled that the organization be led by a general committee rather than a president, to cultivate the appearance of democracy. Baldwin was learning the political game and learning how to expand the base of his party. The general committee of the Reform Association reflected that, with new faces joining the old stalwarts of liberalism. Among those new faces was that of George Brown, a vigorous Scots immigrant who, with his father Peter, ran a Presbyterian newspaper in Toronto, the *Banner*, that offered valuable support to the Reform cause.[6]

The new organization seemed to be gathering impressive strength. Its first general meeting was held on 25 March amid the glitter of the ballroom of Toronto's finest hotel, the North American. The large crowd was treated to five hours of speeches and seventeen resolutions on responsible government and the Metcalfe crisis. But the Reform message could be summed up in ten seconds of Baldwin's speech that night. All Reformers demanded, he said, was the British constitution: "Not by one hair's breadth short of that will we ever be satisfied." He sent the Reformers out of the meeting ready to fight the good fight. The association leased rooms at Front and Scott Streets and from there spread the word across the province. By summer at least twenty-two local branches had been created across Upper Canada.[7]

Lord Metcalfe was also busy with political preparations. Despite the hopes of some Reform leaders, Metcalfe saw the break with his old ministers as final. "Whatever may happen," he wrote Lord Stanley in November 1843, "I do not mean at any time to take back Mr Lafontaine or Mr Baldwin. Both are intolerable." His problem was to find men to fill their places, preferably Frenchmen. The parliamentary session limped toward its end on 9 December 1843 with no government in place. Dominick Daly sat alone on the treasury benches or, rather, he did not sit, having developed a convenient illness that kept him from the House, what J.H. Dunn called Daly's "Parliamentary complaint." Whatever the nature of his "illness," Daly was hard at work on the governor's business. More than a month before the resignation of the ministry, Daly had attended a dinner party in Kingston at which some of Metcalfe's most important advisors were present—Edward Gibbon Wakefield, Denis Viger, and Dr. John McCaul, the principal of King's College. Also present was Denis-Benjamin Papineau, brother of the rebel leader of 1837, Louis-Joseph. Daly asked the younger Papineau to advise his brother to return from exile in Paris as soon as possible. The governor had a place for him. Louis-Joseph Papineau did not rush back, but the suggestion indicated how ruthless, perhaps desperate, Metcalfe was. He would invite the prime traitor, Papineau, into his government if it meant keeping Baldwin and LaFontaine out.[8]

Metcalfe cobbled together something resembling a government in the days after Parliament recessed. William Henry Draper and D.-B. Viger were sworn in as executive councillors, but not assigned portfolios, so that they would not need to seek re-election. The *Examiner* was surely correct, however, that this makeshift left Canada a despotism ruled by Metcalfe, "her constitution . . . rolled up like an old coat and thrown under the table for the dogs to lie on." And it was difficult even to find dogs to lie on it. Viger was supposed to rally French-Canadian support to the government. Yet his offers to virtually every prominent Lower Canadian politician were rejected. It would not be until August 1844 that he found a taker for his cabinet prizes and a dubious trophy at that, the erratic D.-B. Papineau who became commissioner of Crown lands. Denis Papineau's only real claim to prominence was his brother's name.[9]

Reformers were naturally delighted with the stumblings of the "no government," which Baldwin ridiculed as "the thing—I know not what to call it the shadow of a shade which some call an Administration." His confidence was buoyed by the establishment of two new Reform newspapers in the metropolises of the colony. The major liberal journal in Toronto, the *Examiner*, had fallen on hard times and had fewer than 700 subscribers at the beginning of 1844. Although it was taken over by a bright young publisher, James Lesslie, that February, Reform supporters did not feel they could wait for Lesslie to revive the *Examiner* with an election call possible at any moment. Instead they offered to finance the twenty-five-year-old George Brown in founding a new liberal paper. Baldwin himself advanced £50. In March Torontonians were purchasing the first issue of the *Globe*, a fiercely partisan but always interesting Reform organ. Meanwhile Hincks had decided to fill a void in Montreal. Like Hincks, Baldwin recognized the importance of an English-language liberal paper in Montreal. He could not avoid some pangs of anxiety, however, remembering Hincks's betrayal when operating the *Examiner*. "I am far from wishing to express any ungenerous distrust of Mr. Hincks," Baldwin wrote LaFontaine, "but he certainly went wrong in 1841/2 and we have therefore to protect ourselves as far as possible against a similar want of judgment on his part or that of any other." This was as far as Robert ever went in expressing his resentment over Hincks's bolting of the party. His caution could not restrain Hincks at any rate. Hincks went ahead, and on 5 March the first issue of the *Pilot* appeared. As might be expected, the *Pilot* would become among the most lively and readable, and at times most scurrilous, newspapers in Canada—a fair reflection of its proprietor.[10]

The two journals joined into a paper war that raged until the autumn. Gibbon Wakefield fired the first shots with a series of letters published in England by the *Colonial Gazette* and then reissued as a pamphlet, *A View of Sir Charles Metcalfe's Government in Canada*. Hincks quickly countered with a letter to the London *Morning Chronicle* under the pseudonym of "A Supporter of the Late Canadian Administration." In February Viger rushed out his *La Crise Ministerielle et Mr. Denis Viger*, which was considered important enough to hurry through the press at Kingston and speed to Lower Canada by stage. Hincks once more fired back with an attack on Viger, *The Ministerial Crisis: Mr. D.B. Viger, and his Position*. The most eloquent of all the screeds was a series of letters published in Reform papers and later as a book, a collection known as the "Legion Letters." The use of the pen name "Legion" fooled no one; it was widely known that the author was R.B. Sullivan. A long gloss on the meaning of responsible government, the letters summed up the Reform faith: "When Canadians obtained Responsible Government, they got the life and soul of the Constitution with it."[11]

The pamphlet war was only one part of the struggle in this bitter pre-election campaign. The Reform leaders took every opportunity, legitimate or illegitimate, to propagandize. Baldwin, for example, traded on the goodwill created by his unsuccessful university bill to obtain an invitation to the annual meeting of Toronto Methodists in January 1844. In July Baldwin and Hincks toured Lower Canada to meet liberal leaders and encourage the troops. While there they lobbied Metcalfe's man in French Canada, D.-B. Viger, but with no success. Reform even extended itself further. In September William Young, speaker of the Nova Scotian Assembly, visited Upper Canada. Baldwin tried to demonstrate the general import of their issues by feting the Nova Scotian leader. That was the thrust of Robert's comments, the general, intercolonial good that responsible government represented, at a gala dinner for Young held at the North American Hotel in Toronto on 23 September.[12]

It was not all so genteel. The party's greatest success came with a victory in a by-election in Montreal in April. The sitting member had res-igned his seat and two prominent Montrealers stepped forward to claim it: a promising young Irish Catholic lawyer, Lewis Thomas Drummond, for the Reformers and William Molson of the wealthy brewing family for the Tories. Hincks took the Reform campaign in hand, and a colourful, raucous campaign it was. There were large bilingual rallies, equally large drinking parties, and frequent torchlight parades that snaked through the centre of the city. The most effective, but also most ethically dubious, tactic was Hincks's organization of the Irish working class in their Griffintown ghetto. As the campaign got underway in March 1844, Tories began to hear rumours of Hincks's work with the Irish, "des bêtes féroces en guénilles au service de Francis Hincks," the ferocious tattered beasts as conservative organizer J.-G. Barthe called them. Hincks's inducements of money and liquor paid handsome dividends. LaFontaine was to address a Reform rally on 27 March, but scores of Tory bully boys arrived to disrupt it. Out of Griffintown marched the Irish, arrayed in tight columns, and the terrified Tories fled without a fight.[13]

By election day, 11 April, with both sides supported by armed and organized gangs, it was obvious that serious disruptions were likely. The Tories occupied the poll and Reformers surrounded the occupiers. The returning officer, A.-M. Delisle, staved off bloodshed by adjourning the election until 16 April, but tempers were no cooler then. Rival gangs clashed at the polls and elsewhere in the city that first day of voting. The magistrates called out the troops for the second day, with the results that usually followed military intervention. The troops marched into McGill Street where a Reform crowd had gathered. The soldiers mounted their bayonets and charged. When the troops fell back, a boatman named Julien Champeau was lying on the cobblestones with a neat triangular wound in his stomach and another in his side. Reform politician and doctor, Wolfred Nelson, was kneeling beside Champeau trying to stem the bleeding. Nelson's efforts were to no avail. Champeau died in the early hours of Sunday, 21 April 1844. The voting was almost a side issue as the liberal, Drummond, overwhelmed Molson by 1383 votes to 463.[14]

The Reformers had learned about electioneering at the knee of the master, Lord Sydenham. Some had little stomach for it, however. LaFontaine withdrew from the campaign as the violence mounted while Baldwin watched anxiously from Toronto. Those on the scene added copious doses of sugar to their accounts when they wrote to the leader. Hincks assured Baldwin that the Tories had always been the aggressors and that while some workers from the canal construction site outside Montreal "did come in <u>against our will</u>," they were unarmed and (miraculously) non-violent. John Ross—whose brother had gone down from Belleville, Upper Canada, for the election—admitted that Irish canal workers had been involved in fighting, but he attempted to colour it to appeal to Baldwin. The Tories had been so violent, Ross claimed, that "the Canal men were necessary there, just as the shanty men were in Hastings" in Baldwin's own election. Baldwin could not claim to be ignorant of the truth, nevertheless. The member for Bytown, Stewart Derbishire, observed some of the violence and heartily approved because he believed it would end the sway of Tory thugs in elections. "Hincks is playing the D-l in Montreal . . . I think he is completely breaking up what we call the 'Blood & Guts' Party." Hincks himself became more forthcoming after the election. In May he wrote Baldwin that after establishing the *Pilot* he realized that another step was necessary. Reformers needed protection against Tory intimidation. Out of this realization grew an alliance of French-Canadian liberals with Irish canallers.[15]

Robert's role was one of selective blindness. Perhaps the issues in this crisis were so fundamental that they drove from his conscience his usual scruples about the use of violence. He made no attempt to rein in Hincks during the campaign or to set down guidelines for electioneering. He did criticize his colleague, after the fact, but his strictures were notable only for being substantially wide of the mark. In late May he wrote to LaFontaine to express satisfaction that the tone of the *Pilot* was improving. "I did not altogether like all his papers during the contest but of course we must make allowances for the fiery oven into which he was cast." To criticize the "tone" of editorials amid the violence in the streets was akin to criticizing the troops for not keeping their bayonets polished.[16]

Despite Reform victories such as Montreal, Metcalfe was quietly building his moderate party. He had attracted to his cause some business-minded Reformers including Isaac Buchanan and William Hamilton Merritt. Merritt had been alienated from Reform, at any rate, because Baldwin had rejected a scheme to improve compensation for shareholders of the Welland Canal after the canal was taken over by the government in

1843—shareholders such as Merritt and his friends. W.H. Draper, also lining up with the governor, had no compunctions about promising Merritt what he wanted. That was all that was needed for Merritt to jettison his party and join what Draper smugly called "the good cause."[17]

Egerton Ryerson was an even more important recruit. Long-time spokesman for Methodism in Upper Canada, principal of that church's Victoria College, a leading educational reformer, and one-time advocate of liberal causes, Ryerson was among the best-known men in the province. He was as aristocratic in appearance and demeanour as the governors he served despite his dissenting religion, an imposing man with a halo of well-coiffed hair girding a high, broad forehead, and dark eyes above his disapproving mouth. Ryerson had gone to visit Metcalfe in January 1844 and become convinced, so he claimed, that true responsible government was best defended by supporting the governor. This was a conversion of the first order. Ryerson was a political manager's dream come true. His religious certainty blended seamlessly into his personal certainty. Egerton Ryerson believed devoutly in Egerton Ryerson and he was able to bring others to share that belief. The "pope of Methodism," as he had sometimes been derisively titled, had become cloaked in political invulnerability by 1844. For decades to come he would manoeuvre with skill and often ruthlessness through the shoals of Canadian politics and while others rose and sank, Ryerson remained pristinely on the surface.[18]

Now he launched a bitter and brilliant assault on the Reformers. In the first of several pamphlets he produced that year, a carefully crafted diatribe called *Sir Charles Metcalfe Defended Against the Attacks of His Late Counsellors*, Ryerson linked present-day liberals to the rebellion of 1837 and charged that their leaders were, perhaps unwittingly, pushing Canada toward independence. The issue, thus, was escalated from a local quarrel to an attack on Britain itself. "It is no longer a question between Mr. Baldwin and Sir Charles Metcalfe, but between Mr. Baldwin and the imperial authority."[19]

As always, this was an effective tactic. Ryerson was only the most famous of many Canadians who professed liberal values, but responded with reflex fury when they imagined that the British connection was being endangered. It was a reflex that Metcalfe encouraged at every opportunity as he responded to loyal addresses from various parts of the province or spoke personally to gatherings of faithful Britons. Sometimes his posture was that of the martyred patriot, standing against impossible odds: "Whether my contest be with a malignant Minority, or with a Majority of the House of Assembly, or with the whole Colony run mad, my duty must be the same. I cannot surrender Her Majesty's Authority, or the supremacy of the Mother Country." At other times he was the wise and terse leader of the great majority of the loyal. In August he received an address from 209 inhabitants of Drummond County. They congratulated him for resisting the attempt "to degrade the representative of Her Majesty to a party tool." The late ministers, they went on, represented "a party tending directly . . . to the result of separation from British connection and rule." Sternly and sadly, the governor responded that "you have accurately described the designs of the late Executive Council."[20]

Like so many ordinary Canadians, Baldwin felt deeply the reflex to support the British connection and understood its potency in politics. That understanding was not shared by all his colleagues. Metcalfe's response to the Drummond electors outraged leaders of the French Party. LaFontaine and A.-N. Morin wrote to Dominick Daly to express their disappointment over what the governor "has been thus advised by his councillors to advance against our colleagues and ourselves." It was a nice turn of phrase that combined justified anger, a promotional message for responsible government and, perhaps, a touch of black humour. It was also the justification for their announcement that they were resigning their commissions as Queen's Counsels, the honorary title granted by the governor to senior lawyers. Baldwin was clearly taken by surprise and thought the action was unwise. After all, Queen's Counsel was not an office, he pointed out to LaFontaine, it was "but a rank in our profession." Nor did it have anything to do with responsible government. Such recklessness, and perhaps pettiness, threatened to undermine public confidence in the judgment of the Reformers and to twist their battle of principles into a contest of a personal nature with the queen's representative. Yet, on 10 September, Baldwin and J.E. Small joined their Lower Canadian colleagues in resigning as Queen's Counsels. He had no choice, he felt. As he told LaFontaine, "[T]o have omitted following your resignation would under all circumstances be productive of worse consequences."[21]

It was typical of Robert's strong sense of party, and his loyalty to his putative leader, LaFontaine, that he followed against his own better judgment. In this case the loyalty may have been misplaced. The furor over the Queen's Counsels only strengthened Metcalfe, who already was riding a crest. By turning the contest with his late advisors into one over loyalty, he had begun to rally public opinion. The formation of a ministry, albeit after nine months of trying, helped. On 3 September Metcalfe introduced his ministers. Despite the long gestation, the infant was a homely one. There was only one member of the Assembly from Upper Canada, Tory Henry Sherwood, because no one else could be convinced to take office. Metcalfe had to make do with legislative councillors "Sweet William" Draper and William Morris, a prominent Presbyterian layman. In Lower Canada, only a political unknown, a Montreal lawyer named James Smith, could be found to take the post of Attorney General East. It was not much, but it was a ministry of sorts and it gave a certain representative lustre to Metcalfe's rule. He pressed the advantage. On 23 September the Assembly was dissolved, with election writs to be returned by 12 November.

———≫•≪———

Amid the seemingly endless pre-election skirmishing, the politician Baldwin had to make room for the grieving Baldwin. His father had gone to join Eliza, but Robert had to soldier on with the family business of duty and reform. Nevertheless, his mind could only deal with his anguish by erecting pain into a cult, and by setting aside time to celebrate its sacraments. By 1844 he was practising his private religion. He was both solitary enough, and political enough, to keep it from the public eye. The following year, however, he did reveal the outlines of his worship in a letter to his mother and his aunt.[22]

On 31 May Robert celebrated his wedding and his past. As he and Eliza had in 1827, he walked from Russell Abbey, where he had lived while Eliza was exiled in New York, to the site of the Sullivan house. The house had since been moved to Yonge Street and Robert followed it there in his morbid recreation so, he said, "to put my hand at least on its once familiar walls." Later he went by carriage to Spadina "over the same road by which we were that day driven home" and spent the afternoon "in visiting the old haunts about dear Spadina so full of the past & so dear to the recollection of us all." Haunts, indeed. With Eliza still somehow at his side, he picked a sprig of lilac from the first tree on the right-hand side of the entrance to Spadina, the same tree from which they had each plucked sprigs those many years before. The sprigs of 1827 had been carefully retained and would be buried with Robert.

This ritual gave him some constancy in a life whose moorings had been destroyed with the deaths of Eliza and his father. He had been so shaken by William Warren's passing that he been unable to write to his daughter, Maria, then studying in Quebec, to tell her of the tragedy. Ritual gave him a new anchor and provided him with as close to pleasure as he could achieve after his losses. It was on those pilgrimages along the wedding route and in Eliza's locked room where he pored over her letters, his scriptures in the cult of death, that Robert found his reality— not on the campaign trail.[23]

<hr />

He nevertheless had to take to the campaign trail. He had his choice of ridings for the fall election. He could certainly have been returned again for Rimouski, which he had visited during his Lower Canadian tour in July. Reformers in Middlesex, Upper Canada, had invited him to be their candidate. It was closer to home, however, that he settled. LaFontaine vacated the Fourth Riding of York to return to Lower Canada and Robert decided to stand there. It was still the safest Reform riding in western Canada and its security freed Robert to worry about other constituencies. There was much to worry about. In another traditional and nearby liberal seat, the East Riding of Halton, the old and the new in the party were in direct conflict. Three candidates sought the Reform nomination. Caleb Hopkins was a blunt, craggy farmer, a veteran of the pre-rebellion party. John Wetenhall was an up-and-comer, a young lawyer who embodied the new, business-like liberalism. William Notman was a party workhorse, a grey functionary. Hopkins had been in disfavour with the leadership since he voted against the Reform ministry on the seat-of-government issue. Perhaps it was that bitterness that produced suspicions, or perhaps they were well founded, but there were also rumours that old Caleb was secretly consorting with the governor's men. He retained strong support from traditionalists even so, and two nomination meetings left the East Halton Reformers deadlocked over a candidate. During the second of those meetings, in Nelson township on 7 September, Hopkin's supporters charged that the party establishment was tampering with the nomination process, and they stormed out of the hall. The rump convention then named Wetenhall as the standard bearer, but even they recognized that their action lacked credibility. They opened negotiations with the Calebites and the two sides agreed to refer the matter to arbitrators, including Baldwin. The referees quickly, and unsurprisingly, ruled that Wetenhall had been properly nominated.[24]

The arbitration settled nothing. Hopkins was convinced that he had been cheated by the very leader of his party, and he determined to run without official sanction. Baldwin was acutely aware how damaging such a rift could be and he sent *Globe* publisher George Brown and another Reform worthy from Toronto, Thomas Ewart, to sort out East Halton. They were hardly unbiassed observers, representing Baldwin's hostility to Hopkins. They applied pressure to all of the principals to unite but Caleb, of course, refused. Brown and Ewart nevertheless went ahead to mount another, carefully managed, nomination meeting that obediently confirmed Wetenhall as candidate. Brown tersely reported to his leader "in a word we found it necessary to blackball Mr. Hopkins." Baldwin still hoped for party unity and wrote to Hopkins asking him to stand aside in the interests of the greater good.[25]

As was usual with Robert's ventures in power politics, this one ended badly. Hopkins would not back down from a party leader who, he now believed, had betrayed him and true Reform. The rupture in the party and Baldwin's crude attempts to force his will on East Halton were well publicized not just there but across the province. Equally damaging was the truth that Baldwin could not successfully impose his authority. It was the very worst of both worlds in which he was seen not only as a dictator, but an ineffective one. The dogged Hopkins stayed in the race, he and Wetenhall split the Reform vote, and Tory George Chambers was elected. Nor would Caleb Hopkins forget his grievances. He would nurse them for the next seven years until he would have a final revenge on Robert Baldwin.[26]

The disaster in East Halton was but a microcosm of the general election. Baldwin's much vaunted Reform Association proved ineffective in organizing a campaign. The governor's men, on the other hand, were both well organized and fervent. They even had a battle hymn, sung to the tune of a familiar ditty, "The Fine Old English Gentleman":

> So let our loyal shouts go forth, let traitors hear and quail,
> And British hearts will leap for joy on every hill and vale;
> And though the Baldwin clan may howl, though loud the
>   hyena roar,
> We'll rally round Old Square-toes, and give him one cheer more;
> The fine Old Square-toed gentleman, all of the present time.[27]

Well might they cheer. The song captured the essence of their successful campaign. It turned a Reform insult to Metcalfe, the slur that he was "Old Square-toes," into a term of endearment and it made clear that the only issues in this election were loyalty to Britain and Sir Charles himself. Baldwin's earnest attempts to talk of universities and electoral reform and responsible government fell on ears deafened by huzzahs for the fine Old Square-toed gentleman.

Metcalfe's party had more tangible advantages, as well. Despite Hincks's efforts, or perhaps spurred on by them, the ministerialists mounted superior firepower. Beginning in early summer, Orange mobs persistently attacked Reform meetings, driving off the opposition and passing loyal addresses of their own. Typical was the rally at Bradford, Simcoe County, in June, when Baldwin had to flee an Orange mob, leaping over furrows in farmers' fields, while the Orangemen whooped after him. He escaped, but some of his followers were not so lucky. One was knocked from his horse by a barrage of stones and another was severely beaten.[28]

When polling began, Metcalfe used the power of his office to assure victory. Sir Charles pre-empted them where Reformers might have had superior force. In Dundas County, Upper Canada, it was rumoured that the opposition was going to bring in canal navvies to control the polls. Instead of waiting for conflict to develop and then sending the troops, Metcalfe dispatched soldiers before the election and voting took place under the sway of their bayonets. The canallers did not come and the government candidate won easily. In the two-seat constituency of Toronto Reformers complained of bribery, partiality by the returning officer, and the disqualification of legal voters, all in the interest of the successful government candidates, Henry Sherwood and William H. Boulton. The Reform newspaper, the *Examiner*, was even more outraged by the quality of the Tory victors than by Metcalfe's manipulation of the election. The *Examiner* could not believe that respectable Torontonians had voted for Boulton, "the gambler and horse racer! the frequenter and encourager of the Theatre and its concomitants!" The morality of traditional Reform was empty rhetoric in a contest dominated by the greater morality of British connection.[29]

The grandest conflicts, of course, were in Montreal. Hincks's successful use of the mob in April had made that inevitable. The atmosphere was near hysterical as voting began for the two Montreal seats. A man who described himself as a "good Protestant" wrote to the governor's secretary on 20 October that he had evidence that the "Papists of Ireland," joined by French Canadians, were going to descend on Montreal "to murder the orangemen, protestants and all that will vote contrary to their wishes." And they were prepared to murder cheaply. He reported that each of the scoundrels was being paid five shillings plus passage to Montreal. The good Protestant would perhaps have been more comfortable had he known of the preparations taken by the ministerialists. To counter Hincks's bullies, they had organized the Loyal Protective Society. It spawned secret paramilitary groups in the various city wards, groups that gloried in dramatic names. Those in St. Lawrence ward, a group led by the later-prominent historian, William Kingsford, called itself the Cavaliers. They were ready when the canallers did come. The combined efforts of the Loyal Protective Society, the cavalry and the 93rd Highlanders turned back the Irish on the first day of voting. The next day, according to military intelligence, Reform candidate Lewis Drummond went out to the Lachine Canal site and told the workers that Tories had burned a Catholic church and "that their comrades had been abused and were bleeding in the streets." Some 400 navvies marched into the city but they were routed in McGill Street by the cavalry and 30 were arrested. The liberals had failed utterly to re-establish the control of the streets that had won the election in April. Both of their candidates went down to defeat.[30]

Defeats were rare in Lower Canada, however. Members of the French Party captured twenty-eight seats against thirteen for the ministerialists, and one non-aligned member. The Baldwinites, in contrast, had more than their share of defeats. Robert won Fourth York and carried with him some prominent Reformers such as S.B. Harrison, Malcolm Cameron, J.H. Price, and J.E. Small. Overall, however, the results were disastrous. At the most optimistic count, there were twelve Reformers returned in the west, along with one independent, the erratic Colonel John Prince. The governor could count on twenty-nine conservatives. The front rank of the Reform Party was devastated: Hincks lost in Oxford, Dunn in Toronto, James Durand in West Halton, William Buell in Leeds, H.J. Boulton in Niagara, and William Hume Blake in Second York.[31]

Baldwin and his party had surrendered much of the ground gained since 1841. They were again perceived by many Upper Canadians as "Ultras" for their attacks on Metcalfe. Their performance as a government, terminated before much of their legislation could be passed, was also held against them. Some of that legislation, especially the attempts to reform the university, Upper Canadian municipal government, and the assessment system in western Canada, had stirred resentment from various groups and the vote to move the capital to Montreal was unpopular with almost everyone in Upper Canada. For the taste of moderate people, they had tried to do far too much. For the left of the party, they had done too little. Dissatisfaction on the left may explain Reform defeats in such traditional strongholds as the two Haltons, Lennox and Addington, and Oxford. The exiled Lower Canadian rebel, Dr. E.B. O'Callaghan, summed up radical opinion on the LaFontaine–Baldwin government: "[T]hey went out of office . . . without having as far as I can recollect, passed one measure into a law to extend, or to render more secure the liberties of the people."[32]

Had that been put to him, Baldwin would have answered that he was concerned with shaping a real party out of the movement that men such as O'Callaghan supported. In 1844 he had done some of the preparatory work, creating a more modern institutional form in the Reform Association, and trying to mute the evangelical enthusiasm of some old Reformers. The party was still at best a work in progress, though. Baldwin's often-clumsy attempts to impose unity, as in East Halton, did more harm than good. He ended with two Reform candidates competing with each other in Dundas, East Halton, Middlesex, and Lincoln North. The Baldwinites lost all of these races. His reputation was considerable among politicians. He had shown that between 1841 and 1842 as he won over politicians, one by one, and built a majority in Parliament. His appeal was far weaker for the public or even the party rank and file, as his election defeats in 1841 and 1842 painfully testified. The virtues of the gentleman were most apparent to middle-class politicians who themselves had pretensions to these same virtues. They won less respect on the hustings where more flamboyant attributes succeeded and where voters looked for concrete accomplishments.

Sir Charles Metcalfe was victorious and he won, as well, the gratitude of the home government. On 2 December 1844 Lord Stanley wrote to advise that the queen would confer on him a barony of the United Kingdom. Henceforth he would be Baron Metcalfe of Fern Hill, in the county of Berks. It was not an honour he would long enjoy for once again the peculiar curse of Canada would strike down a governor. Sir Charles' cancer was advancing rapidly. It had been serious enough the previous spring that Stanley had dispatched a famous physician, George Pollock of St. George's Hospital, London, to treat Metcalfe with the most current remedy, chloride of zinc. Pollock stayed until year's end, when it was clear the treatments had failed. Metcalfe was in intense pain from above the right eye, down the cheek, to the chin. His eyesight was failing and he was having difficulty opening his mouth to eat.[33]

In February 1845, Sir Charles wrote to an old friend, Dr. Wallick of Calcutta, India. The letter gave a poignant picture of his suffering, and his courage.

> I am now unable to write to you with my own hand, having lost the use of my eyes . . . This misfortune is the consequence of a complaint in my face . . . which has baffled surgical skill, and resisted the most powerful caustics. I have reason to fear that it is incurable . . . if I consulted merely my own inclination, I should again seek tranquillity and repose at home; but mischief might follow my departure from this country, and while this is apprehended I cannot desire to desert my post.[34]

He did not desert, but he did become debilitated. By November 1845 he was blind and paralyzed. He had to be carried aboard the steamer *Prince Albert* to begin his journey home, at least more fortunate than his predecessors Sydenham and Bagot in being able to fulfill his desire to die in the quiet of the English countryside. However pathetic his departure, many Reformers could not find it in their hearts to be gracious. The *Globe* spoke for them when it admitted, "It would be sheer hypocrisy to conceal the unfeigned satisfaction with which we announce the event . . . we heartily congratulate the country on the departure of Lord Metcalfe from Canada." LaFontaine said he would remember Metcalfe as a liar and headed his letter to Robert on the departure with an exultant flourish: "Lord Metcalfe is gone!!"[35]

Illness and death had scarred Robert, had left his being a mere shell. It was ironic, then, that illness and death did so much to aid his political career. When all had seemed lost in the fall of 1841, Sydenham was struck down and his system fell with him. Out of the ruins of the Sydenhamite coalition, Robert built the first LaFontaine–Baldwin government. When all seemed lost again in the fall of 1844, Metcalfe lost his ability to govern and his coalition began to founder. Pain was laced through even the greatest of Robert's victories.

1. ROBERT BALDWIN (1804–58)

Turning everything into responsible government

❖

Courtesy of Toronto Public Library

2. AUGUSTA ELIZABETH (ELIZA) BALDWIN (1809–36)

She was all a husband's love could wish her

━━◆━━

Private Collection

3. MARGARET PHOEBE BALDWIN (1771–1851)
AND MARIA BALDWIN (1828–1866)

The mastermind of our family

Courtesy of Toronto Public Library

4. WILLIAM WARREN BALDWIN (1775–1844)

One of the most beloved heads that ever a family were blessed with

Courtesy of Toronto Public Library

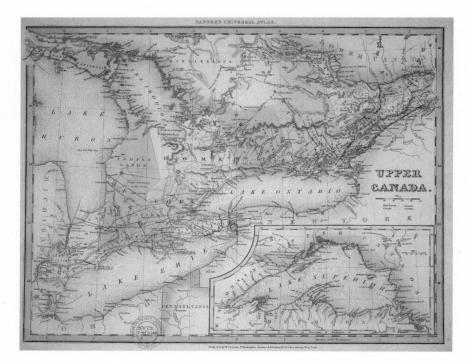

5. UPPER CANADA (1858)

The place where Baldwin triumphed and failed

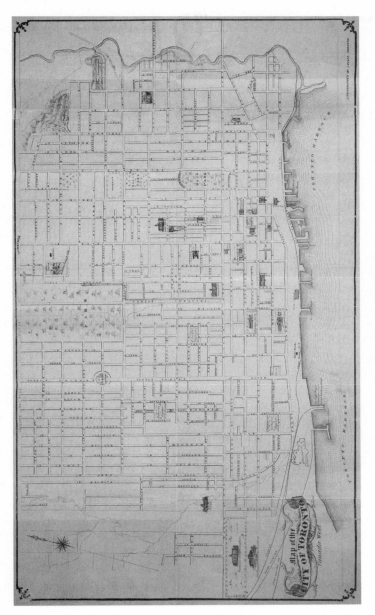

6. CITY OF TORONTO (1858)

Home—my own dear home

Courtesy of Toronto Public Library

7. CHARLES EDWARD POULETT THOMSON,
BARON SYDENHAM AND TORONTO (1799–1841)

The greatest coxcomb . . . and the vainest dog

8. SPADINA HOUSE (REBUILT 1835)

Country home, blessed retreat

Courtesy of Toronto Public Library

9. LOUIS-HIPPOLYTE LAFONTAINE (1807–64)

Meeting in a spirit of peace, union, friendship, and fraternity

Mr. PUNCH TURNETH WOODMAN, AND LAYETH HIS AXE TO THE ROOT
OF A ROTTEN OLD TREE.

10. MR. PUNCH CHOPPING DOWN THE "HUMBUG" TREE OF
RESPONSIBLE GOVERNMENT (*PUNCH*, 1849)

Tory magazine takes the ax to the responsible humbug

McCord Museum M930.51.1.46

Chapter 11

Turning Everything into Responsible Government

In the politics of the Union, the greatest of all virtues was patience.
That Robert had in abundance, at least for the events of this world.
He was only impatient to see the next world, to see Eliza. She had
been dead for eight years. It was June 1846.

Robert Baldwin was in an unusually playful mood Monday afternoon
8 June 1846. He leavened his speech to a warm, somnolent House with
self-deprecating humour. "There was an ancient who was said to turn into
gold every thing he touched," Robert joked, "and I am sometimes said, in
like manner to turn everything I touch into Responsible Government."[1]

Robert was more comfortable in opposition than in government,
and at least as influential. He pressed constantly during the second
Parliament for recognition of the principles of responsible government,
and he was largely successful. A good deal of what he touched also turned
into nationalism. His vision of Canada became ever clearer. It was to be
governed on British ideals, through responsible government. It was to be
bicultural, a dream which underlay his patience with French-Canadian
strayings. And it was to be *Canadian*, a new nation of the north that
blended the best of British, French, and North American qualities.

Robert had campaigned during the 1844 election on behalf of
Canadian nationalism. He travelled west to the London district that
September to tell a Reform convention for Middlesex county that,
"I . . . wish to see a provincial feeling pervade the whole mass of our
population . . . to see every man belonging to us proud of the Canadian
name, and of Canada as his country." It was a theme he would return
to frequently trying, as with responsible government and justice for
French Canada, to erode opposition by the endless drip of his reminders.
He found occasion in 1846 to urge, during debate on a school bill, that

the province should move toward employing only "native Canadian teachers." That nationalism could inspire a rich-blooded rhetoric that gave the lie to his reputation as a simple British imperialist. Hear him on the militia in 1846:

> There was little doubt but that the militia would perform their duty if called on; they have never been backward in defending their country from a foreign foe. We want no foreign bayonets here . . . to redress our grievances; no . . . [we] are proud of . . . [our] institutions, our institutions are our own, and we need no assistance. . . . I am proud of the connection of Canada with that mighty Empire; I love the Mother Country, but I love the soil on which I live better. . . . As a Canadian, my anxiety for Canada, is the ideal of my idolatry, and it was because I believe that the best interests of Canada would be promoted by its connection with Great Britain, [that] I advocate that connexion as the best source of prosperity, that I wish that connection to continue.[2]

The civil list was the issue that showed his nationalism most consistently. The Act of Union had provided for a permanent civil list that paid the salaries of government officials and judges, and was beyond the control of the legislature. This was anathema to Robert, because it offended both his liberal and his nationalist sentiments. As soon as Parliament reconvened in December 1844 he began his fight, moving an unsuccessful motion to declare the civil list unconstitutional on the grounds that no monies could be appropriated without consent from the provincial Parliament. He and LaFontaine returned to the issue in 1846, raising it at every opportunity that spring. Their efforts were rewarded when the House in June 1846 accepted the principle that only the provincial Parliament could grant a civil list. The following year Britain conceded and repealed the offensive section of the Union Act. Again, the question here for Baldwin was both liberalism and nationalism. The two were yoked in his mind. This new Canada was a liberal Canada, a Canada of basic freedoms and control by the representatives of the people; however, nationalism could override even liberalism. Baldwin's politics were very much ones of small government, modest expenditures. Yet national pride was an even greater good. His government in 1843 had created a Geological Survey under William Logan to assess the natural resources of the colony. When funding of the Survey came before the Assembly in January 1845, Robert bubbled with enthusiasm. He "felt a great pride and satisfaction in Mr. Logan's being a native Canadian, and would gladly vote any reasonable sum of money to be placed at the disposal of the Government." The House was rightly aghast at this unprecedented show of generosity by the parsimonious Baldwin. Such was the depth of his national feeling.[3]

<hr>

The energy and passion that Robert brought to his beloved issues were all the more striking, given both his characteristic stolidity and the distractions around him. Ill health dogged him all too often. There were the depressions that were becoming more frequent and more serious. In the spring of 1845, for example, he was unable to leave his home, except to carry out the ritualized remembrance of Eliza on their wedding anniversary. The following winter he caught measles and was confined to the house for some weeks. There apparently were complications because he remained very weak. He left Toronto by stagecoach for Montreal on 10 March to attend the parliamentary session. He was too feeble to make the journey without breaks and therefore arranged to stay with the Brockville Reformer, Andrew Norton Buell, to rest. Alas, the roads were desperately bad and Robert's coach was upset four times between Toronto and Montreal. Already weakened, he now had a shoulder injury to add to his misery.[4]

Family responsibilities could not be neglected despite his physical ailments. While he was still recovering from the ill-fated coach trip, he had to set off again, this time for Quebec, in June 1846. The children were to return to Toronto for the summer from their schools in that city. Robert's mother was in a panic, certain the children would not be safe unless their father went to fetch them. With the session barely over, Robert put aside his aches and went to Quebec. Arrangements for the children's travel were always complicated, and sometimes the source of irritation. Robert's cold severity only added to what must have been a source of anxiety for the children. For example, young Eliza, then fourteen, was spending Christmas 1845 in the bleakness of the Ursuline Convent of Quebec. The dreariness was hardly relieved by a letter from her father, taking her to task over her travel accounts. "It is not that I doubt your proper application of the money, but because a matter of business ought to be disposed of in a business like manner by every one who deserves to be interested in it." He advised her to consult her brother Willy, also studying in Quebec, since "His was sent in quite a business like manner and gave me great satisfaction." The lecture then turned to her spelling and detailed critiques of her letters to her grandmother and sister. As an afterthought, he wished her a merry Christmas.[5]

Family relations could be much warmer than this. Robert was always especially glad to see his father's younger sister, Aunt Anne Maria Baldwin, when she visited from her home in New York. She had been a bridesmaid at Robert and Eliza's wedding and had a special place in his heart as a result. She had gone to New York in 1807 to live with her sister Elizabeth and brother-in-law John Jordan Morgan. The connection gave Robert a strong emotional link to the New York relations, the Morgan and Dix families. Daughter Maria had a great adventure when she went to visit New York and then went on to Washington to stay with Senator John Adams Dix and his wife, Catherine. In Washington Maria and Catherine visited First Lady Sarah Childress Polk, and a proud Maria was able to play political informant, assuring her father that Mrs. Polk had guaranteed there would be no war between the United States and Britain, despite the current tensions over borders.[6]

There was no doubt about Robert's commitment to family and his affection for its members. He remained, all the same, a stereotypical Victorian paterfamilias. He proudly assumed his father's place. As he wrote when seeking information from Ireland for a family coat of arms, he was now "the head of the senior male branch" of the family in Canada. Commonly, at the time, such a head was a benevolent sovereign who kept an emotional distance from his family subjects. The sovereignty extended to the imposition of parental ideals, to the demand for perfection. Eliza would have to grow wearyingly familiar with her father's expectations.[7]

Robert did not always live up to the ideals he held out to the children, including that of disposing of business in a business-like manner. The family land business suffered because of politics. Brother William Augustus floundered in his attempts to manage the land. Robert promised in 1845 to rush home to help as soon as the parliamentary session ended, but politics again took precedence. As a result, the business was handed over to the law firm to manage, with Lawrence Heyden employed as confidential clerk for land matters.[8]

At least as troubling was the Reform Party infighting. Much of it swirled around the rivalry between two party newspapers, the *Globe* in Toronto and the *Pilot* in Montreal. Both had been established in March 1844—the *Globe* by George Brown, the *Pilot* by Francis Hincks—to carry the Reform message in the metropolitan cities. The common purpose did not long last. Brown and Hincks competed for support of their papers, influence in the party, and dominance of their political ideas. Brown was a liberal of the modern British free-trade school. More, he was a dogmatic Protestant voluntarist who burned with a deep suspicion of popery and its sway in Canada. He quickly emerged as the champion of Protestant Upper Canada. Hincks, as always, was flexible; resident in Lower Canada, he made his peace with French Canada and Catholicism.

The *Pilot* was not a viable business enterprise in the crowded English-language press of Montreal. During the year ending in February 1845, revenues fell £410 short of the expenditures of £1646. The party, and Baldwin personally, had to subsidize Hincks's paper. Naturally that irritated Brown and his supporters who believed the party was paying for Lower Canadian domination. Hincks, in turn, believed that Brown was scheming against him. Although he had lost Oxford County, Upper Canada, in the election of 1844, Hincks still claimed the seat for the future. Brown's interference there set off an explosion of paranoia in September 1845. Hincks wrote to Baldwin that Brown had been in Oxford

> exerting himself not only against the Pilot but against me personally—His object is to unseat me for that Co. & . . . to substitute himself. He purposes also to substitute [William Hume] Blake for you as leader. My information can be relied on. My friends are enraged and look on him as a thorough Scoundrel.

Neither of the substitutions took place, but the sniping between the party papers continued throughout the opposition years. In the spring of 1847, for example, the *Globe* charged that the *Pilot* was cowardly for opposing a monument to Lord Metcalfe in Montreal, erection of which would produce violence, Hincks was certain. Later that year Brown cast scorn on Hincks for supporting the building of a "palace," the official residence for the governor. The constant harassment was enough for Hincks to decide that his losses were too great—some £700 of his own money according to his account, as well as his patience—and to leave journalism. Or so he told Robert. In fact he continued to operate the *Pilot* and remained its editor until he was appointed to the new Reform ministry in February 1848.[9]

Baldwin kept his patience, if not his money. Perhaps his equanimity was increased by the realization of the greater crises outside the family and outside politics. The provincial economy was struck blow after blow in the 1840s. The Empire had long protected the entry of colonial goods into the British market. High tariffs against foreign products gave the colonies substantial price advantages in timber, grain, and other imports: however, the new industrial Britain no longer needed the colonies as markets or as suppliers. Britain was the world's greatest economic power and could flourish in a climate of free trade. Thus, from 1842, the home government began to strip away colonial protection. The result was a series of economic panics in Canada, and a good deal of despair about the future. "We are in the same condition as a man suddenly precipitated from a lofty eminence," said the president of the Toronto Board of Trade "We are labouring under concussion of the brain."[10]

The anxiety was sharply increased by the migration of Irish from famine. The failure of the potato crop and the spread of epidemic diseases devastated Robert's ancestral homeland. The lush fields that had once provided support for the most densely populated country in Europe reeked with the rot of Ireland's staple. Those fields soon were reconquered by the deep grasses that surrounded abandoned cottages, as the people died or fled. In 1847 more than 100,000 of those desperate people escaped to British North America. Many perished on the voyage, but the rest washed up on the shores of the Province of Canada. More than 90,000 people arrived that summer at Quebec and most found their way up river. At Montreal the government erected sheds and tents to receive them , and doctors and nuns struggled to deal with the misery. From the end of May to 21 August 1847, the *Pilot* reported, 7150 immigrants had died and more than 26,000 had been treated for illnesses.[11]

Life carried on, amid tragedy. Death wagons collected bodies in Montreal every evening as ship-borne diseases spread. About the time the wagons were preparing to roll out for the grisly task, on the last Thursday in July, some 400 guests were mounting their carriages to go to the Governor General's residence, Monklands. It was a large family home, built in the Scottish style by lawyer Samuel Cornwallis; not a grand dwelling for a governor, but the best the province had been able to obtain when the capital shifted to Montreal. The guests rode out past Mount Royal to Monklands in the hundreds. Once there they were ushered to the esplanade behind the house, and from there followed a footpath through the meadow below and into the trees where, a newspaper enthused, "a temporary court was established." The site presumably was far enough from the rough misery on the docks for the dignitaries to forget the dying.[12]

The immigration crisis did compel everyone in Canada eventually to come to terms with the issue. Robert Baldwin had been the president of the St. Patrick's Benevolent Society in Toronto in 1846, so his involvement in immigrant relief was to be expected. He had long opposed pauper immigration, but he recognized that paupers would now come and that provision had to be made for them; hence, his personal and financial involvement with the relief effort. He contributed £25 to Irish relief, £10 to the Toronto fund for destitute widows and orphans, and £5 for Highland Scots who were also suffering from the potato blight. This was, however, hardheaded generosity. Robert had told the Toronto city hall gathering that created the relief organization that the arriving Irish peasants had to be moved out of the city. Once removed, they should be settled on the land rather than employed on the canals, since "You cannot compel them to keep their money. The labourer on the public works will save very little." Indeed, Robert had been an enthusiastic supporter of the Tory government in its suppression of Irish labourers on the canals, labourers who rioted for better wages and living conditions. Robert's trip to the old country a decade before may have made him a better

Irishman, as he claimed, but it had not erased the gulf of class between him and the destitute immigrants from Ireland.[13]

———

It might be expected that the tensions would be reflected in politics. What was most curious was the ambiguous character of the politics of the period. The animosities in Montreal itself grew worse, if that were possible. Religious, ethnic, and political differences blended into a bitter stew; one that boiled over at every opportunity. In August 1845, for example, there were two serious riots precipitated by the oratory of a visiting Presbyterian preacher, whose enthusiastic denunciation of popery offended local Catholics. There were bloody municipal election riots in March 1846 and March 1847. These riots cut across class lines, merchants and professional men joining labourers in the brawls. There were peculiarly elite forms of dispute, however. In this climate, small things could produce great anger.[14]

Baldwin and other members of the House were shocked by an illustration of elite violence on 25 March 1845. That evening the squinting little Reformer from Quebec, Thomas Aylwin, got into a dispute with the "perpetual secretary" Dominick Daly over who was responsible for stirring up religious hatred in the province. Aylwin, in the course of the argument, said he had read a pamphlet about the Orange Order that was lent to him by Daly. Daly said he did not remember such a pamphlet, but Aylwin insisted Daly had given it to him. Red-faced, Daly shouted, "Sir! It is false." Aylwin shouted back across the floor, "What do you say?" "I say that it is false," replied Daly. Aylwin was silenced, but the affair was far from over. The next morning Daly and Aylwin met along the river to settle the dispute with pistols. Shots were fired. Fortunately, Daly missed; Aylwin was so near-sighted he could hardly have been expected to hit his opponent.[15]

Even those strongly opposed to duelling could not always escape elite retribution. Francis Hincks was a thoroughly modern man and considered duelling a barbaric vestige of the aristocratic age. He ignored challenges when they came his way. That did not discourage those who had exaggerated ideas of honour. In January 1846 the *Pilot* printed a letter charging that Patrick McKeon had been a Tory spy when he worked in the office of Reform lawyer Lewis Drummond. McKeon was now a clerk under Daly, and the *Pilot* alleged he was in reality "Mr. Daly's agent for intriguing with the Irish." McKeon could get no satisfaction from Hincks, so when Hincks left his office on Place d'Armes at 5:00 p.m. on Tuesday, 13 January, a furious McKeon attacked him from behind, knocking him down with a club and continuing to beat him while he lay on the cobblestones. McKeon was unrepentant when hauled to court and fined £3; the attack, he told the magistrate, was completely justified because Hincks had defamed him.[16]

Baldwin could understand such behaviour since his father was a duellist, but he could not condone it. Fortunately, there were concerted efforts on all sides to avoid confrontations of this sort, to bring some measure of peace to a troubled colony. Those efforts were assisted by the appointment of a new governor. As Charles, Lord Metcalfe, left for England to die, Charles Murray Cathcart, the second Earl Cathcart, commander-in-chief of British forces in America, was sworn in on 26 November 1845 as administrator of the province. He would be designated Governor General in April 1846. As with General Jackson, who had assumed office when Sydenham died, Cathcart was an amiable military man with little interest in politics. Outside of the military, his one passion was geology. He discovered the cadmium mineral, greenockite, which was named for his courtesy title, Lord Greenock. He was happy to leave politics to his ministers, and thus the Draper government enjoyed all the powers of a responsible government. Cathcart's benign rule helped to quiet partisan bickering. The opposition became as welcome at official functions as the government. In May 1846, for example, Baldwin and LaFontaine mingled with their foes at Earl Cathcart's levee for the queen's birthday at Monklands. The respective strategies of the parties helped, as well. The government was well aware that it had been returned in 1844 because of Metcalfe's efforts, not because it was popular. The receiver general, William Morris from Brockville, had told his son in November 1844 that he would only take a short lease on a residence in Montreal, since the ministry's future was so dubious. That led the government to drift to the middle, to identify itself as a moderate force that accepted the broad outlines of responsible government. The Reformers read the same message from the election. Hincks had written from Montreal that same November 1844: " Moderation is the order of the day here. The plan is to let the Enemy fall by their own weakness." That was advice that suited Robert very well. He reined in LaFontaine as much as he could and tried to maintain a low profile. By January 1846 the Montreal *Gazette* was complaining that there was "not a single animosity to keep us in liveliness. . . . Our old stock Aversions, Mr. Baldwin and Mr. Lafontaine, have long been so quiet, that they have ceased to offer food for a single paragraph." That quietude extended into the parliamentary session of 1846 where Robert worked to provide constructive opposition.[17]

The strategy was helped by the weakness of the government. Lord Metcalfe had alerted the Colonial Office in the spring of 1845 that, in his view, Draper hardly had a party. "I do not know that, strictly speaking, he can be said to have a single follower. The same may be remarked of every other member of the Executive Council." It did not get any better for the Tories. There was open hostility between ministers during the 1845 session, and the government suffered several humiliating defeats on important votes. So ineffective was the ministry that the *Examiner* could crow in March 1845: "The Great Government Measure of the Session, The Dog Bill Carried—The Muskrat Bill Lost." The fiasco continued in 1846, with the ministry being defeated on several revenue measures and its most important bill, on a university for Upper Canada. Draper himself hung on until the spring of 1847 when he left politics for a judgeship. The party was by then openly divided between "Gowanites" and "MacNab men," the pragmatic conservatives of Orange leader Ogle Gowan and the Tories of Sir Allan MacNab.[18]

Baldwin's success did not rest only on Tory ineptitude. His was a special role in the House, and that strengthened his credibility. He was the acknowledged expert on procedure, British procedure. His comprehension of parliamentary practice was seemingly encyclopedic, and he could rise to brilliance in his explanations to the House. One early example in the second Parliament was on 19 December 1844. The issue was a petition against the election of two Tories, Charles De Bleury and George Moffatt, as members for Montreal, on the grounds that they had engaged in electoral irregularities. The debate was a mundane one, full of partisan carping— until Baldwin intervened. His defence of the petition was effulgent, a stream of precedents, logical inferences, and historical references, all phrased with precision and, at moments, elegance. That the petition lost by two votes does not dim the lustre of his performance. His expertise was given credence by his reputation for honesty. There was an impressive demonstration of the point on 22 March 1845. Robert was replying to some Tory claims that Reformers engaged in "factious opposition." He took the slur personally and demanded to know of any case in his entire political career when he had used any "indecent means" to advance the fortunes of his ideas. This brought cheers from the government, as well as the Reform, side of the House. He went on to point out that he had supported government measures on the judiciary, against the majority of his own colleagues. "And was it to be said after all this that I . . . have given the hon. Gentlemen opposite a factious opposition?" George Barker Hall, the Tory member for Northumberland South, spoke for everyone when he shouted, "No not from you."[19]

He earned a rather different reputation as well. He was slow and heavy, and his slowness could drift into sleep at times, a condition not unfamiliar in depressives who have difficulty sleeping at night. It was on 27 March 1845 that he voted on a motion despite being asleep. The Montreal *Gazette*, rarely kind to Robert, was at least sympathetic when he nodded off on the evening of 5 May 1846:

> On Tuesday night, Mr. Cauchon [member for Montmorency] first wearied, and then fairly emptied the House. While delivering his frothy inanities, Member after Member dropped off; and finally, we believe, the Ministerial Benches were left with only three occupants, and the Opposition Benches were almost equally thin; Mr. Baldwin even, a model of patience, first falling into a real or sham sleep, and then, in despair, getting up and joining one of the numerous groups that were wiling [*sic.*] away their time by a sip of coffee, or (those who liked it) of something stronger in Dolly's bar.[20]

He might be excused simply because of the character of the House itself. A correspondent for the *Globe* noted in 1847 that the Assembly chamber, furnished with easy chairs, seemed "almost inviting to repose rather than exertion." That same correspondent, George Brown himself, gave a remarkably candid and accurate picture of his leader. Robert, he said, was a statesman of great diligence. He rose early to read parliamentary papers and rarely missed a minute of House sessions. In the Assembly he was deferred to by the ministers who were forever "hanging on to him" seeking his opinion on rules or the drafting of bills. His leadership of his own ranks was cautious and even passive, the *Globe* claimed, designed more to avoid mistakes than to seize the initiative.

> He has no enthusiasm about him, he inspires none. The country politician who comes to town to consult the great Reform leader, proud of his mission, receives a sad check when he encounters the cold, courteous, self-possessed Mr. Baldwin . . . when he comes away, the visitor feels that the business he especially came upon has been satisfactorily settled, he has got all he actually needed—but there is a want unsatisfied, he has been shown no confidence. Mr. Baldwin never shows a card more than is necessary.[21]

It was a perceptive analysis. What Brown could not know was what was hidden by the coldness. He could not know how little self-possession Robert really had, living out his father's dream, thinking more of the dead than the living.

Robert's caution and his willingness to see merits in government proposals set him in conflict with other Reform leaders. So, too, did his views on policy issues. The differences among Reformers on economic questions were profound and omnipresent. They could be put aside in the struggle for responsible government, in hostility to Tories, and in mutual self-interest. They did not go away, however, and an economic crisis such as that of after 1846 would bring them to the fore. Farmers, merchants, financiers, and landowners all had their own interpretations of the best course to steer Canada out of its dire state. Britain's adoption of free trade brought out both supporters and opponents in the colony. John Young, a Montreal merchant and a Reform cabinet minister in 1851, published a manifesto in April 1846, which argued that Canada could only prosper with complete free trade. The *Pilot* and the *Globe* echoed his argument, and a Free-Trade Association sprang up to advance the cause. Some present and past Reformers lined up on the other side. Isaac Buchanan, once a liberal turned Sydenhamite, wrote to the *Times of London* that free trade meant Canadian independence, for "no man could show any, the slightest *interest* British America will have in continued connection with this country." Cousin Robert Baldwin Sullivan spoke to the Mechanics' Institute in Hamilton, Upper Canada, in November 1847 and suggested industrial development, behind provincial tariff walls, as the only sensible future.[22]

It was difficult for a party leader to avoid the shoals. The task was made all the harder because Robert was uncertain in his own mind. In 1845 he opposed discriminatory duties in favour of Britain on the grounds that such duties hurt consumers. Duties should be for revenue only. It was "wrong to set up artificial restrictions for the advantage of particular parties." One could hardly ask for a clearer expression of free-trade philosophy. A year later, in March 1846, he was still telling the House that he did not fear commercial changes. At least he did not fear them unless they affected his farmer constituents. Three days after his "no fear" speech he seconded a motion by a government member asking Britain to retain protection for Canadian wheat entering the British market. When Aylwin complained that the motion was irregular because no notice had been given, the stickler for parliamentary niceties, Baldwin, told him ordinary practice would have to be dispensed with because this was a matter of "paramount importance." His course grew ever more erratic on the trade question. On 17 April he gave an agitated address to the Assembly about the need to counteract the "evil effects" of recent changes in British economic policy. He believed, he said, that in the abstract free trade was correct. But Canada had flourished under protection and had no reason to celebrate its removal. Yet a few days later he was voting against a series of motions from a select committee that proposed duties on dye woods and foreign wheat. To cap this curious career, he agreed to serve on a committee to prepare an address to the queen about the repeal of the Corn Laws. The committee report, which came to the House on 12 May 1846, deplored the loss of the "Protective Principle, the very bases of the Colonial Commercial System" and warned that Canada might fall to the United States if abandoned by British commercial policy. Baldwin had done a splendid job of debating both sides of the issue.[23]

Necessity finally resolved the matter for him. He had studied the entrails all that troubled year, and come to the conclusion that Canada must make the best of the new situation. On 11 November 1846 he was beginning the long campaign that would bring him back to power in 1848. He travelled by coach from Toronto west to the town of Dundas, where hundreds of Reformers from the riding of East Halton had gathered to greet him in a roughly hewn hall at Boggis' Hotel. Robert told his followers what must be done. Canada must meet the free-trade era "with manly self-reliance." Farmers had lost their protected British market and they must not be "saddled" with duties that might advance "the separate interests of any other class of the community." The die was cast; Britain would never return to the old colonial system. "Let us shake off the imbecility of childhood and stand erect like men, and I feel assured that Canada will be found equal to the emergency." Nationalism was the consolation in this uncertain time.[24]

He had been pulled back and forth by different interests in the country and in the party on free trade. That was far from the only issue where it was difficult to find the middle ground. He was prepared to accept economic ideas antithetical to his own if he thought there was a consensus on them. That was the case with primogeniture. The landholding Baldwins believed in passing down estates intact to the eldest son. When a bill came before the Assembly in 1845 to abolish primogeniture and provide for more equal distribution of estates in cases where property owners died intestate, Robert warned there were dangers in splitting up farms; however, he would support the bill because 90 percent of Upper Canadians wanted such a change. There was rarely such a clear-cut opinion, and that meant Robert would come into conflict with important Reformers on economic questions. Mining speculation was one. The *Globe* was very concerned about speculative ventures around Lake Superior that attracted a good deal of attention in 1846. They were dangerous financially and they reeked of political favouritism, the *Globe* charged. Those were sentiments Robert could share. Unfortunately, his other Reform newspaper baron was up to his ears in the mining speculation. Francis Hincks gloated to his leader in March 1847 that "I have been very fortunate in my Mining operations having cleared $4500 on stock."[25]

The division in the ranks was awkward, but at least it allowed Robert to follow his own inclinations. Nevertheless, it could be costly. The House session that began on 2 June 1847 was marked by bitter exchanges over economics. The independent member for Essex, Upper Canada, John Prince, voted almost consistently with the Reformers. Or he did so before June 1847. He introduced a bill to incorporate the British

North American Mining Company, which carried on its activities in the mineral rush area of Lake Superior. The bill drew angry opposition from Baldwin, Aylwin, and J.H. Price. They claimed the bill was no more than "spoliation" of the public, a scheme to gain public lands at fire-sale prices, and to speculate dishonestly in stock. Who was involved in this alleged fraud? The partners included Colonel Prince himself; the Attorney General West, Henry Sherwood; Reform backbencher B.-H. Lemoine; and Francis Hincks. Prince wrote in his diary after the second reading: "Carried my own & Hincks's Mining Bills after a stormy debate & <u>factious</u> opposition from Baldwin & Aylwin."

That was far from the end of it. The House was in committee on the mining bill on Friday, 23 July 1847. The measure would make the company a limited liability corporation, whose owners were only responsible to the extent of their investments. Interestingly, the sides had lined up rather differently two years before. Then Aylwin had sought to establish the Quebec Forwarding Company as a limited liability corporation, while Hincks in the *Pilot* viewed the concept of limited liability "with much alarm." Now Hincks's own company embraced the alarming theory. Baldwin and Price attacked it as unfair, indeed immoral, not to take responsibility for all the debts one had contracted, and Price moved an amendment to require full financial responsibility. Tory W.H. Boulton scorned them. To oppose limited liability was to oppose investment and was "an antideluvian [*sic.*] doctrine." Robert was not embarrassed. "[I] am willing to bear the odium of being considered an antedeluvium (laughter); I will vote for the amendment on the old fashioned principle that men were bound in conscience, and ought to be bound in law to pay all their debts." It was a nice thrust, but the amendment could muster only seven votes in this capitalist House, and the mining bill passed easily. The dispute cost Baldwin John Prince's support. He crossed over to the government benches that July.

Limited liability was only one of many issues on which Robert opposed some of the important figures in his party and in the House. In July 1847 there was debate on a master-and-servant bill that gave employers greater power to punish runaway servants. Prince enthusiastically supported it since in "the wild Western country" where he lived, near the American border, it was easy for servants to escape.

Robert, however, believed that it was "one-sided—all for the master . . . while professing mutual protection, it did not protect the servant in a single instance." Again, Robert was in the minority, even in his own party. It was not always so, since Robert could often count on the support of farmers in the Reform ranks. They helped him to defeat attempts to remove the limit on the interest that could be charged for loans. Again, many rank-and-file Reformers rallied against a bill introduced in 1847 to abolish dower rights, the entitlement of widows to a portion of their late husbands' estates. Robert denounced Solicitor General Cameron for the measure, since "the main object of this Bill was THE INJURY OF WOMAN, and to despoil them of the trivial rights they now held, and I will earnestly oppose it to the last." The bill was soundly defeated.[26]

These were little more than holding actions. Many shared Robert's unease about the direction of economic and social change. Historian Peter Gay talks of members of the European bourgeoisie recoiling from "an alarming lack of anchorage, a universal anarchy of thought, an unhealthy speed of existence." It was that sort of sentiment that the old Tory William Macaulay expressed when he wrote in 1847:

> The electric telegraph seems to be extending itself every where. The world will get all its news now at once, which will not be half so pleasant as when it came, driblet by driblet, after long expectation—Indeed what with steamboats, rail cars, electric telegraphs, & so forth, the next generation will be altogether a different kind of race from our dull plodding generation.[27]

This "new race" would live in a world where values were changing, where relations between people were changing. Increasingly those relations would be measured by the value of exchanges, by money values. Landed property itself was the greatest check on such a development since land ownership gave people the option of using markets in their own way, rather than being appropriated into them. It was land that underlay the "civic humanism" that motivated people such as Robert Baldwin. In that philosophy, man was a political creature who achieved satisfaction by engaging in politics and serving the public. The "new race" would assume man was an economic animal, driven by the need to increase exchange value and largely defined by the relationship to the market.[28]

His principles could still win out, especially when his foes were divided against themselves. A singular triumph during the second Parliament was the defeat of Tory attempts to create a provincial university on their principles. Robert had tried in 1843 to establish a provincial institution free of Anglican control, and the issue remained a deeply emotional for him. A non-sectarian university was a liberal dream, and an important symbol of provincial nationalism. The very ferocity of the abuse he received from his own church about the university only added intensity to his purpose. He had the opportunity to display that intensity in the spring of 1845. William Henry Draper had come to the bar of the House in 1843 as solicitor for Anglican King's College, to argue against Baldwin's university bill. Now, as leader of the government, he discovered there was a swelling demand in Upper Canada for a more liberal institution of higher education. He accordingly introduced a bill in early March to erect the University of Upper Canada. It mirrored many of the provisions of Baldwin's legislation, but made financial concessions to religious colleges. If Baldwin was surprised, Draper's conservative friends were even more so. Anglican Bishop John Strachan, long an admirer of Draper, was flabbergasted. He wrote to inspector general William Robinson to ask "by what alchemy he [Draper] could have been made to think favourably of a measure which in my opinion is even worse than Baldwin's." With more and more Tories expressing their unease, Draper tried to brazen it out. He rose in the House on 11 March, while debate was proceeding on second reading, to defend his bill. He belied his nickname of "Sweet William" as he thundered defiance at all his critics, "I must either stand or fall by this measure."[29]

It was wondrously incongruous. Draper had scorned Baldwin's views, had refused to sit at the Council table with him. Now the fate of his great measure rested on Baldwin. If Robert would support the bill, it might pass despite High Church anger. Robert kept his silence until the afternoon of Saturday, 22 March. The government was wobbling, and now Robert contrived an opportunity to speak to the university question. During debate on a motion to grant supply, Thomas Aylwin surprised the members by asking that the House go into committee on the university bill. The point was to give Baldwin the chance to deliver a long, carefully prepared speech. He assailed every detail of the proposed university, but his argument boiled down to this: there were two major objects to any such legislation, and this bill failed to satisfy either. The first purpose ought to be to assure youth of all religious denominations the right to a liberal education. All this bill offered was a proliferation of small, inadequate religious colleges. They would end up, he said, offering diplomas that were, like so many American degrees, worthless. The second purpose was to give "satisfaction to the country." The storm of protest from all sides made it clear that object was not being met. The bill should be allowed to die as quickly as possible.[30]

The ministry appeared ready to die instead. William Robinson resigned his cabinet post, probably on Strachan's urging. Henry Sherwood was perhaps the most able member of the government. The Solicitor General was tall, handsome, gifted—and unreliable. His announcement that he could not support the university bill on final reading doomed it. Draper had no choice but to swallow his pride, and the university bill. So much for "stand or fall."[31]

Draper tried again in 1846; however, he faced even stronger opposition. Robert had determined on a comprehensive campaign. A great meeting was held on the evening of Tuesday, 3 February at Toronto's Congregational Chapel on Adelaide Street. Some 900 people crowded into the church to demand an open, liberal university with no religious tests. A permanent lobby group, the University Reformation Committee, was established. With attacks from both the left and the right, Draper's new bill was doomed. Robert's motion of 29 May to kill the measure was joined by Tories such as William Robinson and Henry Sherwood.[32]

By the 1847 session William Henry Draper had departed and the burden of the university fell to the young receiver general, the member from Kingston, John Alexander Macdonald. He was ungainly and unpretty, his bulbous nose betraying his proclivity for heavy drinking. He was not a great success as a lawyer or a businessman, and the Reformers saw his quick elevation to cabinet as a sign of Tory desperation. Macdonald was a good deal cleverer than they took him for and, once he had determined the university question must be settled, he did the political groundwork. He toiled assiduously to win over the warring religious factions. Strachan and the Anglicans were offered the lion's share of the university endowment, but the other religious colleges got a share of the wealth. There was no centralization in Toronto, as Baldwin had planned; instead, the colleges could remain in their provincial towns. For those not likely to go to college, Macdonald offered grammar schools in each district of Upper Canada.[33]

It was a well-thought-out plan, and it garnered support from Bishop Strachan, Egerton Ryerson of the Methodists, the Church of Scotland, and the Roman Catholic Church. Macdonald perhaps overreached, however, when he tried to enlist Baldwin. The young minister praised Robert's contributions to education as he introduced the university bill on 9 July 1847. Robert was having none of it. He was grateful for the compliment, but he found this bill radically deficient. "It has been among the early dreams of my boyhood that the day would come when his country would be blessed by an establishment affording those high educational advantages, which I myself, as much as anyone, felt the want of, as well in the pursuit of my profession, as in other several walks of life." Macdonald's bill betrayed these dreams. Splitting up the endowment among small religious colleges was really "sweeping the University off the face of the earth, and giving the country in its stead a few paltry institutions." He would withdraw from public life, he said, if the people disapproved of his opposition, but oppose he must. He need not have worried. Strachan, under pressure from the council of King's College, withdrew his support and many Anglicans in the House dutifully followed their bishop. When the bill came up for second reading on 26 July, a chastened John A. Macdonald announced that he was withdrawing it.[34]

It was a negative sort of victory. There was no university, but at least there was not a High Church university. Robert won the same sort of victory on responsible government. By 1847, Canada did not have a genuine responsible government, but it did have at least grudging acceptance of the concept by all parties. Robert had continually returned to his political nostrum, arguing its merits at every opportunity. Early in the first session of this Parliament, for example, he had expressed his anger over the ministers sending petitions to committees rather than acting themselves:

> I am for giving Ministers all the support they needed
> Ironical cheers from the ministerial Benches . . .
> or all they deserve rather, but I will not aid them to escape from

responsibility; and believing this was an attempt to do so, I shall give the motion my decided negative.[35]

He had already won a convert. William Henry Draper, aware that a government could no longer be managed from the Legislative Council, ran for an Assembly seat in a by-election in February 1845. He was also mindful that to win support in Upper Canada and among French Canadians he had to compromise on the constitution. He told voters in London, Upper Canada, that he would govern on the principles of responsible government. It remained unclear what that meant. Draper never cobbled together a party, so party government did not prevail. More, the ministry suffered a plethora of defeats, sometimes on money matters, and yet this responsible government clung to office. Still, Draper had a free hand to govern under Lord Cathcart, and free-trade Britain was increasingly willing to let Canada find its own course. When William Ewart Gladstone became Colonial Secretary in early 1846, his undersecretary, James Stephen, advised him that Canada had a British governor and British trade laws, but it nevertheless was almost a separate self-governing state. Later that year another Colonial Secretary, Lord Grey, sent a dispatch to Sir John Harvey, Lieutenant-Governor of Nova Scotia, instructing him to change his executive council only when it was unable to "command the confidence of the Legislature." It was "neither possible nor desirable to carry on the government of any of the British provinces in North America in opposition to the opinion of the inhabitants."[36]

Even the staunchest of Tories had to realize the game was essentially over. As late as September 1846 the Montreal *Gazette* was still denouncing the "Lafontaine-Baldwin theory" as unsound and unworkable. Four months later, after the publication of Nova Scotia liberal Joseph Howe's letters to British prime minister Lord John Russell, the *Gazette* sadly conceded that responsible government was an irreversible reality and that Canada had become a democracy. That was perhaps farther than Robert himself was prepared to go. As he told the House during its last session in June 1847, "We, Mr. Speaker . . . are the true Conservatives—we have defended the Constitutional principles and usages of the British System from the sacriligious [*sic*.] hand of Her Majestys advisers." In doing so, he had indeed turned everything into responsible government.[37]

Chapter 12

There Must Be No Question of Races

Loyalty, he found, was the rarest of commodities. Yet he must be patient, he must try to understand why those he had sacrificed so much for could contemplate casting him aside. There was only Eliza. She had been dead a decade.

The core of Robert's political strategy, and of his hope for his native country, was the alliance of French and English. Liberal-minded citizens of both ethnicities would find common ground on responsible government. They would create a unique polity, bicultural and bilingual, that might draw on the genius of each people. It was a remarkable vision for someone who spoke no French, who had little familiarity of the lower province beyond the environs of Montreal. Indeed, he had only once visited his own constituency of Rimouski, a fleeting introduction while electioneering in the summer of 1844.

The vision had been conjured up from his political calculation, that such an alliance was the only way to win good government. Yet it was not simply political; it was also the product of his recognition that French Canada had suffered great injuries and deep insults, of the sort that an Irishman could understand only too well.

He was not naive; he knew how difficult it would be to realize his vision. He was just beginning to know Louis LaFontaine, in November 1840, when he wrote to his new colleague about the demands and the dangers in the relationship. He was about to read to some pamphlets that LaFontaine had sent, "with that attention which the consideration of every thing so important as I understand this to be to our Lower Canadian fellow subjects—demands from us." He underlined the dangers: "There is, and <u>must be no question of races</u>. It were madness on one side, and guilt, deep guilt on both to make such a question." French

Canadians would isolate and endanger themselves if they made ethnicity the centre point of their politics, while Upper Canadians would suffer the shame of the ignoble if they discriminated.[1]

Robert strove to create and maintain the alliance formed in 1840 and to explain its importance to his followers in Upper Canada. It was no easy task when he had to choose between the sensibilities of Reformers and those of Lower Canadian liberals, as he did in 1843 on the question of moving the capital to Montreal. There were always rumblings from the English about "French domination"; however, the nastiest twists of the knife came from the French Canadians, those Baldwin sacrificed so much to placate.

The twists came in quick succession, beginning in the winter of 1844. It was the strange twilight time, when the Reformers had left office after their break with Metcalfe, and old Dominic Viger was shopping about for ministers to create at least the facade of a ministry. Robert was at home that February, trying to be cheerful about the newly minted Reform Association, but troubled by the party infighting. The Reform Association was the modern form of campaign organization favoured by those Robert called "the new lights," while some Reform veterans were suspicious of it and of the newcomers. All this was transpiring while Robert was suffering the cramps and other indignities of dysentery. Worse, he had recently lost his father. Then he heard of unrest among some Lower Canadian liberals who were tempted by the fleshpots of office. He anxiously wrote LaFontaine to sort things out and to have some French-Canadian leaders provide letters reaffirming their commitment to the alliance, letters Robert might read publicly to the Reform Association. As it turned out, Viger and Metcalfe lured few notables, which did not matter. Metcalfe would win the 1844 election without a viable ministry.[2]

The defeat in that election naturally led to unrest. The French Party had succeeded in returning a majority of members from Lower Canada, but Baldwin had failed in Upper Canada. The logic was clear to many. French Canada ought at least to explore whether there was more to be gained, more protection for their culture, by linking up with the government than remaining in opposition with Baldwin. Many of the "liberal" members from Lower Canada were by inclination conservative and had been cajoled into the Reform alliance only by LaFontaine's assurance that it was the best guarantee for their continuance as a people. It was Étienne-Pascal Taché, a long-time liberal member for L'Islet, who captured that truth when he told the House in 1846 that "Nous sommes dans nos habitudes, par nos lois, par notre religion . . . monarchistes et conservateurs . . . treat us like brethren, and not like bastards."[3]

"Sweet William" Draper was more than willing to embrace his French brethren. His enthusiasm for a bicultural Canada tended to wane when he was out of office, and wax when he was in government. Now the French were brethren who could breath life into this breathless ministry. The first session of the new Parliament, in the winter of 1844–1845, was also the first in Montreal. As in Kingston, Parliament was in makeshift accommodations. It used the upper floor of the St. Anne's market on Place d'Youville. Members had to make themselves heard over the din from the market that continued below and outside during parliamentary sessions. Place d'Youville was a bustling place, with Boutillier's potash warehouse and several stores. Only the broad sweep of McGill Street on the west gave some dignity to the setting. It was the perfect setting, all the same, for the new, accommodating Toryism that Draper hoped would give longevity to his ministry.[4]

⸺⸱⸺

The fact that the capital was in Montreal helped to keep attention focused on French Canada. Upper Canadian members had straggled into Montreal in November 1844 for the first session of the second Parliament. Only a few, such as Robert Baldwin, were content to be there. The reluctance of many to leave their home province was exacerbated by their welcome at the new capital. It was winter there and some Montrealers relished the impression made on the visitors. The Montreal *Gazette* struck a note of hardy superiority when it claimed that it was "not so cold as to 'astonish the natives,' but quite sufficient to 'give a new wrinkle' to our parliamentary visitors from the 'sunny south' of Toronto." In fact, it was cold enough that several issues of that paper were barely legible because the printing ink had thickened after freezing.[5]

The unfavourable impression of the metropolis was more firmly fixed when it quickly lived up to its reputation for violence. As Parliament opened on 28 November, the city was bracing for municipal elections. The polling was not to begin until Monday, but the fighting started on Saturday night, 30 November. The local Tory organization, the Loyal Protective Society, was out in full force to intimidate the opposition. That Saturday night the first victim, an Irishman named James Fennell, was shot to death near the walls of McGill College. The murderer was a young conservative partisan, Charles Colburn. On Monday, heavily armed mobs thronged polling places, with the Loyalists largely successful in driving off the Reformers. The worst violence was in the dockside Irish ghetto of Griffintown. Tories invaded the slushy streets while Reform defenders fell back into a ramshackle frame house. As the furious Loyalists besieged the building, the liberals inside fired rifles from every window. James Fennell was revenged when a Tory, John Johnson, fell dead in the street. A typical Montreal election came to its ritual end the following Wednesday with the mass funeral for James Fennell and, the next day, that of John Johnson.[6]

There was more to Montreal than cold and blood. By the 1840s it was the largest city in British North America, surpassing Quebec, with a population approaching 50,000 people. It was the hub of Canadian commerce and Saint-Paul Street was at its centre. It was there that merchants from Upper Canada came every spring and fall to buy imported goods and arrange for sale of their wheat and potash. Montreal's commercial pre-eminence was embodied in the first railway built in the colonies, which ran from the south shore of the St. Lawrence at Laprairie to Saint-Jean on the Richelieu River. It was built to carry cargo, but the Montreal smart set took summer excursions on the new marvel to link up with elegant pleasure boats that plied Lake Champlain.[7]

The largest city in British North America was still a small town for the powerful. The social, economic, and political leaders lived and mingled in close proximity. An Assembly member weary of oratory could leave the market cum Parliament and visit all of the important institutions and many of the important people within a few blocks. He might find some of his delinquent colleagues a few streets to the east at Dolly's Chop House where members of both houses retreated for the good food provided by proprietor R.P. Isaacson (whose Tory allegiances did not deter Reformers from enjoying his fare) and then mount to the third floor for whiskey and cigars. In the immediate vicinity of Dolly's the wandering politician might try to influence opinion at the offices of two newspapers, the *Courier* and the *Transcript*, or drop in on municipal officials at Montreal city hall. Strolling north on Saint-François-Xavier Street he would come to Montreal's most impressive public space, Place d'Armes. The site was dominated by the massive buildings of the City Bank and the Banque du Peuple, and the even grander cathedral of Notre-Dame de Montréal with its 227-foot twin towers. More modest was the building housing Francis Hincks's *Pilot* newspaper. Turning east along Saint-Jacques he could see that French and English still mixed in the city. Tetu's Hotel was a popular choice for visiting politicians of both ethnicities. The very symbol of Anglo-Saxon domination, the Bank of Montreal, was nestled among office buildings where Louis LaFontaine, A.-N. Morin, and George-Étienne Cartier had their law offices. And nearby was the home of the venerable French-Canadian leader, and Sir Charles Metcalfe's chosen one, D.-B. Viger.

Our wandering politician would get an even stronger sense of how small the elite was when he walked south on St.-Gabriel Street. The centre of francophone radicalism, the Institut canadien, was nearby the home of Peter McGill, president of the Bank of Montreal, and the offices of the conservative anglophone newspaper the *Herald*. The mix was flavoured by the law offices of a rising star, the young Irish Reformer, Lewis Drummond. Refreshed, the politician would make his way back to the legislature along the main business thoroughfare, Saint-Paul Street. The oracle of Tory opinion, the Montreal *Gazette*, was there. So too was the grandest hotel in the city, Rasco's. It had been established in the early 1830s by Francisco Rasco and quickly became the city's most stylish lodging house. It had a grand concert hall where important touring artists performed, many meeting rooms, and accommodations for eighty-four guests, including Robert Baldwin, who took up residence for the first parliamentary session in Montreal. Robert and Louis LaFontaine met often at Rasco's to plot strategy.[8]

If elite Montreal was a small circle, the errant legislator might have noticed an even smaller, inner clique—that of the French-Canadian leadership. Party conflict could be fierce among them, yet political leaders of all stripes socialized together and drew tight to protect the interests of French Canada. The Saint-Jean Baptiste Society had been formed a decade earlier to celebrate and enhance the Québécois nationality. During the first session of Parliament in Montreal, meetings of the society brought together political foes such as Tory cabinet minister D.-B. Viger, president of the organization in 1845, and the liberal A.-N. Morin, a member of the society's governing council. Indeed, the ties were often a good deal more intimate. Cartier, a rising light among French Reformers, married the daughter of Viger's lieutenant, Raymond Fabre. Blood was much thicker than the water of politics.[9]

That was Robert Baldwin's problem. The close relations among French-Canadian politicians on both sides of the House, and their common passion to defend their nation, meant that the Reform alliance was always on slippery ground. A confusion of ideology and "race" was hammered into the very structure of the Union. That was true even of Robert's closest ally, Louis LaFontaine. In 1842 he and Robert had been attempting to establish responsible government. Even then, LaFontaine was confusing matters with his ethnic concerns. He had been offered a post in Bagot's ministry in early September, but declined because, he explained to the governor, Baldwin objected to the executive councillors then representing Upper Canada. LaFontaine contended that as a member from Lower Canada he himself had no right to object to whatever councillors were chosen from the upper province. This was a peculiar version of responsible government, but it was an accurate illustration of French-Canadians' views. They were prepared to forego the party solidarity that lay at the root of responsible government in the interest of protecting region and ethnicity. They would respect Upper Canada's autonomy and would expect Upper Canadians to respect theirs.[10]

This was the concept known as the double majority that would dog the politics of the Union until its very end. The simplest rendering was the belief that each section of the Canadas should have the say on those matters crucial to its identity. More elaborately, double majority came to suggest that issues of provincial concern should be passed only with concurrent majorities from each section. There was support for the theory from the beginning of the Union and, equally, there was artful avoidance of it. When LaFontaine and Baldwin established their ministry in September 1842, they each interpreted the constitutional arrangements to their satisfaction. LaFontaine pretended there was a double majority, referring to Baldwin and himself as co-premiers. Baldwin, however, deferred to LaFontaine as the leader, the sole leader on the British model. Pragmatism required Robert to accept the duality of Canada, whatever his ideological assumptions. The Union government was always one of parallel structures, with two Attorneys General, two Solicitors General, and so on. Given that practicality, double majority was fated to persist as an ideal for French Canada.

It was inordinately difficult to govern without French-Canadian support. Despite their prejudices, the Tories had to woo the French. In that first session in Montreal, Upper Canada was largely ignored while Draper introduced a bounty of legislation for the lower province. The school system and local government were reformed. The first steps were taken to encourage the conversion of land from seigniorial to freehold tenure. The most powerfully symbolic action was on the legal restrictions against the use of the French language. The issue was indeed symbolic, since members routinely spoke French in Parliament and the courts accommodated the language. Yet it rankled many that Durham's scheme to assimilate the French Canadians lived on in official form in the language prohibition. A gesture about language, then, would be welcomed. It was awkward since the imperial cabinet in London had discussed the issue in the summer of 1843 and agreed unanimously that there should be no concession on language, that the policy of anglicization remained firm. Metcalfe had to shore up his ministers all the same, and that meant shading his instructions from Britain, without actually defying them. The ministry brought forth an address to the home government on 20 December 1845, asking that the restrictions on French be removed. The movers were a suitably peculiar pair for a peculiar procedure: Denis Papineau, the ne'er-do-well brother of the 1837 revolutionary, and the Montreal businessman, George Moffatt. Everyone was prepared to play along, for reasons real or political. When the address came to a vote on 31 January 1846, one newspaper reported, "The whole House immediately rose amid a great clapping of hands." The Legislative Council hurried it through, and the address was dispatched to Britain. Prime Minister Robert Peel's sullen anger over the defiance was countered by the political recognition that rejection would throw Canada into turmoil. Britain did delay a favourable response for a full year. Still the symbolic deed was done.[11]

The Tories could not always hide their antipathy to the French and that would spill out in minor insults, such as the refusal to accept petitions in French, despite the recent address to Britain, or to reform election laws in Lower Canada that worked against the French Party. The careful efforts by Metcalfe and Draper were undercut by thoughtless insults. As the address was still under consideration by the Legislative Council, on 17 February 1845 the clown princes of Toryism, Henry Sherwood and Allan MacNab, showed their Anglo-Saxon colours. A Lower Canadian member of the Assembly, Joseph Laurin of Lotbinière, brought forward a petition from some constituents. Solicitor General Sherwood interrupted the startled Laurin to point out that the petition was only in French and therefore could not be considered while section 41 of the Union Act, which proscribed the use of French in Parliament and representations to Parliament, remained in force. French-speaking members were understandably both angry and confused, and a vigorous if unhelpful debate ensued. Then it was the turn of the rotund hero of 1837, the Speaker of the Assembly, Sir Allan MacNab. The Solicitor General was correct, he found, and therefore the petition could not be considered. The ruling was appealed, but upheld by a vote of thirty-one to thirty. There must be no question of races? A similar ethnic divide occurred when LaFontaine attempted to overturn election results in Montreal, where the usual chicanery had influenced the outcome of the last vote, and to improve the election laws in the lower province. The ministry's enthusiasm for justice to the French collided with its self-interest in protecting the system that gave it seats in Lower Canada. The Tory troops were whipped into line to maintain the status quo in which French Canadians were beaten and killed and denied the right to vote.[12]

What the Draper government did have in its favour was a dramatic shift in attitudes among the French-Canadian elite. Before the rebellions, many prominent politicians and journalists had foreseen French Canada thriving with liberal self-government and a vibrant francophone nationality. The defeats of 1837 and 1838, the threats posed by Lord Durham, and the Union itself, all shook that faith. The man sometimes called Quebec's first intellectual embodied the changing attitudes. Étienne Parent was the long-time editor of *Le Canadien* newspaper and an ardent advocate of liberal political reform. However, during the 1840s he lost confidence in a liberal solution. He had come to believe that French-Canadian nationalism was inconsistent with the materialistic liberalism championed by people such as Durham. He wrote in 1842 that the national question was now the primary issue, and political matters came far behind in importance. The commitment to a nationalism that was based on "traditional' values and that was to be the sole mission of French-Canadian leaders was shared by the Church. Indeed the Catholic Church, as the institution that survived rebellion and Union largely unscathed, gained new strength and asserted its social leadership in areas such as education.[13]

Ultramontane nationalism, deferring to the wisdom of a conservative church, was a threat to Baldwin's vision of a bicultural Canada with liberal political institutions. So too was the other cross-current in French Canada. Some young activists began to look to Europe for a politics of nationalism. There they found a liberalism more advanced than Baldwin's, and more secular than the Church could tolerate in Canada. This minority view found its focus on 17 December 1844. Some 200 young francophones—students, lawyers, and journalists—crowded into the chambers of the Société d'histoire naturelle in Montreal to found a new organization, the Institut canadien. They plunged into political, social, and economic studies, only awaiting a charismatic leader to make them a serious challenge to LaFontaine and Baldwin. There was another element in the mix. Montreal and Quebec had long competed for pre-eminence. Some ambitious Québécois resented Montreal's dominance of the liberal movement under LaFontaine.[14]

These were promising signs for the government. The newspaper that expressed the views of the Catholic hierarchy, *Les Mélanges religieux* of Montreal, had supported Metcalfe during the election of 1844 and stayed onside afterwards. As the parliamentary session began, another paper, the traditionally liberal *Le Canadien*, urged support for the government on the grounds that the Lower Canadian majority should act with the Upper Canadian majority; that is, double majority.[15]

Missteps by Reformers also helped the government. Many Protestants harboured profound suspicions about Catholics and felt deep unease about being politically aligned with papists. The discontent broke into the open just as Parliament was convening. The Toronto Reform paper, the *Examiner*, published excerpts from the controversial English polemicist, John Rogers, who contended that the chief factor retarding the progress of Christianity was popery. With no apparent embarrassment, the leader of the Orange Order and staunch Tory, Ogle Gowan, denounced the Reformers as anti-Catholic. Soon there was warfare within Reform ranks as Francis Hincks and the *Pilot* supported the rights of Catholics while the *Examiner* and the Toronto Presbyterian paper, the *Banner*, castigated popery. The verbal volleys lasted into the summer of 1845. The religious controversy was deepened by the regional. Isaac Buchanan, a one-time Reformer who defected to Metcalfe in 1844, decried Baldwin's "mawkish liberalism" in pandering to every French-Canadian prejudice.[16]

Mawkish it might seem to some, but Robert's sentiments were deep and real. On 6 February 1845 LaFontaine moved second reading of his bill on Lower Canadian elections. The ministry's opposition brought down Baldwin's ire. He was visibly angry when he rose to enter the debate and his emotions grew stronger as he talked. He warned of dire results if future elections were held under the present rules and challenged if the government was prepared to take responsibility for "the scenes of violence and bloodshed that might take place." Ever sensitive, Inspector General William Benjamin Robinson shouted, "Yes." Robert was both infuriated and saddened on behalf of French Canadians. They would not long accept "scenes which would deluge their city with blood, and fill the streets with troops." By this point he was in tears and almost inarticulate. Neither his words nor his tears moved the government. The election bill failed.[17]

Robert's support and visible emotions were not nearly enough as French-Canadian fears mounted. Louis LaFontaine felt the hot breath of nationalism on the back of his neck. He knew that criticism of the Reform alliance was building in French Canada after the electoral defeat of 1844. He might have to hurry to stay in front of his followers.

Sir Charles Metcalfe, when intriguing to strengthen his ministry in 1844, had seen LaFontaine himself as a weak link in Reform. As Metcalfe noted, "He is said to be generally disliked for his rude and overbearing demeanour." Certainly, LaFontaine was vain and could be curt with others. The personal, then, conspired with the national to force him to seize higher ground on the "French question."[18]

LaFontaine was prepared to play on the resentments of his flock. Between 1844 and 1846 he kept a list ready for political use. It chronicled the measures affecting Lower Canada that had been decided by Upper Canadian votes. It grew to seventeen items, some important, some minor, but all taken as evidence of Upper Canadian interference in matters that ought to be the jurisdiction of Lower Canadians alone. Yet LaFontaine's list did not account for the cases where Baldwin risked his Upper Canadian support to protect French Canada. LaFontaine had not complained in 1843 when two of the most important measures affecting the upper province—moving the capital from Kingston and land assessment in Upper Canada—had passed over the opposition of most Upper Canadian members. Nothing better exemplified Robert Baldwin's dilemma. He needed to maintain Upper Canadian support if he wished to reassure French Canada about the Reform alliance. However, one reason he had difficulty in maintaining that support was because of the assistance he gave to the Lower Canadians. Rolland Macdonald of Cornwall was an undistinguished member of the House, but he nicely skewered Baldwin on one horn of that dilemma during an 1846 debate on funding the judicial system of Canada West. Thomas Aylwin launched into one of his intemperate attacks on Upper Canadians. When Aylwin's boozy tirade was finished, Macdonald said he was waiting to hear from the member for Fourth York. Baldwin "pretended to represent the whole people and patriotism of Upper Canada," yet he sat silent before these insults. Macdonald warned that he "was not the only person who was watching the movements of the hon. Member the people of Upper Canada generally had their eyes upon him, and I would tell that hon. Member that a repetition of this conduct would send him from Upper Canada to Rimouski once more for a seat." Caught in this circle of suspicion, though, it was not altogether clear that Baldwin could rely on Rimouski either.[19]

Robert knew that there were persistent overtures to the French from the Tories, and that many of the Lower Canadians were ready to listen to offers. At the centre of much of it was René-Édouard Caron. Caron was a lawyer then in his mid-forties but with a long political pedigree. His father had sat in the Lower Canadian Assembly as had Caron himself. He was now mayor of Quebec and speaker of the legislative council. His appointment to the latter post by Metcalfe had been one of the bones of contention between the governor and LaFontaine and Baldwin. Caron had been wooed to accept a cabinet post in 1844, but demurred then. By 1845 Caron was the spokesman for a Quebec City cabal that LaFontaine called *la réaction*. Behind Caron was the strategist of the group, the clerk of the executive council, Étienne Parent. Their purpose was to oust LaFontaine as leader of the French Party. An alliance with Upper Canadian Tories seemed one way to do that. LaFontaine was well aware of the plot and tried to head it off by becoming more publicly nationalistic. He worked the double majority into his speeches and his pet newspapers talked of an arrangement where each section would choose its own ministers and agree not to impose legislation on each other. The message was garbled, however, since LaFontaine felt it necessary to continue to express his commitment to the united party and Baldwin.[20]

In the summer of 1845 William Henry Draper sounded out Caron on terms for an alliance. Caron prudently advised LaFontaine of the approach before meeting with Draper in Montreal. They recognized that LaFontaine was a roadblock. He could not be brought into government because of Metcalfe's animosity. Yet he had a sizeable following so he could not be ignored. The compromise to make the deal palatable included LaFontaine's appointment to the bench and Draper dropping his French loyalists, Viger and Papineau, with all their dirty linen, from the ministry.[21]

Caron told LaFontaine of the plan, but he rejected it. Significantly, however, LaFontaine conceded that if an administration were formed that had majority support among Lower Canadian members, he would leave politics rather than oppose it. He would never divide French Canada. It was a very different message from his public commitment to Baldwin and Reform. It was enough to embolden Draper and Caron. Sweet Draper dripped his honey on Caron. He would take care of LaFontaine so he could leave politics honourably. Baldwin,

Draper suggested, was tired of politics and ready to retire, so he was not a problem. LaFontaine, Draper pointed out, had endorsed double majority, so that policy was a legitimate basis upon which to reconstruct the government. The honey was so appealing that it promised to catch some important game. Prominent Reformers such as Augustin Morin were influenced by the argument that double majority would truly protect French Canada and the belief that LaFontaine would approve a ministry based on the principle. So the threat built through the fall despite private and public cries by Hincks about the absurdity of double majority. Why were Baldwin and LaFontaine silent, Hincks wanted to know. LaFontaine undoubtedly avoided speaking out because of his ambivalence about whether double majority was worth the destruction of the Reform alliance. Robert remained in numb silence because of his habitual tortured sensibilities. He could see that his dream of a new Canada was in mortal danger, yet even so he believed that French Canada had the right to decide its own destiny. As it developed, it was all moot. Metcalfe's health was ever worse and his incapacity made it impossible to proceed with any fundamental reconstruction of the government. Without his support and advocacy with Britain, it was hopeless to proceed. Discussions were broken off by the end of November.[22]

Robert could not yet relax. There was continuing turmoil in the Lower Canadian ranks. The erstwhile rebel chieftain, Louis-Joseph Papineau, had returned from exile in the midst of the Draper–Caron negotiations. Papineau had consorted with French leftists in Paris while banned from Canada, but he had lost none of his aristocratic demeanour. He was just short of his fifty-ninth birthday, yet he was vigorous, handsome, and compelling. His dress was immaculate, his curly hair cropped short, his eyebrows permanently raised in an attitude of detached disdain for all below him. Papineau was the French-Canadian paradox walking, the proud seigneur who carried the past with him, the advanced liberal who represented the dream of a new nation.

The Reform leaders exchanged anxious letters about the implications of Papineau's return, LaFontaine surveying the ground in Montreal, Robert trying to puzzle it out from Toronto. As Papineau began his journey to Canada, LaFontaine recounted with relief the rumour that Papineau would approve of the current Reform approach and, blessedly, would not return to politics. Robert and LaFontaine then agreed it would be best to maintain a discreet distance as the old rebel settled into Montreal. Others streamed to welcome the great man, but the party leaders bided time and tried to read the entrails. The Draper–Caron negotiations changed that. Baldwin might have thought the matter at an end when the talks broke off in November. But, then, he did not see the letter that LaFontaine wrote to Papineau on 6 December 1845. Papineau had made encouraging public noises about LaFontaine's political behaviour. Gratified, LaFontaine wrote to say that he wished to brief Papineau on recent correspondence, correspondence "d'une haute importance." The talk would have to be at LaFontaine's home, since he was too ill to venture out. Indeed, LaFontaine spent much of that winter of 1845–1846 confined to his house, tormented by rheumatism.[23]

LaFontaine's flirtation with Papineau, alerting him to the offers by Draper, was only part of the political stew in Montreal. While Baldwin in Toronto made an unsuccessful attempt to learn French, Hincks had been visiting LaFontaine in September 1845 with a scheme to reverse the Caron strategy. He thought they could extract Draper from the ministry, where he was distrusted by more extreme Tories, and lure him into alliance with the Reformers. Publicly, Hincks tried to play off the factions of the French Party. His newspaper, the *Pilot*, tacked artfully through the political waters. It contended that *Le Canadien* and the Quebec *réaction* were irresponsible for advocating double majority and an alliance with the Tories. LaFontaine, however, had always supported double majority and, the *Pilot*, enthused, that was statesmanlike. Further, since most Lower Canadian politicians supported it, Hincks was prepared to accept double majority. But it would certainly fail. It took a supple mind to keep all these ideas in the air at the same time.[24]

Robert Baldwin's mind was not supple. He had a single and simple program. He let some of the roils subside before he wrote LaFontaine on 16 October to warn him against the dangers of siren songs. There was no genuine interest by Draper and the Tories in double majority. "Depend on it there are no scruples about governing by any majority—however made up." At any rate, there was no reason to chase after untried and impractical innovations when so much had already been accomplished by the Reform alliance, and so many triumphs lay ahead. "I am more surprised at what has been accomplished than disappointed at more not having been done." This was the Baldwinian sense of destiny reasserting itself.[25]

It was not easy to maintain that optimism when disappointments compounded. The Draper–Caron correspondence ended in November 1845 but became public knowledge in April 1846. LaFontaine decided, apparently without consulting his colleagues, to lay the correspondence before the House of Assembly. His decision, so he said, was precipitated by Caron's plan to publish the documents in a pamphlet. Yet it appears that LaFontaine was the one who raised the possibility of publication when he met Caron in Montreal on Sunday, 8 March. Caron said he did not think it wise. LaFontaine went ahead and prepared a précis of the affair and passed it on to Caron. It was then Caron decided to make ready his own version since he felt that LaFontaine made the business sound more serious than Caron, now in full retreat from his earlier enthusiasm, contended it had been. So LaFontaine tried to trump him by going directly to Parliament.[26]

It was a messy business and a treacherous one for so direct a politician as Baldwin. He may not have known about LaFontaine's deception. If he did, he nevertheless felt obliged not only to support his colleague but to defend his rather tarnished honour. Government members attacked LaFontaine in the House for revealing private correspondence and for reading such material into the parliamentary record. Colonel John Prince of Essex, Upper Canada, flailed about in his usual fashion, turning the whole affair into a demonstration of unreasonableness of French Canadians. They had the golden opportunity to share power and they had niggled it away with petty differences until the negotiations collapsed. Prince unwittingly gave Baldwin his line of defence. Robert began by boring the House with a long list of British precedents for the sort of action taken by LaFontaine. However, he then turned Prince's comments on the Tories, in an effective parliamentary performance. Prince had shown French Canada the true face of conservatism. Baldwin had no doubt that "the opposite side would gladly take the votes of his hon. Friends, but he doubted whether they would give much in return." Lower Canadian members could only agree even if Prince tried to regain the initiative by calling Baldwin "the most impracticable minister the world ever saw" and warning the French Canadians that they would destroy themselves by allying with "the impracticables of Upper Canada." Prince's sputtering could not disguise the reality that Baldwin had come out of the affair with more credit than either his liberal colleague or the government.[27]

The ministry was desperate enough to try again. Governor General Cathcart, who succeeded the dying Metcalfe, authorized Draper in June 1846 to approach the French-Canadian liberals. Draper was as ruthless as he was anxious. Denis-Benjamin Viger, the veteran politician who had grown even older in his alienation from French Canada while serving the Tories since 1843, was ousted from cabinet along with the most rabid francophobe, Henry Sherwood. With those most obnoxious to the French gone, the pursuit of Caron could begin again. LaFontaine, at least, was more cautious than he had been the prior year, or so he claimed. When he looked back on the affair in April 1847 he told Joseph-Édouard Cauchon that he had abstained from offering Caron any advice and did not even see the correspondence with the ministry. His colleague A.-N. Morin was not so discreet. He had been willing to consider a cabinet post in 1845 and was similarly seduced by the prospect of power in this round of talks. Indeed he called a meeting that August in Montreal to discuss the possibility with a set of flexible liberals including George-Étienne Cartier, Wolfred Nelson, É.-P. Taché, Benjamin Holmes, Jacob DeWitt, and Lewis Drummond, a set of business-minded and largely conservative members of the French Party. Caron himself was absent in Quebec. The pliant group was interrupted by the arrival of Francis Hincks. While the others chatted and smoked their cigars, Hincks took Morin aside and persuaded him that Tory offers could not be trusted. Hincks carried the day and the second round was over.[28]

As in 1845, both the motives and the actions of the chief players remain obscure. The only account of the decisive meeting in Montreal is by Hincks, and that version, not surprisingly, makes him the hero. Cousin R.B. Sullivan was not convinced. He provided Robert with his assessment, couched in his usual florid prose. Caron was "a false sneaking knave" and Parent was "not fit to be Clerk in a lime Kiln." As for Hincks, he had worked both sides of the street on double majority in the *Pilot*. After all Hincks was in Montreal and dependent on Lower Canadians for his political, and journalistic, future. "Let us not blame him, but for heavens sake let him not act for us—his position forces him into a species of double dealing." On the basis that it takes one to know one, Sullivan's evaluation may have been accurate.[29]

Robert was not so concerned with who said what to whom, but with the future of French Canada. He had written to LaFontaine on 10 August that the protection of French Canada was more important than even political liberalism itself. The politics of race, and that was the essence of this affair, could only bring disaster. This was no glib attempt to shore up the alliance, for it echoed the letter of 1840 that had warned "there is and must be no question of races."[30]

Even Robert's patience grew short when it started up again the following year. Twice burned, Draper now had the new governor, Lord Elgin, initiate negotiations in February 1847. They first tried Morin, remembering his longing for office. Elgin's brother and aide, Colonel Robert Bruce, hand-delivered a "confidential memorandum" to Morin. Morin was weary of it too, and declined. Then they moved to Taché, with no greater success. Finally they fell back on the perpetual object of desire, Caron, who tried to involve Papineau. There was more interest in Quebec than in Montreal, driven by the former's jealousy of Montreal dominance. It was possible that French liberalism could split along geographic lines, so a worried LaFontaine began again to equivocate. Caron wrote him in April, insisting LaFontaine was crucial to the success of any new alignment. LaFontaine did not reject the idea, he merely said that he was too ill to take part in a reconstruction of the government. At any rate, LaFontaine suggested that Caron could certainly manage the matter easily enough without his help. Perhaps this was tongue in cheek, although LaFontaine was not famous for the sharpness of his wit. It was an equivocal, a political response.[31]

LaFontaine's ambivalence did not matter. The ministry itself tired of Caron's escalating demands and broke off negotiations at the end of April. The third round had ended like the first two. It embarrassed everyone involved, provided the occasion for much ill-tempered and petty invective in the press, and further discredited an already feeble government. Baldwin, at least, was satisfied. He congratulated LaFontaine that things had concluded so well for the party and the country. "[H]ad it terminated otherwise neither you nor I would live to see the last of the fruit that would have been produced from the mischief that would have been thus sown." He was less metaphorical, more blunt, when the issue arose in the House. Edward Ermatinger, a Tory from Middlesex, Upper

Canada, tried to prevent the embarrassing correspondence from being tabled in the Assembly. Baldwin's long controlled anger finally spilled out on the unfortunate member for Middlesex.

> [H]e admired the consistency of Mr. Ermatinger's conduct with his politics [and] his character, for he had always been an advocate of the suppression of the truth, and a supporter of arbitrary power. He belonged to a party which would ever suppress information, and crush every thing by the strong hand of power. He gave him great credit for courage in sticking to his coldness.[32]

Ermatinger cowered as the opposition benches erupted with cries of "Hear! Hear!" and derisive laughter. The House got the documents, Ermatinger got his treatment, and Baldwin got the last word on the Draper–Caron fiasco. Or almost. A group of chastened Quebec City politicians formed the Constitutional Committee of Reform and Progress. At their meeting on 30 July 1847, sixty-six members passed resolutions deploring the government's attempts to lure in French Canadians, and praising the performance of the late LaFontaine–Baldwin ministry. The chair of the meeting was René-Édouard Caron.[33]

※

Robert Baldwin was a trusting man. He believed in honour and assumed others shared his belief. All too often that trust was unmerited. The wavering French Party was hardly the first example. He had trusted Poulett Thomson, as he trusted the Britain that Thomson represented. Yet Thomson had lured him in, trapped in the neutrality of office like some insect in amber, while the governor built his own party to eclipse Baldwin's.

Robert had trusted John Rolph, a political colleague and personal friend. He had welcomed Rolph as his companion in the dangerous task of acting as intermediaries between Sir Francis Bond Head and the rebels gathered outside Toronto in November 1837. Only Robert was not in on the complicated games being played. He had not understood that Governor Head was only jockeying for time, not sincerely trying for a settlement. Nor did Robert know that Rolph had whispered to the rebel chieftain, Samuel Lount, to ignore Head's overtures and prepare to storm the city. When the emissaries returned to Mackenzie and Lount with a new message from Head, Rolph this time went off with Mackenzie, whispering something Baldwin could not catch. Only later did Robert learn that his colleague was telling Mackenzie that he would return to the city and rouse rebel sympathizers there. Small wonder Robert would retire to his home during the rebellion, feeling betrayed by both sides.[34]

The dilemma of trust reached into the Baldwin clan itself. The strength and importance of family rested on more than property. Family was bound by affection and by mutual obligation. Robert felt that obligation even when it was not reciprocated. Witness his relationship with Robert Baldwin Sullivan. Sullivan had a particular pull on Robert as not only a first cousin but as the brother of Eliza. Robert loved and protected Sullivan despite his cousin's personal and political failings. Sullivan was Robert's polar extreme, a charming and outgoing man, an orator who enthralled audiences with his flowery speech and his well-cultivated "country Irish" accent, a drinker and roisterer—and a political opportunist. His sense of family obligation was not well developed. In the spring of 1836 Robert was grieving Eliza's death and struggling through the executive council crisis with Francis Head. Sullivan administered the final wound. When Robert and his colleagues resigned, Head reconstructed the council on unregenerate, unresponsible lines. Among those to accept his call to office was Sullivan. Yet, far from denouncing his cousin's betrayal, Robert congratulated him on his post and he urged his father to forgive the renegade. "And oh above all things let not the political differences interfere with the cultivation of [family love]—but on the contrary where such unhappily exist always forget the politician in the relation."[35]

Again in 1841, when Robert resigned office on the principle of responsibility, Sullivan (then commissioner of Crown lands in Sydenham's ministry) remained in office. Sullivan came home to the political fold when it was to his advantage, when his cousin formed a government in 1842. Now Sullivan was the most partisan of Reformers. He would leave office with Robert and LaFontaine in 1843. But few, looking at his performance since 1836, would see it as an act of principle. One Tory, John Macaulay, expressed the common cynicism about Sullivan in 1843.

> How beautifully consistent are the entrée and the exit of
> President [of the executive council] Sullivan. He came in high
> & fierce under Sir Frank [Head], against the very moderate
> principle of the first Baldwin Ministry and he goes out equally
> fierce in favour of an out & out responsibility principle . . . See
> to what point a disregard of political honesty may soon lead a
> clever man.[36]

Through all the twists and turns, Robert continued to practice law with
Sullivan. That too had its tribulations. Sullivan was a bad businessman,
and not always scrupulously honest. As commissioner of Crown lands
before the Union, for example, he had woefully neglected the state's
business and he had lent out public funds to members of his department
and deposited government money in his own account. He was equally
feckless in the law business, having difficulty keeping track of accounts
or collecting them. Robert was patient with his partner-relative, even
though he knew many of Sullivan's problems sprang from alcoholism.
That made him a liability as a politician, as well as a lawyer. His tongue
loosened when he was drinking, and he could embarrass the party with
his intemperate comments. "For God's sake," LaFontaine implored
Baldwin in December 1843, "try to prevail on Sullivan to amend you
know what I mean." And a month later Hincks insisted Sullivan must
take the temperance pledge to abstain from alcohol. "There is no end to
the reports here [at Kingston] about him. He is utterly ruined unless he
takes the Pledge." To Robert's relief, Sullivan did join a total abstinence
society in February 1844. Rumours persisted that Sullivan periodically
fell off the wagon and in the spring of 1848 the rumours were confirmed.
He had, a relative wrote, "broken out again."[37]

Still, against his own better judgment, Robert once again accepted
Sullivan into the Reform cabinet of 1848. In September of that year he
sent him to his reward, appointing his bibulous cousin to the bench.
It was at no small cost, clearly, that Robert preserved family ties and
his emotional link to Eliza. But it was a cost he willingly paid, for he
retained a naively idealized conception of family. Despite the example of
R.B. Sullivan before him, he could still write in 1843, "[W]e cannot too
sedulously cultivate family union & affection it affords a circle within
which we may hope to be at least free from treachery."[38]

Chapter 13

An Enlarged View Must Be Taken

Responsible government was no longer a chimera. It existed and, if he played the game well, it would be his to exercise. How proud Eliza would be. It was a decade since she went.

The longer the second Parliament dragged on, the more it seemed likely that Reform would win the next election. Robert Baldwin worked hard to assure that would be so. With responsible government so near, the Holy Grail now visible, he scouted new alliances that would guarantee victory. One of those scouting expeditions showed how anxious he had become, how the importance of the result could compromise his political judgment. He was actively pursuing the Tory of Tories; Sir Allan MacNab.

The men had been enemies long before the Union and they had shown each other the most savage hostility in the House. They had only two things in common: a dislike for the government and a lust for power, albeit for different reasons. LaFontaine had seen MacNab's discontent with Draper conservatism and several times since 1844 had suggested to Baldwin that something might be worked out with the "gallant knight," as MacNab's admirers called him. The opportunity came in 1846 when MacNab accepted the post of adjutant general of militia from Governor General Cathcart. Cathcart had not confirmed MacNab's choice of deputies with the government, and the ministers rejected them. A furious MacNab resigned the position.[1]

Francis Hincks and the *Pilot* immediately began to fish the troubled waters with charges that MacNab had been the victim of government "foul play." Robert dithered for some time, but finally agreed to join the wooing of MacNab. The issue became whether Sir Allan should resign his seat. Some spiteful Tories claimed that MacNab had accepted the position of adjutant general and therefore should follow custom by resigning and seeking re-election. Robert found a rationalization in the belief that MacNab had never functioned in the position. In a letter to LaFontaine, he wrote:

> I of course would not commit myself or wish others to commit themselves to a false principle for the sake of any momentary triumph over an opponent whether he were in the ministry or not. But it is clearly a question of which an enlarged view must be taken and while, on the one side a full bona fide and absolute acceptance must be given its constitutional effect . . . on the other a mans seat ought not to be knocked from under him upon any little contemptible nicety.

Robert was overlooking that he had spent much of his career arguing the necessity for scrupulous respect for constitutional niceties.[2]

Sir Allan was ready to deal. He came to see Robert in Toronto that December and won assurance that the Reformers would support his struggle to keep his seat. The visit made Robert uncharacteristically enthusiastic. The government would not survive the next session, he was sure. He asked LaFontaine to call all Reformers to Montreal two or three days before Parliament reconvened to plot strategy. What he did not count on was the long delay before the House met. The government let a full year pass between sessions, long enough for Tory anxieties to build. Robert delegated Henry John Boulton, himself a former Tory, to act as an intermediary with MacNab and his followers. As the recess trailed on, more and more Tories decided it was too dangerous to break with the government. By the time the House finally did meet, on 2 June 1847, the MacNab strategy was clearly inadequate to defeat the ministry.[3]

There was enough sting in the ploy to hurt the government, nevertheless. On the first day of the session, William Benjamin Robinson took his seat after a by-election in Simcoe County, Upper Canada. Two ministers, Dominick Daly and James Smith, had issued the writ for that election. Baldwin rose to ask if the seat of the Speaker—Sir Allan MacNab—was vacant since the speaker ordinarily issued writs. He requested the writs be tabled and there proved to be two, one from MacNab as Speaker dated 4 July 1846 and one from Daly and Smith dated 6 July 1846. The latter requested the Clerk of the Crown to provide an election writ under the independence of parliament act since the Speaker had allegedly vacated his seat. Robert was delighted at this "extraordinary situation: . . . here was a warrant assuming that there was no Member for Hamilton and no Speaker, and there was a gentleman in the Chair professing to be both." The best the ministry could do was buy some time by agreeing to produce the documents on the case at a future session. Attention was further diverted that day when William Henry Draper announced that he was resigning his seat to go to the bench.[4]

Robert would not let go of it. On Friday, 4 June he was back hammering away at Daly and the Crown clerk, Felix Fortier. The ministry tried to prevent Robert from questioning Speaker MacNab, but enough Tories bolted to sustain Robert's motion to do so. MacNab managed to present himself as a humble man wronged, while Baldwin made Daly appear both incompetent and malicious. The government decided to reduce its losses and Baldwin's motion that MacNab had not, in reality, vacated his seat was carried by a vote of seventy-two to one, with only the perverse Tommy Aylwin dissenting.[5]

The MacNab affair hurt the ministry, but did not topple it. Nor did it lead to a Tory-Reform alliance. MacNab continued to sniff about, offering fanciful suggestions for a coalition. He insisted that the very epitome of reaction, John Hillyard Cameron, be included in a joint Tory-Reform ministry. When that found no enthusiasm he settled for retention of the Speakership should Reform come to office. The intoxication of power was never better illustrated than by the fact that it was not until January 1848, in the midst of the next election, that Robert finally washed his hands of MacNab. However Robert rationalized it, it had been a sorry affair, at least as unprincipled as Draper's pursuit of Caron. After all, there was a basis for claiming some ideological common ground between the Tories and the French Canadians. There was none in the case of Baldwin and MacNab. There was only political opportunism. Standing a few seats shy of toppling the government and thus reversing what he saw as the unjust verdict of 1844, Baldwin let his anxiety propel him off the pedestal and down among ordinary politicians. A shrewd ordinary politician, however, would have chosen more likely game than Sir Allan and might not have come home empty handed.

The pursuit of MacNab was part of what amounted to a two-year election campaign. It had begun in the summer of 1846 when Hincks reminded Baldwin about how ineffective the party organization had been in the last election, and insisted that the leader get out into the country to assure that such a failure did not reoccur. Robert did so with an enthusiasm he had never shown before. The scent of ultimate success was in the air. Indeed, the odour grew ever stronger. No only could Robert sense victory, he knew it could be a sweeter one than before. The Reformers would be able to govern without the constant harassment they had endured from Sir Charles Metcalfe when last in office. A new governor was appointed, and he seemed promising. James Bruce, Earl of Elgin, arrived in Montreal on 29 January 1847. He made his ceremonial entrance into the city the following day. Montreal greeted him in characteristic fashion. The streets were clogged with snow and Elgin's one-horse sleigh struggled into the city along the almost impassable road from Monklands. Nevertheless, there was a grand procession awaiting him, led by the mayor John E. Mills. Despite the weather, it was a triumphant passage along Great St. James and Notre-Dame Streets to Government House where Elgin was sworn in. For Baldwin, more important than the pomp was that Elgin came armed with instructions to concede untrammelled responsible government. In future, governors would be strictly neutral between parties and must recognize that their ministers would be justified in resigning if the governor refused their advice. Robert was indeed close to the kill.[6]

Elgin was still a young man, thirty-five at his appointment, but he had impressive credentials. His brilliance had been attested to at Eton and Oxford, and he had moved on to a political career in the British House of Commons and then, on the death of his father and older brother, in the House of Lords. His experience included nearly four years as governor of Jamaica. Elgin was a political conservative, but Baldwin could overlook the awkward fact, given that Elgin, shortly before he left for Canada, had married Lady Mary Lambton, eldest daughter of the late, sainted Lord Durham. Robert could actually overlook the new governor, for Elgin was an unprepossessing little man in person. He was short, as stout as Robert himself, and nearly bald. A closer look, however, showed a man with steely determination. His eyes were cold and piercing, his mouth tight and severe, his whole countenance stern in its frame of iron-grey muttonchops. He looked what he would prove to be, a statesman of intelligence, courage, but scant sympathy.[7]

The Durham connection, Robert was certain, was the way to Elgin's favour. A few days before Christmas, 1846, Robert sat in his study at the Front Street house and composed a lecture on the subject to Louis LaFontaine, who was home in Montreal for the holidays. He urged LaFontaine and the Lower Canadians to flatter the Governor General; his wife; and his brother and secretary, Colonel Bruce, who was being rushed by Tories anxious to introduce him to all of the pleasures of Montreal. As Robert told LaFontaine, it was fortunate that the Elgins were in French Canada since "you beat us hollow in the art of making yourselves agreeable." Apparently LaFontaine and his colleagues were not as impressive in strategic thinking, for Robert felt the need to school them in the basics of dealing with authority.

> In all this there must be exercised a sound discretion and a delicate appreciation of persons & things, their feelings & positions. I certainly believe that I am as little inclined to yield in the mere courtier spirit to the pleasure of those in power as any man and still less to become a panderer to their self love. But mankind must be taken as we find them and allowance must be made for the prejudices of education & habits and a judicious discretion observed not only to avoid offence to such prejudices & habits but in order if possible to make a favourable impression on the parties themselves. This is perfectly compatible both with respect for the Superior towards whom it is used & manly independence in oneself. Within these legitimate bounds let us endeavour to make a favourable first impression if we can.[8]

Robert was scrupulous in deferring to LaFontaine as the party leader, yet he wrote to him as if he were a rather dull underling. Robert's own unease spoke here, as well. He was convincing himself that the compromises made in the name of electoral success were honourable ones.

He had already begun to follow his own advice. He commenced a measured march toward the next election, accepting invitations to speak in East Halton and Norfolk, but declining those from Brantford and

Niagara because, as he told LaFontaine, he did not want to appear to be mounting a general "tour of agitation." Tories knew that he was doing exactly that and their press warned that the dinners were building reform support. As the *Globe* commented about one Tory paper, he "appeals to his readers against his friends being eaten out of office."[9]

Dundas was a few hours' ride west of Toronto and Robert trotted there on Wednesday, 11 November 1846 for the meeting with the Reformers of East Halton at a large wooden tavern. The faithful crowded in, tables pushed to the walls to accommodate chairs for several hundred, buzzing with excitement as they digested their roast dinner and prepared to absorb their leader's wisdom. It was not the sort of setting in which Robert was comfortable for he liked neither crowds nor the reek of tobacco and beer that permeated the room. Nevertheless, the occasion was important and he rose to it. The Durham strategy for winning the Governor General was the core of his address that evening. The Reformers of East Halton, he pointed out, had been the first, back in 1839, to mount a demonstration on behalf of "the Text-book of British Colonial Rights," the Durham Report. The Durham strategy was the starting point for an articulation, the clearest articulation, of his political creed, an articulation so important that it was published as a pamphlet and circulated throughout the Canadas.[10]

Durham had come from Britain and that was evidence of Britain's goodwill toward the colony. So too, Robert imagined, was the Metcalfe crisis. A series of imperial statesmen—Russell, Peel, and Stanley—had all endorsed the basic concept of responsible government. Had any of them been governor in place of Sir Charles, there would have been no crisis. Nor should the Halton Reformers despair about a conservative government in Britain. No British Tory was as reactionary as the Canadian Tory, who had been "nurtured under the numbing influence of the old colonial system." So long as Canadians shouldered their responsibility and held to the Durham faith, they would prevail.

Their cause was destined to triumph but, if they wanted that triumph to come soon, they must follow a careful political course. The key words were moderation and unity. Baldwin had always been moderate. He challenged anyone "to put their finger on a single act of my political life that deserved any other designation." Moderation was no shapeless thing. It meant fighting for the rights handed down by their ancestors, but always fighting with the weapons provided by the constitution. "<u>Union is strength</u>." They could not expect him to carry on with the heavy burden of leadership unless the party was united. Accept the necessary implications of being a political party. Try to find candidates who are acceptable, but support the party candidate whomever that might be. Their friends in Lower Canada, who made victory possible, had the right to expect no less.[11]

When he sat in his study at Spadina, though, he knew that unanimity in Upper Canada was chimerical. He admitted to LaFontaine in a letter in 1847, "We are not materials so easily combined as yours in Lower Canada." He was working steadily, however, working in the fashion that best suited his temperament. He could deliver a good party speech, as the East Halton oration had shown. His preference, all the same, was to stay at home and rally his lieutenants by correspondence. Letter after letter warned the faithful of the deadly perils of dissension in the ranks. He told LaFontaine that he believed the message was having effect, even if some eastern counties remained "backward" in their political understanding. They would do well in Upper Canada when the dying government finally gave up the ghost and an election was held.[12]

Unhappily, it was not only backward counties that nursed dissension. The newspaper war between the *Pilot* and the *Globe* continued to tax Robert's patience. Some Upper Canadians deeply resented the favour shown to Hincks and his paper. William McDougall was a rising star on the the more radical wing of the party in Toronto, and himself a budding journalist. He spoke for many in his opinion that the *Pilot* was out of touch with the sentiments of Upper Canadians and that it was an instrument of Montreal dominance over the party. George Brown said amen. The *Pilot* was being subsidized as a party organ, at the expense of his *Globe* and other papers. In western Canada Reformers could subscribe to the *Pilot* for only two dollars a year, while the *Globe*, competing in the market, had to charge five dollars. Brown could also have pointed out that even with subsidies the Montreal paper was chronically financially unstable.[13]

The arguments did not sway Baldwin. The party had to have a voice in Montreal and, for better or worse, the *Pilot* was it. He would continue to raise funds to keep the journal in business. Indeed, he had more ambitious plans for the party press. In 1847 he was exploring the possibility of supporting a newspaper in London, England, perhaps the *Morning Chronicle*. He believed that Reformers had "undervalued" the importance of representing their views at the imperial capital, a truth he had discovered by bitter experience back in 1836. It never came to fruition, but the idea demonstrated that Baldwin's political instincts were sharpening as he neared power. When in government he would consider going farther. In the spring of 1848 he and the young Toronto Reformer, Hume Blake, discussed taking over the *Globe* and converting it, as Blake said, into "a permanent organ of the party & now of the government." Again, the plan fell through. What it showed, even as only a wisp of an idea, was that Baldwin understood the need for political parties to become institutions if responsible government were to succeed.[14]

That party institution was still an elite one under Baldwin. He spoke often of the "people," but within the Reform Party the role of the people was to support the leadership and the candidates. As they prepared for an election, Robert had to stifle incipient democratic impulses so as to maintain his control. The old Reformer from Halton, James Durand, was one who challenged Baldwin's monolithic view of party. Durand contended that delegates to nominating conventions were obligated to vote as instructed by their township meetings. Baldwin was having none of this. Durand had to understand that the only obligation of delegates was to decide on the man "most likely to secure the success of the cause." Durand's theory would prevent the party from finding ridings for notables. That, of course, may have been exactly what democrat Durand had in mind.[15]

How frustrating for the party liberals to watch Baldwin find safe harbours for his chosen. Hincks's defeat in Oxford in 1844 worried Robert, and he thought of moving Hincks to a safer constituency, Norfolk; however, soundings there made it clear that Hincks would fare no better. Robert then decided the riding would be suitable for another notable, the recent recruit, Henry John Boulton. The leader wrote to a local organizer that he first thought of putting Boulton in the East Riding of York, but then Hume Blake was nominated there. He held consultations with Price, Sullivan, and Blake—all Torontonians, none with any ties to Norfolk county—and they decided to place Boulton in Norfolk. It was a remarkable demonstration of a leadership-dominated party, as well as of Baldwin's willingness to sup with the devil in the interests of victory. Boulton, the urbane Toronto aristocrat, would be imposed on the farmers of the county. And what an unlikely Reformer he was. His clan was the very core of the old Family Compact. He himself was the persecutor of William Lyon Mackenzie in the 1830s, a Tory of the Tories. The good folk of Norfolk would have to swallow deeply. Obediently, they did so, nominating Boulton and electing him in 1848.[16]

Baldwin was busy not only finding ridings for important recruits but taking constituencies away from the unfavoured. He apparently was undaunted by the fiasco in East Halton in 1844, when he blackballed Caleb Hopkins and ended up giving the seat to the Tories. It was again Halton in 1847, this time the West riding, which had now been retitled Waterloo. James Durand had lost this traditional Reform seat in 1844. Baldwin was not prepared for another defeat there and so Durand had to go. Robert circulated a list of acceptable candidates to local organizers, a list that did not include James Durand. Robert's personal favourite was a long-time activist, Adam Johnston Fergusson, and he was duly nominated in April 1847. Durand felt betrayed after his years of service, as well he might, and even Baldwin recognized the need to soothe him. He had written to Durand before the nominating convention to thank him for his past efforts and to urge party unity. It was a gracious gesture, except that Baldwin had sent copies of the letter to prominent Reformers in Waterloo. Durand was humiliated by this advertisement of his ouster. He was still a Reformer, he wrote Baldwin, and would continue to recognize Robert as his leader, but he would not support Fergusson. Once again, as in 1844, Baldwin's attempt to play political boss had alienated a strong and effective liberal. And the result was the same. James Webster took the riding for the Tories.[17]

The scent of power was intoxicating stuff, even for so stolid a man as Robert Baldwin. There in the Toronto study, amid his books, he dreamed exotic thoughts. They could waft him far away from his rock principles. He would now welcome almost anyone, however aberrant, into his caucus as he demonstrated with MacNab and Boulton. Preparing for the 1847 session of Parliament, he was musing to LaFontaine that they might pursue yet more mossy-backed Tories, members of the British Party in Lower Canada. He would even welcome the arch traitors themselves, Denis Papineau and Viger. Heady with the scent, he suggested they attempt to defeat the newly appointed Attorney General East, William Badgley, in his by-election in Missisquoi. Baldwin admitted that had had never believed it proper to contest elections that arose simply by acceptance of office. Yet he rationalized this was somehow different because it did not involve the re-election of an incumbent but the election of a new member. He was forced to admit the real reason: "And we have too a ministry so weak as to make every vote a matter of the utmost importance." The artful justification was wasted. Badgley was elected; Viger and Papineau stayed where they were. The Reformers would have to be patient and win their victory the old-fashioned way, at the polls.[18]

The economy and immigration were more important than political games, at any rate. The Tory ministry avoided the House until June 1847. The sour odour of a sickly government was made more rank by unseasonable heat, and by death. Ship fever was in the harbour, so close to Parliament. The smell emanated from musty ideas as well. That spring, thinking about the session ahead, John A. Macdonald had written to the Orange leader, Ogle Gowan, despairing over party divisions. The Compact wing of the Tory Party, what Macdonald called the "Toronto clique," was growing stronger and it would make the ministry "stink in the nostrils of all liberal minded people" and assure a Reform victory in the next election. Macdonald's own accession to office as receiver general in May did little to arrest the decline.[19]

Baldwin's major concern was the governor, not the ministry. He knew that in Nova Scotia the liberals were being tarred with personal antagonism to the Lieutenant Governor, and he saw Tories in Canada trying out the same canard. That might influence the new viceroy, and so Reformers had to be prepared for Elgin "throwing himself into the melée not perhaps as openly in defiance of all constitutional decency as Lord Metcalfe did but as thoroughly as he possibly can consistently with the forms of constitutional etiquette." Elgin had, after all, taken a leading role in the approaches to Caron and Morin, and that certainly put him at least on the edges of the melee. Robert would have worried all the more had he access to Elgin's private correspondence with the Colonial Office. The governor denounced the "unnatural alliance between the Baldwin & French factions" and complained of their bitterness toward him, presumably in reaction to the Caron negotiations.[20]

Whatever Elgin's private opinions, all groups tried to win his favour. Macdonald was anxious to keep the governor out of the grasp of the

Compact Tories and courted him with all his boozy charm. Baldwin was urging a reluctant LaFontaine to put aside his well-founded suspicion of viceregal politics and join in the wooing of Elgin. The governor could not help whom he was, could not escape the prejudices that were engrained by his background, and LaFontaine must make allowances for that. Neither of the liberals saw the irony in their positions. Both, from their different perspectives, were reading partisanship into Elgin's early actions in Canada when, in fact, he was simply doing his job as a responsible governor. Within the limits of Baldwin's "constitutional etiquette" it was Lord Elgin's task to support whatever ministry was in office. As for the Reformers, it surely was the task of a political party in a responsible regime to woo the electorate, not the governor, and assume the governor would play his part in a non-partisan fashion. LaFontaine was closer to the appropriate posture than Baldwin, albeit for the wrong reasons, in assuming that they should go about their business and let the governor go about his.[21]

The Reformers did go about their business during the parliamentary sitting. It was clear to everyone this would be the last session before an election, what with a new governor, the failed negotiations with the French, and an ever-weaker ministry. The old market building was crowded with the eighty-four members of the House, eighty-four uneasy, uncertain men, sweating in their frock coats, tempers on very short leash. And there was the cholera. The barque *Syria* had arrived at Quebec from Liverpool on 14 May. Nine passengers had died of cholera en route and fifty-two more were ill. Every day more died in the dockside hospital, alarmingly close to the parliamentary chamber itself. The misery compounded as more ships arrived, overwhelming the medical facilities at Quebec and upriver at Montreal. The *Pilot* reported on the conditions in mid-June. "The state of the immigrants at the sheds is really awful. Language is inadequate to describe the misery and wretchedness that prevails there. Twenty-five were buried on Sunday, and six died yesterday morning. The food is altogether unfit for the poor famishing wretches. Hard, black biscuit, surely is not proper food." To make matters worse, the weather suddenly changed from oppressive heat to bone-chilling cold.[22]

Through it all some retained their certainty. Robert Baldwin had his strategy and would pursue it with consistency. When he moved the Reform amendment to the ministry's address in reply to the speech from the throne, he launched into an extended eulogy to Lord Durham and expressed his hope that Elgin would help to achieve Durham's lofty ideals. Not everyone took so elevated a tone. Gowan of Leeds had no love for Baldwin since Robert had tried to suppress the Orangeman's power base four years earlier. Gowan attacked where Baldwin's strategy was most vulnerable, the attempt to cloak the Reformers in the mantle of Lord Durham while still placating French Canada. Gowan thought the House might be interested in hearing some passages from the Durham Report, and he read into the record the most inflammatory, anti-French extracts. There was more literature that might enlighten the Assembly. Now Gowan resurrected the Caron correspondence, from which he drew the lesson that the French were more than willing to desert Baldwin, and that Robert was only saved because the ministry itself abandoned the matter. It was time to face the truth, Gowan insisted. The French-Baldwin alliance was simply one of convenience. Baldwin himself was no man of principle. He had always resigned from office over patronage, a somewhat hyperbolic charge, but one that stung. And what did Baldwin do when he could not dine at the government trough? He "lends his aid like an itinerant mountebank to agitate the Province from Huron to the Ottawa! Where was the great principle at stake?"[23]

Gowan's tone was more suited to this session than Baldwin's. It was Pierre Chauveau from Quebec County, not Robert, who took on Gowan. He reminded the Orangeman about a town in the United States that still remembered French invasions during the colonial wars. There, parents threatened unruly children with the cry, "Rouville and the Frenchmen!" The government backbenchers were like those children, kept in line by cries of "Baldwin and the Frenchmen!" Both Gowan and Chauveau would soon find the old threat was losing its force. The ministry could barely maintain a majority as once staunch supporters began to desert an obviously sinking ship. The ministry's incapacity prevented the passage of controversial legislation, such as John A. Macdonald's effort to resolve the university question.[24]

Baldwin had his way on his pet grievance: the civil list. It was an essential principle of responsible government, despite Gowan's cynicism on the issue, that patronage rest in the hands of the colonial ministers, and its funding rest with Parliament. The Assembly had requested that the civil list be ended and salaries be placed under parliamentary control, but Britain had ignored the request. Henry Sherwood of Toronto, who was the de facto premier after Draper's departure, guessed that Britain did not want to be engaged in "constantly tinkering with the union Act," and so had delayed action on both the civil list and French language disabilities until it was ready for a general overhaul of the constitution. That was not good enough for Baldwin. The civil list was crucial to the operation of a free government, yet the House's request had been reserved by the governor, neglected by Britain and ignored by the Canadian executive. "Why, it was bundled home with all the trifling turnpikes and charity Corporation Acts, and not a word has since been heard about it, and not an Enquiry made as to it by the Provincial Administration!" He thought he knew why. "It might be however that the gentlemen opposite had other engagements on their hands of a more urgent character, negociations with friends without, and friends within." Baldwin carried the day. A new address to Britain was adopted on 28 June and, later that year, the imperial Parliament passed legislation giving Canada control over its government and civil service salaries.[25]

Baldwin tried to establish that, even if Britain acted on the civil list, there was no legitimate government in Canada to manage it, only a set of factions struggling over power. For example, on 17 June he harassed Inspector General Cayley over the case of Samuel Jarvis who was accused of cheating Aboriginal people out of £800 while serving as Superintendent of Indian Affairs. Cayley said that, as a personal friend of Jarvis, he would attempt to explain the case. That bemused Baldwin. How could Cayley be two people at once—the member speaking personally and the spokesman for the government? The confusion was all too typical of this sorry executive.

> [I]t would be very desirable to know which of the hon. gentlemen opposite was the leader of Her Majesty's Government. There seemed to be great doubt on the point, especially among the Hon. gentlemen themselves. ... The Opposition were not particular—they were willing to take any of the Hon. gentlemen opposite, but I do trust they would lay their heads together and select someone to speak the sentiments of the Government.

Cayley did not need to consult. He popped up to advise Baldwin, "I, at any rate, am not the leader of the Government."[26]

Robert was growing impatient as he waited for power, and it showed in debates. In early July he made an unsuccessful attempt to impeach

D.-B. Papineau, and in the argument he went well beyond what he himself had defined as acceptable parliamentary speech. Papineau, Baldwin charged, "stood convicted by his own counsels of being the incompetent officer, the imbecile, he was reputed to be." This was the same individual Robert was prepared to recruit into his party a few months earlier. He painted the whole government side with a broad brush of contempt. There were no principles there, just self-interest. They were "all making their way over the stile with something of the same spirit as a flock of sheep getting into a clover field." Even worse, they were wolves in sheep's clothing, claiming to be conservatives when they made unacceptable appointments, degrading the Legislative Council, and behaving unethically. And he claimed the mantle of true conservatism for himself and his constitutional loyalists.[27]

Some of his followers must have cringed, for they did not all share Baldwin's embrace of conservative values, and certainly not the title. For the moment, such differences were muted by the prospect of power. They could appreciate the leader's new-found aggressiveness, his wit and self-control. The base had been laid for the campaign to come.

——◆——

The Baldwin who shaded his principles as he sensed the closeness of responsible government was the aberration, seduced by that heady siren. He had always been the steadfast arbiter of morals for his friends and family. It was typical that Robert Sullivan would turn to his cousin Robert for advice and help in 1824. Sullivan was worried about his younger brother Augustus who had fallen into "wretched habits." He was sure that Robert could sort out the boy. In 1839 it was R.B. Sullivan himself who needed sorting out. Sullivan was in trouble, presumably because of his excessive drinking. Uncle John Spread Baldwin had called on Robert to counsel the errant Sullivan. J.S. was grateful that Robert had been so kind to Sullivan, that he had shown him true religious feeling. Robert did so at a time when Sullivan was still part of the Tory oligarchy that was trying to thwart Robert at every turn. And, just as MacNab was a politician who had to be bought every Monday, Sullivan was a relative who had to be rescued at least as often.[28]

Chapter 14

The Phrase or the Content

It would be prudent and fitting to stop here, now that responsible government was accomplished. Little more was needed than to fill up the great achievement with the few institutions of national culture that would complete it. How proud Eliza would be. She had been dead nearly twelve years.

The third Parliament of the Province of Canada convened on Friday, 25 February 1848. Lord Elgin and his brother Colonel Bruce rode in from Monklands along the snowy streets to the old market building. At precisely three o'clock that afternoon the governor strode into the legislative council chamber where the councillors and the newly elected members of the Assembly waited. Elgin's military finery was a dash of colour in a sea of black suits. His flash was soon gone; he announced that he would give the Speech from the Throne on Monday, but now the Assembly should gather in its own chamber to elect a Speaker.

The House set down to that business at 3:30 p.m. Inspector General Cayley and the independent member for Essex, John Prince, nominated Sir Allan MacNab for speaker. The vote demonstrated how much had changed in a few months. MacNab's nomination was defeated, yeas nineteen, nays fifty-four. Then Robert Baldwin and Louis LaFontaine proposed the name of A.-N. Morin. He was elected without opposition. The only question now was when the government would change.[1]

In 1852, a European sage would write words that were all too apt as this fully responsible Reform government was about to assume office:

> Men make their own history, but they do not make it as they please; they do not make it under self-selected circumstances, but under circumstances existing already, given and transmitted from the past. The tradition of all dead generations weighs like

a nightmare on the brains of the living. . . . The social revolution of the nineteenth century cannot take its poetry from the past but only from the future. It cannot begin with itself before it has stripped away all superstition about the past. The former revolutions required recollections of past world history in order to smother their own content. The revolution of the nineteenth century must let the dead bury their dead in order to arrive at its own content. There the phrase went beyond the content—here the content goes beyond the phrase.[2]

Robert Baldwin delivered to Canada his greatest gift that winter of 1848: a sturdy and workable form of government that would give the country a firm political base. However, he was not the man to move on with a quiet revolution, not the man to bury the dead and find poetry in the future. Those heady days of victory began his triumph and his ultimate humiliation.

The second Parliament had been prorogued on 28 July 1847 and a prolonged election campaign began. Baldwin chose his issues carefully. The university question was an emotional one in Upper Canada, combining visions of the province's future with religious divisions. He gave it a prominent place in the campaign and mustered ostensibly non-partisan support from a broadly based university reform committee that issued an address in December endorsing Baldwin's late university bill and rejecting Macdonald's. Responsible government and its virtues, of course, were a constant theme. What gnawed at Baldwin, though, was party unity. Dissension could ruin this opportunity and he worked hard to silence it. As he had written to James Durand in April, there was a "general break up" of the old political order and Reform had to seize the chance now or be ruined. The government's negotiations with the French had shown that time was short, that Lower Canadians would not wait for Upper Canada to pull itself together. "What use they will say of our waiting for your defeat, when defeat is already made certain by the internal dissentions among yourselves . . . see how you are cut up."[3]

Reformers remained fractious and internal feuds sometimes spilled out into the open. As the campaign began in earnest in December 1847, two Toronto liberal papers were sniping over the ancient rebel, William Lyon Mackenzie. The *Globe* did not want a potential Reform government to offer him a special amnesty and could not understand sympathy for a traitor. The *Examiner* supported Mackenzie and, condescendingly, pointed out that *Globe* publisher George Brown had not been in Canada in 1837 and could not possibly understand the situation. The controversy petered out without much damage, but it was a forewarning of how explosive the issues surrounding Mackenzie would be.[4]

Robert had much to preoccupy him in his own riding without controversy elsewhere. The old constituency of Fourth York was now called York North. It was still the same mix of small towns and prosperous farms. What was new was the opponent. The Tories put up Hugh Scobie, editor of the Toronto *British Colonist*. Scobie was merely the tail of his campaign manager, the fiercely partisan and abusive Tory William Boulton, member of the Assembly for Toronto City. Baldwin, along with James Hervey Price in First York, was a special target. The conservative press kept up a barrage of attacks on the Reform leader, and predictions of his defeat. The Montreal *Gazette* thought that he would "again have to take a flight toward the Arctic Circle, but, by no means with a certainty of finding a constituency on this side of Labrador." Baldwin deserved to be ousted because his liberalism was something like disloyalty and his "private virtues" did not compensate. "If Mr. Baldwin's private character is to be an excuse for his conduct to Lord Sydenham and Sir Charles Bagot, we say 'a plague upon your virtuous men. Let us have a rascal or two who cannot afford to play false.'"[5]

The assaults from Boulton were less delicate, for he was that sort of rascal the *Gazette* favoured. Boulton's most egregious assault attacked Baldwin and the Reformers for "slavish submission to the French faction," and called all free-born Britons to resist the "set of Tobacco smoking, dram drinking, garlick eating Frenchmen who were so stupid as to refuse to be educated . . . foreign in blood foreign in race and as ignorant as the ground they stand upon." The Tories spent heavily and worked to draw away individual Reformers who might believe that Baldwin had neglected his riding. One Reform organizer, Eli Gorham of

Newmarket, reassured Robert that the defectors were few: there would always be some "Renergates" he pointed out. And Robert's supporters struck back at the enemy. David Willson, the patriarch of the Children of Peace at Sharon, issued a broadside that urged voters to reject Boulton's slanders and allow him "to enter into the SWINE, and run with violence downhill, and be remembered no more." Baldwin canvassed vigorously but evinced great confidence. His broadside to supporters emphasized not just victory but the need for "an overwhelming majority."[6]

The majority was certainly substantial. The returns in January 1848 gave Baldwin 363 votes to Scobie's 102. Across Upper Canada the Reformers won a majority for the first time, if a scant one: 23 of 42 seats. As usual, the French liberals did better with 33 of 42. There were casualties and near casualties. Robert had organized Reform notables, including Brown, to campaign in Oxford for Francis Hincks since Hincks did not travel down from Montreal for the nomination and headed to Ireland during the election. The result was a closely contested vote that was not finally resolved in Hincks favour for some months. In Waterloo, Baldwin's handpicked candidate, Adam Fergusson, faced hundreds of ineligible voters who had been bribed by the Tories. Reform agents in one township were beaten while four others were kidnapped. The conservative incumbent was returned, not surprisingly, but the House of Assembly overturned the election and Fergusson got his seat. In Lower Canada the candidates in Champlain riding, Turcotte and Cauchon, were hauled down from the hustings and beaten, and a savage riot ensued at Marchildon's tavern. The polling at the market hall in Trois-Rivières had to be suspended when voters for liberal Antoine Polette were beaten and thrown out of the building; that election also had to be decided in the House. And there was, as always, Montreal. When voting began on 11 January 1848 the rival mobs were in the streets, seizing polling stations where they could. A Reform parade passed a Tory tavern, the Royal Oak, and the marchers pummelled the building with stones. The inmates responded with pistol fire. That was enough to bring out the troops who tried to control the sporadic violence for the rest of the day. The next morning the outnumbered Tories cried uncle and their candidates withdrew. That was almost the end of it. Triumphant Reformers marched through the city stoning the houses of known Tories.

The tactics launched years earlier by Francis Hincks were triumphant, for the moment, in Montreal.[7]

The victory was indeed substantial. Robert worried it might be too large. He suggested to LaFontaine that such an unwieldy caucus "will require tenfold caution in management of it." He was blunter to Sandfield Macdonald, a powerful Reform chieftain in eastern Upper Canada. The party had to pull together and follow a moderate course. If radicals were not prepared to do so, they could find another leader. And they would produce "another upset of the coach" that would leave them wandering in the wilderness until they learned "more practical wisdom." Tories took comfort in the same difficulties that Robert foresaw. The Montreal *Gazette* was sure that the Reform Party was "too heterogeneous in its composition, too divided in its objects, to join in anything like a coherent whole."[8]

Still, there is no greater force for cohesion than the taste of the fruits of power. Reformers watched with anticipation as Lord Elgin delivered a Throne Speech on 27 January, the dying gasp of the doomed Tory government. The stately dance of parliamentary niceties had to be completed, so on 3 March John Prince and Robert Christie moved the address in reply to the Throne Speech. Baldwin and LaFontaine countered with an amendment that would spell out the basic principle of responsible government.

> We feel it . . . to be our humble duty to submit to His Excellency, that it is essential to the satisfactory result of our deliberations on the important subjects to which His Excellency has been graciously pleased to direct our attention, and on other matters of public concern, that Her Majesty's Provincial Administration should possess the confidence of the House and of the Country, —and respectfully to represent that that confidence is not reposed in the present Advisers of His Excellency.[9]

The amendment carried by a vote of fifty-four to twenty. The next day, Saturday, 4 March, the old ministry resigned. The promise land had been reached. A government had fallen on a vote of confidence and a new party government would be formed. That Britain did not yet accept the result and viewed it as a mere "experiment" did not alter reality on the ground in Canada. Responsible government was established.[10]

LaFontaine was called to form a new ministry on 7 March. Stitching together a cabinet had been ongoing for some weeks. Robert's initial list of possibles included twenty-four names. He and LaFontaine winnowed it down to eleven, with the unwelcome assistance of Lord Elgin who insisted on including R.B. Sullivan in the executive, because of Sullivan's long service—and, perhaps, his shaky allegiance to Reform. The cabinet disappointed many Reformers. The turncoats Sullivan and Caron were ministers, and four of the eleven were from the Legislative Council. It was a curious way to begin a responsible regime with four councillors in the upper house, removed from daily scrutiny by the elected members. The parliamentary session itself was unimpressive. The new ministers, under the practice of the day, had to seek re-election. It was not possible to accomplish much under the circumstances, although the Montreal *Gazette* reported that Baldwin and LaFontaine, while they were technically not members, stationed themselves behind the Speaker's throne to direct their troops. So the session wrapped up quickly, ending on 28 March. Robert was re-elected without opposition in York North and the other ministers were also returned. The real governing could begin.[11]

That beginning was inglorious. The first bill passed was to establish the inspection of butter in Montreal. Tory Henry Sherwood crowed about the mountain labouring to bring forth a mouse and sneered that the butter bill was "a great feather in their caps." But Baldwin had no intention of attempting a legislative agenda. The new government had to be organized and the badly managed public finances put in order. Hincks was the right man for the job and set to it. He convinced the British government to help shore up the province's credit with the Bank of England, and he won agreement from Baring Brothers in London to market Canadian debentures. The financial record keeping was reorganized so that books of various departments corresponded with each other. Canada joined with New Brunswick and Nova Scotia to finance the survey for a possible Quebec to Halifax railway, a railway that Hincks saw as important for long-term economic growth. And both Hincks and Baldwin agreed with Lord Elgin on the advisability of seeking reciprocity, an agreement with the United States for free movement of goods across the international border. Hincks continued to prepare ambitious plans. In December 1848 he presented the cabinet with a set of proposals that would form much of the most important legislation over the next two years: an act to improve management of the public debt; an act to support railway development by government guarantees of loans; reform of municipal government; and creating a consolidated municipal loan fund that would allow communities to borrow for public works. It was an integrated and progressive plan for a new Canada.[12]

It was not enough for some. William Hamilton Merritt criticized the new ministry because of the preponderance of lawyers who were unlikely to understand the real needs of the country. That would become a familiar critique over the life of the government. The radical Reform paper, the Toronto *Examiner*, often complained about lawyer-politicians who were mostly concerned with protecting the privileges of their craft and who made the law a "profitable mystery" with their arcane language and forms. The opposition to lawyers in Parliament was one signal that politics and the political public were changing. The free-trade revolution, the birth of the railway, and the first stirrings of industrial capitalism broke the single-class perspective of traditional politics. In the past, groups within the professional-gentry elite had vied for power. Now Merritt was not alone in thinking that the ruling class was no longer capable of guiding a society in flux. As always with Merritt, there was an ulterior motive. He was angling for a place at the trough. Private criticism of Baldwin and the lawyer clique was balanced by Merritt's fawning on the leader. He was anxious, he told Robert in March 1848, to help "in working out your system" and making Canadian finances as strong as those of the United States. His defection to Metcalfe four years earlier was forgotten. Robert was prepared to overlook it, or pretend to, as well. Merritt was a trimmer and an opportunist, but he had a business reputation that would serve the government well. He was the ideal person to pursue reciprocity. Accordingly, he was welcomed back into the fold in the fall of 1848, entering cabinet as president of the executive council.[13]

Baldwin had always found patronage to be one of the most distasteful aspects of governance. It often involved putting favouritism ahead of merit in filling offices. It swamped him with importuning letters and angry complaints. And it was a dangerous bog, full of political perils, as the collapse of his first government had shown. Yet it could not be avoided and it had to be addressed immediately. He tried to ease the burden by decentralizing patronage. In the Eastern District of Upper Canada, for example, John Sandfield Macdonald, newly appointed to cabinet, was given a free hand to fill such posts as lockmasters, postal clerks, and land officers. Robert also delegated much of the Crown business, such as patronage in the Chancery Court, to his old firm in Toronto, now run by Adam Wilson. It was never enough. Both the *Pilot* and the *Globe* wanted substantial turnover in the personnel of the public service since, as the *Pilot* contended, many officers were "creatures" of the Tory ministry. The *Globe* insisted that the purge had to go to the top, with the removal of the superintendent of education, Egerton Ryerson. Ryerson was a toady to Toryism and a threat to the young of Canada. "He would convert the children of the Province into the most pliable tools of an arbitrary system." Baldwin may have privately agreed, but he was not prepared to snatch that nettle, and Ryerson stayed on. The newspapers' blood lust was shared at the grass roots. Ordinary Reformers wanted a strategy of appointing only liberals, not the "temporising policy" of the last Baldwin government, as John Steele of Brantford demanded. Others had more self-serving goals. W.B. Richards was a prominent in eastern Upper Canada who complained of having his patronage recommendations ignored in favour of those from Francis Hincks's "clique around Montreal." Charles Robinson of Thora township put it most bluntly. "I am frequently asked by the one what is Mr Baldwin going to do for us & by the other what has Mr Baldwin done for you—of course I cannot give a very satisfactory answer to either of the queries."[14]

Patronage was one reason why Baldwin, even in the flush of victory, harboured resentment about the political career into which duty had cast him. On 27 February 1848 he wrote from Montreal to Maria, who was at home in Toronto. It was her birthday and his absence stirred in him "all the bitterness of that absorption into political life that has come upon me during the last few years. I feel this more deeply when they occur on the blessed Sabath [*sic*] the only day that I can claim even a reprieve from the worry of politics."[15]

A substantial part of the worry stemmed from economics. Canada had been reeling for years as Britain dismantled the preferential tariff system that had sheltered colonial exports to the home country. The impact was as much psychological as substantial. A deeply rooted colonial mentality made it difficult for merchants to imagine how they could prosper except under some imperial umbrella. Canadian merchant capital was unprogressive but political. Its protection against the uncertainty of crops and long-distance trade was not improvement in its practices but an alliance with the state. That alliance had broken down in the 1840s as Britain withdrew its protection, first from timber, then from grain. The Tory government from 1844 to 1847 had been buffetted by waves of economic crisis, declining revenues, and surging debt. Baldwin and LaFontaine inherited all this. Trouble piled on trouble. That spring of 1848 they discovered that the bookkeeper of the Bank of Upper Canada had absconded with bank funds, and the bank's solicitors, William Boulton and Clark Gamble, had run up huge debts they could not repay.[16]

John Henry Dunn, acting as their agent in London, England, summed up the dilemma. The province needed public works to stimulate the economy and the government needed them to retain popular support in Upper Canada. Yet borrowing for public works could lead to collapse of Canada's credit. Hincks's reform of the management of public finances helped. So did an initiative to seek reciprocity with the United States, an enterprise begun in the summer of 1848 when LaFontaine and Sullivan went to Washington to feel out sentiment there. While reciprocity was not achieved until 1854, its mere possibility helped confidence in the economy. So too did rumours of British intentions to repeal the Navigation Acts. They were the natural complement of the preferential duties of the past, requiring colonial, protected cargoes to be carried in British ships. With the duties mostly gone, Canadians could see no reason why they should not be able to seek out the cheapest transport, of whatever nationality. Elgin reported that talk of the repeal of the Acts "has been hailed with unanimous acclamations here." The following year Britain responded by removing the Navigation Acts and, symbolically, spelling the end to the old trading empire. A final piece was immigration policy. Britain felt compelled to ship out as many Irish as possible from their ravaged homeland. Earl Grey at the Colonial

Office, with usual British tact, assured Elgin that the mother country intended to tutor "the wild ignorant natives of the west of Ireland" in "the arts of industry of which they know nothing" so they would become useful emigrants. Canada, in turn, was allowed to take measures to discourage paupers and sick migrants. The Canadian Parliament passed immigration legislation in 1848 and 1849 that increased the head tax on immigrants, on a sliding scale that depended on the number of days immigrant ships had to stay in quarantine. Shipmasters also had to give sureties that their passengers were not paupers. It was a set of useful measures. However, what really made a difference was the gradual improvement of the economy as trade with Britain recovered and that with the United States flourished.[17]

Baldwin understood little of the fine points of economics. As a result, he usually gave Hincks his head. That was amply proved when the inspector general presented to the executive council his memorandum on immigration and the public works in December 1848. The modest title cloaked a general program for economic development, a program that would move Canada far from Baldwin's world of property holders and small government. Hincks was proposing a fundamental shift in land policy to facilitate industrialization. Baldwin and Sullivan, when they were in Sydenham's ministry in 1840, had wanted to employ free land grants to allow the poor to become yeomen. Hincks would use them to settle workers along the canals where they would form a permanent paid labour force. Robert sat silent at the Council chamber as Hincks laid out his vision and won commitment from the ministry for his extended plan. As always, Robert's relationship with Hincks was complicated. He was an old friend. His wife had sheltered the Baldwin children when the wounded Robert retreated to Britain in 1836. Hincks was smooth and persuasive, and he appeared to understand things that Robert did not. Yet it is not safe to assume that acquiescence meant approval. Back in September, Baldwin's friend from Brockville, W.B. Richards, thought the leader was nearly ready to step down because of disagreements with Hincks. As well, during the period that Hincks was preparing his great memorandum, Robert was sunk in depression. It had been a difficult year and the pressures of governing had overwhelmed him. He was ill again in October, under the care of family physician and friend, Christopher Widmer. It was another form of withdrawal; his solution when the world was too taxing.[18]

———⊷⊶———

The assumption of power had also made Robert master of his beloved law. He had been part of the law and it had been part of him since the rambunctious four-year-old had scurried after his father on the way to the courts in little York. The law had been an element of the family business and the subject of dinner-table conversation. However, it was much more. William Warren Baldwin had entered the craft to enhance his income. He was one of five notables who, without formal legal training, were licensed by executive fiat of Lieutenant-Governor Hunter in 1803 to ease a shortage of lawyers. Once he had practised and absorbed the law, he came to understand its importance as the buttress of civil order and as a pillar of the ordained hierarchy in society. He explained that to young law students in 1823. The Juvenile Advocate Society had been established at York two years earlier as a forum to discuss legal issues. When it was suggested that membership might be extended beyond those entering the profession, William Warren warned against the idea.

> [H]uman society is formed of so elegant a web that every violence done it makes a breach which however repaired will long remain a blemish. In all [society's] rich tapestry distinction is necessary; this is nature or more properly speaking the order of providence. . . . As the division of labour tends to improve and perfect an art so the division of society tends to polish and perfect mankind in those arts which embracing religion, morals, and science are as it were the machinery of progressive embellishment and happiness of a people.[19]

The law was an art, a rank in society, a vital thread in the social fabric. Robert Baldwin, studying with his father, breathed in these values in the law office and in the Juvenile Advocate Society. He saw his father serve the profession as treasurer of the provincial law society from 1811 to 1815, in 1820 and 1821, from 1824 to 1828 and again from 1832 to 1836. It was a role Robert himself would assume in 1847 and 1848, and between 1850 and 1858. The treasurer was effectively the chair of the leaders of the society, the "benchers." The Baldwins, father and son, were the guardians of the profession for nearly fifty years. Robert played an important part in the legal community throughout his career. He was only twenty-six when he was elected a bencher and chaired a committee to revise the by-laws of the law society. His reforms transferred authority for internal affairs of the society from the judiciary to the benchers. In 1833 he continued his work to gain full independence for the profession by chairing a committee that set out forms of discipline for law society members. He sought, as his father had urged, to improve and perfect the practice of law, and thus the progress of mankind.[20]

Robert foretold his interest in university reform with his concern for legal training. He had been an avid participant in the Juvenile Advocate Society and continued to urge better education for young lawyers. In 1832 he convinced the convocation of the Law Society to authorize study classes and he quickly acted to establish the Trinity Class, so named because it first met in the spring or Trinity term. Each Thursday evening students gathered at the Society's headquarters, Osgoode Hall, to debate and study. Robert also served on a committee in 1833 to stock the Osgoode library, in part with donations he himself made. Again in 1850 he took time from politics to help choose books for the library.[21]

Osgoode Hall had special meaning for him because of his father's role in its creation. William Warren had been involved from the beginning. When the Law Society set up a committee in 1820 to obtain plans and estimates for a building, he served with J.B. Robinson and Henry John Boulton. Although the benchers were divided by politics into Reform and Tory factions, they could work together for the common good of the law. Cost scuttled this attempt, but five years later the elder Baldwin was asked to draw up plans for a building. Although he had no formal training as an architect, he already had designed several houses and the new jail and courthouse on King Street. His idea was to develop the headquarters in stages as finances permitted. A professional architect, John Ewart, would proceed with a modest first stage, based on William's plan, in 1829. The Law Society took possession of the edifice in 1832, but William was not finished. He designed a group of chambers, that were fittingly called the "Baldwin Chambers," with accommodation for law students, an addition that was completed in 1834. And he kept a close eye on the costs of the project as head of a finance committee. William Warren Baldwin would be remembered as one of the fathers of the law in the province. Fittingly, the convocation decided to honour him with a posthumous portrait to be displayed in Osgoode Hall. Robert was given the choice of artists and, in keeping with his nationalist sentiments, he chose a Canadian, Théophile Hamel. The portrait was received by the Hall in June 1850. Robert loved and served the law, but even there his father looked down at him.[22]

The victory in January 1848 returned Robert to the office of Attorney General West, in charge of the law on a day-to-day basis. He brought to the ministry his knowledge of the law, both Canadian and British; his diligence; and his determination to make the law work effectively. Yet his conservatism and his belief in limited government militated against that. Overall, the provincial bureaucracy grew through the 1840s. When the Reformers first took office in 1842 there were 95 civil servants at government headquarters. When Baldwin left office in 1851, there were 176. The number outside the capital swelled from 342 to 704. Yet Robert tried to operate the increasingly complicated legal machine with no permanent staff in his office. He imagined he could oversee the courts, deal with patronage, and manage the political process, all without even the resources he had available in his private practice. His was a Dickensian administration, the Attorney General at his desk in a small office in Government House, scratching out replies to letters in his cramped hand.[23]

Partly because of his parsimony in regard to his office, Robert's departmental administration had not improved since the first government. Complaints were legion about letters not answered and decisions not taken. Take the sad plaints of the deputy postmaster general, Thomas Allen Stayner. He wrote to provincial secretary James Leslie in April 1850 to seek his help. The story had begun two years earlier, Stayner explained, when he gave Baldwin a claim for £137.28 by the post office against William Rorke. Rorke, the former postmaster at Picton, Upper Canada, had fallen into insolvency and taken post office funds with him.

Some months passed with no response after Stayner contacted Baldwin, so Stayner went to see the Attorney General. Baldwin blamed the agent he had entrusted with such matters, and promised to appoint an agent who would be more diligent. In October 1849, with still no resolution, Stayner heard that one of Rorke's sureties, who guaranteed the debtor's financial reliability, had died. In fear that they would lose the claim, the official again wrote to Baldwin. Now, as he contacted Leslie in April 1850, not only had there been no satisfaction, there had not even been an acknowledgement. Stayner had been berated by the postmaster general, James Morris, for not collecting the debt and was feeling rather badly treated by his political masters. Could Leslie do anything? A week later Leslie reported that he had talked to Baldwin and proceedings were now underway.[24]

Robert might plead that his office carried many heavy responsibilities. Among them was supporting, guiding, and even disciplining local law-enforcement authorities. The duty often sat uneasily with his ideal of decentralized authority. When presented with a case of alleged misconduct by a sheriff in 1849, Robert appointed a commissioner to investigate, but made clear the limitations on such inquiries. Sheriffs were responsible at law for their conduct and "it is not the object of inquiries like the present to substitute the Executive Government . . . for the ordinary tribunals of the Country."[25]

His views on many legal matters were conventional, if well-informed. Among the mounds of paper he shuffled at meetings of the executive council were recommendations for mercy in capital cases, advanced to him from judges and juries. His recommendations were invariably accepted by the cabinet, probably a reflection of his orthodox views on capital punishment. During his second term as Attorney General, some three-and-a-half years, about half of death sentences were commuted to life in prison, the same proportion that would be commuted by his successors in the next three-and-a-half years.[26]

As a private citizen Robert was often generous with supplicants who approached him for financial assistance. As Attorney General and leader of the ministry, however, his ideology trumped his munificence. He and the cabinet shared a belief in maintaining narrow limits on government charity. Baldwin had shown strong interest in both education and temperance, but that did not preclude his rejection of a invitation to advance both causes. Rev. T. Osgood requested in September 1849 that government provide assistance in restoring the building of the Seaman and Strangers' Friend Society in Quebec City, so that it might house a school and a temperance hall. This was not the business of the province, Baldwin contended, however splendid the cause.[27]

When charity was extended, it was often dispensed with ill-grace. That same month, September 1849, Baldwin presented the Executive with the case of a Mr. Beattie, lockmaster on the Cornwall Canal in eastern Upper Canada. Beattie was standing on a lock on the evening of 21 August when the steamer *British Queen* began to drift dangerously off line. Beattie frantically tried to wave the ship off, but it crashed into the lock, throwing Beattie into the water and to his death. He left behind a widow and three children, a family with no means of support. Robert and the cabinet refused to accept responsibility for the accident, but did agree to pay Beattie's salary up to 1 January 1850, a princely £12.10. The politicians were hardly more charitable with a group of Maliseet and Mi'kmaq traders who had come to Quebec, only to be struck by cholera. It left them "in a starving condition and without means of returning home." Council, as in the Beattie case, made clear that the people had no valid claim on government but, "out of our charitable instincts" they would be provided with provisions worth £25. They were lectured that this was not a precedent and would not be repeated. Presumably the Maliseet and Mi'kmaq traders either got home or died of disease and starvation since no further impositions on the goodwill of government were recorded.[28]

The Attorney General's responsibilities sometimes extended outside Canada's borders. In late 1849 Robert was embroiled in an incident that tangled up Canada, Britain, and the United States. The steamer *Canada* carried a cargo of various goods from Buffalo to Detroit, only to be seized by American customs officers as soon as it arrived at its destination. It had violated an American law that forbade foreign vessels trading between two US ports. Baldwin was a Canadian nationalist, and his instincts would be to defend his fellow citizens. However, the only course of intervention he could see was for the province to buy back the ship from the Americans. His thrifty liberalism now conflicted with his nationalism. Fortunately, he could fall back on another of his allegiances: imperialism. The British government had a bond giving it the option of purchasing the *Canada*, apparently because of some past service to its owners. Robert could, thankfully, let greater powers sort it out. He was always cautious—a nationalist, but no jingo.[29]

There was a more homely international, of sorts, dispute the following year. The citizens of the Magdalene Islands in the Gulf of St. Lawrence petitioned the queen to be permitted to secede from Canada and join Nova Scotia. They complained that they paid heavy duties to Canada and received nothing in return. They had no common interest with agricultural Canada, while their fishing and foreign trade complemented those of Nova Scotia. Most serious were their complaints that Baldwin's government had failed to provide even a minimum standard of law and order. While Canada stood idly by, drunken sailors from Cape Breton terrorized the islands and murdered the inhabitants. Without policing, the community was at the mercy of the brigands since, for long periods, "the most of the Inhabitants were absent from these Islands to the Labrador, to the great fear of the Female sex." The queen was unsympathetic, despite their sad tale, and there is no evidence that Baldwin or LaFontaine did anything to improve their security. Local law and order, for him, was a local matter; true, he did not extend his decentralist philosophy of local initiative to countenance secession. The Magdalenes stayed put.[30]

Closer to home, Robert had the responsibility to provide legal advice. Sometimes the advice satisfied neither his correspondent nor Robert himself. That was the case in September 1850 when municipal officials in Kingston were attempting to deal with "bad characters" at the so-called French Village, a shantytown haunt of the disreputable. Charles Damien had been stabbed to death after a dispute in a brothel. The murderer was, allegedly, one Joseph Matthieu. The Kingston authorities faced stolid silence from the "bad characters" who had witnessed the stabbing. How could they compel witnesses to appear at the assizes? Baldwin could offer no help. There was no way, he replied, to compel witnesses to appear or to attach conditions to their recognizances. Again, two threads of his belief system were pulled in opposite directions. He believed in local responsibility for local matters, but recognized that the law, as it stood, prevented the local authorities from carrying out those responsibilities. Yet his innate legal conservatism made him inordinately reluctant to tamper with the law as he had inherited it. He did nothing to repair this or other deficiencies in the law, a law often ill-suited to a pioneer community.[31]

He was more helpful when requests did not require tinkering with the system. Unlike many public figures, he did not attempt personal gain from his frequent advice about interpreting and applying the law. In February 1851 he was approached by Reform politician William Notman. There was a dispute in his riding about whether the Great Western Railway could cross a private road without paying a fee. Baldwin sorted out the legalities for Notman. Two weeks later the politician reported to Baldwin that the railway was now executing the proper legal instrument. Notman enclosed a fee for the Attorney General's legal services. Robert immediately replied that he did not offer advice to earn a fee, and returned the money to Notman.[32]

There was a curious twist to Robert's parsimony. He was unable, for most of his tenure, to carry out one traditional responsibility of his office; that was to represent the Crown at the assizes across Upper Canada. One reason was that he was needed at the capital to carry on the business of his bare-bones ministry. Political duties as party leader also kept him in the capital. So too did his frequent bouts of ill health. He had intended to travel the legal circuit in the fall of 1848, only to be laid low by illness. Whatever the reasons, the result was additional cost to the province. He had to appoint Queen's Counsels to represent the state at trials.[33]

The practice left Baldwin open to political attacks. A debate in the House on the public accounts in June 1851 turned into an assault on his prosecution of the public business. Several angry Tories charged that Baldwin was appointing young, inexperienced political friends as Queen's Counsels. John A. Macdonald and his Kingston crony, Henry Smith, denounced Baldwin for letting his political role occupy his time, so that he neglected court business and cost the province large sums for the fees paid to his surrogates at the assizes. Smith thundered that the Queen's Counsels were "a wholesale system of bribery and corruption" while "[t]he country would rather see the Attorneys' General attending to their proper business than making long election bills which nobody wanted." Reformers leaped to the defence. James Curran Morrison of York West contended that, if the Tories were charging Baldwin with corruption, "not one man in ten will believe it." Robert chose not to defend himself, but rather public life as a calling. If public servants were treated as "thieves and rogues and robbers" they were likely to behave as such. If they were held in high regard, they would behave with integrity. The issue was sent to a special committee that reported on 30 June 1851, the day Baldwin told the House he was resigning. It found no irregularities in the justice system.[34]

The debate was about more than legal fees. The Tories were making political hay, but they were doing so from a particular perspective. They could not fathom that government was undergoing seismic change. The little government of the past, where responsibilities were so few that executive councillors could absent themselves for many weeks at a time, had transmuted into something more complicated. The administration was more demanding and the politics more involving. It was no longer possible for an Attorney General to mount his horse or climb into a carriage to follow the legal caravan about the province, leaving his duties at the capital behind. Robert may have understood this, but he was not reconciled to the new politics that he had helped to bring on with responsible government. Certainly politics in Upper Canada had always been a blood sport. Yet it was, for the most part, a game played by gentlemen with understood rules and limits. The stakes of government were higher now, with politicians in total control, virtually unchecked by the Crown. Responsible government had raised expectations of government, and those in turn would lead to demands for change and little patience for the sort of cautious governance that Baldwin represented. He understood the principle of responsible government, but was blind to its political implications.

One change he could countenance. There was near unanimity among lawyers and judges that reforms were needed in the court system. Robert had discouraged his young colleague from Toronto, William Hume Blake, when Blake had urged the party to push for judicial reform in 1845. Baldwin's conservatism had been reinforced by the political judgment that the time was not ripe for the opposition to pursue such basic changes. In 1848, though, he was convinced by the opinions of those he respected in the legal profession. He delegated Blake to work on the legislation that eventually created important institutions. There was a new Court of Common Pleas. The bench of the Chancery Court, which dealt with equity matters—mostly property cases such as trusts, estates, and bankruptcies—was expanded from one to three members. The system was capped with a Court of Error and Appeal. Blake appears to have been responsible for the Chancery reform, while he and Baldwin shared drafting on the other matters. Robert again demonstrated his peculiar conservatism. He did not embrace far-reaching reforms, yet when he became convinced of their necessity he could contemplate them. The considered opinion of legal practitioners was one powerful factor in persuading him, believing as he did in local responsibility.[35]

Solicitor General Blake was given the honour of introducing the legislation in March 1849. The bills did not face strong opposition, but they were delayed by the outbreak of rioting in Montreal in April. It was outside Parliament that a groundswell of concern developed. Chancery was the source of most anxiety. The appointment of the justices for the expanded court produced outrage among radical Reformers. Mr. Justice Burns was appointed in preference to J.H. Boulton, by now a radical darling. Worse, Blake became Chancellor for Upper Canada, heading the court. It appeared he had laboured mightily to create a job for himself. Chancery as an institution was unpopular as an expensive, complicated, and lawyerly affair. James Lesslie of the left-wing *Examiner* had no doubts. "[T]he Court of Chancery I cannot but regard as a public nuisance—an Engine created to rob the people professedly to subserve the interests of equity." Lesslie told William Lyon Mackenzie that the failure to appoint Boulton had been a gross miscalculation by Baldwin. Boulton was now "plaguey riled" and would fight the government in the Assembly.[36]

Robert was not insensitive to the criticism outside the House. He pressed Blake to simplify the practices of Chancery and to reduce the costs of court proceedings. This was whistling in a wind of complexity. The reforms of 1849 may have improved the court system, but they clearly made it more complicated and more costly. For many ordinary Upper Canadians, it seemed that lawyers had constructed a vast machine whose main purpose was to generate lawyers' fees. Perhaps Robert's instincts in 1845 had been correct; that general judicial reform was a political swamp into which the prudent did not venture. The thought must have crossed his mind in June 1851 as he sank into the quagmire that was the Chancery controversy.[37]

The judicial reforms of 1849 did not signal a conversion to legal liberalism. Several examples of Robert's conservatism also demonstrated that the full implications of responsible governing had not been grasped, even by him. In April 1849 Lewis Drummond, soon to become Solicitor General East, introduced a bill in the House to limit the boundaries of contempt of court, a power often used to silence newspaper editors. Drummond's initiative roused Mr. Baldwin's ire and set off a storm in the Reform camp, with cabinet ministers denouncing each other. No cabinet solidarity here. Baldwin pulled his bulk out of seat to condescend to his Lower Canadian colleague. Drummond, he charged, had offered no proof of judicial excess and warned that the bill touched "an important branch of jurisprudence which, interfered with, might have a dangerous tendency." As for the press being punished for comments on court proceedings, Baldwin came down solidly on the side of authority. Freedom of the press was a lesser concern than the integrity of the courts. Drummond, clearly perplexed, said he had discussed the bill with Solicitor General West Blake and received encouragement to proceed. Maybe so, said Blake, but the Solicitor General really agreed with Baldwin. Hincks did not. As a long-time journalist he was outraged by Baldwin's approach, which amounted to a star chamber. The delighted opposition was content to allow Reformers to flail at each other. When it was sorted out, Baldwin's conservatism prevailed. The bill was withdrawn.[38]

That same month the government was again divided over the treatment of debtors. That was something of a litmus test for liberalism. Advanced populist liberals wanted to protect ordinary people from draconian measures to collect debts. More conservative men uphold the sanctity of property and abhorred debt in any form. The debate began when two Reform backbenchers introduced a bill to strengthen debt collection, allowing sheriffs to sell all of a debtor's property save beds, clothing, and cooking utensils. Henry John Boulton, once a High Tory and now a flaming radical, moved that the bill be read three months hence, effectively allowing it to die. His motion passed easily with support from cabinet ministers William Hamilton Merritt and James

Hervey Price, as well as most Tories, only too happy to create mischief in the Reform ranks. Baldwin and Blake voted no. Baldwin's vote suggested he was willing to strip away traditional protections granted to debtors.[39]

The ideological divisions widened a few days later when Boulton and Wolfred Nelson, member for Quebec City, moved to abolish imprisonment for debt. Their teamwork told how strange politics had become, with a former member of the Family Compact co-operating with a former rebel of 1837. Once again the ministry was a picture of confusion. Blake was the first up, to suggest the government would likely present legislation on this matter later in the session, so the present bill should be withdrawn. Baldwin made this sound unconvincing by denouncing the Boulton bill. It was absurd, he charged, to talk of abolishing imprisonment for debt when it was obvious there was no alternative remedy for creditors. Hardly had Baldwin sat down when LaFontaine announced his support for the bill. The newly minted liberal, W.H. Merritt, and the authentic radical, Malcolm Cameron, assistant commissioner of public works, joined LaFontaine, while Blake was with Baldwin. W.B. Richards, the Reform member for Leeds, Upper Canada, wondered what had happened to responsible government. The ministry was divided against itself and some members were apparently inventing pending legislation on the spot. In their confusion, the ministry was in danger of leading their followers "into a trap." The bill eventually moved off to committee where it died quietly. There was no sign of Blake's promised legislation.[40]

Backbenchers attempted again in 1850 and 1851 to abolish imprisonment for debt. It was clear they were expressing the opinion of the majority of members, but Baldwin managed to bottle up the bills in committee so that they never re-emerged for debate. On 13 June 1850 he gave the House a clear explanation of his position. Perhaps, "if we were about to commence the formation of society, it might be a question whether it would not be better to refuse to sanction any process for the collection of debts by law whatever." However, Canada was not in such a state of nature and no one had the right "to pull down a system, without doing anything toward building up another." This was not simple callousness toward debtors but rather an attempt to maintain a balance in the absence of alternatives that might protect property.

Robert could not have disagreed more with laissez-faire liberals such as Francis Hincks. Hincks had contended, in a debate over usury in March 1849, that "He was prepared to repeal every law giving any protection to any person, because he thought they were not founded upon sound principles." Hincks, and others like him, assumed markets and rationality would sort things out. Baldwin, in contrast, was less trusting of minds and invisible forces. He fought to retain necessary protections for many groups: for property owners by laws to compel payment of debts; for debtors by limiting interest rates; for women by retaining dower rights; for individuals by limiting the corporate rights of businesses. He might, as in the case of imprisonment for debt, recognize that existing protections for creditors were excessive, perhaps unjust. Even so, unless viable alternatives were found to present practice, as with the judicial reforms of 1849, and as with responsible government itself, he was not prepared to tear down the existing edifices of protections and mutual obligations. That pragmatic conservatism set him off from the liberal ideologues of his party. He was both a conservative and a Reformer.[41]

Robert still drew income from the law practices of Baldwin and Son as well as Baldwin and Sullivan. He rarely went to the office, leaving the business largely to Adam Wilson and R.B. Sullivan. Yet his name on the letterhead could create political embarrassment. There was much dismay among Reformers in the town of Beaverton, northeast of Toronto, and its environs in the fall of 1849. Baldwin's firm was suing John Bruce of that town for costs incurred in a court case. Bruce claimed he could not pay and begged Baldwin for more time. Meanwhile, local party supporters were up in arms, angry that their Attorney General should be suing one of the most prominent Reformers in the district. Wearily, Baldwin did not even attempt to explain his relationship with his old firm. He simply wrote to his correspondents in Beaverton that he was cancelling the debt and asking the law office to charge the costs to him. So much for principled pursuit of debtors.[42]

Whatever the vexations caused by his law practice, Robert remained committed to the law as an institution. He was anxious to retain his standing in the profession. One symbolic action was the resumption of the title of Queen's Counsel that he, LaFontaine, Small, and Morin had resigned in 1844 in protest against Governor Metcalfe's attacks on them. It was all indeed symbolic since the resignations had never been officially accepted and Baldwin himself had thought the gesture unwise at the time. Given all that it was difficult to know how to handle the matter, the sort of nicety that deeply troubled Baldwin. He worried over it once the ministry was established and Reform vindicated. He struggled to find the words, to reach an explanation that somehow made sense of their resignations, and undo them with honour. His explanation of why they should resume their professional rank, written to James Edward Small, was laborious. The tender of office to LaFontaine and Baldwin by the Governor General "is in itself a removal of the unjust imputation of which we have had so much to complain. And as such imputation was general and not particular such tender is in effect a removal of it as well as from you and Mr. Morin as from us." This may not have made much sense to Small and the others, but they all happily again became Queen's Counsels. It did satisfy Robert's conscience and permitted him to resume an active role among the benchers of the Law Society.[43]

His legal conservatism and the pressures of politics created a great tangle in the penitentiary affair. The penitentiary at Kingston, Upper Canada, had been constructed on the most modern lines and was the pride of the province when it opened in 1835. A great, grey brooding structure, it was intended to frighten potential miscreants by its very appearance. That apparently did not work, since the penitentiary population swelled nine-fold between 1835 and 1848. The institution became a subject of concern in the 1840s as rumours spread of abuses by the warden, Henry Smith, and his staff. The charges included corruption, violent abuse of prisoners, and even sexual misconduct with female inmates by the prison doctor. All of this faced Baldwin when he took office. He quickly appointed a five-man commission to investigate with a legislative councillor, Adam Fergusson, as chair. The dominant members of the commission, it soon emerged, were two newspapermen, William Bristow of the Montreal *Times* and George Brown of the *Globe*. Robert recognized the explosive nature of the affair. The penitentiary was an important institution. The commission was made up of Reform loyalists and they were investigating a warden who was a prominent Tory and whose son sat in the house for the conservatives.[44]

The commission's report was a damning indictment of Smith and his staff, but it attracted little attention since it was delivered in the midst of the crisis and rioting in Montreal in the spring of 1849. This suited Baldwin. He did little about the recommendations beyond removing Warden Smith, and there would be no legislation to reform the penitentiary until 1851. The politics of the situation were too explosive to plunge in, especially when so many other troubles faced the government. As well, the suggested reforms were too modern, based too solidly on contemporary liberal thought, to appeal to him. Brown and Bristow had made a trip to the United States and returned with the most advanced American ideas about prison management. Robert might agree with their suggestion for less physical punishment, but wonder at the recommendation that each prisoner be kept initially for six months of absolute solitary confinement, or even at the stress on industrial labour to train convicts. These grew out of an ideology of human nature that believed in the ability to remould people, where Baldwin's conservatism rested on tradition and historical experience. The liberal capitalist George Brown saw the penitentiary as a place to break lower-class prisoners of the habits inculcated by their former proletarian environment. Their defiance would be smashed by solitary confinement and they would be educated as citizens of industrial society by prison labour. It was an approach that might have suited New York, but it was decidedly premature in pre-industrial Canada. Baldwin, a pre-industrial man, was in no hurry to implement it.[45]

Far more challenging was the lingering issue of amnesty. LaFontaine had long felt strongly that there must be a general amnesty for those convicted or exiled for their roles in the rebellions of 1837–1838. Indeed, he threatened Lord Elgin that he would resign from the ministry in 1848 if amnesty were not granted. Robert was much less ardent, but he supported amnesty because of its legal simplicity. It was too difficult, he told Elgin, to deal with all the different categories of offenders, such as those dealt with under that attainder act, those transported, and all the other complex dealings. A general amnesty was clear and efficient. He did fear the political repercussions of proposing amnesty. His fears were unfounded. When a bill for a general pardon came to the House in early 1849, there was no opposition, as everyone seemed relieved to put the painful past behind them. Indeed, it was treated like a funeral: "[T]he Bill being signed by His Excellency the Governor General, all the Members sat uncovered while it was read."[46]

If Robert thought that was the end of it, he was sadly mistaken. Long before the rebellions, Robert Gourlay had aroused the authorities in Upper Canada by questioning their management of the province. He had been hounded out of Upper Canada in 1819. From his home in Scotland he had kept at successive government to redress his financial losses and his political persecution. When Baldwin assumed office, Gourlay wrote to remind the premier that he had presented petitions to the House on Gourlay's behalf in 1846. Now Baldwin was in position to settle the matter. Robert tended to put aside difficult and embarrassing matters, so it was some months before he replied to the old reformer. He would be happy to help, he assured Gourlay, "but when you were in this Country last it was impossible to ascertain from you what you did want; and I confess I am as little able to understand you definitively now." Certainly Gourlay's resentments tended to pour out of him in a great tangle, but reasonably enough, he pointed out that Baldwin had presented his petitions in 1846. Surely he had understood them. In the end, they remained confused by each other and there was no resolution to the grievances of the father of Upper Canadian reform.[47]

Gourlay had been succeeded, in the 1820s, by Marshall Spring Bidwell as the inspiration for reform. Bidwell had helped to shape oppositionists into something like a political party when he served as Speaker of the Upper Canadian House of Assembly. After the abortive rebel assault on Toronto in 1837, Bidwell had been threatened with arrest by Sir Francis Bond Head, and forced into exile, although Bidwell had taken no part in the uprising. Before fleeing he had placed his property and family in Baldwin's safekeeping. Their closeness was forgotten as Bidwell soured in his imagined Babylonian captivity. Despite his success as a lawyer in the United States, his sense of injustice grew deeper, and so did his feeling that his erstwhile friends in Canada were doing nothing to right the wrong. Bidwell peppered Canadian politicians with demands for redress. J.H. Price, for one, grew weary of Bidwell's sense of martyrdom. Price thought that the former leader would do well to remember that, whatever the costs of voluntary flight, there were many—including Price himself—who stayed and suffered. One who stayed, Robert Baldwin, was more patient and was genuinely anxious to help Bidwell. Robert arranged to have Bidwell's pledge to Governor Head, that he would never return, cancelled during the first Reform ministry. Now he pleaded with the exile to come home and offered him the Crown business on any assize he might choose. Bidwell wavered, then refused the offer.[48]

Yet Bidwell twisted his own decision to remain in the United States into another example of persecution. Somehow, his former friends had betrayed him. Baldwin was astonished, and wounded, by Bidwell's accusations of ingratitude, relayed through Brown. As Price said, "Baldwin feels heavily Bidwell's reflection on him." Yet Robert still tried to find a solution satisfactory to the prickly Bidwell. In September 1849 he approached Bidwell's unofficial agent in Canada, Egerton Ryerson. Perhaps the old leader had been misled by suspicions whispered to him by troublemakers. "I know that I have never afforded any just grounds for such suspicions," Baldwin said. Indeed, Robert was prepared to renew a commitment he had made as early as 1843. Bidwell should return, familiarize himself with the practice of law in the province, and then assume a post as justice of the Court of Common Pleas. Apparently it was too much to ask that Bidwell make the effort to come up to speed with legal changes. So, as with Gourlay, no accommodation was found. And again as with Gourlay, the failure stamped Baldwin as a reactionary, an enemy of the glorious Reform tradition of pre-rebellion times. Delicious, this man frozen in tradition should be charged with abandoning it.[49]

The radical critics had more grounds in Baldwin's handling of amnesty for William Lyon Mackenzie. Robert had never liked Mackenzie, whose extreme ideas and provocative behaviour offended both Robert's politics and his sense of decorum. Nevertheless, they had worked together for a common cause until 1837. Their disparate Reform enterprises were under one roof in central Toronto, Turton's building that was owned by William Warren Baldwin. "Radical Hall," as it was dubbed, by 1836 housed the Baldwin's Constitutional Reform Society, at the moderate end of the liberal spectrum, and William Lyon Mackenzie's *Constitution* newspaper at the radical end. The co-operation ended with the rebellion, and Robert never forgave Mackenzie for that stain on Reform.[50]

One after another, through the 1840s, proscribed rebels had been permitted to return to Canada. By 1847, only Mackenzie and the Lower Canadian, Robert Nelson, remained under the ban. Mackenzie was comfortable enough in New York City, writing for the *Tribune* newspaper that was edited by his friend, Horace Greeley. Yet he longed to return to Canada and was angry at those who prevented it. He reminded Baldwin in February 1847 that general opinion now was sympathetic to the rebels and wondered, "how long, Sir, am I to be proscribed and outlawed by 'responsible government'?" Mackenzie was certain that he knew why he had not been pardoned: "Baldwin & his friends." The rebel leader was undoubtedly correct. His treatment infuriated radicals and tainted the whole regime with a reactionary cast. James Lesslie, the ultra-liberal Toronto newspaper editor, saw the affair as illustration of the fundamental weaknesses of the ministry. "There is a want of nerve—a timidity."[51]

Mackenzie was finally free to return after the general amnesty and did so in 1849, to be greeted by Tory riots and effigy burnings. He was poor and jobless and sought tangible recompense for the wrongs that he imagined had been done to him. He demanded three years' of parliamentary salary that he claimed was due him. Baldwin was unsympathetic and further widened the gulf between them by the peremptory and pedantic tone of his reply.

> I do not conceive that it is at all essential . . . that lengthened Epistolary correspondence should be entered into by the different members of the Government with parties setting up claims upon the Province . . . Neither does it form any part of my official duty to advise persons upon the nature & extent of their claims . . . Ministers in this Country not being supplied with the means of securing the assistance of private Secretaries your acquaintance with public business will convince you how impracticable it would be to undertake to answer all the letters that may be addressed to them.

It went on. Mackenzie tried to regain his property seized during the rebellion, but was refused the right even to see the records by Sheriff

Jarvis of the Home District. He complained to Baldwin who was icily correct in his reply. "Whatever was done by Shff. Jarvis was I suppose done under the authority of Civil process and I do not see how within genl amney [general amnesty] the Crown has any interest that would give it a right to interfere in the matter."[52]

Baldwin had been despairingly disapproving of the rebellion. Nevertheless, he found it possible to work amicably with some of the revolutionaries. LaFontaine, after all, was implicated in the troubles. George-Étienne Cartier and Wolfred Nelson were rebels who became trusted associates. The special animus was not for all those who took part in the long past insurrection, since Baldwin could appreciate the frustration of French-Canadian liberals. He extended no such understanding to Mackenzie. Mackenzie was a smasher, not a reformer. He was no gentleman with his histrionics and his lower-class affiliations. Mackenzie was so unacceptable that it was easy for Robert to undervalue the old rebel's popularity and influence. Mackenzie returned to Canada disillusioned with the United States after close-hand experience and ready to support the British system and try to make it work better. Robert saw only Mackenzie the destroyer and refused to make the gestures that might have reconciled him to the ruling Reform Party. It was petty and insensitive of Baldwin to treat Mackenzie with contempt. Worse, it was politically foolish. Mackenzie would return to the House in 1851 and prove what a dangerous enemy he could be.[53]

Many things confounded Robert's practise of the law, whether as private lawyer or as Attorney General. He struggled with the politics of it, and the personalities. He put economy before efficiency. He had too many duties and too many illnesses. He could rise to cope with the content, as he did in the judicial reforms of 1849. That, however, was a circumstance where common opinion in the profession and his eager young colleague W.H. Blake stirred him into action. For the most part, it remained the phrase, the idea of the law that moved him, that roused his passions.

Chapter 15

Anglo-Saxons to the Struggle

Politics was about principles, Robert believed. It was a belief that would be sorely tested this troubled year. The memory of Eliza was a comfort as never before. She had been dead for thirteen years, but never gone. It was 1849.

The year began well enough. Montreal's weather was mild on New Year's Day and conducive to levees, private visits, and ample quantities of mulled wine. Robert and his colleagues were refreshed by the opportunity to spend Christmas with family and friends, and forget partisan bickering for a few weeks. The mood was raised even more by hopes for a better future. Those who preferred to whistle by graveyards professed to believe that a corner had been turned. The Speech from the Throne in the provincial Parliament, delivered by Governor General Lord Elgin on 10 January, would point to signs of commercial improvement and laud the country's "uninterrupted tranquility." The Address in Reply from Robert Baldwin's ministry was even smugger. Canada had avoided the turmoil that tore Europe in 1848, a truth that spoke of Canadians' "love of order, and of the attachment they bear to their institutions."[1]

Canadians had good reason to hope this was true, but even better reason to doubt it. There had been precious little tranquility over the last decades. The Rebellions of 1837–1838 had destroyed the old political order in the colonies of Upper and Lower Canada and thrust Canadians into the challenging experiment of living together, English and French, in the new Province of Canada. The new era was ushered in by widespread violence that marked the politics of the decade, especially in the capital itself. This was, as one observer called it, "the Montreal way of electioneering."[2]

Political partisanship was given a bloody edge by several developments. One was the hostility between English and French who now were balanced off in the new province. It was particularly difficult to work through the ethnic relationship when United Canada was buffeted by the waves of economic change set off by Britain's conversion to free trade and the consequent abandonment of the protection of colonial imports to the mother country. As the Empire dismantled first the timber preference and then the grain preference, the colonial economy lurched about. The effects were real enough as exporters struggled to adjust. And they were psychological, the fear both rational and irrational that periodically swept the business community. One modern historian has argued that, at least at the end of the decade, the home government bought the loyalty of the English middle class by shifting the economic burden of empire onto the colonies through free trade and troop reductions. Certainly many in Canada believed that.[3]

Wholesale prices fell by 30 percent between the beginning of 1840 and the end of 1843. They rallied and retreated in a pattern of economic futility, only to stabilize somewhat in 1847. This was the 1840s, however, and every silver lining had a cloud. Just as the economy seemed to be recovering, the Irish famine migration washed over British North America. The Province of Canada was the destination for about 90,000 of the starving and disease-ridden refugees. It was truly a time of horror as the Irish emigrants huddled in the immigration sheds on Grosse-Îsle in the St. Lawrence and on the outskirts of Montreal, Toronto and other towns. Official estimates at the time were that 12 percent died on the ships or in quarantine. Many more expired in hospitals ashore. Canadians could now add a new collection of fears to their economic anxieties. They feared the disease the refugees carried and, indeed, there were severe epidemics of ship fever and cholera in 1847 and 1849. They feared the economic impact of so many destitute people and the economy did collapse once again. They feared disorder and disorder did assault society. Catholic Irish and Protestant Orangemen fought their ancient battles across British North America on 12 July 1847. Again in 1849, the Orange celebration of 12 July was marred by widespread violence, including battles in Saint John, New Brunswick, and on Upper Canada's Welland Canal—battles that left many dead.[4]

Political change dogged economic and social change. Baldwin and some of his liberal compatriots, from the mid-1830s on, saw responsible government as the solution to the political ills of the colonies. Most conservatives were equally fervent in their opposition. Their concept of the British constitution was rooted in the importance of property and in the "representation of interests rather than individuals." In Britain, the monarchy and the aristocracy checked democracy. Such limitations were absent in Canada. Therefore it would be disastrous to good government and destructive of property to surrender imperial authority to a mere majority in the House of Assembly. Britain nevertheless, with great reluctance, granted responsible government. Tories expected the worst.[5]

The difficulties of politics in a bicultural state, economic uncertainty, the famine migration, responsible government: conservatives felt victimized and betrayed in so many ways. Above all, they felt battered by change. John Beverley Robinson had been a central figure in the Family Compact. As the woes of the 1840s piled up, he barely knew whether to be angry or simply melancholy. He wrote to his friend John Macaulay in 1843: "I wish I could go to sleep & forget all that happened since Sir John Colborne left Canada [in 1839] . . . but the world is no worse than it was only once we were a little more heroical & respectable than the generality of mankind. The age of simplicity cannot be expected to last long while steamers & railways are flourishing."[6]

The Speech from the Throne promised a busy legislative session. The young Reform ministry planned to assume control of the post office from Britain, increase representation in the Assembly, reform the judiciary and municipal government, create a University of Toronto, reorganize finances and the provincial debt, and provide a fund to support schools. That this was indeed a new era was signalled when Lord Elgin delivered the speech in both English and French. Baldwin's hope that Canada would become a place of justice for both its peoples seemed to be one step closer to fruition.

Alas, all the ministry's bold plans were obscured by the one measure that would attract most of the attention—providing compensation to those Lower Canadians who suffered property losses during the Rebellions of 1837 and 1838. The issue was not new, for claims had been made as soon as the uprisings had been subdued. The previous Tory government had paved the way to dealing with the matter. During the House session of 1844–1845, some £40,000 had been appropriated to pay claims from Upper Canada. As well, a commission was appointed to determine what losses should be compensated in Lower Canada. The Reformers now were prepared to act on the report of the commission.[7]

Louis LaFontaine rose in the House on Tuesday, 13 February to introduce the final reading of the Rebellion Losses Bill. He proposed to honour claims for losses, except from those convicted of treason, and to issue debentures for £100,000 to meet the obligation. His friend Baldwin was curiously silent as the debate raged on. There was, inevitably, speculation that he did not support his colleague's measure. If so, he kept his own counsel. Some support was given to the speculation by the fact that he did not speak in the House on the resolutions for weeks, only intervening once on 19 February to set Sir Allan MacNab right about a technicality on how the legislation should be introduced. His first substantive comments did not come until 27 February, after LaFontaine had accepted amendments that ruled out compensation for anyone convicted or banished for their part in the rebellions.[8]

Conservative members, having resisted at all stages of the measure, were still attempting to prevent the inevitable passage of the bill. Henry Sherwood of Toronto and Colonel John Prince of Essex both demanded that it be delayed until the opinion of the people could be ascertained. Apparently Prince, who had won fame for summarily executing prisoners during the rebellion, already knew the tenor of that opinion for he announced that he would rather cut off his right arm than consent to payments to Lower Canadians. Lord Elgin, who personally opposed the Rebellion Losses Bill, understood the basis for Tory indignation. "[T]he opposition leaders," he wrote to the Colonial Secretary, "who are very low in the World at present, have taken advantage of the circumstances to work upon the feelings of the old loyalists as opposed to Rebels, of British as opposed to French, and of Upper Canadians as opposed to Lower."[9]

Feelings both inside the House and outside became fevered, as the compensation bill was entangled with English-French antagonisms, Tory bewilderment over responsible government, bitter memories of the rebellion years, and the ongoing commercial depression. Two of the more volatile members were the Solicitor General West, William Hume Blake, and the rising conservative star from Kingston, John A. Macdonald. They clashed frequently in the House, Macdonald's broad Scottish burr trying to drown out Blake's shrill rhetoric. Their animosity went beyond words on Friday, 16 February. Macdonald was infuriated by Blake's attacks on the character of Tory leaders. Those attacks had set off a fistfight in the public galleries the previous day, an affair so violent that the ladies present had to be escorted to safety behind the Speaker's chair. That Friday, while both partisans were still in the Assembly listening to the debate, Macdonald sent a message to the Solicitor General, challenging him to a duel. They left the chamber to prepare. The Speaker got wind of it and ordered the Sergeant at Arms to apprehend the two. Macdonald was quickly rounded up and delivered to the House, but Blake could not be found until the following Monday. The would-be duelists were brought before the bar of the Assembly and required to pledge peace. Outside the House there were effigy burnings, threats of violence, and talk of joining the United States, where, presumably, rebels would never be compensated. Newspapers such as the Toronto *Colonist* and the *Patriot*, and the *Hamilton Spectator*, speculated openly about the prospect of annexation.[10]

More explosive yet was the return of William Lyon Mackenzie in the midst of the excitement over the Rebellion Losses Bill. He was the last of the 1837 rebels to receive amnesty and the most potent symbol of the issues that still troubled the country from the time of the revolt. He set out in March 1849 on a tour of Upper Canada, planning to deal with business in his capacity as executor of several estates. Everywhere angry mobs and burning effigies greeted him. The culmination came in his old home city of Toronto. He received threatening letters, warning him, as one said, to "Dread it by pistol, by dagger, by club, and by poison." A large crowd gathered on the evening of 22 March, while city magistrates looked on benignly. They smashed the windows of the house where Mackenzie was staying and marched to the homes of W.H. Blake and Robert Baldwin where effigies were burned. The Baldwin children were sheltered by, of all people, Robert's old nemesis Bishop Strachan. The gentry could still rally beyond partisanship, it seemed.[11]

The crowd was in the street again the following night, once more lighting the darkness with flaming effigies. A prominent Reformer, James Lesslie, told Mackenzie that the Tories were really trying to intimidate Lord Elgin so that he would dissolve Parliament before the Rebellion Losses Bill became law.

The Tory efforts were in vain. The large Reform majority easily passed the Rebellion Losses Bill. The stage was set.

―――◆◆◆―――

It was a routine day for the Assembly that Wednesday, 25 April. Members voted on the third reading of a bill about construction of aprons on mill dams in Upper Canada, and some housekeeping items. The only matter of substance was a tariff bill. It was being rushed forward because the first spring ships were about to arrive at Quebec. The inspector general of Finance, Francis Hincks, told the House that it was imperative to pass the tariff bill immediately so that the early ships would be subject to the new rates as later ones would be. Members agreed and the tariff passed third reading in the Assembly and hurried through the Legislative Council without opposition. The Governor General had already been alerted and agreed to come to Parliament to sign the bill.[12]

Lord Elgin and an aide made the 4.8-kilometre trip from Monklands, bumping along a rutted road in the governor's handsome four-in-hand. He arrived at Parliament by late afternoon. The members gathered in the Legislative Council chamber to witness the signing of bills. Along with the tariff measure, Elgin signed several pieces of legislation, including the Rebellion Losses Bill. Elgin himself contended that it was simply convenient to approve all at once. Opponents thought the ministry was trying to slip the controversial bill through without anyone noticing. One witness claimed that the clerk read it in "a low tone, with the intention of attracting as little attention as possible." If that was the intention, it was a resounding failure.[13]

As Elgin signed the offensive legislation, boos and hisses rang down from the public galleries and a number of men rushed from their seats and into the street. Elgin emerged from the market building about 6:00 p.m. to return to Monklands. A crowd of some hundreds had gathered, with their weapons ready. Elgin mounted his carriage through a volley of rotten eggs and stones. The mob chased the carriage as it fled along McGill and St. Antoine Streets. The governor finally escaped to Monklands without serious injury.[14]

The Tories were well prepared as illustrated by the special edition that the *Gazette* hurried onto the streets. "The Disgrace of Great Britain

Accomplished, Canada Sold & Given Away" screamed the headline. The newspaper announced a meeting at the Place d'Armes for 8:00 p.m. and urged, "ANGLO-SAXONS TO THE STRUGGLE NOW IS YOUR TIME." It warned ominously, "The puppet in the pageant must be recalled, or driven away by the universal contempt of the people."

The *Gazette*'s call to gather was supplemented by others. Fire engines paraded the city, ringing their bells. The crowd that began to gather overflowed the Place d'Armes and the meeting was rescheduled for the Champs de Mars. A cab raced through the city with a man holding on to the top. He had liberated a bell from the fashionable restaurant, Dolly's Chop House, and was ringing it and shouting, "To the Champs de Mars, to the Champs de Mars. Elgin has signed the bill." The Champs de Mars was at the eastern end of the downtown core, a space that served both as a military drill ground and a public park. By eight it was filled with thousands of men, many of them carrying torches. Augustus Heward, an insurance and commodity broker and nephew of Chief Justice J.B. Robinson of Upper Canada, was the first to speak. Other notables in the Montreal anglophone community followed him: Hugh Montgomerie, a merchant and a captain in the militia; John Esdaile, a freight and produce broker; James Moir Ferres, editor of the *Gazette*; George Mack, a lawyer; Alfred Perry, a manufacturer. These were the firebrands. Less inflammatory rhetoric came from the proprietor of the city's largest export-import firm, George Moffatt, and MLA Colonel Bartholomew Gugy, although their very presence gave a patina of respectability to the proceedings.[15]

The meeting adopted a resolution condemning Lord Elgin for signing the bill. Then it was on to Parliament. As the mob streamed west toward St. Anne's Market, the House was in committee, discussing a bill to create an appeals court in Lower Canada. Joseph Laurin of Lotbinière was speaking in support when a stone crashed through a window of the chamber. The stone became a fusillade and the members scurried for cover. There was a thunderous crashing as part of the mob, led by Alfred Perry, used a fire-company ladder to batter down the doors. Men burst into the hall brandishing clubs. Burly Alex Courtnay, clad in a blanket coat, mounted the dais and took the Speaker's chair. "I dissolve this House," he shouted and the destruction began. A great pyre of papers and broken benches was built in the middle of the floor. The intruders threw clubs at the chandelier and the globe lights along the walls, igniting the pyre and flames spread through the chamber and into the parliamentary library. William Snaith Jr. and a Mr. Hargrove rescued a large portrait of Queen Victoria that hung above the Speaker's chair and some rioters made off with the mace. All else was lost. The flames that leaped high above the doomed building lit up the whole of Montreal.[16]

Troops had been stationed at the Bonsecour Market and they secured the street in front of the Parliament to allow access for the fire engines. Yet it appears neither the troops nor the firemen did anything to save the building or intimidate the crowd. Lord Elgin would explain to Colonial Secretary Earl Grey that there was a reluctance to have the troops act for fear of making the situation worse. That may be so, but there may also have been a fear that the troops would disobey orders. One member of the garrison, interviewed many years later in his old age, remembered that most soldiers were sympathetic to the Tory crowd and "when we were told the night before that there would be trouble if the Governor came down to sign the bill, we promised that if we were ordered to fire our rifles would be discharged in the air." This may have been an old man's rambling, yet Elgin's own aide-de-camp, F.A. Grant, made clear at the time that he was supportive of the Tory cause. Hincks was certain the troops would refuse to fire on the mob. When he was in London mustering support for the colonial ministry, he told Earl Grey that the garrison commander, Major General Charles Gore, ordered his men not to fire on the crowd even if ordered to do so by the magistrates.[17]

No lives were lost although it was a near thing for some. Several members had to slide down drainpipes and columns to reach safety. A number of others were trapped on a balcony outside the Legislative Council chamber, unable to get down from the second floor and endangered by the flames behind them. Conservative partisanship, strangely, saved the lives of some Reformers. A rumour ran through the crowd that Tory leader Sir Allan MacNab was among those on the balcony, although in fact he had escaped out the front of the building. A ladder was fetched and the parliamentarians were saved. Meanwhile MacNab had retreated to his hotel, Donegana's. The mob would pay him tribute there. Perry, the mace in hand, led the crowd back along

Notre Dame Street toward Donegana's. Perry later noted that the mace, "the emblem of dethroned dignity," gave him an air of authority and encouraged the crowd to follow him. This was "lawless law" in action. At the hotel, they presented MacNab with the mace and roundly cheered him. Their business done, the mob began to disperse.[18]

A few hours of relative calm ended by daybreak when the police arrested the ringleaders, Heward, Montgomerie, Esdaile, Ferres, and Perry. They were taken to police offices in the basement of the Bonsecours Market. A crowd quickly gathered, shouting its intention to free the prisoners. When the police tried to move Perry by cab to military headquarters on Dalhousie Square, his supporters attacked the vehicle, threw it over and cut the harness. Perry assured the crowd he was safe and, followed by the mob, went with the police to Dalhousie Square. The festivities continued outside the Government House on Notre Dame Street where protestors jeered and assaulted ministers who were coming and going. The *Montreal Herald* reported that "The Hon. J.H. Boulton was an especial object of derision, as he ran off, his small figure was well coated with unsavoury eggs." Meanwhile, the arrested rioters were finally settled in jail. Dolly, the proprietor of the famous Chop House, arrived with two waiters to treat them to roast meat, sweets, and wine.[19]

Sporadic violence continued through the day and darkness emboldened the Tories all the more. The first major attack was on the office of the liberal newspaper, the *Pilot*. Then a mob marched on Louis LaFontaine's residence. It was a splendid target, isolated on a ridge above St. Antoine Street. This was no random act. A party of about 500 marched in orderly fashion up St. Antoine, obeying the instructions from parade marshals. There was an attempt to burn the house, a fire quickly extinguished, and the inside was ransacked. Then it was on to other targets. Soldiers drove them off when they attacked the home of Reform MLA Lewis Drummond. There was better success at a rooming house on St. Antoine Street, where Reform cabinet ministers Robert Baldwin, J.H. Price and Malcolm Cameron lived during parliamentary sessions. The crowd smashed all the windows there and, warming to their work, did the same at the dwellings of MLAs Wolfred Nelson, Francis Hincks, Benjamin Holmes, and John Wilson. Allies of the mob heaped indignity on indignity. John G. Dinning held the mortgage on LaFontaine's house and that afternoon of 26 April he wrote to the politician insisting on full payment of mortgage and interest. Dinning was outraged that Perry and the others had been arrested. He warned,

> [S]hould the Govt. injure the hair of any man's head, belonging to those, <u>who are now determined</u> to see no treason live in the Country, there is every probability that your house will be the next to be committed to the flames. . . . In such a position you will oblige me by at once sending to my office for a regular a/c [accounting] and Interest a/c and on ascertaining the balance send me a check therefore. . . . P.S. You are of course aware that your policy of Insurance, in case of a fire caused by Citoyens, is useless.

LaFontaine ignored the demand. So, too, the House of Assembly, meeting in the Bonsecours Market, gave short shrift to Sir Allan MacNab's version of "make the victim pay." He provided notice that day of a motion "to make the loss sustained by the fire of the preceding night the first charge on the sum voted to be paid out of the Rebellion Losses."[20]

The arrest of the five crowd leaders continued to rankle and to produce threats of mass destruction. The government's attempts to secure order did so as well. On 26 April, LaFontaine asked the mayor and the police superintendent, William Ermatinger, to enroll special constables. They were unable to find volunteers among the respectable elements who usually served. So the next day the governor appointed the commissioner of public works, Étienne-Paschal Taché, as commissioner of the peace, authorized to organize a special police force. A number of French-Canadians citizens, as well as Irish navvies from the canal works, were ready. Gustave Papineau, son of the rebel leader of 1837, reported that a crowd of 500 to 600 French Canadians had gathered at the office of *L'Avenir* newspaper, ready to attack the Tories if they rioted again that night. Instead, they were enrolled in the new police, issued arms, and set to drilling that evening at Bonsecours Market. There had already been some skirmishing near Dalhousie Square in which French Canadians and Tories had exchanged fire. At least three men were wounded. Angry oppositionists responded to the ringing of fire bells and mustered at the Haymarket. The city was now on the verge of civil war. There was nothing for the government but to back down. The English crowd began to march toward the Bonsecour Market to disarm the French Canadians, but Major General Gore and Colonel Gugy halted them in front of the Ottawa Hotel. Gugy mounted the steps of the hotel and pleaded for calm, promising to disarm the special constables and free the five prisoners. The government had capitulated. The liberated leaders were paraded through the streets to the cheers of a delirious throng.[21]

Every gesture by the ministry was trumped by the mob. On 28 April Henry John Boulton and Joseph-Édouard Cauchon moved an address of loyalty, expressing support for the Governor General. There was a furious debate marked by Tory attempts to attach an amendment that blamed the government for the recent riots and by dire warnings from Colonel Gugy that the whole country could be "deluged in blood." The main motion finally passed although one reformer, Alexander Tilloch Galt from the Eastern Townships, and the old rebel, Louis-Joseph Papineau, joined the Tories in opposition. The attempt to deliver the address to Elgin set off the mob once more. The governor came into the city by carriage and awaited the members of Parliament at the ancient Château de Ramezay, now serving as the Government House. Troops and police guarded the Bonsecours Market and the lane leading to Notre Dame Street and Government House. The security was so tight that a soldier stopped a conservative independent member, Robert Christie of Gaspé, as he tried to enter the market. Christie advised the soldier that he was a member but, as the outraged Christie told the House, the soldier answered, "How the hell can I tell if you are a member or not?" Christie finally made his way in to complain to his colleagues. The members then set out for Government House, to be assaulted by stones rained over the troops onto the politicians. Robert and LaFontaine sheltered under their hats and covered their faces as stones rattled on the paving in the all too familiar music of Canadian politics. A magistrate read the Riot Act, and the military cleared a path for the members to Government House where the address was delivered. A plain stone building, the Château de Ramezay had stood since 1705, protected by its stout fence and thick walls. Every inch of those defences were necessary that day, as Robert and LaFontaine sheltered in the garden from the mob fury outside. It was a shaken Lord Elgin who received their address. He had been attacked on his way into town, despite a cavalry escort, and pelted with eggs and rocks. It was worse as Elgin returned to Monklands. The cavalry tried to plow a passage through the crowds clogging the streets, but there was little hope of protecting the governor's carriage. Near St. Lawrence Hall, a trooper ran over a man and the mob turned from derisory to furious. Perry, newly freed from jail, was nearby and he would later claim to have been the first to hurl a brickbat through the window of the carriage. Missiles battered the coach and anyone who tried to protect it. The police magistrate, Colonel Ermatinger, and Captain Jones of the cavalry were injured. Elgin fled, his horses at full gallop, pursued by a motley armada of impressed vehicles, carriages, cabs, and trucks, even water carts. Elgin was overtaken at the corner of St. Lawrence and Sherbrooke Streets. His carriage was pummeled until its sides collapsed and his brother, Colonel Bruce, suffered a severe head wound from a stone. They finally broke through the mob and escaped up Côte-des-Neiges to Monklands. A military guard and barricades kept the mob out, but also kept Elgin in. He did not dare to enter Montreal again. When Parliament was prorogued on 30 May, the deputy governor, Major General Rowan, was sent in Elgin's place.[22]

It was dangerous business, supporting Lord Elgin and the ministry. Delegations of Reformers came to Montreal from Toronto, Kingston, and Cobourg, Upper Canada, to deliver addresses. Robert, LaFontaine, and the governing party feted them with a grand dinner at Tetu's Hotel on the evening of 9 May. Legislative Councillor Adam Fergusson was in the chair and a distinguished company had gathered to celebrate their loyalty. The speakers of both Houses were there, as were many members of the legislature and leaders of the Upper Canadian delegation including George Brown, and prominent Toronto business leader, W.P. Howland. According to the *Gazette*, their "hip-hop, hurra-ing" attracted a crowd in front of the hotel. The gathering may have been less spontaneous than that, since some of the protestors arrived with pistols and a battering ram. The mob began to gather about 9:00 p.m., contenting itself with jeers for two hours. Near eleven, stones were flying and then the doors were attacked with the battering ram. A side door gave way, but the Reformers beat back the intruders. Both sides would claim the other opened fire first. Whatever the truth, those inside got the better of it. At least two, perhaps three, of the rioters suffered bullet wounds. The Reform sharpshooter was William Hume Blake, Solicitor General West. It was as measure of the time that few seemed to think it strange for a law officer of the Crown to be engaging in a gunfight on the streets of the capital. It was Colonel Hay and the Nineteenth Regiment that finally ended the affair and cleared the street.[23]

The troubles in Montreal had their fainter echoes across Canada. There was fear of a major riot in Toronto in early May, but the Tory crowd was confined to effigy burning and street parades, thanks to the presence of troops called out by the mayor, George Gurnett. Elgin's effigies were in flames in Newmarket, Cobourg, Hamilton, Napanee, and other towns in Upper Canada. In Sherbrooke, Lower Canada, the effigy was dragged by the neck to the Magog bridge and dumped into the water below to cries of, "Here goes the Governor General." Orangemen near Port Hope, Upper Canada, had their own form of protest, attacking the premises of a Reform supporter and maiming his cattle—cutting their sides and hacking off their tails. There were fears that worse could happen. Reformers in Markham and Newmarket, near Toronto, reported that local Orangemen were well armed with guns from the militia. Godley Eckard warned Baldwin that Orangemen in Markham "are making their boast of turning their arms upon the government in case that any of their gang should be brought to justice for what they have already done." More fanciful were the stories of spies and mysterious figures. Reformers at Holland Landing, Upper Canada, claimed that the effigy burning there was led by "two strangers with long coats such as described, in the Montreal papers, at the burning of the parliament House." The paranoia was understandable. Men more respectable than the Orange mobs were contemplating violence. Samuel Jarvis Jr., scion of a Family Compact line, wrote to his mother in May that, "I wish they would catch old Elgin & string him up as a caution to other traitor Governors." Henry Sherwood, an independent-minded Tory, moved a motion in the Assembly to move the capital from Montreal. He then had to flee the city because of threats to his life. And, once again, in June, LaFontaine's mortgage holder advised him to remove his belongings from the house on Craig Street to avoid provoking the dwelling's destruction by a mob. After all, Dinning pointed out, LaFontaine still had not paid off the amount owing, so it would be Dinning who would absorb the loss.[24]

The struggle was mostly rhetoric and petitions. Many Tories joined the British American League that had been formed in Montreal that spring under the leadership of Montreal merchant George Moffatt. The League had the potential to increase tensions, especially given that among its first officers were some of the ringleaders of the Montreal riots, including W.G. Mack, H.E. Montgomerie, and John Esdaile. However, as the League extended across the province it became an ineffective debating society, torn between those who wanted constitutional reform to check French influence and those who leaned toward more extreme solutions such as annexation to the United States. Meanwhile, the ministry was organizing vigorously to give the impression of widespread support for Lord Elgin and for government policy. Robert Baldwin personally financed petition campaigns. Both parties sought to influence British opinion. In early May, the Tories dispatched William Cayley, member for Huron, Upper Canada, who had good connections in the home country, and reinforced him with Sir Allan MacNab, who boarded a ship for Britain on 21 May. The Reformers countered with Hincks. The Canadian delegates lobbied vigorously in London and carried their arguments to the dance floor when both were invited to a festive ball at Buckingham Palace on 13 June. There is no evidence that they made a difference in British policy, but diplomacy was clearly preferable to fisticuffs. And, at home, disease helped keep people out of the streets. Cholera was rampant from early summer to autumn, taking a heavy death toll especially in Montreal and Toronto.[25]

Perhaps the worst was over. It was devoutly hoped that was true, since Britain was withdrawing troops from Montreal as a matter of economy; apparently the Empire could not afford a replacement for the crumbling Montreal barracks. LaFontaine and Baldwin tried to compensate by creating a regular mounted police force that June, despite Tory threats of violence should the police be deployed. Adam Ferrie, a legislative councillor, was delegated to warn the ministry. The Tories, he advised, were unhappy about police replacing soldiers since they were certain that the troops would not fire on the crowds and police might. The changes went ahead and the police had to deal with the usual mayhem. There was fighting on Notre Dame Street when Orangemen celebrated the twelfth of July. Eight days later a dispute between an Orange restaurant owner and a Catholic near St. Anne's Market concluded with the Orangeman drawing a pistol and the Catholic dead in the street.[26]

Alas, it was soon apparent that politics could stir the familiar emotions. A concert by the European singers Toffanelli and Madame Laborde on 18 July was disrupted when some young French Canadians called for "La Marseillaise." Enraged Tories attacked them and the fighting spilled out into the streets. The city mob had gathered and joined in, not only denouncing France, but giving groans for Lord Elgin. There were dark rumours of more trouble to come and officials took them seriously. LaFontaine called on militia colonel and cabinet colleague Étienne-Paschal Taché to fortify and provision the premier's home in anticipation of further attacks.[27]

The government's decision to proceed against those who had burned Parliament set off a new crisis. Warrants were issued to arrest the arsonists on 15 August. Immediately as the news began to circulate, handbills were posted throughout the city calling on members of a hitherto secret society, the Briton's Club, to prepare for action. The arrests were made with little resistance and eight ringleaders were committed to the jail. It would not go so smoothly when the mob took to the streets on the evening of 15 August. The military was outnumbered and outmanoeuvred as crowds gathered at various points in the city centre and erected barricades across major streets. The main front, meanwhile, was at LaFontaine's home. The Reform leader gloried in his resemblance to Napoleon I. Now, hunkered down in his fortified dwelling, surrounded by heavily armed friends, he would experience battle himself. The mob arrived soon after nine that night, with much uproar and threat. According to the conservative press, physical violence began when someone inside fired on the crowd. Captain George Augustus Wetherall, the special magistrate, contended that the first aggression was from the rioters who pelted the house with stones, broke through the gate to surround the home, and fired a shot at the defenders. Whoever began the violence, LaFontaine and his colleagues ended it. A volley of shots drove the crowd back. As they retreated, they assisted their wounded. Eighteen-year-old William Mason was beyond anyone's assistance, however. He was dead, and rumour had it that it was Louis LaFontaine himself who had fired the fatal shot.[28]

The death of Mason reignited the city. The thoroughfares were aflame on the following evening, with a crowd surging down Notre Dame Street, smashing the street lamps as they went. At the Place d'Armes, barricades were thrown up. Placards flowered on every pole.

MURDER ! !
THE
FIRST ANGLO-SAXON BLOOD!
TURN OUT
TO A MAN, TO THE
FUNERAL
THAT YOU MAY REMEMBER FOR EVER
THE MURDERED VICTIM
AND THE GLORIOUS CAUSE.
TO-MORROW MORNING, AT TEN O'CLOCK
THE BODY OF THE YOUNG MASON
WILL BE CARRIED FROM CRAIG STREET TO THE GRAVE.
LET THE SHOPS BE SHUT.

The shops were indeed shut the next morning along the route of the procession. Angry men with red scarves and ribands marched behind the coffin and lined the streets. Again, fires troubled the night in various parts of the city. The inquest into Mason's death at Cyrus' Hotel only made matters worse. LaFontaine was exonerated but, after his testimony, the Seventy-first Highlanders had to rescue him from an attacking mob. Innkeeper Cyrus saw his hotel go up in flames.[29]

Even some Tory leaders had had enough. Merchant George Moffatt and William Badgley, the member for Missisquoi, Lower Canada, co-operated with Mayor Fabre to raise a force of 200 special constables. Relative calm returned to Montreal. Much of the political excitement shifted to Upper Canada when Elgin announced a tour of the west. Toronto oppositionists greeted the news with placards calling for demonstrations when the Governor General came: "[L]et your eggs be stale and your powder dry!" As the tour date drew near, in mid-September, there were large anti-Elgin meetings in Brockville, London, and other towns. Posters in Toronto claimed that hundred of "armed CUT-THROATS" had been hired, presumably by the Reformers, to slaughter the loyal inhabitants of the city and burn their homes. Conservatives needed to arm themselves. There were more than words and dark suspicions in the pioneer community of Bytown, the lumbering centre on the Ottawa River. Reformers called a meeting on 17 September to prepare an address of greeting to Elgin. They were attacked by a Tory crowd and a great battle of rocks and bullets ensued, the affair that became known as "Stony Monday." One young Tory, David Borthwick, was killed. The threats and violence rallied many Upper Canadians to their governor. Elgin began his tour at Port Dover and he was escorted along the way by hundreds of supporters. Wisely, though, he cancelled plans to visit Bytown.[30]

Robert Baldwin thought that he understood what this was about. He was certain that Montreal Tories were stirring up trouble in Upper Canada. They were attempting to discourage any attempt to move the capital from Montreal to the west by demonstrating there was no guarantee of peace there. Robert did not want to believe his own province was as susceptible to violence as was Montreal. He had been making the case for Toronto as the new capital, he reported, and begged for order there so as not to dash his hopes. "Depend upon it, the time is now or never."[31]

He need not have worried. Most of the ministry agreed that the first necessary step toward stability was the removal of the capital from Montreal. The cabinet met with Elgin on 26 August. The Governor General urged time for reflection since LaFontaine was opposed to a move, Upper Canadians wanted an alternating capital with the first tenure in Toronto, and other Lower Canadian ministers insisted on relocating first to Quebec. Elgin told Grey, in condescension, that the ministry was "somewhat impressionable" in their frightened anxiety to leave Montreal. A week later, he too was convinced by the continuing Tory threats. The city was impossible. Britain was withdrawing troops. The mayor was under the influence of the old rebel chief, Papineau. And continuing the capital in Montreal, or even moving it first to Quebec, would only reinforce the impression of French domination over the government. The decision was taken. The capital would alternate, every five years, between Toronto and Quebec. By the time the move was made, there was more regret than anger and, on 20 November 1849, Elgin quietly moved his family into Ellah's Hotel at King and York Streets in Toronto while his official residence was being prepared.[32]

There was still the threat of annexation, the desperate measure spawned by the Rebellion Losses Bill. The Annexation Manifesto was published on 11 October 1849. It bore the name of more than 300 men, among them prominent business and political figures including: John and Peter Redpath of the sugar-refining dynasty; John and William Molson, brewers and merchants; J.C.C. Abbott, lawyer, businessman, and future prime minister of Canada; Alexander Tilloch Galt, later a Father of Confederation; French-Canadian political leaders, Louis-Joseph Papineau and Antoine-Aimé Dorion. The movement rallied the support of *Rouges* radicals, followers of Papineau, whose leading newspaper, *L'Avenir*, had been espousing annexation since at least February. A number of English-language newspapers also promoted annexation, among them the *Herald* and *Witness* of Montreal, *Le Canadien* and the *Morning Chronicle* of Quebec, and a new Toronto paper, the *Independent*. This time, however, the ministry, led by Baldwin, was decisive. Government appointees and militia officers who endorsed annexation were removed from office. Reform radicals, with their sympathy for democratic institutions, were whipped back into line. The annexation movement proved to be a brief outlet for anger and disappointment.[33]

More important was the economy. There was an upturn in 1850 and there was new hope in reciprocity negotiations with the United States, although they would not result in a treaty until 1854. And there was a grand financial adventure in which all political stripes could enroll. The railway age began in earnest, and soon a mania for railway construction would become the great political pastime. It was that arch-Tory, Sir Allan MacNab, the abettor of the Montreal mob, who captured the new spirit in 1851 when he declared, "[A]ll his politics were Railroads, and he would support whoever supported Railroads."[34]

There was no single cause for all this. The strands that wove together the fabric of Canadian society contributed to the crisis.

Laws apply to all and protect all. That is the premise of modern western societies. That premise had little traction in Canada in 1849. Lord Elgin, who viewed the colony with the shrewd eye of the informed outsider, commented as the rebellion-losses issue built toward its climax: "[I]t has been so long the practice here that animosities should rule by intrigue and corruption if possible, and failing this, by violence and external help, that things cannot be expected to find their level without shocks that sometimes assume the proportion of earthquakes."[35]

This was a philosophy that had long animated the elites. The Canadas had a tradition of societal leaders acting directly in extralegal ways. Carol Wilton studied thirty cases of conservative political violence in Upper Canada between 1818 and 1841, cases in which legal authorities approved of vigilante or mob action or turned a blind eye to them. Lawyers and law students could take part in riots such as that in 1826 when a mob destroyed Mackenzie's newspaper office in York. That was because the legal establishment saw the purpose of the law as maintaining the traditional hierarchical order.[36]

Group violence was common beyond the elites and, by the 1840s, had come to threaten the social order as Orange-Green riots and labour unrest erupted across British North America. Baldwin believed that "lawless law" must be extinguished if political and social progress was to be achieved. During the first Reform administration in Canada in 1842–1843, he tried to outlaw the processions and the party symbols of the Orange Order so as to prevent violent confrontations. More modestly, he encouraged the Governor General to express his approbation to local authorities who resisted extralegal activities. The legislation against processions failed because magistrates and juries either refused—or were afraid—to act against Orangemen. And backwoods officials were often powerless to control vigilante and mob power.[37]

Direct action was the way of things in Montreal. The January 1848 provincial election showed the boldness of extralegal forces and their degree of organization. On 11 January liberal lawyer Charles Drolet led a force of armed men down Notre Dame Street toward the polls. They were fired on from the windows of the Royal Oak Tavern, a well-known haunt of conservative supporters. Lord Elgin thought there was a "perfect understanding between the more outrageous and respectable fractions of the Tory party" in Montreal. The events of January 1848 remind us this was true on the liberal side as well.[38]

The Rebellion Losses Bill was seen as so unacceptable, so beyond the bounds of legitimate parliamentary jurisdiction, that it was natural and necessary for conservatives to take direct action. The *Gazette* described the burning of the Parliament building as "the destruction of the Sodom and Gomorrah" in which the outrageous bill had been conceived. The unfolding of the crisis offered a tacit consent to this view. The government and local authorities were unable to act decisively against the rioters. Those arrested were never brought to trial. The special magistrate charged with maintaining order in the city, Captain Wetherall, resigned on 18 August 1849 because he believed it was impossible to enforce the law. The local authorities were overwhelmed, the use of the military would produce unacceptable bloodshed, and legitimacy had passed to the crowd in the streets. Wetherall's assessment was accurate until the conservatives realized that direct violence would not solve their problems and that other tactics were required.[39]

The incidents in Montreal were unusually large in scope and extended in time. Yet they could be justified as falling within the range of traditional political practices. That was all the more so given the issues at stake: "race" and loyalty. When Alfred Perry burst into the corridor of the Parliament that fateful evening, he confronted a portrait of Louis-Joseph Papineau, who had served as speaker of the Lower Canadian Assembly for many years. "I saw the pictures of Her Majesty and Papineau. The latter was to me like a red rag to a bull." Perry cheered on a man who smashed the offending portrait with a plank and then put his foot through the canvas. It was the symbol of French domination, the raising of a so-called inferior people to power over their "betters." Some weeks earlier, the *Gazette* had reminded the authorities that Britain had precipitated a revolution in the Thirteen Colonies "by establishing a French Canadian nationality" through the Quebec Act of 1774. It was happening again thanks to recognition of the French language—the delivery of the Throne Speech in English and French, the establishment of French law in the Eastern Townships, and the proposal to allow French Canadians easy access to traditionally English lands in the Townships. The French were flaunting their political power while their innate "sluggishness" was inhibiting the progressive Anglo-Saxons. [40]

The Rebellion Losses legislation offended both racial sensibilities and traditional loyalty when French votes rewarded French rebels. The idea of colonial loyalty has mostly been discussed in reference to Upper Canada, with its providential loyalism springing from reaction to the American Revolution and the War of 1812. The Lower Canadian anglophone variant has been treated as either a commercial ideology or an imported one. Donald Creighton, in his classic *Commercial Empire of the St. Lawrence*, admired a merchant class that recognized the geographic logic of the St. Lawrence trading system. The St. Lawrence's empire was linked to Britain's, and the two owed loyalty to each other so both might prosper. Leading scholar of Lower Canada, Alan Greer was less admiring but equally focused on the commercial roots of political ideology. In contrast, historian Michael McCulloch identified Lower Canadian loyalty with adherence to Whig ideals imported from Britain. [41]

In both Canadas, there undoubtedly was much sincerity in conservative professions of devotion to the British constitution and its principles. It was their familiar form of government and it was a stout barrier against the evils of the American system. Such devotion was also self-serving. The British constitution, as imported to the colonies, ensconced Tory elites in power and conceded them economic bounties in the form of land grants and public salaries. It is impossible to untangle the principled and the convenient in the conservatism of the time, but we can detach the experiences of the two colonies. Circumstances in Upper Canada made Toryism a popular political force, as many ordinary yeomen rallied to the pro-British, anti-American rhetoric of the elite. That could hardly be so in Lower Canada, where the large majority of ordinary folk were French Canadian, deaf to the elite's message. The English-speaking merchants and professionals have been called traditionalists by Greer, for their willingness to adjust to the existing order in Lower Canada, or Whigs by McCulloch, for their espousal of British constitutional forms. It is simpler to see them as conservatives who exploited their ethnic advantage to gain commercial and governmental preferences, and remained loyal to the system of privilege that prevailed for so long.

When these twin buttresses of their power and prosperity were challenged, they reacted out of proportion to the threat. Archibald Acheson, Lord Gosford, was sent by Britain in 1835 to resolve the political tensions in Lower Canada. His modest attempts to draw French Canadians into the government produced shrieks of rage and threats of violence from the *Gazette* and the zealous pamphleteer Adam Thom, premonitions of 1849. In the midst of the Rebellion Losses crisis, the *Globe* would note, with shrewd insight, that "The Toryism of Canada has ever founded its tactics on *panics*. To get up a good panic, and work it well has been the point of perfection in their political system. . . . Let the panic be connected with a national crusade against the French Canadians, and the day might be won." Indeed, that tactic had always worked in the past so it was sensible to dust it off again in 1849.[42]

Most conservatives, in both Canadas, did not understand responsible government, and that ignorance led to their miscalculation in 1849. The old panic would not work under the new order. Responsible government effectively had been conceded by Britain in 1846 when Colonial Secretary Henry George Grey, third Earl Grey, laid out the new policy in a dispatch to Sir John Harvey, Lieutenant-Governor of Nova Scotia. In Canada, it was the conservatives, led by William Henry Draper, that held office as responsible government was granted definitively. Yet even young moderates, such as the member for Kingston, John A. Macdonald, failed to grasp the meaning of the change. He still believed that it was the Governor General's program that a ministry must follow. More, Macdonald thought that the regime could function, under responsible government, without significant French-Canadian participation. The election of 1848 and the subsequent formation of a Reform government could only represent a catastrophe for such men. The French had seized positions of power and would hold them to the eternal exclusion of loyal English Canadians. All responsible government had done was to weaken the governor and give the executive absolute control. As the central committee of the British American League contended in 1850, the new system was a "democratic oligarchy."[43]

Loyalty and ethnicity, conservatives discovered, no longer were enough. They had continued to appeal directly to the Governor General and, with no satisfaction there, to Britain: all in vain. Burning down the Parliament had not won the day, either. Tories felt a mix of anger, disillusionment, and fear that they were permanently shut out from power. MacNab placed his confidence in the traditional method of political violence as a counter to responsible government. He told the House on 1 May 1849 that he preferred "being numbered with what they are pleased to term, the mob of this city, than with these who . . . have attempted to justify treason and rebellion, and have insulted the bold and honest defenders of their Queen and country." The *Gazette* advocated independence rather than live under a form of government that provided "no check to party legislation."[44]

Tories rejected responsible government because, unlike in Britain, there was no curb on the democratic oligarchy of executive and Assembly. How genuine was this critique? For some conservatives, at least, there is reason to doubt the sincerity of their attacks on responsibility. By 1850 several prominent Tories were prepared to go much further down the democratic path than was the Reform government. Robert Christie from Gaspé and John Prince from Essex introduced a motion in the Assembly on 28 May recommending an elective Legislative Council and the elective principle for all government offices. The one-time arch conservative, Henry Sherwood of Toronto, wanted confederation of the British North American colonies with an elected Legislative Council. The initiative failed, but Tories tried again the next month with a motion from W.H. Boulton and Colonel Prince to adopt a completely new constitution with the elective principle, representation by population and an elected governor.[45]

The apparent guiding principle was to throw the Reform rascals out, by street violence or, failing that, by whatever constitutional nostrums could be conceived. The true conservatives in all this were those Reformers, such as Robert Baldwin, who sought to transplant a responsible British form of government in Canada, and to cease constitutional tinkering once that was achieved. Nor was the Tory position on the French more consistent. After all the rhetoric about the unsuitability of French Canadians for governance and the fears of French domination, conservatives would recognize that the French held the keys to power. By 1854, a new Tory–French Party alliance had been crafted and formed a government led by, of all people, Sir Allan

MacNab. Lord Elgin had predicted exactly that in 1850, arguing that the French were attached to the Upper Canadian liberals only by "Accident, or, rather, I believe I should say, the artifices of Imperial policy."[46]

The leadership of Toryism weaved and bobbed as it tried to determine a way back to office in the new political era. What of their street fighters? There was a tradition of paramilitary groups in Montreal, on both sides of politics. The Patriotes' Sons of Liberty skirmished with the Doric Club as a prelude to the Rebellion. In the 1840s the Reform Party's mob comprised French-Canadians and Irish navvies, while the Tories rallied in the Loyal Patriotic Society, the Cavaliers, and other militias. The crowd in 1849 kept with this tradition.

Baldwin had survived all this relatively unscathed. His rooming house had been vandalized and he had burned in effigy in many towns across the province, but his ministry had held firm and, for the most part, had held together. He remained calm and deliberate, even though family worries were added to the political. That August, while the streets of Montreal were still battlegrounds, Robert's mother-in-law, Barbara Sullivan, and his son Bob were both seriously ill. Indeed, it was thought Sullivan would not survive. September brought good news about both, just as the political winds were also changing. And the legislature's escape from Montreal meant that Robert could be at home in Toronto, back in the bosom of family.

Chapter 16

Un jeu d'enfants

The fruits of victory were real, but sometimes they had a bitter taste. Still Eliza would have been proud at what had been accomplished and bitterly protective against those who questioned Robert. Could it be fourteen years?

It was the same room, the same council table that he had left over four years previously. Some of the faces around the table were the same, as well. Francis Hincks and Louis LaFontaine assumed their accustomed places as did Thomas Aylwin, although his tenure would be short this time. Among the new participants one was of pre-eminent importance. Lord Elgin sat at the head of the table in place of Charles Metcalfe. And Elgin had his orders from Britain: give this new ministry its head on domestic matters. Elgin was a living symbol of the change that Robert had won.

Adding substance to the symbolism was complicated. Robert willingly accepted criticism for the brief parliamentary session in the late winter of 1848, confident in his belief that it was crucial for the ministry to organize itself and lay out a program. Some things could not be put off. First on the list was patronage, the evil necessity that had so troubled Baldwin during the first Reform ministry. The expectations of the faithful were even higher now, with responsibility established and four years of Tory patronage finally ended. There was more to dole out now as the bureaucracy grew and as major patronage departments were transferred from Britain to the colony, as customs was in 1849 and the post office in 1851. Robert recognized that patronage was not only good politics, but it was implicit in responsible cabinet government. Yet he did not take the next step to make patronage truly part of responsible government. There was no parliamentary control as the executive shared out offices virtually unchecked.[1]

It might have been distasteful, but Robert dealt with patronage regularly and vigorously. He did not limit his activity to his department but exercised his broader power as party leader, as when he named the members of the new Medical Board of Appeal in June 1851. He personally chose trustees for grammar schools under the School Act of 1850 and appointed local coroners. In many cases, he knew little about the position or the locality, except the political credentials of the appointees. Louis-Joseph Papineau was not far off when, in 1861, he looked back on the second LaFontaine–Baldwin government. He contended that they had been deeply embittered by their defeats in 1843 and 1844 and, in response, adopted the very techniques that Metcalfe had used against them. "To punish bribery, bribery was resorted to. . . . Though they were brighter men than their successors, they have installed bribery in elections and Parliaments, as a necessary ingredient of governing this country."[2]

If the council chamber was familiar, so were some of the issues facing the ministry. Government after government, including Baldwin's own, had struggled to find a system of local government that would be efficient and would satisfy the wishes of Upper Canadians. Robert grasped that particular nettle and, by the beginning of 1849, had drafted a measure. The specific structure was his, but the philosophy behind it emanated from Francis Hincks. Hincks's Memorandum on Immigration and Public Works, presented to the executive council in December 1848, had argued that the province should not fund public works of a local nature. Instead, the government should require municipalities to have sufficient credit and a sinking fund to redeem debt, so that they could take up the burden. Robert could hardly disagree, given his belief in decentralization. Yet he and Hincks had very different assumptions about what such an approach might accomplish. For Baldwin, it was a rational division of power that required municipalities to accept responsibility for their own progress. For Hincks it was a way to free up provincial funds that could then be applied to railway development.[3]

Whatever the disparate motives, Robert successfully pushed through the municipal bill that would become universally known as the Baldwin Act. It abolished the large districts that had been the basis for local government and transferred authority to counties and townships. A measure of local autonomy gave elected township councils unlimited taxing and debt authority. Not coincidentally, the Baldwin Act diminished the authority of the magistracy that had long been a source of influence for the Tories. It was a new political age with rising classes demanding a share of political power. However, it was also an age of uncertainty when nearly every reform measure grated on different interests. Some opposed the Municipal Act because it was too complicated and too expensive. Even those within the family could be critical. Martin Donald Macleod's daughter was married to Robert's brother, William Augustus. He reported that, in his district, the new regime was "not at all palatable to the lads themselves." They were not alone. Baldwin's office was flooded with anxious queries from local authorities who were confused about the qualifications required for candidates for township councils, whether non-residents could vote and other fine points of the legislation.[4]

More telling was opposition from within Reform ranks. The matter of municipal government exposed three distinct tendencies within Reform. Baldwin represented a moderate liberal element that was prepared to countenance change, but not rapid change; that accepted a wider measure of popular participation in governance, but not democracy; that recognized the future was speeding down upon them, but wished to preserve the best of a gentry past. Hincks stood for the rule of the new middle class and the embrace of capitalism. Emerging to challenge both these positions was a more radical set of Reformers who were prepared for democracy and republican institutions, but clung to the values of an agrarian society. One such was Peter Perry. Perry was a veteran of the Upper Canadian legislature before the rebellion who resurfaced in December 1849 to win election for the Third Riding of York in a by-election. He quickly established himself as a leader of the radical wing of the party. In July 1850 he introduced to the House a set of resolutions on municipal government. They advocated the abolition of the property qualification for county and township offices and the extension of the franchise to all persons over twenty-one years who were liable to perform statute labour—essentially all adult males. The resolutions proposed to strip the provincial government of the power to appoint any local officials. Perry cannily pointed out that the ministry was always complaining about the burden of patronage; these resolutions would ease that weight.

Baldwin could not agree to such sweeping changes. They were, he complained, "of a character to change the Institutions of the country" and would undermine the prerogative of the Crown, which was the very essence of the monarchical system. The property qualification for office and voting was a sensible compromise. He wished it were possible to establish an intellectual qualification, but, failing that, property was "the next best mode of regulating the matter." Perry and John Prince, erstwhile Tory, now advanced liberal, attacked Baldwin for abandoning the more progressive position he had taken when opposing Sydenham's municipal bill in 1841. Baldwin now was, according to Prince, "a good, honest, red hot Tory." Robert was furious, insisting it was his critics who had changed, becoming republicans. As for himself, "I have ever defended those principles . . . it had ever been my pride that I had lived and—I hope to God would die a British subject." There was loud applause that echoed around the legislative chamber, and Baldwin was able to defeat the radical resolutions. Perry, though, had the last word. Mr. Baldwin acts as though "he had forgotten there are such beings as the people . . . he had never committed a greater mistake in all his life, than to suppose himself perfect and infalible, or to suppose that when he puts his hat on his head, he covers all the political wisdom, knowledge, and common sense in Canada West."[5]

While Hincks was busy repairing provincial finances and Merritt was making the first overtures for reciprocal trade with the United States, Baldwin turned his energies to education. He had tried in the past to remove the dead hand of Anglican monopoly from university education. John A. Macdonald and William Draper had wrestled with it while the Tories were in office. Bishop John Strachan had been the immovable barrier that prevented any substantial reform of Toronto's King's College. Could a more powerful responsible government break through? Robert was determined to do so. Higher education had become a national goal for him, the way to train up an intellectual elite who could lead Canada to great things. He began to apply pressure to King's as soon as he took office again. He was helped by the change of leadership at King's. Strachan, in a great miscalculation, thought King's was well established and that he could step down. He handed the presidency of the college to Rev. John McCaul on 26 January 1848. Strachan quickly learned he was not infallible. Robert invited his old teacher to a meeting in Toronto and, an hour later, the Bishop stormed out, now aware that Baldwin planned a secularized university. He also had learned that responsible government meant that Baldwin, not the Governor General, would be making decisions about King's. Robert forced through some changes in the governance of the college and, most ominously for the Anglicans, set up a commission to investigate college finances.[6]

The ground was prepared. Robert introduced his university bill to the House on 3 April 1849. Its most important principle, he said, was that it "divested the University of all denominational characteristics." This University of Toronto would be a national institution and therefore it must have the confidence of the people. To earn that, the institution must have no religious tests, no chair of divinity, and a governing structure that would assure "the public that it was not a mere class corporation." The unstated hope, as Baldwin confided to Lord Elgin, was that a financially viable, non-sectarian university would be the single vehicle for higher education in Upper Canada. The Methodist Victoria College in Cobourg would see the wisdom of joining the University of Toronto while the stubborn Presbyterians at Queen's in Kingston would witness their college "die of inanition" thanks to lack of funds. That was exactly what many feared. The Methodist conference remained neutral, but the church newspaper, the *Christian Guardian*, called the bill "the most objectionable ever submitted to the country." Queen's vowed never to yield to a godless university. Anglicans, of course, were outraged— the hurt all the greater when a co-religionist was the author of the evil. Strachan's petition to the House fairly dripped venom against this attempt "to establish a most rigid and oppressed monopoly over mind . . . and to impose on the deluded public a mutilated sort of education." Rev. James Beavan of King's College was more succinct in his petition; Upper Canada would suffer God's wrath if the university bill passed.[7]

The bill did pass, but that was far from the end of it. Victoria College remained in Cobourg. Queen's board of trustees not only rejected merger, but warned that "there is nothing in the Act to prevent Infidels, Atheists, or persons holding the most dangerous and pernicious principles, from being entrusted with the instruction of youth." Strachan, meanwhile, lobbied and raised funds in Canada and Britain to erect a new Anglican institution in

Toronto, that he called Trinity College. Baldwin was gravely disappointed at Strachan's success, warning Elgin that it would be a dangerous precedent. "He points," Elgin said, "to the States where Charters are given to all who ask for them and where consequently University degrees are of no value."[8]

Robert had invested himself in the university question. He would regret that he had not paid similar attention to primary education. There was considerable dissatisfaction with the school law passed by the former Tory government, and no shortage of confusion about how schools were to be financed. In Toronto, the city council and the school board could not agree on how to raise funds for education, with the result that schools closed down in the summer of 1848 and remained closed for a year. It was obvious that something had to be done during the parliamentary session of 1849. However, Baldwin was preoccupied with the university and with the Rebellion Losses crisis. Without much thought, he recruited Malcolm Cameron, the assistant commissioner of public works, to draft a school bill. It was a disastrous choice, politically if not educationally. Cameron, the member for Kent, Upper Canada, was a successful businessman and professional gadfly. He looked every bit the Victorian bourgeois with his tight, jowly mouth and ample mutton chops. His behaviour was capricious, however. He had been a moderate Reformer, opposed to the Baldwinites in the first Union Parliament, but changed his tune when the Reformers took power in 1842. Appointed inspector of revenue, he resigned in 1843 in protest over the relocation of the capital to Montreal. Once again he made peace when Reform regained power. Now, in Baldwin's fit of absent-mindedness, Cameron had his moment on the political stage.[9]

He introduced his school act to the House on 13 April 1849, as the Rebellion Losses crisis was moving inexorably toward its explosion. It received little debate as it went through the House and committee and was so uncontroversial that it was adopted on 29 May without a recorded vote. It was a solidly liberal measure that decentralized the school system. Control over teachers, curriculum, and textbooks was devolved to the township level. It was altogether consistent with Baldwin's approach to governance. However, it tweaked the nose of a powerful bureaucrat: Egerton Ryerson, superintendent of education. Ryerson believed that Cameron had "concocted a singularly crude and cumbrous school bill" whose major purpose was to force Ryerson himself out of office. The new legislation stripped the superintendent of his power to enforce uniformity in education and passed that power to unqualified local people. It removed the clergy as school visitors and did not require the use of the Bible in schools. To make matters worse, Ryerson had submitted a draft bill to the ministry in February, but Hincks and Merritt did not read it and Baldwin admitted he had merely glanced at it. Ryerson told Baldwin he could not continue when his office had been rendered "nugatory." So powerful was the superintendent, so extensive was his network of political friends that Robert quickly retreated. Even though the act was clearly Baldwinian in its approach, Robert agreed to suspend the bill and allow Ryerson to draft the new, centralizing school act that was passed in 1850.[10]

The Cameron Act was more popular with local people than with Ryerson. John Buchanan of Colchester, a community on the shore of Lake Erie, was one who preferred the 1849 bill. The more power that was devolved to ordinary Upper Canadians, the better. "The People . . . ought not to be controlled by Chief Superintendent in the erection of their School houses." Even Baldwin's campaign organizer from Sharon, David Willson, expressed his strong support for a decentralized school system. The public enthusiasm for the bill ought to have warned Baldwin that the Cameron situation was a political thorn. Instead, Cameron was allowed to marinate in his resentment. Finally, in December 1849, Cameron submitted his resignation. He would claim that he been ignored by colleagues, not consulted on cabinet changes, and rebuffed in his attempts to have the government reduce costs. Robert was puzzled since Cameron had told him that it was business concerns that led to the resignation. It got worse. J.-É. Cauchon, member for Montmorency, Lower Canada, warned LaFontaine that Cameron was furious, charging his cabinet colleagues with being arbitrary and tyrannical. "They seemed determined to force me out and they have. I was willing to go out and say nothing but they will not. They force upon me explanations and the country shall see who is to blame," Cameron warned. When the opposition raised the resignation in the House, Robert took his usual legalistic stance. Constitutionally, he lectured, the Crown does not explain its motives when cabinet changes are made. At any rate, "the public was not interested" in private reasons for resignations. Those comments were neither politic nor true. The public was very interested. Radicals such as James Lesslie of the *Examiner* pounced on the issue of retrenchment of public spending as the real issue here. Others responded because of Cameron's personal popularity in parts of the province.[11]

The Cameron imbroglio struck a government that was already unsteady, despite the accomplishments achieved in 1849. The decision to move the capital from Montreal was inevitable, after the riots that spring and summer, but it had a heavy cost. Robert thought that rotating the capital, every five years, between Toronto and Quebec City was a reasonable compromise. Some French reformers disagreed, believing that once the capital moved west it would never return. That suspicion cost the ministry two members with the resignations of Louis-Michel Viger and R.-É. Caron. Others reluctantly made the best of it. Backbencher Joseph-Édouard Cauchon told LaFontaine that he had a strong stomach and therefore could tolerate a move to Toronto. Fearing some Montrealers would be less flexible, troops guarded the movement of government records and property in October and November.[12]

The political troubles may have been balanced by the personal advantages. Robert would be home. He could stroll to the Parliament buildings on Front Street and to consult the governor. Elgin lived in temporary quarters at Elmsley Villa, near Grosvenor and St. Vincent Streets, while Government House was being refurbished. LaFontaine was nearby at the Wellington Hotel. They all settled in contentedly in late November. It had not been so easy when Elgin first visited Toronto on 9 October. Robert had done what he could to assure the governor's safety and comfort. Lawrence Heyden, Robert's brother-in-law and agent, was put in charge of arrangements. It was cloak-and-dagger, given the still simmering Tory rage. There would be exchanges of telegraphs to keep Heyden posted on the likely date of Elgin's arrival. Robert was especially worried about the attitude of the Tory mayor, George Gurnett, and wanted Heyden to keep a sharp eye on him. "If Mr. Gurnett is in Toronto telegraph me 'Yes' or as soon as he comes do so." As it developed, Gurnett behaved well, arresting ringleaders of the Tory mob who gathered in the evening of 9 October to denounce Elgin and drag his effigy through the streets.[13]

Time at home could only ease, not remove, the growing political burdens. Radical criticism of Baldwin and his ministry increased day by day. A controversy erupted in 1848 at the provincial lunatic asylum in Toronto, with the board of commissioners denouncing the newly appointed medical supervisor, George Park, for his arbitrary leadership style. R.B. Sullivan was delegated to assess the situation and, on his advice, Robert dismissed Park in January 1849. Park was a close associate of the radical John Rolph, who took up his cause in the *Examiner*.

> Our blood boils with indignation at such atrocious conduct. We have hunted for a precedent in the history of Tory government in the country. . . . we are humbled in finding none. The Tories have, in too many instances, been unmerciful to their political opponents; but not an instance like this, of treachery and abandonment <u>towards</u> their friends—It is without its parallel. Our motto must be—<u>Measures not Men</u>.[14]

The *Examiner* would continue to snipe at the government from the ultra-liberal flank. It printed weekly letters from William Lyon Mackenzie, most critical of the Baldwin administration. By November, the editor, James Lesslie, was confiding to Mackenzie that, "I am determined to drive the ministers into doing their duty—or out of office." No longer could Baldwin's character shield the government from criticism; measures, not men.[15]

Responsible government had unleashed expectations, especially the pent-up needs of advanced liberals. A loose coalition was slowly coalescing against Robert: a mix of pre-1837 radicals, small-government agrarians, and advocates of democratic reform. Robert failed to recognize the danger such a bloc could represent, and was insensitive about the actions that could further alienate the radicals. Henry John Boulton, one-time Compact Tory turned Reformer, had played a constructive role in finding compromises on the Rebellion Losses Bill. Baldwin determined to reward him with a seat on the bench, only to botch the matter. News leaked out about the pending appointment, raising the ire of some Reformers who could not forget Boulton's past. When the moderate Reform paper, the *Globe*, joined the chorus of dismay, Robert backtracked and withdrew the offer. Boulton fretted in the palatial comforts of his Toronto mansion, Holland House, until he could tolerate no more. He wrote Baldwin in January 1850 to charge the leader with ingratitude and dishonourable behaviour. He had been "sacrificed by treacherous friends." Boulton was one more recruit to the radical caucus. The attempt to regulate medical practice by licensing doctors was another stumble. One staunch Reformer, F.B. Morley of Cooksville, wrote to Baldwin to warn him of the widespread opposition to the bill. It would "create a monster monopoly by the Medicine Men" and drive out the traditional practitioners so beloved by backwoods people. That issue would arise again in the House sessions of 1850 and 1851, each time to cries of betrayal from rural folk.[16]

Hincks, among others, was uncertain the government could survive as the troubles piled up. He was increasingly frustrated. Baldwin was too passive in the House. He was, Hincks told George Brown, "a tame debater." Baldwin and LaFontaine were inefficient, allowing debate in the executive council to drag on when a single minister acting with vigour could resolve the matters at question. They seemed to dither endlessly about administrative appointments. Hincks's impatience boiled over at the council when he snapped at Baldwin, "I could form an administration in 24 hours." The criticism stirred up in Robert the old fear that he really was not cut out for politics. He was ready to resign, he told Hincks, who quickly tried to patch things over, pleading that Robert's resignation would ruin the party. Robert stayed on, and Hincks discovered how difficult the leader's job was. Baldwin delegated Hincks to recruit John Ross for the cabinet. Ross was a lawyer and businessman from Belleville whom Robert had appointed to the legislative council. Ross would shore up support in eastern Upper Canada as the government tried to repair the damage from resignations in December 1849. Ross had declined the post of Solicitor General when Baldwin offered it in September, and Hincks had no more luck. Serving in the ministry was not a great plum as 1849 ended. Small wonder that a worried Reformer like Cauchon would describe the government as "un jeu d'enfants."[17]

Robert had been preoccupied that autumn with rooting out annexationists from the militia and from government posts. He was also worried about them in his own ranks. There was a by-election in the East Riding of York County to replace Hume Blake, now raised to the bench. The Reform candidate was Peter Perry. Perry was one of the "Old Reformers," a veteran of eleven years in the Upper Canadian Assembly. He had supported Baldwin and responsible government in the 1840s but, as with so many others, he had been disappointed by the conservatism of the new Reform government. By 1849 he was a democrat, a republican, and not prepared to disavow annexation to the United States. He was a formidable challenge to mainstream Reform. Although uneducated, he was intelligent, a fine speaker, and supremely self-confident. His fierce appearance, accented by heavy, dark eyebrows and a powerful hooked nose, added to his impressive presence. For once, Robert recognized the threat and acted quickly. He wrote to Perry from Montreal in October, warning the candidate that annexation was the breaking point for membership in the party. "[T]here remains in my opinion no room for compromise. . . . All should know therefore that I can look upon those only who are for the Continuance of the Connexion [to Britain] as political friends—those who are against it as political opponents." Perry was unimpressed and even ridiculed Baldwin. At an election meeting in Markham, Perry read out Baldwin's letter and asked those who supported Baldwin to raise their hands. No one did.[18]

Perry's election in York East on 4 December was hailed by the *Examiner* as a victory for the "Reform and Progress Party" over the "Government party." Robert saw the ferment within Reform first-hand when he attended a dinner held at Powell's Tavern on Yonge Street to honour his friend James Hervey Price. It was a gala affair, 200 liberals gathered to feast, drink, and toast their colleague. Along with Baldwin, Hincks and Merritt represented the ministry. The pleasantries came to a bitter halt when both Hincks and Price used their speeches to attack the *Examiner* and what that paper pleased to call the "Young Canada" party of advanced liberals. The assistant editor of the *Examiner*, Charles Lindsey, tried to respond, but was harassed by Hincks's heckling. Robert sat in uncomfortable silence. The radicals had their say, all the same, at hastily organized township meetings that had been inspired by Perry's victory. Throughout the central districts of Upper Canada, local people gathered to complain about the government and demand rapid change.

James Davidson of Niagara exulted to William Lyon Mackenzie that "the district is all 'alive and <u>kicking</u>'" about retrenchment of government expenses and law reform. Even members of the ministry were influenced by the uproar. John Sandfield Macdonald, Solicitor General and rising star, visited the *Examiner* offices in Toronto in late January 1850 to discuss reform ideas and express his admiration for Mackenzie, the symbol of liberal unrest.[19]

Perry's election was troubling. The next by-election was a disaster. John Wetenhall of Halton, Upper Canada, was appointed assistant commissioner of public works and had to seek re-election. The contest brought some of Baldwin's chickens home. In 1844, he had installed Wetenhall as Reform candidate for Halton, blackballing the Ultra incumbent, Caleb Hopkins. Hopkins was only too glad to respond to radical entreaties and seek his revenge. So too was Malcolm Cameron, bitterly resenting his treatment by the ministry. As the *Globe* sarcastically reported, after his resignation,

> Malcolm was immediately made a martyr, and it was resolved that all his grievances should be represented in the Halton election in the person of Caleb Hopkins. Accordingly, Mr. Cameron posted off to the County, pinned this wretched Caleb to his coat-tails, and told off *ex cathedra* a catalogue of the iniquities of which his late colleagues had been guilty.

The yeomen of Halton were more convinced than the *Globe*, and Hopkins won decisively. The disaster became a tragedy. Wetenhall, always moody and lethargic, was cast into madness by the vicious campaign. The morning after, he stumbled into the hotel room of a reporter, Charles Clarke, carrying a lantern and staff and asking, Diogenes-like, for an honest man.[20]

The triumphs in York East and Halton encouraged the radicals to take the next step. They already had a name. David Christie, a farmer and activist, and Peter Perry had talked about wanting men who were "clear grit," that is pure in principle, for their movement. The *Globe* picked up the term to deride the Ultras, but they proudly embraced it. So Clear Grit it was.[21]

The first planning meetings for the new faction illustrated its curious mix of tendencies. They met at the office of a young lawyer, William McDougall, whose King Street office was hardly an invective's throw from Baldwin's own law firm. Charles Clarke, associate editor of the Hamilton *Journal and Express*, was only twenty-three. Christie was barely thirty. Lindsey of the *Examiner* was thirty-one, while *Examiner* editor, Lesslie, was fifty. With them were the hardened political veterans, Perry and Cameron. They were attempting to yoke the old reform tradition of pre-rebellion days with modern concerns informed by the Chartist movement that had roiled English public life for over a decade. Traditional agrarians were seeing common cause with liberal professionals. That mix posed more dangers for agrarians than they imagined for modern liberalism was on a path to financial and industrial capitalism, a path that had no lane for farm folk. For the moment, however, they could find common ground on cheap government, free trade, ending Anglican privilege, striking through legal complexity and a new panacea: manhood democracy. And the heady excitement of casting down a conservative enemy: Baldwinism. Yet no more than Baldwin did they speak of social class. Clarke, in particular, believed that the people could be one, once the press and a common educational system had awakened them.[22]

They gathered to celebrate and chart the future in a grand convention in Markham. Farmers and small merchants came in from across Upper Canada for the 12 March 1850 meeting and its successor convention in Whitby a few days later. At Markham they adopted a broad platform of liberal reform including secularization of the Anglican clergy reserves, cheap government, abolition of the Court of Chancery, extension of the franchise, and repeal of primogeniture. Their enthusiasm whetted, the Grits at Whitby called for election of all officials, from the governor to the lowliest local functionary. This was a head-on assault against some of Baldwin's fundamental beliefs. He could not accept general democracy since he thought those without property lacked the stability and stake in society necessary to exercise the franchise responsibly. He had just reformed Chancery and believed it an essential part of the legal system.[23]

The Clear Grit surge was assisted by the immobility of the government. Robert was often depressed early each year, and in 1850 a debilitating attack drove him into seclusion at home. Rumours spread quickly, rumours that damaged an already weakened ministry. Was he going to resign? Some supporters tried to convince themselves it was just overwork that troubled the leader. John Ross wrote jokingly to Baldwin that he needed to pass a ten-hour law. Others, including enemies, knew there was more to it. Lesslie reported that Baldwin was suffering from "an affection of the head." Only LaFontaine and the provincial secretary James Leslie had direct knowledge of how serious the attack really was. They went to see Baldwin at his home on the afternoon of 6 March 1850. Robert tried to be cheerful, but admitted he was suffering acutely. To their alarm and astonishment, Robert suddenly burst into tears. The stolid, stoic Baldwin was dissolving. LaFontaine tried to convince him that a dark room in his home was not a place where he would get better, but Robert refused to leave his family. In the end, all LaFontaine could do was take away all the official papers from the Baldwin home so that Robert would be required to rest fully. It was a frightening time for LaFontaine as much as Baldwin for, as Wolfred Nelson told him, Robert's retirement would be "an incomparable calamity."[24]

He came back to his responsibilities that spring of 1850, compelled by a familiar sense of duty. After all, there was entombed in his memory the much more painful return, when he re-entered politics scant weeks after Eliza's death. He was not his father, try as he might to be, and he knew that politics was a strange and treacherous country for someone who viewed the world in simple moral terms. When he first entered the Assembly in 1829, he faced that stark reality. The most obdurate of the Tories he confronted was his boyhood companion, James Hunter Samson, now the member for Hastings, and their friendship did not survive the political differences. Robert was relieved, if embarrassed, by his own defeat in 1830, and the years divorced from electoral politics were his happiest. The law and Eliza were more than enough to fill up his life. His estrangement from politics became estrangement from his party. The rough-and-tumble politics of the 1830s was distasteful, and political brawlers such as Mackenzie were more so. Certainly, he was comfortable with some, such as the de facto leader of Reform, Marshall Spring Bidwell, and his close friend, J.H. Price. Others, Mackenzie, Hopkins, and the like, were neither politically nor socially acceptable. Robert was convinced there could be little progress toward reform while such men dominated the discourse.[25]

It was not all gloom. Robert knew that support for the idea of responsible government was growing, slowly but steadily. As early as November 1832 the prominent Quebec newspaper, *Le Canadien*, had asserted that peace and harmony in government was only possible if the executive had the confidence of the Assembly. His spirits were buoyed when a new governor, Sir Francis Bond Head, arrived in Toronto on 23 January 1836, the reputation that proceeded him reflected in the placards that lined the streets that day, "Sir Francis Head, A Tried Reformer." What he would remember of the time, though, was that Eliza had died only twelve days before Head's arrival and little more than a month before Robert began his ill-fated and short-lived career as a member of the executive council. He had been driven from his mourning, again by duty, as his father, Bidwell, and John Rolph insisted he must grasp the opportunity of the executive position, the opportunity to advance responsible government.[26]

Duty discharged, he was able to create the fonder memories of his visit to Britain that year. There was his father's college friend, Dr. Coles in Dublin, who entertained him with stories of William Warren Baldwin's student pranks, and the Hincks family who made him feel at home in Belfast. It was true, all the same, that he could not put the Eliza's death behind him. His family, however loving, forced the memory to the fore. His mother, Phoebe, wrote to him while he was in Cork, Ireland, with welcome news of the children and a prod about duty.

> How shall I my Dear Robert say all that we feel for your dear little ones—they are truly deserving *each & every one* of a Father's tenderest feelings; & we bless God that they have a Father, so capable of directing their every step through life & pray, *earnestly* pray that they may be spared to *you & you* to them— . . . Willy is delighted with his school . . . Maria's fondness for reading increases; she however plays a good deal & joins Willy in flying his Kite; now his favourite amusement . . . you will find your little

Eliza, the same affectionate little creeping plant you left her; she grows every day more like her dear Mother.[27]

Robert returned to Toronto to wrap himself in his memories, only occasionally venturing into the political realm at meetings of his father's Constitutional Reform Society, a vain attempt to insert a moderate voice into the cacophony. He could remember, in 1850, the healing within the family. It was interrupted by the call to duty. His summons by Sir Francis Head to bear a flag of truce to the rebels north of Toronto plunged him into events that would be echoed in 1850. He, his children, and his parents were as alarmed as other Torontonians with the news of an impending rebel attack, alarm heightened by the bells that were set ringing throughout the city to rouse loyal defenders on the night of 4 December 1837. The next day, as they ventured out, they found the shops and workplaces closed. Robert was at home when Sheriff Jarvis arrived with the Lieutenant-Governor's request that he carry a message to the rebel camp. As always, duty overcame his reluctance and at 1:00 p.m. that afternoon, he and Dr. John Rolph set off to meet the insurgents at Gallow's Hill, 1.6 kilometres north of Bloor Street. Rolph would betray Robert's trust then, as the Rolph-inspired Clear Grits would later, when he used the flag of truce secretly to advise Mackenzie and his officers to attack the city without delay. Forgotten was the warmth of friendship and Robert's happy visit with Rolph's family in England the previous year.[28]

A plague on all their houses might have been his motto, but duty called again. He joined with a prominent lawyer from eastern Upper Canada, George Morss Boswell, to defend some of those tried for treason in April 1838. They were successful in winning acquittal for Dr. Thomas Morrison. The case of John Montgomery was more difficult, since the rebels had convened at Montgomery's Tavern. The state was represented by its highest legal officer, Attorney General Christopher Hagerman, a bloodthirsty Tory of the most obdurate cast. Robert opened the case for the defence and ably presented a long series of witnesses who testified to Montgomery's innocence of any part in the rebellion. It was to no avail for the jury deliberated only briefly to decide on a guilty verdict. The trials over, Robert found there was no escape from public life. The Durham

Report, new connections to Louis LaFontaine and his Lower Canadian colleagues, and the onrush of the Union of the Canadas ended the quiet of his life for more than a decade. He remembered it all as he returned to his duties in the spring of 1850. Most of all he remembered the loss of Eliza for his annual rite of grief and joy on their wedding day was near.[29]

The "Great Ministry," as its followers would dub it, took office at a time that indeed demanded greatness. The first Speech from the Throne lauded the peace and order that blessed the country. That boast, of course, would soon be belied by the crisis over the Rebellion Losses Bill. However, that melee would be far from the only challenge facing the new government. The first was a great scare, the fear of an Irish invasion. That was the beginning of a series of insurrections and apprehended insurrections that made governing interesting for the Great Ministry. The Irish, the Ojibwa on Lake Superior, the peasants in Lower Canada who fought the school laws, the rioters protesting the Rebellion Losses Bill, and the supporters of annexation were joined by the usual discontented such as the Welland Canal workers and railway labourers. Many seemed unimpressed by the new form of government. Many, such as the Ojibwa and the school rebels, seemed not to grasp the subtleties of progress. While the ministers did not face the revolutionary wave surging across Europe in 1848, they had little room for complacency.[30]

There was a poignancy mixed in with anxiety as Robert Baldwin read the dispatches from military commanders about the threat of an Irish uprising. After his 1836 trip to Ireland he felt closer to his ancestral homeland and better understood its grievances. Yet he could no more countenance Ireland's secession from the British Empire than Canada's. There were dark rumours of Canadian Irishman joining an insurrection to support the upheavals at home. Belligerent public rallies were held that spring in Quebec City and Montreal, the militants urged on by Louis-Joseph Papineau. The plot came to nothing, although rumours continued to filter into the government well into 1849.

Robert had good reason to take the threats seriously. Many Irish immigrants were lower class, a Celtic peasant culture that was alien to that of the Canadian majority. Such people lacked land, which Baldwin believed to be the measure of commitment to the society, and they formed a restless proletariat. They all too often engaged in the violence of the oppressed, violence that seemed irrational to the established society. Their ranks had grown and their discontent deepened by the flood of poor and desperate immigrants who fled the Irish potato famine in 1847. It was no great stretch to imagine them capable of treason and rebellion. Certainly, as Attorney General, Robert had to deal with numerous cases of Irish disorder. Sometimes it was in the form of criminal activity. In the Oakwood area of Upper Canada, northeast of Toronto, there was what locals called a "Murder Committee," led by one Patrick Doyle, that was able to commit murder with impunity since the magistrates were afraid to pursue the desperados. More common were traditional forms of vengeance such as the maiming of cattle, which usually involved cutting off the ears and tail and sometimes slashing the sides of the unhappy beasts. But Baldwin's reluctance to interfere in local matters left little for the executive to do to control the activities, which were clandestine and often had the approval of the local community. He could offer rewards for information leading to convictions, but few had the courage to claim them. That problem extended well beyond the Irish. Intimidation of witnesses or community support of criminals made it difficult to convict for some categories of crime. At the last assizes where he acted for the Crown, in the County of York in October 1851, nineteen people were tried for riot in five different cases. Six men were bound over for the next court session. All of the others were released, in most cases because witnesses failed to appear. Baldwin's rule of law remained a phrase with little content.[31]

Robert and his government were on the cusp between the old and the new, between pre-industrial Canada and the modern nation. The railway was a great rattling intrusion into Baldwin's garden. He had been reluctant to support railway construction through the government guarantee of loans, but the modernizer Francis Hincks had his way. The Guarantee Act of 1849 thrust the Great Ministry into the midst of the new railway age, as a guarantor of loans for railway construction. It did not change all of the old ways of thinking, however. The government continued to permit construction under the traditional contracting system that had created chaotic labor relations on the canals. The exploitative hiring practices, under which workers were forced to shop at overpriced company stores and were often cheated out of pay, provoked violent reactions among workers building the Great Western Railway. Labourers outside Hamilton went on strike twice in the first six weeks of 1851. They patrolled the railway works carrying clubs and drove off anyone who wished to stay on the job. The mayor of Hamilton and the inhabitants of the city petitioned the governor for military aid to control the workers. The petition was passed on to Baldwin who had no hesitation in lecturing the city fathers about local responsibility for law and order. Hamilton, he insisted, must organize a police force capable of suppressing riots. Only if that proved inadequate, would troops be made available. His theory was sound enough, but in the case of a town threatened by thousands of navvies, no local police force was likely to be sufficient. He had merely delayed the matter. In April 1851 Hamilton did organize a police force and, predictably, it was ineffective. Later that month troops were authorized and arrived on the scene in June to intimidate the workers.[32]

The Mackenzie riots of March 1849 in Toronto were expressions of old hatreds embodied in traditional forms. More and more often, it was the clash of the traditional and modern that confronted Baldwin and his government. Between 1845 and 1847, there had been extended debate in the House about the incorporation of mining companies. Baldwin had been opposed, but Francis Hincks had reached across the chamber to like-minded Tories and pushed through exploitation of mineral resources in the North. Neither Baldwin nor Hincks had mentioned the existence of First Nations people who occupied the areas to be mined; however, the residents made themselves felt in 1849. As a mining company prepared to develop its property at Mica Bay on the north shore of Lake Superior, a considerable force of Ojibwa gathered to resist the development. Baldwin received numerous warnings of impending conflict and was quick to dispatch troops to the site. Where was his usual reluctance to intervene in local matters? Perhaps his respect for property outweighed his belief in local responsibility. Or perhaps even Baldwin had been seduced by the promises of the modern age. In September 1850 the executive council authorized negotiations on the Aboriginal land claims, and used the occasion to lecture the Ojibwa, a lecture couched in the language of the new. The First Nations must not "expect excessive remuneration for the partial occupation of the Territory heretofore used as hunting grounds, by persons who have been engaged in developing sources of wealth which they had themselves entirely neglected." Robert himself would confront some of the offenders at the York assizes in October 1851. Facing trial were some white men and two Ojibwa chiefs, charged with crimes ranging from riot to conspiracy. Baldwin agreed to drop the charges against the two Ojibwa and to stay those against the white men in the interests of facilitating treaty negotiations.[33]

Robert was bewildered and torn by the conflict between the old and the new. There was demand for economic progress, a desire shared by most of his close colleagues. Yet he could see his world, the gentry world, the beloved world, being pushed back into history. It was easier for him to resist the excesses of progress when whites were being victimized rather than First Nations. Sailors had traditionally protested against conditions aboard ship by deserting once they reached Canadian ports. Shipping interests in Quebec City urged the Legislature in 1849 to adopt more draconian legislation against desertion. Baldwin and some of his Upper Canadian colleagues were able to bottle the legislation up in committee and prevent its enactment. The unfair treatment of sailors by profit-maximizing ship owners was a relatively easy issue for Robert. More difficult were cases where anti-modern protests attacked those areas where Baldwin himself believed in progressive reform. He strongly held that Canada must have modern educational systems that could advance its infant nationhood. Not everyone agreed. Lower Canada was agitated for half a decade by opposition to the School Act of 1846. Both French-Canadian and Irish peasants in communities along the St. Lawrence River rose up against assessment for school taxes. Assessors were assaulted and driven out of villages. The homes of school trustees and the schools themselves were burned in some communities. Louis LaFontaine struggled to suppress the insurrection, sending troops into the most troubled areas. Here the conflict was writ large between traditional local people and the modern centralizing bureaucracy. Robert might have begun to understand the complexities, indeed the impossibilities, of reconciling continuity and change.[34]

Fortunately, there was always home and the garden. Amid the turmoil of annexationism and the move of the capital, Robert received the happy news that his winter pears had won first prize at the Provincial Agricultural Fair.[35]

Family, as much as pear trees, continued to sustain him. During the fall of 1848 and on into the winter, Maria lived with Robert in Montreal, acting as his secretary. Her sharp mind and her bilingualism were invaluable. So too was family support in the days of his dark dogs of depression. In the fall of 1850, Robert had another attack, although one less debilitating than the depression of the previous spring. The children tried to buoy his spirits, taking turns reading to him. Depressed or not, however, he remained Mister Baldwin. The readings were not fluff but serious books such as Thomas Babington Macaulay's recently published *History of England from the Accession of James II*. The uplifting history and the familiar voices worked to lift Robert back to some equilibrium.[36]

Chapter 17

Infidels, Socialists, and Others

The memories stayed with him. For months he had immersed himself in them, reading Eliza's letters over and over. He had moved painfully between his room and Eliza's, her room and temple that he had maintained sacrosanct, admitting no one until he ushered in their eldest daughter, Maria, on her twenty-first birthday in 1849. The memories were of Eliza. She had been dead fourteen years.

He pulled himself out of the sea of memories and returned to his office in the spring of 1850. There was much to be done, many reforms still to be accomplished. The memories were of those few years when Robert had seemed genuinely alive. They were of the family, who sustained him in his loss of Eliza and in the turmoil of politics. They were of the painful, but fulfilling, last year of their marriage. He had seen her off, full of hope, in May 1835. His father would accompany her to New York where a different climate and the warmth of the American family would help her to recover her strength. The hope was dashed. She came home still weak and pale. While Eliza was fading all the year of 1835, he nursed her and comforted her and loved her. They had the Front Street house to themselves. Spadina had been damaged by fire, and Robert's father and mother moved there while they rebuilt. It was piercing hard to watch Eliza lose strength. Yet, in Robert's romantic inner self, it may have seemed a fitting part of their story. They had a novelesque love affair, rising above family opposition and social disapproval, two souls eternally joined. Such romances often ended in wrenching, moving tragedy. When they were apart in 1827, Robert had written to Eliza: "I feel as if I loved you (after the words of our own prayer) 'next to God' & yet whatever is the reason when I attempt to put on paper a description of my emotions—it looks so cold & meagre that I get quite out of conceit of it & imagine that I cannot really feel it because I cannot really express it."

He had now found a way to express that love, in the tortured blackness of depression.[1]

———◈———

Toronto was very nearly as gloomy as was Baldwin in the spring of 1850. The city was victimized in mid-May by a fire that began in the kitchen of a home on Adelaide Street and spread to consume many buildings on the commercial thoroughfare, Yonge Street. A rainy spring, with considerable flooding, gave way to a resurgent winter that month when heavy snow fell on Toronto and environs. A few days later, Isabella Clark Buchanan, the wife of Robert's brother William Augustus Baldwin, died at their home, Mashcoutah, on Yonge Street. As his father had noted, Robert grieved such losses more deeply than anyone else, for family was the one protection against an alien world.[2]

It was not all shadow. Even Robert had to feel excitement and pleasure when the provincial Parliament resumed at the refurbished building on Front Street on 15 May. The shabby relic of the Upper Canadian Parliament was shiny as new, especially the upper house. The walls of the Legislative Council chamber were pleasingly painted in pea green with white edgings and decorations. Along the walls were red hangings with gold fringe. There were luxurious seats for the members who would deliberate under the stern stare of Queen Victoria's rescued portrait on the west wall. Although the Assembly met in less imperial surroundings, their chamber was also clean and new—and not on fire. Torontonians were certainly impressed, for a large crowd gathered in the street, so many people that the honour guard from the Rifle Brigade had difficulty clearing a path for the Governor General's carriage. It was all in good spirit, though, this was no mob like the one that had assailed Lord Elgin in Montreal. As Elgin made his way to the Legislative Council chamber, Robert and the other commoners crowded in at the back of the room to hear another Throne Speech promising progress and prosperity.[3]

The political world was still a small one. The Baldwin home on Front Street was two doors away from that of the Reform judge, William Hume

Blake. Between them was a house rented by the member for Cornwall, the highest of High Tories, John Hillyard Cameron. The neighbours got along amiably enough, despite the invective they hurled at each other in Parliament. The atmosphere was friendly, too, on the early morning of 7 June when Robert and members of both houses of the legislature scurried aboard a steamer that bore the unfortunate name of the *Chief Justice Robinson*. The steamer left Brown's Wharf for the mouth of the Welland Canal, W.H. Merritt's great work to join Lakes Erie and Ontario. After almost two decades, the canal was finally being declared finished. Lord Elgin and local municipal officials met at Port Dalhousie on the Lake Ontario shoreline for the ceremony and then the whole party went up the canal to Merritt's hometown, St. Catharines. From there a cortege of thirty carriages took the dignitaries to the town of Thorold, and another steamer, the *Britannia*, for a voyage to Merrittville and a grand celebratory dinner. That voyage was somewhat dampened when, near Merrittville, Alexander Duff was ramming a charge down the muzzle of a cannon for a salute, only to have the weapon discharge. Fortunately, two physician-politicians, Pierre Davignon and Étienne-Pascal Taché, were in the party and they tended to the wounded gunner. Despite the tragedy, the dinner was a great success with Robert, speaking from the high table, praising the bipartisan support the canal had received. Forgotten was the angry political infighting over the project during the 1830s.[4]

The debate on the Speech from the Throne, in May, made it evident that the opposition, both Tories and radical liberals, was feisty and had grasped some popular issues with which to pummel Baldwin and his ministry. Three matters preoccupied the critics. One was the clergy reserves, that vast store of lands set aside by the imperial authorities to support the Churches of England and Scotland. Many Reformers were unhappy that the speech had made no commitment to secularize the clergy reserves. Another was alleged French domination. Radicals were sure that real reforms for Upper Canada were blocked by Lower Canadian conservatism. Finally, there was the Court of Chancery. Radicals attacked it as expensive and confusing for ordinary people. Caleb Hopkins expressed a growing sentiment in Upper Canada when he insisted that the country would be better off if there were no lawyers in Parliament. Then there would be fewer mistakes such as the Chancery.

Robert's defence of the court and of Chancellor William Hume Blake, his plea to give the court time to prove itself, fell on deaf ears. The ministry was able to whip most of its members into line to defeat amendments to the Speech, but it was clear the waters ahead were going to be rough.[5]

There were tensions even within the ministry. J.H. Price and Francis Hincks wanted to deal with the clergy reserves before they became an albatross around the government's neck. Louis LaFontaine, on the other hand, feared that agitation over the reserves would stir up opposition to the powers of the Catholic Church in Lower Canada. He warned his brother-in-law, J. A. Berthelot, that the 1850 session of Parliament might be "une débâcle politique." That was also the opinion of the major *Rouge* newspaper, *L'Avenir*, which feared attacks on Catholicism by the "infidel and socialists" among the radicals. That may have been an exaggeration but it was evident that anti-Catholicism was cresting in Upper Canada. It would become a frenzy that autumn, propelled by the so-called papal aggression scare in Britain. The Vatican's decision to re-establish an ecclesiastical hierarchy in Britain was considered a threat to Protestant ascendancy, both in England and Upper Canada.[6]

The ministry tried to avoid the clergy reserves controversy by stalling for time. Petitions were pouring in from townships across Upper Canada, demanding that the reserves be appropriated, and the Anti-Clergy Reserves Association was created in Toronto with support from many Protestant churches and a group of political players including Malcolm Cameron, James Lesslie of the *Examiner,* and George Brown of the *Globe.* Some gesture had to be made. On 18 June 1850, the commissioner of Crown lands, J.H. Price, introduced a set of resolutions on the reserves, but as a private member, not on behalf of the government. This was a gesture of loyalty to Baldwin for Price, a Congregationalist and devout advocate of religious equality, had been the loudest voice for government action to appropriate the reserves. These resolutions proposed a breathing spell through a petition asking Britain to grant Canada the authority to legislate about the reserves. That did little to appease the radicals who believed Canada already had such power.[7]

There was some gentle jousting the first day of the reserves debate, but both government supporters and opposition were waiting to hear what Baldwin and LaFontaine had to say. Robert did enter the lists on the afternoon of 19 June. He was tense and testy, recognizing how dangerous the matter was for the government. Price had admitted to the House that the cabinet was divided, so Baldwin now had to patch over the differences. He did not make a good job of it. He began by attacking those who claimed members must vote to secularize the reserves because their constituents desired such a result. Lulling the opposition into a stupor with an extended dissertation on the ideas of British theorist Edmund Burke, Robert rejected the concept of delegate democracy. "Another idea has been thrown out in the discussion of this question out of doors, equally erroneous. It was that members were bound to follow the mere opinion or wish of the majority—a false principle either in politics or morals, to which I will never subscribe." Every measure had to be assessed "on its own intrinsic right." He argued that government must protect minorities as surely as it did majorities. Without such sensitivity there was despotism. He was not personally opposed to endowments for religious purposes, but he was troubled that the Act of Union, in its provision for the reserves, had mixed up state and church in a fashion dangerous to both. Yet he was equally alarmed at reckless attacks on a system created by the Crown for religious purposes. If the reserves could be stripped away by the "mere will of the majority," then no property rights were safe. Now that he had shown that the lands properly belonged to the religious authorities, he then mused about allocating them to educational purposes instead. As John Hillyard Cameron would remark, Robert's speech would have led most listeners to believe the Attorney General was going to vote against Price's resolutions. Instead, Robert would support the resolutions so that Parliament would have time, while Britain dealt with the request to give Canada jurisdiction, to consider the best disposal of the reserves.[8]

Robert would not emerge unscathed from this diversion. Henry John Boulton had always been an irritant for Baldwin—as a Family Compact stalwart before 1837 and now as a Clear Grit nettle. Boulton threw Baldwin's own words at him. During the last election, he pointed out, Baldwin had told his constituents that when a minister differed from his cabinet colleagues on an important policy, he must resign. Clearly someone should be resigning since both Baldwin and Price had admitted the ministers were divided on the reserves. All Robert could muster in reply was an ad hominem attack on Boulton's "Republican schemes," a flaming red herring since Boulton was citing both Baldwin and British practice. Robert mumbled that he still stood by his election statement "but circumstances have changed and it was impossible to see what circumstances might turn up." Boulton might well think that the only change in circumstances was that Baldwin's statement in 1847 was theoretical, while his about-face in 1850 was the real politics of governing. As Tory Henry Sherwood remarked, Baldwin had never appeared so embarrassed as he did that day.[9]

Sherwood hoped to add to the ministry's discomfort when he demanded to hear LaFontaine's views. Instead, LaFontaine tried, without success, to have the House adjourn. The ministry was reeling, fighting off a fusillade of opposition amendments. Finally, he could evade no longer and entered the debate. Despite his attempts to avoid committing himself, LaFontaine came off better than his fellow Attorney General. He was clear. He would vote to ask Britain for jurisdiction but he insisted that, when the matter was finally settled, the reserves must be applied to religious purposes. It was not so much a matter of religious rights as of property rights: "[T]here was a wide difference between considering a settlement of a question not final, and being ready to repeal every act by which the private vested rights of private individuals had been acquired, of which there was too much now-a-days." LaFontaine was more successful than Robert in shifting the discussion from religious inequality to the sacredness of property. Lord Elgin told Earl Grey that LaFontaine had been splendid, taking a "neutral and commanding position." Reformer Joseph Curran Morrison was less generous: "[A] rather singular spectacle was presented to the House by the two Attorneys General. One of them spoke in favor of the resolutions with the intention of voting against them, while the other spoke against them with the design of voting for them." In the end, on Friday evening 21 June, both Attorneys General voted for the resolutions, as did a majority of the House.[10]

Anti-Catholic and anti-French sentiments continued to curdle politics. The necessity, and the capacity, of Catholic and Protestant, British and French, to live together was the essence of the Baldwinian formula for Canada. That was now endangered, in part because of radical impatience in Upper Canada, in part because of the "papal aggression" agitation in Britain. The "papal aggression" had its Canadian counterpart in the cry about "French domination." A typical piece of anger and derision was the comment by a Toronto city councillor in February 1851. Toronto was trying to reverse a provincial decision to move the capital to Quebec City, as provided in the rotating capital arrangement. "Mr. SMITH thought the Council should concentrate its efforts to an attempt to produce an impression upon Mr. Lafontaine, for Lafontaine rules Baldwin, Baldwin rules Hincks, and the three together rule the Governor General."[11]

Even strong supporters of the ministry were alienated by fears of Lower Canadian hegemony and Catholic presumption. Malcolm Cameron's school act of 1849 had been repudiated by Baldwin because of school bureaucrat Egerton Ryerson's opposition. The act that replaced it in 1850 gave stronger support for Catholic separate schools in Upper Canada. That was worrisome for Protestant Reformers such as George Brown of the *Globe*. Brown's suspicions increased with news of the "papal aggression" excitement in Britain and by the end of 1850 the newspaper was attacking Catholic privilege in Canada and expressing concern over the course of the LaFontaine–Baldwin government. In January 1851, Louis LaFontaine mused over whether religious and ethnic tensions would lead to the breakup of the Reform Party and the creation of new alliances. He found it difficult to imagine how French Canadians could coexist in a party with men, such as Brown, who were "fanatiques en matière religieuses." As it played out, the animosities would indeed lead to new political alliances, once LaFontaine and Robert were gone. Yet, whatever the particular political alignments, there was no escaping Baldwin's logic, for Canada could only function as a bicultural entity.[12]

The law was equally central to Robert's system of beliefs. It too was under attack. Advanced liberals wanted a legal system that was trimmed down to essentials, stripped of its complexities, lawyerly jargon, and professional monopoly. The Court of Chancery, newly reformed by Baldwin and Blake, was the prime example of what was wrong with the law, in the view of radicals. Personal animosities entered into the matter, as well. Boulton had expected to receive a judgeship as reward for helping shepherd the Rebellion Losses Bill through the House. Baldwin decided not to appoint him. Attacks on Chancery were Boulton's revenge. He had widespread support, as Chancery had become a symbol of waste and elite arrogance. Robert was worried enough about the discontent that he sought information from Blake, now the chancellor of the court, about how costs were being reduced. Robert's attempts to defend the court during a raucous debate in the House did little to silence the critics. Caleb Hopkins asserted that the people wanted cheap law, but the House was full of lawyers who would protect their own selfish interests. Edward Malloch, a Tory from Carleton county, claimed that the whole country wanted Chancery abolished, but the public will would be thwarted by French votes.[13]

There was a general attack on the legal system and its expense. The law had become a surrogate for all the popular discontents of the day. Robert could only sigh when he received a letter such as that from William McVity, clerk of the peace in the town of Barrie. McVity wanted the qualifications for jurors removed from legislation. Without that provision, he and the local officials, "could have returned many persons better qualified in point of intelligence than some of those selected, had a discretionary power been given, but were obliged to return some Highland Scotch, and Frenchmen, who could not speak English, as well as several coloured men."[14]

More typical was H.J. Boulton's bill, presented on 14 May, "to alter, simplify and amend the Practice of the Law, and to diminish Law expenses." He wanted to suppress "all useless, formal and unnecessary words, not tending to elucidate the subject." Robert attacked the measure as lacking "deliberate attention" and a large majority of the House agreed in rejecting it. Nevertheless, there was a chilling reminder in a rebuke from John Wilson, the member from London, Upper Canada. If the lawyers in Parliament opposed law reform, he warned, "they would be excluded from this House."[15]

The cry of "retrenchment," the demand for smaller, cheaper government, extended well beyond the courts. The legislature received petitions from many counties and townships in Upper Canada, as well as from individuals, all demanding reductions in the cost of government. The petitions were echoed in the House by private members' bills. Proposals included reducing the salaries of cabinet members, eliminating the post of Solicitor General, and removing the Attorneys General from the cabinet. Prince wanted to ask the imperial government, rather than the colony, to pay the Governor General, and failing that to reduce his salary substantially. Sir Allan MacNab, still an imperialist despite his behaviour during the Rebellion Losses crisis, shouted that he would never accept such a proposal; it was a matter of loyalty to support the governor. Prince sneered that $2500 a year was more than enough to pay the governor to do nothing. The speaker of the legislative council was not spared. Boulton thought that he should receive no more than £250. Prince agreed, since he "did not see why he [the speaker] should receive £1000 a year, for sitting for three months with a cocked hat on." Boulton also wanted to save money by keeping the capital in Toronto, rather than moving to Quebec. He was shouted down by Lower Canadian members but remained defiant. "Yes, they might shout, but he could tell them that the Upper Canadians would not submit to Lower Canadian domination."[16]

The uproar over retrenchment offended Baldwin's sense of how politics ought to be conducted. The government was quite ready to consider cost reductions, he said, but "I deprecate the practice of appealing to the dollar prejudices of the community," and stirring up "popular agitation and excitement." As for the alternating of the site of the capital, he also found it an unnecessary expense. However, the legislature had made the commitment to alternate Toronto and Quebec and that was like a treaty with Lower Canada. It was one more sacrifice in the cause of a bicultural Canada.[17]

⟞⟝

The government held its majority through all the dissension and passed its legislation. For Robert, all the same, it seemed as if upheaval never ended. He had entered politics in 1828 to confront, as his election address contended, "this important and alarming crisis." The crisis still appeared alarming. The faces had changed, but the central question of good government versus bad had not.[18]

He remembered many of those faces from the House in 1830, when he had his first brief experience there. Among the large Reform contingent was a preponderance of young men. Robert was one of two Reformers in their twenties, while most of the others were in their thirties and forties. The few grey heads included his father. Some of his compatriots there would become friends, as close as Robert let anyone. William Buell, the merchant and journalist from Leeds county in eastern Upper Canada, would often extend his hospitality when Robert was riding the court circuit in later days. Others would be lifelong antagonists, among them William Lyon Mackenzie, Caleb Hopkins, and Peter Perry. There were more American-born among them than Upper Canadian, and more farmers than lawyers. The Tories across the floor were similarly youthful, although only one was American born and lawyers predominated there. Robert would see few of them again in public life, except for John Beverley Robinson, who would remain a dominant figure as chief justice of Upper Canada.[19]

Memory told of the differences as Robert contemplated the legislature in the spring of 1851. He was no longer the youngest member, but was of an age with most of the parliamentarians. They were an older group than those of 1830, the typical member now in his mid-forties. That profile fit all factions except, curiously enough, the most radical. The Clear Grits were a grizzled group of political veterans. Henry John Boulton, whose high-pitched rhetoric jarred on Robert's ears with great regularity, was now sixty-one. Caleb Hopkins was another nemesis, a blunt, stern farmer who seemed to be an eternal presence at age sixty-six. Peter Perry, John Prince, and after a by-election victory in April 1851, William Lyon Mackenzie, were all in their late fifties. Unfortunately for Robert, age had not diminished the vigour of these firebrands. That was true of their Lower Canadian equivalent, Louis-Joseph Papineau. At sixty-four, Papineau was as formidable as ever. He joined his radical republican politics to a daunting presence. His angular, stern face was topped by a shock of white hair that stood straight like a mohawk cut, his hand was often thrust into his black coat in a, probably conscious, imitation of Napoleon Bonaparte. He was a constant counter-attraction to LaFontaine's moderation for young francophones. Similarly, the elderly Clear Grits exerted a pull on some of Robert's own backbenchers such as young Joseph Curran Morrison from York West and the habitually restless John Wilson of London, once a Tory, now an unreliable Reformer.[20]

Even Robert could recognize that there was some truth to the charges of domination by lawyers. As he looked over his own Reform caucus from Upper Canada, he saw a majority of lawyers and, unlike in 1830, not a single full-time farmer. Professional men—lawyers, doctors, notaries—had elbowed aside agriculturalists and now represented over two-thirds of the legislators. Businessmen made up most of the rest. There had been a class revolution since Robert first sat in the House, a revolution in which liberal professions and their business allies had seized control of the political process. Some of those liberal men, such as the lawyers John Prince and H.J. Boulton, and the businessmen Malcolm Cameron and Peter Perry, Clear Grits all, claimed to speak on behalf of the "people" and thundered at the government in populist terms. The people were still mostly agrarians, however, and it was far from evident that liberal professionals and businessmen actually had much in common with the rustics.[21]

A striking difference from 1830 was the confusion of political alignments. In Robert's first parliamentary term, political parties were just gelling. There were certainly tensions and disagreements among those on the Reform side, but they usually acted together. The Tories were cohesive. Now, in 1851, political groupings were becoming ever more confused and confusing. Responsible government had solidified the concept of party politics, and legitimized the role of the opposition. The ground rules had been established, then, but it would take much painful experience to work out exactly what that meant. Robert had long understood both responsibility and party politics. However, he saw that as the end of things, as an established political process that gave Canada all it needed: the very model of the British constitution. In the spring of 1850, when his cabinet colleagues, under pressure in the House, were prepared to consider establishing an elected Legislative Council, Robert threatened to resign. The draft of his resignation letter advised Lord Elgin that, "To any and every measure calculated to lead to such an end Mr. Baldwin feels it his duty both to his Sovereign and his Country to offer the most uncompromising opposition." The ministry backed away from the proposed reform. Later that summer, constitutional change was once more before the House during a discussion of municipal reform. Robert again drew his line:

> I have always striven to obtain British institutions—I have
> sought to gain for my countrymen the full and complete

enjoyment of British freedom, under the institutions of Britain—
for I am convinced that her institutions were calculated to afford
them real, solid advantage, but if they were swept away—if they
became intoxicated with republican principles, the man who lived
to see the day that change was made, would live to rue it.

His passionate defence of British institutions, as they existed, was more
than a rational judgment of comparative advantage. The constitutional
status quo, once responsibility was achieved, was a tribute to his father.
William Warren had raised his son to constitutional loyalism. Together
they had advocated for responsible government as a final settlement for
all colonial grievances. When Robert tried to explain to the House how
his principles had been derived from his father, he came near to tears.
He struggled to control his emotions and told a hushed assembly that,
"I have defended those principles—I have ever cherished that love—it
has ever been my pride that I have lived and—I hope to God I will die
a British subject." The House exploded into applause that rang around
the chamber for several minutes.[22]

Some did not share Baldwin's sense of completion. Peter Perry
insisted, "responsible government in itself is not a reform, but a principle
of government." Malcolm Cameron was more explicit. "The boon of
Responsible Government was never sought for as a finality, but as a
means to an end, and that end was the liberalising of our institutions."
Here was the line drawn between Baldwin's conservatism and the
pretensions of the new liberalism.[23]

Robert's own faction, the Upper Canadian Reformers, was only about
sixteen strong, and some of those were doubtful. The major division
within Reform was between its two most prominent leaders, Robert
Baldwin and Francis Hincks. Hincks, as with Perry and Cameron, saw
responsible government as only a means of facilitating more fundamental
reforms. His reforms were economic. Robert could remember, with
some regret that he had not grasped the full significance of the words,
when Hincks had remarked in 1843, "We are now fighting the battle of
the Middle Class against the aristocracy." That battle was waged with the
rhetoric of free-trade liberalism. Hincks told the House in 1849 that he
was "prepared to repeal every law giving any protection to any person,

because I think they were not founded upon sound principles." Those laissez-faire principles, however, could accommodate government support for private economic development. The stern political economy that would strip "any protection" from individuals was combined in Canadian liberalism with faith in a growing, activist state, the state that created railways and canals to underpin development. While agrarians were calling for retrenchment, Hincks increased provincial expenditures by 75 percent between 1848 and 1851.[24]

The political alliance of Baldwin and Hincks did not obscure their differences on the nature of the state, the economy, and individual rights. Throughout the 1840s they had disagreed publicly on economic fundamentals. Hincks, in 1841, had wanted a bank of issue to increase the money supply. Baldwin had successfully opposed it. Hincks had advocated removal of the statutory limit on interest rates. Baldwin had successfully opposed the attempt. Robert was unable to stem the tide of applications for limited liability charters, applications that Hincks loudly supported. Limited liability was an important instrument of infant capitalism in a capital deficient colony, for it allowed companies to expand far beyond the limits of the individual wealth of their owners, who would not be personally responsible for all the debts of their companies. During a debate over one bill of incorporation in 1847, Robert said his opposition to limited liability was based on the belief that there was a moral obligation to repay debt. That was indeed an old-fashioned principle when the growth of the province and the new economic circumstances created by British free trade ushered in a new era. The railway became both the solution to Canada's problems and a symbol of modernity. Robert and Hincks each recognized that railways offered great opportunities. In 1849, Robert seconded Hincks's motion to proffer government guarantees for railway loans. Yet Robert was suspicious of any overly rapid development and of the financial probity of some railway schemes. A few days after the introduction of the Guarantee Bill, he unsuccessfully opposed the incorporation of the Toronto–Simcoe–Lake Huron line whose money-raising plans sounded to him like "a lottery scheme." The following year he was alarmed by private legislation to permit municipalities to take stock in the Great Western Railway. He suffered not only defeat but embarrassment. His cabinet colleague,

Francis Hincks, moved an amendment to allow municipalities to invest in all railroads, not just the Great Western. Baldwin found himself in a minority of eight members, which included six French Canadians and one English liberal from Lower Canada, and Mr. Baldwin.[25]

Hincks wished to repeal all protections that shielded people from the operation of the free market. Robert disagreed. His vision of society was an older one in which the various ranks or stations were bound together by mutual obligation, not just by market principles. Individual protections and aristocratic concerns for the property order came together in his ideology. That was apparent in the long debate over dower rights in Upper Canada. By common law, a wife was entitled to an estate for life after the death of her husband, equal to the third part of his "lands and tenements," including rents, mineral rights, and other property. The husband's alienation of any such property did not affect the wife's dower claim on it, unless she had explicitly agreed to the sale. There were two attempts, in 1847 and 1849, to amend the dower law. The Tory businessman, John Hillyard Cameron, then Solicitor General in the conservative government, tried to remove the effective veto power over sale of family property that wives could exercise through the threat of their dower rights. Cameron thought it profoundly unjust that the law placed a husband "entirely at the mercy of his wife as to the sale of his property" and even more unjust to a purchaser who, in all innocence, might find himself involved in legal complications if a widow claimed her spouse had not obtained her permission to sell property over which she had dower claim. More, the ability to sell property and thus free up capital was essential in a progressive society. Not so, said Baldwin. Flashing uncharacteristic anger, he argued that a wife might dedicate years of "care and assiduity" in acquiring property but "the pitiful provision" of the dower law was her only claim on the fruits of her labour. "[T]he main object of this Bill was THE INJURY OF WOMAN, and to despoil them of the trivial rights they now held, and I will earnestly oppose it to the last." The majority of the House was swayed by Baldwin's vehemence. Two years later, in 1849, independent member George Byron Lyon tried again to remove the power of widows to make demands on those who had purchased family property. Once more Baldwin led the opposition that defeated the measure.[26]

Baldwin the widower may have been more sensitive than some to the plight of widows. There was more than protection of the innocent in this, though. Laws such as those creating the right of dower, were ancient parts of the property order. They were checks on the rapid transfer of land, on what Baldwin called, in another context, "the evils of subdivision of properties." Real property was the basis for independence, for the rational freedom upon which the social order was founded. At the same time, Baldwin recognized there were few absolutes in politics. He was enough a liberal to concede the force of rough democracy. His stand on primogeniture illustrated this. That law, by which the eldest son inherited his intestate father's property, was an issue that separated liberals from conservatives. The question had long alienated the Baldwins from their fellow Reformers who wished primogeniture abolished. Yet when a bill was introduced into the Assembly in 1845, calling for equal distribution of the estates of those who died with a will, Robert warned of the dangers of dividing property, but nevertheless supported the bill. The large majority of Upper Canadians opposed primogeniture and so Robert agreed it must go, whatever the risks. That bill failed but, in 1851, a saddened Baldwin himself introduced the legislation that abolished primogeniture in the case of intestacy.[27]

The defence of dower rights and the nostalgic adherence to primogeniture were reflections of the bridging role that Robert Baldwin played in Canadian life. He recognized that change was inevitable, that politics had become more broadly based and that the economy was no longer simply about land and trade. Yet, as he told the House in 1845, on constitutional principles, "We . . . are the true Conservatives." Responsible government, for him, was the salvation of much of traditional society. It would bring political liberty without social revolution. In assessing the heritage of responsibility, Hincks and other modern men were more perceptive. The power of traditional elites was finally broken and government was handed over to new men. The structures of government were modernized. The creation of a bureaucracy and the application of a spoils system, based on party loyalty, ended the old divine right of civil service. Government gained new popular legitimacy. It was able to increase its revenues dramatically and thus its ability to intervene in the economy.[28]

As these changes rolled out, Hincks grew more restive. Baldwin was necessary, for his spotless reputation shielded the government. However, Hincks often felt more akin to some of the ministry's opponents than to the Attorney General. In 1849, for example, Hincks and Sir Allan MacNab were in England to lobby the imperial government, each presenting their side of the Rebellion Losses Bill. Whatever their differences, though, they made common cause on industrial development. Hincks helped to sell stock in MacNab's Great Western Railway, in return for "a very handsome bonus." It was railways that eventually emboldened Hincks to impose his vision of the economy and the state on Baldwin. In the spring of 1851 the two clashed in cabinet over Hincks's plan to create a municipal loan fund under which municipalities could borrow money to support railway construction. Robert thought this a reckless proposal and doggedly fought it in the executive council. It would encourage debt and it would permit usurious interest rates of up to 7 percent on municipal bonds. On 24 April Hincks wrote to Baldwin, demanding he stop his obstruction and warning that, if he did not do so, it "may possibly produce serious consequences." Robert continued his opposition, and Hincks took his case to LaFontaine. Robert's behaviour was unacceptable on several counts, he told LaFontaine. It was intolerable of him to oppose "a proposition emanating from the minister peculiarly responsible for this branch of policy." As well, the cabinet supported Hincks and was only deterred from acting by Baldwin's harassment. Hincks recognized that public support for the government would be eroded if Baldwin left, so he was prepared to resign over the matter. The bluff worked. After considering resigning himself, Robert wrote to LaFontaine in an ill-disguised capitulation. He said if Hincks would yield one point—a proposal to employ municipal bonds as deposits for bank credits to railways—Baldwin would cease his opposition. Saving a last measure of face, he wanted LaFontaine to know that he was not "concurring in" Hincks's legislation, but simply "acquiescing" to it. Whatever the words, it was defeat. Hincks's model of an active state supporting capitalist development would prevail, and thousands of kilometres of railways would be laid out across Canada. Perhaps it was some consolation to Robert that, even by the time of his death in 1858, Hincks's Municipal Loan Fund had led to crushing debt on many municipalities and chronic fiscal instability.[29]

There might have been sympathizers with Robert's conception of a land-based economy, a low-debt fiscal regime, and a small but compassionate state. The gulf of class prevented either Baldwin or his potential allies from reaching out to each other. The Clear Grits and some more moderate Reformers could not see beyond the social divide, and they framed their politics by certain symbolic differences. One such was the attempt to incorporate the medical profession in Upper Canada and outlaw "quack" doctors. Robert enthusiastically supported the medical incorporation bills that were introduced between 1849 and 1851. The measures drew violent dissent from the backwoods and rural members of the House. Robert was inundated with complaints from his own constituents who charged the 1849 Incorporation Bill would "increase the evils of Medical Despotism," at the expense of what another petitioner described as trusted "old Medicine men" of the "Thomsonian or Botanic system of Medicine." One of the grounds of concern was that midwives would be prohibited from practicing, since they not only delivered babies, but often supplied medications. A Lower Canadian conservative, John McConnell of Stanstead, told the House he had only been ill once in his life and two doctors had failed to cure him. He had survived thanks to the ministrations of an old woman who employed roots and herbs. The outcry led to the defeat of the bill. In 1851, though, modernization had gained support and the legislation was only thwarted because Mackenzie led a filibuster against it, which lasted until Parliament prorogued.[30]

That continuing struggle over the law was another symbolic divide. Robert had no sympathy for those who wished to simplify legal proceedings, or to reduce the influence of lawyers. Cries for simpler procedures were foolish, he told Reformer William Notman in 1850. "If the hon. member wished to render everything so simple he must reduce us to a state of barbarism." Robert was missing the point. Whether complaints about legal complexity came from Reformers, Tories, or Clear Grits, they were not some know-nothing barbarities. The law, like the medical profession, had become symbolic of a general complication and mystification of human relations. This was a sentiment not so far removed from Robert's own concerns about a modernizing economy. His failure to appreciate this allowed the anti-modern sentiment to become translated, for many, into class consciousness with Robert himself the target. It was a Reformer from Sharon, in Robert's own riding, who wrote to Mackenzie in May 1851 that things would get better only when "we can get the Lawyers thrown out of the house of Parliament, and get good, honest politicians like yourself . . . The watchword is to be no lawyers, more farmers and mechanics."[31]

The radical critique did recognize a significant difference between Baldwin's view of the state and of rights, and the emerging popular perception in Upper Canada. The German philosopher, G.W.F. Hegel, thought there was a fundamental flaw in early nineteenth-century England: "[O]bjective freedom or rational right is rather *sacrificed* to formal right and particular private interest." That same flaw was embedded in the Baldwin system. Property rights, and the power of property ownership, as well as a static view of the law as an institution, informed Baldwin's understanding of the role of the state and his hope that responsible government was a final constitutional settlement. The Clear Grits, disillusioned Reformers, and even some Tories sought to expand "objective freedom" and to imbue formal rights with some content suitable to the times. Both the critics and Baldwin, in the end, would lose out to a new set of private interests—those of liberal capitalists and their corporate power.[32]

The small Clear Grit group was always in Robert's sight, and in his thoughts. They had a far greater capacity to disturb than their legislative numbers might suggest. That was especially so by the spring of 1851 when Mackenzie was returned to the Assembly. His election cost the government dearly for not only was he a formidable opponent, but he cost the ministry the support of the colony's most influential newspaper, the *Globe*. Publisher George Brown chose to contest the by-election in Haldimand County in April. There could hardly be a greater contrast between Brown and his chief rival, Mackenzie. Brown was a tall, substantial man with an impressive set of muttonchops, a quiet but commanding voice, and a cultivated Edinburgh accent. Mackenzie was still the bantam rooster, a fiery little Scot, full of loud and compelling rhetoric, given to exaggerations and insults that disgusted the staid Mr. Brown. Brown felt that Mackenzie was only one opponent, for the ministry was another. Two Reformers also contested the by-election and Baldwin did nothing to discourage them. Brown felt betrayed by a government he had served through his newspaper, and humiliated when Mackenzie defeated him. Brown's bitterness over the Haldimand election added to his unease over Catholic and French influence, with the result that he would become a critic of the ministry and, after the departures of Baldwin and LaFontaine that year, would make common cause with some of the radicals he had scorned.[33]

The Grits were thrust up by the confusion and change of recent years. The social dislocation of the time had been manifest in the Rebellion Losses crisis of 1849 during which Tory merchants and others tied to the old imperial trading system rose up in anger and fear of unpredictable change. The Grit rebellion was less violent but equally a response to the uncertainties of the age. It was an expression of populist concerns, particularly among agrarians in Upper Canada. Populism is a political form that draws broad lines between "the people" and the elites who are imagined to oppress them and ignore their needs. Populists are hostile to existing institutions that are instruments of their oppression, and are impatient with the slow, formal ways of decision making. They no longer identify themselves with the existing political or social order; instead they find their identity in opposition to the "other" against which they contend. They have little confidence that the existing political order can resolve the problems facing them. They feel the existing political parties are insensitive, incompetent, or corrupt. They are alarmed by rapid economic and social changes. And they are given voice by new ways of expressing political views.[34]

All of these conditions were present between 1849 and 1851. The Clear Grits expressed a popular disappointment that responsible government had not produced the expected reforms and that the Reform ministry itself had seemed to become part of the complex and costly system that agrarians had fought to overthrow. Complaints over grievances such as those with the legal system were met by either indifference or elite condescension. Baldwin's curt dismissal of demands for a simpler, more understandable legal system as reducing "us to a state of barbarism" was characteristic of the elite's failure to understand the needs of the people. Such insensitivity gave little confidence that the existing order would deal effectively and fairly with the volatile economic situation.

These concerns might have remained muted had not new forms of expression emerged at the very moment. One was the multiplication of newspapers, thanks to rising literacy levels and technological advances, particularly faster presses that could produce long press runs cheaply and make the news reports more current. Established papers such as the *Examiner* and new voices such as the Toronto *North American*, launched in 1850, publicized the Clear Grit movement. Equally important was responsible government itself, which focused more attention on the provincial Parliament and raised expectations for its performance. Once accomplished, responsible government did provide a finality of sorts, although not the finality Baldwin had imagined. The Reform coalition had been created to fight for responsibility and was held together by that goal. Its achievement made the Reform alliance a relic, and freed radicals to speak out for what they termed real reform. Robert Baldwin's Reform Party had been itself a populist movement against the Family Compact system, but once in power it became institutionalized and thus produced a new populist backlash.[35]

Robert struggled to find a strategy for dealing with the Grits. At times he tried to silence them by preventing their legislative proposals from receiving debate in the House. At others, he argued the case with the Grits. Sometimes he just ignored them. A newspaper reporter noted Robert's treatment of a question from H.J. Boulton in July 1850. "Mr. BALDWIN, the only member of the Administration present made no reply, but after listening to the hon. member, returned to the study of a book before him." The Grits were hard to ignore, all the same. They were active and noisy, and they developed a platform that had considerable populist appeal. Peter Perry and Caleb Hopkins introduced a motion in August 1850 that summed up much of their ideology. The resolution asked for a constitutional convention. It would consider extending the franchise, removing the property qualification for membership in the House, setting fixed times for Parliament to meet, creating an elected Legislative Council, election of the governor, banning any expenditure of public money without approval of Parliament, ending the imperial veto over colonial legislation, and exploring federation of the British American colonies. The political reforms were one aspect of Grit policy. They were intended to end the dominance of a political class that controlled the upper house and influenced Assembly elections through the power of property. They also reflected the confident nationalism of colonial people who had weathered their abandonment by the imperial economy. The second aspect of their policy was economic and social. There must be dramatic retrenchment of government spending and vigorous pursuit of reciprocity with the United States so that farmers would have a reliable market. Primogeniture and usury laws must go, a gesture to the businessmen such as Perry. There should not be any special privileges in the legal system for lawyers; every man ought to be able to access the courts on his own terms and in his own language.[36]

The spirit motivating many of the Grit reforms was the same as that underlying their legal demands. Ancient political practices and formalities were preventing rapid solutions to the peoples' problems. The *North American* complained that, "In the opinion of the Government, the prerogative of the Crown (that is, their own power), is of infinitely more importance than the rights of two million of enlightened citizens." The *Examiner* summed up the problem: "Mr. Baldwin is behind the times." Perry sought change to break class rule. Baldwin and his clique had "an *odour* peculiar to a certain class not a thousand miles from the 'capital city.' viz., strong love and admiration of *self, high rents* and *monopoly*." These reforms united the two factions that made up the Clear Grit movement, the agrarians and the emerging middle-class businessmen. Like the Reform alliance itself in the 1840s, some common goals and a common enemy could obscure the real differences between the aspirations and the class identity of the two groups.[37]

The Grits edged ever closer to republicanism as they sought to eliminate imperial complexities from government. They found some unlikely allies. In 1830, when Robert looked across the floor he saw a thoroughly predictable lot of Tories. Their mantra was simple: King, Empire, Church. Now they were a puzzling mix. Some hewed to the old line. Sir Allan MacNab, grown ever more florid and pompous, had put aside his 1849 flirtation with radical dissent and was again true blue, albeit with the added colouration from railway fever. John Hillyard Cameron, Robert's doughy-faced neighbour, was also a Tory of the old school. Others were puzzling. Boulton and Papineau argued for constitutional change, including an elective Legislative Council, that would give Canada, in Boulton's words, "practical independence." Robert was not in the least surprised. What did shake him was support for the motion from Henry Sherwood, Tory member for Toronto. Sherwood recanted his lifelong opposition to radical reforms such as the elected upper house. Robert tried to spike such talk. There was no need for "organic changes" in the constitution for Britain had given Canada all the authority it needed to legislate on its own affairs. The constitutional tinkerers would push Canada to a break with Britain and that, "I consider . . . black ingratitude, hateful ingratitude and injurious to the character of Canadians at this present time, to discuss the separation of this Province from England." Robert's loyalism fell on some deaf ears as the speech from Sherwood's Toronto colleague, Tory William Henry Boulton, demonstrated. Boulton dismissed Baldwin's "clap-trap" since Canada had not received the full British constitution. He was now prepared to go all the way to a complete elective system, including the governor. The United States, he claimed, was better off and happier with its republican constitution. Canada's present system of government was nothing but a tool in the hands of the Reform Party.[38]

Some Tories in the House, such as W.H. Boulton and Henry Sherwood, and some conservative luminaries outside Parliament, including the Orange leader, Ogle Gowan, and Toronto businessman, John William Gamble, had overcome their repugnance toward American republicanism and now were prepared to think the once unthinkable. The year 1849 had changed everything. Responsible government, the failure of the Tory insurrection in Montreal, and the routing of the annexationists, all had seemed to foretell of a new "family compact," this one of Reformers. The monarchy, represented by the governor, had been the bond of the empire, but Elgin had smashed that link with his behaviour in 1849. Casting about for an alternative, some Tories looked south. There were several disparate interpretations of the merits of republicanism. Hugh Willson, editor of the pro-annexation newspaper in Toronto, the *Independent*, believed that there were "more conservative principles" in the American system, in contrast to Canada's "badly regulated Colonial Democracy, divested of every Conservative principle." Others such as Sherwood, believed republicanism was one of several possible solutions. He advocated British North American union as a way to swamp the French and abort the executive absolutism of the current Canadian regime. Failing that, conservatives should embrace the inevitable democracy and work to avoid its excesses. Gamble believed that Canada was now in the grips of a dictatorship with all power resting in the executive. The American system of checks and balances prevented any one branch of government from seizing too much authority.[39]

Robert recognized that there was no Tory Party anymore, but a ragtag alliance of Compact supporters, annexationists, republicans, and some whose politics was business. Sadly, he also saw that the once solid French Party was fraying around the edges. The Lower Canadian Reformers had never been primarily about ideology. Protection of the French nation and its language was what bound them together. So long as Robert and his Upper Canadian coterie were useful in that protection, the Reform Party would hold together. Religion was part of the equation. The Catholic Church had become a more critical part of French-Canadian identity by mid-century, its role enhanced by the very vehemence of the rising anti-Catholicism of the day. Reform attitudes toward the Jesuit estates illustrated the new centrality of religion. The estates were substantial landholdings that had been seized by Britain after the Conquest. There was an extended debate in the 1840s over what should be done with the revenues from the estates. In 1843 LaFontaine was of the opinion that they would have to be divided between Catholics and Protestants in Lower Canada. Yet in 1846 he supported A.-N. Morin's attempt to have the House limit the use of the Jesuit funds to the Catholic Church.[40]

Some of the Lower Canadian reformers were liberals. Most seemed ready to see manufacturing become the driving force of the economy. Most supported mass education as a tool of progress. Lower Canadians were as likely as Upper Canadians to catch railway fever. LaFontaine was enthusiastic about Hincks's Guarantee Act of 1849, and Joseph-Édouard Cauchon, the member for Montmorency, rejected Baldwin's caution about state and municipal financing of railways. This was not a class-conscious liberalism, however. The two leading figures in the French Party were both from modest backgrounds. LaFontaine was a carpenter's son, and August-Norbert Morin a farmer's. They rose in the social order thanks to talent and good educations. Once they achieved prominence in the law and journalism, they did not share Hincks's bourgeois consciousness. LaFontaine came to believe that the ancient feudal order in Lower Canada, the seigneurial system, should be abolished, but not because he foresaw the triumph of the middle class over the aristocracy. In fact, he professed to believe the seigneurial system had served a useful purpose in the past, not just for the lords but for ordinary people as well; however, progress now required its demise.

Political liberalism did not always accompany economic liberalism. LaFontaine was prepared for modest progress beyond responsible government. Others such as Morin were more conservative. His views were not as evident in Parliament as those of LaFontaine for Morin was a reserved man who spoke and understood little English, and rarely entered debates. Yet there was no doubt that he believed constitutional change had gone as far as was prudent. The United States, so often the model for other members, was a dangerous, anarchic, violent, and crassly materialist place to Morin. Equally, J.-É. Cauchon sounded like Baldwin when he urged caution about change since he did not believe in destroying what had stood the test of time.[41]

All the French-Canadian members agreed on some basics. They represented a nation protected by the federal nature of the Union, in which two equal states were conjoined. At the same time, their nation was threatened. Upper Canada exploited the lower province and used it as a cash cow to pay Upper Canadian debts. There was a powerful streak of anti-French and anti-Catholic bias in many Upper Canadians. Lower Canadian members howled in rage against slurs such as that thrown by John Prince in July 1850. He was supporting fellow radical H.J. Boulton who was still angry over not receiving a judgeship. Boulton, Prince observed, had said "that Mr. Baldwin was a boy in petticoats when he was a man at the bar." Prince wished "the Attorney General, West, would now throw off the petticoats and French influence altogether . . . and take a stand as a good, practical reformer like he was formerly."[42]

LaFontaine was hardened to such gibes. He was more concerned with the divisions within his own province. Papineau had gathered around him a group of young activists and intellectuals who met regularly in the Institut canadien in Montreal. These *"Rouges,"* as they came to be known, had absorbed advanced liberal ideas and viewed LaFontaine and his ilk as far too cautious, either in advancing reforms or in protecting French Canada. Their colour was readily apparent in June 1850 when they held a banquet to mark the feast of Saint-Jean Baptiste. They toasted the sovereignty of the people, European revolutionaries, the Italian patriot Mazzini, Kossuth of Hungary, and the republican United States. They demanded, as the radical newspaper *L'Avenir* had insisted in 1848, on the greatest degree of liberty and equality possible within reasonable limits of public order. Such ideas were infectious and they spread into the French Party. There was no avoiding exposure to this radical liberalism for Papineau represented it every day in the House. Moderates denounced him for endangering the unity of French Canada, but young Lower Canadians listened. Nor was the threat to unity only from the liberal flank. The conservatism of some members challenged LaFontaine's centrism. It was embarrassing when one of his backbenchers, Michel Fourquin of Yamaska, was arrested for joining rioters protesting school taxes. The school disorders were only one manifestation of a reaction against rapid change and modernization. LaFontaine was prepared to see removal of limits on interest rates in the cause of economic progress. Some of his members were even more outraged than Baldwin by such capitalist excesses. Pierre-Joseph-Olivier Chauveau of Quebec County thundered against the tyranny of capital that enslaved the people.[43]

Still, LaFontaine's reputation and his political skills held the French Party more or less intact. Indeed, attacks from Papineau on one side and Upper Canadian Protestants on the other drove most French-Canadian members together. As a result, LaFontaine was unperturbed by the rise of the Clear Grits and their xenophobic Upper Canadianism. So long as the French stayed in their trenches, the Grits were no real threat. He was prepared to bear with much and sacrifice much in the interest of his nation. Among the possible sacrifices was friendship. He liked Robert, and came as close to true intimacy with him as anyone outside the family ever achieved. Yet he would readily see Robert overthrown if it were of advantage to the nation. In December 1850 he mused about this to brother-in-law Joseph-Amable Berthelot. The rise of the Clear Grits probably meant a reorganization of parties in Upper Canada and the end of the old Baldwin Reform coalition. So be it, he wrote, "[D]ans mon opinion, les Bas-Canadiens n'ont rien à perdue."[44]

They had nothing to lose. Upper Canadians of any stripe, seeking to form a government, would have to bite their tongues, suppress their gag reflexes, and make an alliance with the French. Baldwin, however, had everything to lose.

At any rate, he could not see any socialists among the confusing array in Parliament, although there may have been infidels.

———✦———

It was refreshing to escape the political hubbub and retreat into the family. With the capital in Toronto, there could be family meals most days, family entertainments, family talk. Robert could resume his place at the head of the table, a place proudly occupied by young Willy while his father had been absent in Montreal. For a time, there was one empty chair at the dinner table. Robert's second son, Bob, had determined on a career at sea. Robert had found the fifteen-year-old a post on a ship commanded by Robert Ramsay that shuttled between Montreal and Glasgow. Ramsay tutored young Baldwin each evening with a navigation book, and arranged for Bob to enter a navigation school in Glasgow. It was a rather unhappy compromise that placed Bob under Captain Ramsay. Both the Baldwin sons, Willy and younger brother Bob, had been sent to Toronto's Upper Canada College after they completed their studies in the seminary at Quebec. The college was a suitably genteel environment for scions of the landed class. Bob, however, was unhappy and restless. He and a classmate determined in May 1848 to run away to sea. They liberated a sailboat owned by a family friend, Henry St. George, and set out on Lake Ontario. The inexperienced sailors soon found themselves becalmed and had to be rescued and returned home. Bob said he had been trying to get back to shore because he could not abandon his grandmother. Robert recognized that Bob would never be happy unless he pursued his dream, and thus made the arrangement with Captain Ramsay the following year.[45]

Robert had been right to grant Bob his wish. Bob told his sister Eliza that he was as "happy as a cow over a bucket of bran when I am at sea," and apparently no longer worried about separation from his grandmother. The young man studied and worked hard and by 1854 was a mate on a clipper ship bound for Hong Kong and the south seas. In 1856 he won his first command as captain of the *Bramley Moore*, sailing from Quebec to Liverpool. The happy ending was abruptly interrupted in 1858 when Bob came home suffering from polio. He was bedridden just as his father's health was also in serious decline.[46]

William Willcocks Baldwin was more conventional, at least initially. He stayed on at UCC and continued his education at his father's great creation, University of Toronto, in 1850. Willy married Elizabeth McDougall in 1854 and took up farming at a family property, Larchmere in Whitchurch Township, north of Toronto. He was never very successful as a farmer, or indeed at any other profession, but he and Elizabeth gave Robert a granddaughter, a joy quickly diminished by Elizabeth's death in 1856. Willy remarried that same year, to Susanna Mary Yarwood. They would have six children.[47]

Robert went into the city for his parliamentary work, to visit his law firm and to attend church. His relationship with Toronto had always been complicated. He was born and grew to manhood there. His home and his small circle of friends had always been there. Yet the city rejected him politically. It remained under the domination of the civic clique, the Corporation, and the Orange Order. Robert had too often been burned in effigy to feel fully comfortable in his home city. That ambiguity was reinforced by the rapid change Toronto was experiencing. The population had reached nearly 31,000 by 1851, and the business community was expanding even more rapidly. Monuments to commerce were springing up such as the much-admired Bank of British North America building at the corner of Yonge and Wellington Streets, a distinctive edifice thanks to the royal arms over the front door and the large scallop shell that capped the parapet. Yonge Street was also graced by the new Bank of Montreal building, a very loyal copy of a London townhouse. Perhaps the most important addition to the city was the St. Lawrence Hall, erected at King and Jarvis Streets in 1849–1850. The elegant new space was perfect for large gatherings, such as a substantial covered market. Its construction had been made necessary by the massive fire that had destroyed so much of downtown Toronto in April 1849, an ironic echo of the fires raging in downtown Montreal at the same time. Among the victims had been the Anglican St. James Cathedral. For a time, Robert had to make the trek up

Bay Street to the much more humble Holy Trinity Church. There he was face to face with the rough democracy that was elbowing at his society, because Holy Trinity had been built for the masses, with no purchased pews; you sat where you could, even for Robert Baldwin.[48]

There were twelve steamboats and thirty-three schooners registered to the busy Port of Toronto, carrying the products of the city's hinterland to American destinations, and luxury goods to the Toronto wealthy. It was not all modern bustle, though. Wild ducks crowded the skies over the harbour, much to the pleasure of workers in waterfront warehouses who hunted the ducks in their spare moments. And the dominant Orangemen were as bold and raucous as ever. Lord Elgin wrote to a British relative about the Orange celebration on 12 July 1850. "I do not know how the day is to go off, but the gentle savages who consider the day specially dedicated to religion were shouting and firing guns and cannons all about the streets of the town and round this house till midnight last night." Robert could only think with chagrin about his failed attempts to control Orange excesses.[49]

Even home could be invaded by this boisterous new world. The family was all out on a Wednesday afternoon in late August 1850 when Robert's library was broken into. There was little hope of success in catching the culprits. Mayor Gurnett advised Baldwin that the robbery had all the earmarks of the notorious Markham Gang, Upper Canada's first organized crime group. But, then, any mysterious crime was blamed on that glamorous gang of outlaws.[50]

The two daughters were living at home. Maria, twenty-two was ambiguous about it. Her happiest times had been when she was at the convent in Quebec, so happy that she thought of converting to Catholicism. The Baldwin sense of responsibility had prevented that. Instead she came home to be her father's secretary and companion. Maria did try to create her own life. She fell in love with Jonas Jones Jr. and was briefly engaged to him. The young man's father, however, had been a political foe of the Baldwins and a vulgar womanizer to boot. The young woman was torn, anxious to get on with life but uncertain about Jones and about leaving her father. The affair was broken off. Maria had another beau, an American professor named Hume. When he called on Robert to seek permission to wed Maria, Robert curtly refused. Finally there was a doctor from Belleville, Charles Ridley. Their relationship advanced so far that her brother-in-law John Ross was pressing her in 1853 to choose a date for the wedding. Instead, she abandoned Ridley. Her father was ill and she could not leave. As she wrote Ross, "In spite of all my affections for Charley it cannot but be most painful to me to think of leaving Father without one of his daughters near him." Maria had a role to play, the faithful spinster daughter who would see to an aging father. That she would not have chosen that role was no more relevant than Robert's own distaste for politics. They were Baldwins and would fulfill their destinies.[51]

The second daughter, Eliza, was somewhat more fortunate. Her suitor, John Ross, was born in Antrim, Ireland, and transported to Canada as an infant. He articled at law with Baldwin's old friend, Andrew Norton Buell, and became a successful lawyer in Belleville. Ross played a key role in Baldwin's election there in 1841 and continued to perform political services in the years to come. Ross got his reward when Baldwin named him to the legislative council in 1848. Ross was a widower in November 1850 when he wrote to Robert, seeking Eliza's hand. He confessed to his nervousness. He could not continue to visit Eliza without her father's approval, but he feared Robert might think him too old, since he was thirteen years older than the nineteen-year-old object of his desire. He need not have feared. Robert approved, although he warned Ross that the final decision was Eliza's. She had no doubts. He was successful, a Reformer, and as one newspaper described him, "certainly what the ladies would call a *very pretty man*."[52]

Eliza and her pretty man planned to marry at Holy Trinity Church on 4 February 1851. Not everyone in the family was happy about it, for there were rumours that Ross was an atheist, and a low-born one at that. Toronto was enthusiastic, though. The wedding of the Reform leader's daughter was excitement enough, but the promised attendance of Lord and Lady Elgin assured a huge crowd would descend on Holy Trinity. Alas, the throngs were to be disappointed. Eliza came down with a fever, diagnosed as the inflammatory disease erysipelas. Her doctors ordered her to avoid exposure to air, so the grand public wedding became a small private one, held at ten thirty that morning in the parlour of the Front Street house. Family and friends gathered around as Eliza's cousin,

Rev. Edmund Baldwin, performed the ceremony. Robert toasted the bridal couple in his own fashion, in a speech brimming with loyal allusions to the royal family and the queen's splendid example of domestic life. He had the pleasure of his daughter's company for a few more days since her illness prevented the newlyweds from setting off immediately for Belleville. Their ultimate departure filled Robert with memories and melancholy. He wrote to Ross on 27 February: "Three and twenty years ago today I first became a father. The remembrance fills my heart and eyes, and I can only say, God bless you both."[53]

Memories, always memories, more real than today.

Chapter 18

A Reckless Disregard of First Principles

The familiar dilemma faced him. He was pulled between his basic impulses. Duty called him to struggle for his principles, to face the confusion with honour. Self-protection urged him to retreat into home and dreams of the happiness now long behind him. Eliza of memory was awaiting him. It had been fifteen years.

It was the afternoon of Monday, 30 June 1851. Rumours had been spreading, the last twenty-four hours, through the political world and out into the broader community. Throngs of Torontonians hurried to secure seats in the gallery of the House of Assembly to witness the end of an age. There was palpable impatience as the rituals of the parliamentary day played out, with Dunbar Ross of Megantic, Lower Canada, and William Boulton of Toronto giving notices of motion. Indeed, the notices were hardly heard since Robert Baldwin had entered the chamber at 4:00 p.m., and was immediately surrounded by colleagues expressing their concerns and regrets.[1]

Then there was silence. The familiar grey, stooped figure rose to his feet. The voice was, as always, barely audible and now shaky with emotion, but all the same elegant and compelling. There was now in politics, he warned, "a reckless disregard of first principles which if left unchecked can lead but to widespread social disorganization with all its fearful consequences." The evidence of that was the recent vote on the Court of Chancery when a majority of Upper Canadian members had voted, in effect, to abolish the two-year-old experiment. He must resign to alert the country to the grave danger of the "demagog clamour" that was drowning out reason.[2]

He was near tears as he sat down, as were many supporters and opponents. Some could not resist the opportunity to enter the historical limelight, or to serve their own interests. John Prince, never at a loss for words, attempted to reassure Baldwin that his resignation was unnecessary for the motion on the Chancery was merely an "interlocutory" one. Prince went further, making the the most unlikely promise that he would support all of Robert's legislation for the rest of the session. John Wilson of London, Sir Allan MacNab, W.B. Robinson from Simcoe, and Louis LaFontaine all added their regrets, some more sincerely than others. It was left to Francis Hincks to put a political spin on it all. Baldwin was quite correct to resign, but that did not mean the rest of the ministry had to follow. Indeed, Hincks pointed out, he himself could not be charged "with having taken any particularly active part in the establishment of the [Chancery] system."

The players all acted out their parts with fidelity to the script. Baldwin acted on punctilious principles that bemused and confused many. MacNab was the aging soldier, full of pomposity and good fellowship; Baldwin was, the gallant knight said, "a good [and] honorable man, and as loyal a subject as ever drew a sword." And Hincks was the sly opportunist, paying lip service to his leader while disassociating himself from Baldwin's policy and laying claim to the succession.[3]

The family was home for the new year; however, a cloud hung over the beginning of 1851. Robert's beloved mother, Phoebe, was in declining health. That was indeed a dark cloud, for she had been as central in his life as his father. She had taken care of the children in his many extended absences. She was his guide, even in politics. When he contemplated resignation from Sydenham's ministry in 1841, Robert needed his mother's reassurance that he had done the right thing. Phoebe was the first of the women on whom Robert relied for comfort, succor, and release from the pressures of public life and his father's expectations. Eliza, of course, was the next and most important. He knew, from the beginning of their relationship, that his personality and the course of his future were to be shaped by her love. He was sensible about it but certain of the truth. He wrote to Eliza in 1825:

I hope you do not think that I have any <u>merit</u> in any kindness that I shew to your mother—because if you do it would look almost as if you had forgotten that she is or at least will be <u>my</u> mother likewise—at least you have promised to make her so, and I feel that upon the performance of that promise depends the happiness of my future life—not that I mean to say that the loss of it would deprive me of my senses or make me absolutely wretched—I might enjoy comfort nay <u>some</u> happiness, but I should never be <u>happy</u>—everyday convinced more certain of that—I put in this proviso my dear Eliza to take off any appearance of that extravagance with which novels and Romances are cramed and which I abominate—an extravagance which I have always avoided in speaking of you and to you and which I shall always—I respect, I esteem, I love and adore you. I look forward to you as the sweetest source of my future happiness and the kindest soother of any future disappointments and I hope by a constant attention to <u>your</u> happiness to be not unworthy of your kindness—but I do not expect to find you absolutely perfect—I <u>know</u> you will find me very far indeed from being so.[4]

He needed approval from his mother and love from Eliza. The eldest daughter, Maria, was chosen, against her will, to continue the female nurturing of Robert Baldwin. She served him as secretary, nurse, companion, the last in the line of supportive women.

—◆—

How had affairs come to the sorry end with Robert's resignation? The government was strong. True, the erratic William Hamilton Merritt had resigned as commissioner of public works in December 1850. He declared that he could not remain in a government that would not carry out the massive retrenchment of expenses that he proposed. The gloss had gone off Merritt's business credentials by now and his resignation stirred little interest. Otherwise there was not much to disturb the progress of the ministry. Robert returned to the assizes, happy to act as prosecutor when the courts were close to home. He appeared at the York assizes in January and February, with some success in cases involving customs evasion and appropriation of Crown property. It was a good time, despite Phoebe's illness, in the comforting embrace of the family and the law.[5]

That February there was a glittering banquet, hosted by the newly chosen mayor of Toronto, John George Bowes at the splendid Georgian style St. Lawrence Hall. Mayor Bowes, a powerfully built and genial Irishman, gathered the elite to celebrate the city's progress. The leading legal figures, wealthiest merchants, representatives of the clergy, the prominent of the city were all in attendance. At the raised head table sat Lord Elgin, municipal and provincial leaders, and Robert Baldwin. Oysters and beef and wine, all the usual luxuries of such affairs, were consumed before the long list of speakers began their eulogies of the Queen City. Lord Elgin gave his expected graceful, and uncontroversial, speech. Robert then rose to reply to the Governor General. He was as bland as the others but one sentence stood out. "Nothing could be of more importance than the establishment of railroads."[6]

The railroad, the El Dorado of the age, would make Canada competitive with the United States, enrich farmers and manufacturers, and grow cities. Robert shared that enthusiasm, but had nagging doubts about the implications for public debt and the ethics of some railroad promoters. It was those concerns that had led to his conflict with Francis Hincks over authorizing municipalities to go into debt to finance railroads. Hincks's threat to resign in April 1851, and Baldwin's admission of defeat on the issue, meant railroad development would proceed unhindered by financial or ethical concerns. Hincks's secret victory won government support from the many railway proponents on both sides of the House. Hincks and Baldwin welcomed prominent visitors in June 1851 when Joseph Howe of Nova Scotia and Edward B. Chandler of New Brunswick arrived in Toronto to discuss a planned railway from Quebec to Halifax. The Maritimers were invited to the executive council meeting of 16 June, where Howe outlined the potential financial support he had sought from the imperial government. Whatever reservations Robert had about the grand and expensive scheme he kept to himself. And he made his own small compromise with the future. That spring he had purchased shares in the Toronto and Lake Huron Road Company and the Toronto and Guelph Road Company.[7]

Despite the internal tensions, the ministry looked unassailable. Indeed, it looked more and more like a national government. The LaFontaine–Baldwin regime was gathering the powers of a modern state. In January Lord Grey had written to Elgin, granting that the Canadian legislature had the authority to deal with the clergy reserves question. The government now could determine the disposition of the last great tracts of its own territory. Then in April, Canada assumed control of its own postal service. The first Canadian three-penny beaver stamp was issued on 23 April 1851. The stamp symbolized the headlong rush to the future of a country that had hurried from a fur-trade economy to Baldwin's world of land-based wealth to the age of railroads and steamships.[8]

This more modern government, with its reluctant co-leader, had its vulnerabilities. Robert had been aware, from the beginning in 1848, that cabinet building was a difficult, delicate task. Regional interests had to be considered, as did the ideological branches of the Reform coalition, and simple political debts. That had meant including ministers from the unelected upper house. Robert knew that was, at the very least, an awkward compromise, given his commitment to responsible government, government at the pleasure of the lower house. Events trumped principles all too often. When Merritt resigned, he was replaced by a legislative councillor, LaFontaine's Montreal friend, Joseph Bourret. The new cabinet position of postmaster general went to yet another member from the upper house, James Morris of Brockville. Liberal critics did not fail to notice. The *Examiner* tweaked Baldwin in an editorial entitled "Tremendous Rush to the House of Refuge." Legislative councillors led four of eleven ministries. Yet, the paper reminded Baldwin that there were two tests of responsible government. One was the ministry's ability to maintain a majority in the House of Assembly. The other, which the *Examiner* considered even more important, was the necessity that cabinet ministers retain public confidence by being re-elected after they had assumed office. Robert might not have agreed that the *Examiner*'s second "test" was actually intrinsic to responsible government, but he had to recognize that it was consistent with the rough democracy that was incipient as government became modern. It was no smooth cloth, this making of a new state, but a patchwork and some pieces, such as the legislative councillors in the cabinet, did not match the emerging pattern.[9]

There might be embarrassments, and the irritation of the nagging Clear Grit press, but Robert could be confident entering the fourth session of this Parliament on 20 May 1851. The opposition made no amendment to the Reply to the Speech from the Throne, and that often raucous business was over in a single evening. It was the beginning of a productive session that would see 170 acts passed, including hallmarks of this liberal state. One bill permitted the introduction of a provincial decimal currency, while several others facilitated the construction of railways. Little of this was Robert's work, beyond some tidying up of legal administration. The government was apparently strong, but it was already, in many ways, Francis Hincks's government, not Robert Baldwin's.[10]

Robert was struggling with much more than the politics of the ministry. His mother was weakening quickly. The fierce woman, now eighty years old, had seemed invincible: those eyes that penetrated her son's soul, the hard mouth that ordered the family, the strong face that was not at all softened by the lacy fringe of her bonnet. Now she was fading. Faced with the loss of another parent, Robert descended back into depression. He was unable to carry on some of his duties throughout the month of May. It was an already weakened man who was devastated when Phoebe died at the Front Street house on 15 May 1851. Eliza fifteen years ago, his father seven years before, and now his mother, he was without anchors. Phoebe was in his memory in sorrow and in joy. The younger Eliza and John Ross lost their daughter, Mary, in infancy. In 1854 they were blessed with a healthy son. Robert wrote to his daughter: "You say he is like poor little Mary. I always thought she resembled my poor Mother. If like her, he will be like the master-mind of the family, for such was unquestionably my dear Mother."[11]

Robert went to the House every day, although his physical disability was evident to all. Despite his pain, he was able to face up to a raw necessity. On 10 June 1851 he introduced the first reading of a bill to abolish the right of primogeniture in the case of persons dying intestate. His terse comments disguised the personal cost. He was bowing to that same incipient democracy, to the overwhelming opinion of his liberal colleagues and supporters that all barriers should be removed that slowed the conversion of land to capital. His father's words still resonated with him: that there could be only one heir to family property, and that it was the duty of a good custodian to pass on a landed estate that was more substantial than he had received. Yet that ancient wisdom had to give way to popular clamour and to new understandings of social order.

The enmity of his own church added its sting. Robert was caught between Bishop Strachan's High Church pretensions on the one side and the levelling demands of dissenters on the other. Strachan's pastoral letter to the Anglican faithful had not improved Robert's Christmas in 1850. The bishop noted that, "Some of our friends are filled with grief, and others with indignation, on being constantly taunted by our opponents with the fact, that if it were wrong to destroy King's College and establish an infidel institution in its stead, it was a Churchman that did it." Baldwin stood in a long line of betrayers of the church of God for "there was an adversary among the Apostles, and St. Paul had his Alexander the coppersmith." Having been likened to Judas and the apostate Alexander by the Anglican leader, Robert might have seemed shielded from the wrath of the dissenters. Alas, it was not so.[12]

The clergy reserves returned to the House on 23 June 1851 when J.H. Price again took the lead by moving a resolution. Lord Grey had promised that the British Parliament would pass legislation giving Canada authority over the reserves, and Price's motion expressed the colony's gratitude. H.J. Boulton and Caleb Hopkins were furious that the government was still feeding the House the bland gruel of meaningless resolutions, rather than taking action to end the grievous offense that was the reserves. Robert snapped that the Grits were merely trying to embarrass the ministry, since they were well aware that nothing further could be done until Britain passed enabling legislation.[13]

Religious questions would not go away in the fevered atmosphere created by the so-called papal-aggression excitement in Britain, however. The voluntarists pounced on a private member's bill to provide for the management of Anglican properties and diocesan government in Lower Canada that came to the House on 25 June. William Lyon Mackenzie, newly seated from Haldimand, and J.C. Morrison of York West attacked the bill and expressed their opposition to all religious legislation. Hincks was angry that the radicals would deny the Church of England the right to manage its own affairs. Robert was even more adamant. Flushed with resentment, he demanded that the Church of England be conceded the same powers as other churches enjoyed. The opponents were champions of equality, until it came to dealing with the Anglicans. Hincks and Baldwin beat back the amendments moved by Mackenzie and Morrison.[14]

The radicals kept trying, reopening the reserves debate on 1 July with attacks on Robert, who was still in pain from his resignation the previous day. They charged that he was being inconsistent with the strong stand he took on the reserves before he was in office. Tories assaulted him on the other flank for not agreeing to distribute the accumulated funds from the reserves to the Anglican Church. Louis LaFontaine was of little help, for although he agreed to support Price's resolution, he went on to make his familiar argument that the reserves were vested rights that could not be alienated from the church. That left Robert wallowing in his own ambiguities. Whatever changes might be observed in his positions on the reserve question were explained by, of course, responsible government. In the past, ministries had obscured the reserves issue by hiding behind British authority. Now the reserves could be dealt with honestly by a responsible government. Everyone in the House could agree with that. But what was the solution that Baldwin's responsible government would offer? Here the House was left in confusion. "I do not see any more objection to . . . endowments given by the state than by individuals," Robert explained, to the delight of the Anglican Tories, but "I am opposed to clergy as pensioners of the Government," with the voluntarists now nodding agreement. Other denominations had rights to the endowments, as did the Anglicans, but it was up to the people of Upper Canada to decide what should be done with the reserves. It was his last word on the subject, the word of a church adherent who recognized popular opposition to his church's privileges. Yet, he could not forego one of his first principles, that religion was so necessarily essential to an ordered society that it must be supported financially as well as spiritually. Even as the original Price resolution was adopted by the House, he had to know that principle, as with so many other of his principles, was in danger from the popular opinion he could not resist.[15]

Primogeniture, railways, and clergy reserves all reminded Robert of his discomfort in this new world. It was a discomfort that he had brought on himself to a large degree. His friendship and loyalty had put the hand of Francis Hincks, consummate liberal of the new order, on the helm of the state. His responsible government had opened politics up to a much greater influence from popular opinion, a popular opinion that so often rejected his patrician values. This session of Parliament had started so well, but it would demonstrate what he had brought on himself and his order of society.

The most famous, and most vociferous, member of the House was the newest. Mackenzie's triumph over George Brown had warned the orthodox Reformers that they would face a formidable opponent. Mackenzie carried his history, the lost cause of 1837, and the gale force of his personality into the new session. He was determined to see reform as he understood it and to punish Baldwin for leaving him in exile for so long. Mackenzie knew where Baldwin was most vulnerable and most tender, and so aimed his attacks at the judicial system. Less than a week into the session, Mackenzie introduced a bill to create conciliation courts on the model of those in France and Jamaica, which would bring quicker and cheaper settlements and deliver ordinary people from the lawyers who, as one friend of Mackenzie remarked, "unless arrested will shortly swallow up the wealth of the Province." That measure got the briefest hearing in the House, but it was only a skirmish in the battle to come. The old rebel began his head-on assault on 9 June when he gave notice of a motion to abolish the Court of Chancery, put an end to the precedence conceded Queen's Councils and law officers of the Crown in private practice, and to simplify court practice so ordinary people might argue their own cases. Henry John Boulton joined in the attack two days later with another resolution to simplify justice and to adopt the legal code of the state of New York. Robert was aghast. The legal reforms of 1849 had hardly had time to establish themselves and here were members advocating "an entire revolution in our legal system." The motions, each read a first time, ticked away at the back of his mind as the session moved on.[16]

Clear Grits and even Tories often denounced the judiciary and lawyers throughout the session. They drew no blood until the afternoon of 26 June. All the major players were present, Robert reading papers with half an ear on the proceedings, as usual. Then Mackenzie got Baldwin's full attention. His shrill voice cut to the heart of Robert's sense of the world. Mackenzie moved for the creation of a special committee to draft a bill that would abolish the Court of Chancery and eliminate the present form of pleading at common law. His model for legal reform was not Britain but the United States where the states of New York and Ohio had abolished their equivalents to Chancery. Mackenzie added further sting by attacking the appointment of W.H. Blake as Chancellor, suggesting it was a corrupt practice to have members of government raised to the judiciary. He himself had been "fleeced" by the dishonest proceedings of the court where friends of the government had been able to give evidence behind closed doors, "with lawyers at their elbow telling them how they might avoid committing themselves."[17]

Robert was fully alert now. Mackenzie had attacked the beloved legal system, the profession of law, and a personal friend. Still, he tried to calm the waters. Again he pointed out how recently the judicial reforms had been made, and pleaded for the House to give the changes a chance to prove themselves. The Tory Henry Sherwood and the radicals Boulton and Prince all made clear their patience had ended; Chancery had to go. Even a member of the ministry expressed doubts. Solicitor General J.S. Macdonald had flirted with radicals in the past and did so again. The costs at Chancery were excessive, as Mackenzie charged, and taking testimony by affidavit was unjust. Yet he would vote against the motion because the issue was too complicated for a parliamentary committee. There should be a committee of eminent professionals to deal with the defects of the system. Robert could only listen to his colleague with saddened incomprehension.[18]

The vehement debate left the House in disorder, members shouting back and forth, as the vote was taken on Mackenzie's motion. It was lost but Robert was shocked to find that only eight other Upper Canadians had voted with him. It was the solid phalanx of Lower Canadian Reformers who had defeated the motion. A jubilant Henry Boulton leaped to his feet to congratulate the people of Upper Canada whose representatives had sought to carry out the people's wishes. Perhaps Upper Canadians would now recognize the tyranny of the French who thwarted the legitimate demands of Canada West. LaFontaine charged that Boulton was a turncoat who supported the Chancery reform in 1849. That was only "under the bayonets of the Executive," Boulton retorted. The exchange could hardly be heard as members roared, and the Montreal Reformer, George-Étienne Cartier, screamed abuse at Boulton.[19]

———•———

Robert dressed carefully. The face in the mirror was sallow, jowls were drooping lower as the hairline retreated higher. The marks left by political triumphs and defeats were now indistinguishable from those etched by grief and depression. What had become of the young dancer, the happy husband? Straighten the high white collar and the cravat, fleck dust from the waistcoat. Ask Maria to check the document one last time. Summon a servant to fetch the carriage. It was 27 June 1851.

Robert rode up Yonge Street toward Elmsley Villa. He had last been there on the evening of 4 June for a fete hosted by Lord Elgin and his elegant young wife. He strolled the garden chatting to acquaintances while the band of the Seventy-First Regiment serenaded the visitors. A sumptuous buffet was followed by fireworks and dancing. Robert and the older, more dignified guests retired to leave the dance floor to the young. He was too ill and too preoccupied to attend Elgin's "Grand State Levee and Drawing-Room" on 20 June, and this visit was no happy occasion.[20]

He was resigning for his position had become untenable when a majority of Upper Canadian House members had deserted him on the Chancery vote. Lord Elgin was saddened by this end of things, but not surprised. He wrote to Lord Grey the next day to report. Baldwin, he noted,

> is not well, and has, I think, for some time been desirous to leave. If he persists in his resolution the Tories will by their factiousness have driven out of the Govt. the most Conservative public man in U. Canada. They will probably live to rue it. We have a great Railway Dinner tonight at which I attend.[21]

The Governor General apparently missed the irony. He was off to a railway gala after receiving the resignation of a minister whose career had been ended by the modern.

Robert then advised his colleagues in the ministry, some of whom tried to change his mind. To no avail, for his course was set. All that weekend they came to cajole him while the political class of the city buzzed over the surprise. Then it was Monday afternoon in that warm, crowded legislative chamber. His speech was emotional and his voice caught, yet he strove to present his case, his warning to the country, as clearly and logically as he could. He laid out the history of Chancery and the reforms of 1849 in painstaking detail. "It is scarce two years since it became the law of the land, and yet within that short time I found nearly all the members of the profession voting for the motion of the member for Haldimand to abolish the Court of Chancery." When even supporters of the government voted with Mackenzie, it was clear to Robert that he had lost his usefulness.

> The fact that this hon. house should refuse the opportunity of having the measure tested by a few years experience, although the previous one had twelve years to test it, was an evidence that I am no longer fit to occupy the position or attempt to perform the duties of the situation that I now hold. It is my duty to my sovereign, to this House, and to my country, to tender my resignation.[22]

Everyone saw what they needed to see. Radicals believed he had resigned because he knew he had little support among Reformers, or perhaps because he could not countenance the need to secularize the clergy reserves. As one put it, his "Puseyite soul cannot disturb [the Reserves] after all his bunkum speeches in former days." The *Examiner* thought Baldwin had become fossilized in office, content to rule with no real principles. "He is a man of precedents and fictions; with few popular sympathies; retiring in his habits; almost inaccessible; deaf to public opinion unless it speaks through a general election." Now that public opinion had punished him. Papineau thought Baldwin had simply been caught in the patent absurdities of the Union of the Canadas, where one section would always tyrannize the other. His friends were simply puzzled, unable to understood his peculiar sensibilities.[23]

There was something to all these explanations. Robert had a more straightforward version, as he told John Ross.

If the sober mind of the Country is not prepared to protect our Institutions it can't be helped. It was at all events as it appears to me right that that sober mind, if there is such a thing of any considerable weight at present, should be put upon its guard in the most emphatic manner that it was in my power to do against the consequences of that reckless disregard of first principles which if left unchecked can lead but to widespread social disorganization with all its fearful consequences. And as deeds speak better than words my resignation seemed to me the best mode of doing this.[24]

Others were perhaps more concerned with the results than the reasons. Hincks was among those who feared that there would be a disruption of the Reform Party. Perhaps the French would join with the Tories, one correspondent fretted to Baldwin. Lord Grey at the Colonial Office was alarmed by the confusion in the Canadian legislature and worried about the precedent set when LaFontaine and Elgin asked Baldwin to remain as Attorney General without a seat in the cabinet. Their fear was that the whole ministry might unravel if there was an attempt to replace Baldwin now.[25]

Louis LaFontaine soon followed his colleague. He announced in August that he would resign. His departure was voluntary, uncontroversial, and marked by formal tributes that Robert had not received. Yet LaFontaine privately was no more content with the course of events than was Robert. He, too, looked askance at the new government being sculpted by Francis Hincks. Hincks brought in A.-N. Morin, the quiet Lower Canadian, as co-leader and then sought out the Grits. Baldwin's old nemesis, John Rolph, would be welcomed into government along with crusty Malcolm Cameron. By fall, when all the deals had been made, LaFontaine confided to Robert that he was happy to be out of it. "I am getting too old to form part of the School of 'Chisellers.'"[26]

Robert was more forgiving, or at least more loyal to the party. He was immensely relieved to be free of office, he told Ross, and would never take on the burden again. He warned Ross of the terrible cost and advised him to avoid a cabinet post if he could. Still, Robert conceded, they owed the party their assistance. That pull of duty convinced

Robert to enter the lists once again, despite his dread of more political commitment. A new Hincks–Morin ministry was formed in October and called an election for December. Robert agreed to run in his riding of Fourth York, now known as York North. It was more of a gesture than a campaign, however. He did not visit the constituency after his June resignation and declined to attend the Reform convention that was held at Uxbridge on 30 October. He was preoccupied with personal matters. Son Bob, home from sea, was having fainting spells, although his physician, Dr. George Ridley, was confident he would grow out of the condition. Robert and Maria were moving to permanent residence at Spadina. Robert filled his new free time with plans for the estate, content in the isolation of the country setting. It was no surprise, then, that his erstwhile constituents turned against him. At the Reform convention four names were brought forward for the candidacy. Two local men led the voting, with Joseph Hartman of Whitchurch getting eighteen votes, Joseph Gould of Uxbridge fourteen, and two outsiders trailing badly. John McIntosh of Toronto received eight votes, Robert Baldwin one.[27]

Robert's friends in the riding had been begging him since August to come north and stem the opposition tide. His stand on the clergy reserves and Chancery had hurt him badly, and he needed to make a personal appeal to Reformers. Robert finally responded, heaving himself out of his nest at Spadina to tour the riding in November. It was far too late. He met unhappy liberals wherever he went, and he was dogged by an ancient adversary. Secure in his own seat, William Lyon Mackenzie made it his mission to defeat Baldwin in York North and J.H. Price in York South. Mackenzie followed Baldwin about the riding, rallying the people against the former leader. Robert hoped that his reputation and his traditional organization would succeed all the same. Cousin Lawrence Heyden was dispatched to get out the vote, a task he found much more difficult than in past elections.[28]

By the time the voting began, there were three candidates left, Reformer Hartman, Tory Hugh Scobie, and Baldwin. Robert made the journey to Sharon for the declaration of returns on 19 December. It was a crushing repudiation. Hartman had 664 votes, Scobie 327, and Baldwin only 142. Robert's speech exposed his shock and hurt. He deeply regretted, he said, that the ties forged over so many years between himself and the riding had been so abruptly and cruelly broken. It was over.[29]

John Ross and Eliza went down to the telegraph office in Belleville that evening to get the election returns. They were as shaken by the result as Robert. On reflection, though, Ross understood that Baldwin had failed to do the necessary work to win such a radical riding. Robert should have campaigned more vigorously and explained his position on the clergy reserves more clearly. All the same, Eliza was "very indignant" and Ross himself was "mortified." John reported that Hincks was prepared to open up the Niagara riding, one of two the premier had won, for Baldwin. That would be demeaning for Baldwin, Ross thought. Robert agreed and declined to seek another seat.[30]

It was a blessing, so thought Louis LaFontaine. As with Baldwin, he had been ill and was grateful to have the release of retirement. "I cannot but rejoice at the opportunity given you to restore your health, and to enjoy all the tranquility of private life." Indeed, there was a kind of relief mixed with the humiliation as Robert retreated to Spadina, to the familiar house and the familiar memories.[31]

Chapter 19

Hanging by a Most Precarious Thread

Past, present, future: they flowed together in the turbulent stream of memory. It was December 1858, and the wait to join Eliza was finally over.

The hard year of 1851 ended harshly. On the morning of Tuesday, 30 December, Toronto was struck by a fierce storm, the sky lashed with lightening and the city cowered under cold, implacable rain. The next day snow and sleet added to the misery. It was a sign of what was to come as Toronto faced the coldest winter in memory, as punishing as that of 1843–1844, the long winter after the disappointing end of the first LaFontaine–Baldwin ministry.[1]

Robert was as unsettled as the weather. He was no longer a politician, no longer the chief law officer of the Crown. How would he define himself now? He was his father's son. He was Eliza's husband. Had he ever been himself?

His politics were inherited from his father, explained at the dinner table, reinforced by William Warren Baldwin's pontificating at every possible opportunity, hammered into a yoke of heavy responsibility. It never mattered whether those politics fit Robert's personality. Might he, left to his own devices, have preferred the easy Toryism of his uncle Augustus and other members of the Baldwin clan? His inherent conservatism suggested that would have been so, had his father's will been less strong.

His father imposed his politics, and Eliza gave him his emotions. Few of his political supporters or opponents would have recognized the Baldwin who appeared in his letters to Eliza. There he pleaded for emotional reinforcement. He struggled to express the universe of feelings that existed inside him. When she was gone, there was no release save in tears and despair.

Was that all he was: a vessel for his father's ambitions and Eliza's emotions? No. There was something like greatness in his capacity to overcome his personal limitations and his mental disease. There was something like greatness in his understanding of his country; this unilingual, untravelled patrician grasped what others could not; that Canada must be a bicultural society of mutual respect.

Perhaps he could find himself in retirement. Politics had been his life for many years, yet he seemed to settle easily into other pursuits. One was that of landowner. He could not increase his patrimony, but he could improve it. Fifteen metres north of the main house at Spadina, Robert constructed a one-and-a-half storey clapboard cottage. It served several functions. The fieldstone cellar stored vegetables and fruit grown on the estate. The main floor was largely given over to a room for legal files and family papers. Above, facing east, was Robert's library. It was all crowned by a copula that contained, in memory of the conflagration of 1835, a large fire bell. This was a new sanctuary of isolation and memory, where he could study his papers and Eliza's letters and, from the front porch, look out over the family cemetery.[2]

He settled into a routine. He rose early, sometimes by 4:00 a.m., and answered letters and read until breakfast. He particularly enjoyed British newspapers, with which he could renew his and Canada's bonds with the Empire. The day was spent seeing to his garden and to his memory. Robert kept a file called "References of Press to myself, my positions Conduct and opinions," where he tallied the number of times he was mentioned in the newspapers. Household expenses were carefully tracked in a cash and day book. The monthly total in 1856 varied from £33 to £76, unless some major purchase was made when it could soar as high as £346, as it did in January 1857. Modest wages for servants, books, and stationery were the staple items. The stationery was used to respond to requests for loans and for legal business, but not often enough for correspondence with friends. Louis LaFontaine wrote in March 1852 in a ponderously joking tone, wondering whether Robert was still among the living since he did not answer letters. Nor had Robert forwarded some books that LaFontaine had requested in December. Even Eliza was frustrated by her father's isolation. It was the anniversary of her marriage to John Ross, in February 1852, and she had hoped that Robert would come to Belleville for a visit. He would have seen how happy she was, and joined in the joy of her pregnancy.[3]

His solitude began to dissolve when Eliza, John Ross, and grandson Robby moved to a neighbouring property when the capital returned to Toronto from Quebec in 1855. Perhaps to his own surprise, Robert was caught up in the adventure of grandparenting. He was happy when young Robby came to visit and took care to assure the little one's safety. He installed a gate on the back porch of Spadina to keep the boisterous child from wandering too far. When the weather was good, Robert, Maria, and Eliza would take long walks around the property after sunset, enjoying the gardens, woods, and flocks of wild pigeons and hawks. The warmth of family was returning. It was still a family marked by tragedy, alas, for grandson Robert died in 1856.[4]

There were demands that drew him away from Spadina. He kept an office in town at his old law firm. The building at 5 King Street West was a bustling legal centre, overseen by Robert's erstwhile partner, Adam Wilson, and until 1856, by Wilson's new colleague, Larratt Smith. Robert had a modest office above the reception room where he could hold small meetings. To get to the law office when he came from Spadina, Robert would pass the new Anglican university, Trinity College, that Bishop Strachan was building on Queen Street. The cornerstone was laid in April 1851, and enough of the edifice was completed to permit classes to begin the following January. It was a defiant expression of the bishop's will, an imposing structure whose three turrets dominated the skyline. Strachan happily contended that Trinity was flourishing while Baldwin's godless university was failing. The Methodists had refused to join the University of Toronto, squatting sullenly in Victoria College in Cobourg. The Presbyterians were equally uncooperative.[5]

To make matters worse, Hincks had decided to placate religious critics by weakening the University of Toronto into a mere degree-granting institution while teaching was carried on by the colleges. Hincks's new cabinet colleague, John Rolph, now taught medicine at his Toronto School of Medicine. The university's chancellor, Peter Boyle de Blacquière, resigned in protest against Hincks's proposed legislation. The university convocation, trying to make the best of things, met on 25 November 1852 and elected Robert Baldwin as the new chancellor.

Robert was offended by the presumption of the convocation and by the evisceration of his university. He wrote to professor Henry Croft,

> I have heard, as a matter of rumour however only, that I have been elected Chancellor of the University. Such rumour must however I trust be incorrect as the Members must I think through at least one of their number have known I could not under present circumstances accept of that honour. And that being the case such election appears to me so injudicious that I cannot think it can have taken place.

His sarcasm spent, he met with convocation and then wrote a more formal letter that explained why he could not contemplate accepting the chancellorship. It would "imply less hostility than I entertain to the course adopted by the present Government in regard to it or impose on me the obligation of embarking on an active opposition."[6]

As it turned out, Robert's university survived and prospered, despite Hincks, albeit in somewhat different form than he had imagined. It even would, in time, fish in Bishop Strachan's Trinity College. He continued to watch the university with a paternal eye. As treasurer of the Upper Canada Law Society he had a seat on the university senate where he could comment on academic policy. He was sometimes indignant when the university did not live up to the lofty goals he set for it, including its role as a national institution. After a hiatus of several years because of Hincks's policies, a medical school was re-established at Toronto in 1855. All of the previous faculty members were rehired, with the exception of, as Robert put it, the "young Canadian Richardson." James Richardson was the Baldwin family doctor, but the issue here was his nationality. Robert intended the University of Toronto to be a place where Canadians were trained up to leadership and national pride. It was outrageous for a talented young Canadian to be denied a role in that vital process. Robert's nagging was a factor in Richardson's eventual reappointment to the medical faculty.[7]

Robert was a nationalist and a devout Briton, and found no conflict between the two loyalties. He was also always a patrician, filtering his view of the world through that class perspective. His concern for the plight of university professors and senior civil servants was evidence of that filtering.

Robert testified before a parliamentary committee in 1855 on the problems of public servants who were not sufficiently valued by the public. The same year he had lamented that university professors were disadvantaged as compared to the horny-handed workers of Canada. "[T]here can be no doubt," he told his son-in-law,

> that the increase in the expense of living is enormous. We all feel it. And while the labourer and mechanic etc. who can dictate their own terms of remuneration do so it does seem but justice that those who are in a less favourable position in this respect should not be left to become irretrievably embarrassed in the struggle to maintain their position.

Robert's empathy was circumscribed by his social rank.[8]

The practice of law had long since been delegated to Adam Wilson and his associates but Robert maintained his loving relationship with the law as an institution. It was an anchor in troubled seas and a check against the "demagog clamour." He retained the post of treasurer of the Law Society and took direct interest in the major reconstruction of Osgoode Hall in 1857, advancing his father's vision of a palace of justice. Others had to deal with the law in the world, however. Robert was offered a number of legal positions. When Robert Baldwin Sullivan died in 1853, Robert was approached to take his cousin's place as judge of the Court of Common Pleas. The following year he was invited to serve on the commission that was consolidating the legal code and, a few months later, another judgeship was proffered. In 1855 John A. Macdonald asked Baldwin to become chief justice of the Court of Common Pleas. Robert refused all the requests. Sometimes he pleaded ill health. His over-delicate conscience also entered into the calculations. He could not accept a judgeship, he explained to John Ross in 1854, since "the position is one which owes its existence to an alteration in our system of Judicature for which I am peculiarly responsible." The imagined conflict of interest would provide an excuse "for demagogues to chatter upon."[9]

Bishop Strachan may have considered Robert to be something like an infidel, but Baldwin called himself a "High Churchman." As such, he refused to support a campaign in 1854 to have Francis Hincks's brother, the very "Low Church" Thomas Hincks, brought from England to serve as bishop of Kingston. These distinctions did not prevent him from working with representatives from several denominations in the Upper Canada Bible Society, where Baldwin was president in 1856. Nor did he apply any religious test to philanthropy. The great sensation of the age was the "Swedish Nightingale," Jenny Lind, who gave concerts across North America under the auspices of P.T. Barnum. She donated to charity the receipts of her 1853 performance in Toronto. When it was decided to use the funds for a home for destitute children, Baldwin contributed a large lot, some forty-seven metres of frontage on Sullivan Street between Spadina Avenue and Beverley Street. The Orphan's Home and Female Aid Society became a source of pride to the city and a lasting monument to both Lind and Baldwin. Despite his differences with the bishop, he also was generous to the Anglican Church itself. He paid dearly for a pew at the rebuilt St. James, a princely £50, as well as contributing to the rebuilding fund itself. Insults and snubs could not weaken his faith or his allegiance.[10]

Even in his solitude, Robert could not completely avoid politics. His shadow was long, and his imagined influence a subject of concern for radical Reformers. James Lesslie, the Toronto newspaperman, was sure that Baldwin still controlled Hincks and feared that the new ministry would simply carry on the policies of the old. Any compromise with Baldwinism was anathema to Clear Grits. In February 1852 there was a dinner to honour Malcolm Cameron, on his ascension to the cabinet. In an attempt to signal that Cameron was back in the mainstream, Baldwin was invited to attend the gala. His response was formal, but indicative of his feelings toward Cameron and the Grits.

King-St. West, 20th Feb., '52.

SIR—I have to acknowledge the receipt of your note of this day, informing me that you are authorized by the Committee of Management to request my company at a

Public Dinner, to be given to the Honourable Malcolm Cameron, on Monday next, the 23rd instant, and beg to decline the honour intended me.

I have the honour, to be,
Sir,
Your obedient servant,
RBT. BALDWIN.

Mr. Alex Cameron,
Asst. Sec'y to the Committee.

Robert's absence was not enough to satisfy the radicals who resented Cameron's attempt to make peace with Baldwin. John Rolph's ally, Dr. Joseph Workman, was snide about the dinner: "Cameron acquitted himself a small trifle by his good natured attempt to uphold Hincks; and palliate the treason of Baldwin—The people did not pay their 12/6 for stuff of that sort." [11]

Despite the contempt of radicals, there were bids to lure Robert and his reputation back into politics. Whenever rumour foresaw the end of the uneasy alliance that was the Hincks–Morin ministry, Baldwin's name arose. There was buzz in the spring of 1853 that Hincks would pursue his interests in railways on a full-time basis, with Robert returning as premier to clean up the corruption in government. Hincks stayed on and headed the ministry when it faced the electorate in 1854. Moderate Reformers urged Robert to run in Toronto that year against the former mayor John Bowes, who was standing for the Tories despite the charges of corruption in railway dealings swirling around him. Robert refused to leave retirement; perhaps he, as with many Torontonians, was more concerned with the rash of arsons that were tormenting the city than with politics. Once more in 1856, when the conservative administration of Sir Allan MacNab was in shambles, there was talk of bringing Baldwin forward to shape a stable government. Again Robert was unwilling. [12]

Reputation brought unwelcome political overtures, but it had perquisites. Robert was able to exert his influence to gain patronage appointments for his one-time supporters. More abstractly, his reputation won him appointment as a Companion of the Most Honourable Order of the Bath in 1854. His opinion continued to be sought, his approval courted. That was so in the fall of 1854 when the Hincks–Morin government was defeated in the House and replaced by one led by Sir Allan MacNab. The new ministry was a coalition of Conservatives with some Reformers, and mainstream liberals agonized over whether to support it. Baldwin pointed out to one fellow Reformer that, while he would not have entered a coalition himself, he understood that there were conditions that justified such combinations. The country needed steady government and a moderate course, and if that could only be achieved through coalition, the new ministry deserved public support. It was remarkably magnanimous of Baldwin, given his unpleasant history with MacNab. Of course, his generosity may have been influenced by other considerations than pure statesmanship. His son-in-law, John Ross, was one Reformer who joined the MacNab cabinet. Family had always trumped ideology. And perhaps Robert recognized, at some suppressed level of his consciousness, that his Reform Party, from 1841 to 1851, had been a rough coalition of unlikely partners: conservative Francophones; business liberals; agrarian radicals; and Baldwinite Whigs.[13]

Reformers who supported the so-called Liberal–Conservative ministry of John A. Macdonald and George-Étienne Cartier in 1857–1858 called themselves "Baldwin Reformers" or the "Moderate Party." It was understandable that some would try to entice Robert back into the fray. The appeals came from several directions. As a general election approached in 1858, some Baldwin Reformers were alarmed by the machinations of George Brown, now cozily leading the Clear Grits that he had once so vigorously opposed. Fred Jones of Brockville wrote to Baldwin about the radicals who were creating "dissension among the old Reform party of 1841" by pushing for democracy, something Baldwin and his Reform Party would never have countenanced. Robert must speak out to check the Brownites. From the other side, Brown and his Lower Canadian colleague, Antoine-Aimé Dorion, were anxious to enlist Baldwin to their ranks. And there was a middle group of men who wanted to honour their old leader, quite apart from any party considerations. The Legislative Council was now an elective body and Baldwin was lobbied heavily to stand for a Council seat in Toronto. It was a curious business, given Robert's past reluctance and his lifelong opposition to an elected upper house. He pleaded poor health when first approached. Still, duty nagged at him, for he shared Fred Jones's suspicions of the direction that Brown might take the party. In late August he had decided to accept the draft nomination although, he told his daughter Eliza, "[T]he responsibility depresses instead of exciting me." A week later he recanted and withdrew. It was fitting, for resignation had punctuated his whole career.[14]

Robert's claim of ill health was true enough. The illnesses that hampered his government in 1850 and 1851 were precursors of his life in retirement. The spring and summer of 1853 were made miserable by recurring attacks. The drama began on 3 May. The family feared he would not survive, and doctors stayed by his side twenty-four hours a day. It is likely he had a stroke, for his tongue and hand were paralyzed and he suffered fits, sometimes as often as every half hour. Eliza rushed from Belleville to join her sister Maria in caring for their father. By early June, Robert was improving, although doctors were still applying leeches. His mind mirrored his body. He was, Eliza said, "in very low spirits about himself . . . [H]e says he will always be in dread of another attack." That dread deepened when his aunt, Barbara Sullivan, died that summer. Robert was shocked that she succumbed with terrifying rapidity to a simple case of influenza. He imagined himself suddenly taken away, his life and work unfinished.[15]

Louis LaFontaine, no stranger to illness himself, planned to rehabilitate on a European tour. He wrote in September to ask Robert to give up his "obstinacy" and join him and his wife on the trip. It was impossible, alas. Everyone told Robert that he looked much better, but he did not feel recovered. "I am however seldom free for two consecutive days from the disagreeable rumbling noise in my head and I have frequent fits of giddiness attended with a feeling of confusion in my head that is even more distressing than actual pain to a moderate extent. Add to which I find that a very little thing worries and excites me." His body was betraying him. "I manufacture blood and fat too rapidly." He was fighting back, exercising to the point of perspiration, eating bland foods, avoiding worry, and only reading light fare. Still, after his aunt's demise, "I confess when I think of the suddenness of that event I feel my life hanging by a most precarious thread and have no wish to risk having that thread cut in a foreign or distant land far from my family and home." Since 1836 he had romanticized death, the doorway to his reunion with his wife. Now that it seemed imminent, death held fewer attractions for him. His romanticism was channeled into a gothic obsession with disease and decay.[16]

Another death, that of Willcocks' wife, Eliza, was devastating. Robert had loved her like his own children and took the loss much harder than did his son. He was deeply depressed that autumn of 1855. He had dreamed of a happy ending in which he could live with Willcocks and Eliza, and free Maria to marry. The dream was shattered. It was like the loss of his first Eliza, he told his daughter, this passing of someone so beloved and with her the unravelling of a happy future.[17]

The future would not unfold as he hoped, and there was little of his physical past remaining. The city of Toronto was ever larger and livelier, and stranger. Where Robert had trailed behind his father to court, along the eastern stretch of Front Street, there was now the noisy Fair Green. Cattle and produce fairs were sometimes replaced by circuses. P.T. Barnum had come in 1852 with his "Grand Colossal Museum and Menagerie," featuring ten elephants and the wonder of the age, General Tom Thumb, the celebrated midget. This was evidence enough that these were new times. For Robert, the smoke of railway engines may have been even more striking evidence. The machine era had begun symbolically in February 1849 when Lord Elgin, joined by some members of the Reform ministry, rode in a train carriage for the first time, speeding from Montreal to Saint-Hyacinthe on the St. Lawrence and Atlantic Railway. The first passenger train in Toronto left a shed opposite the Sword Hotel on Front Street, a brief stroll from the Baldwin town house, on 16 May 1853. The sturdy engine, dubbed the Lady Elgin, set off for Aurora, north of the city, pulling a box car and a passenger carriage.[18]

New landmarks were being thrust up while old ones disappeared. Russell Abbey, at the corner of Princess and Front Streets, was ancient by Upper Canadian standards, having been built in 1797 by the government official, Peter Russell. The Baldwins had stayed there in 1812 while William Warren tended to the ailing Elizabeth Russell, sister of the deceased Peter. Robert's mother had inherited the house on Elizabeth's death, and it eventually passed to Robert. The Abbey disappeared in spectacular flames in October 1856, another link gone. Beyond John Ross, who remained in government until 1856 and served again in 1858, there were few direct links to the political world either. Some of those few were unhappy ones. Robert had to watch Hincks embrace the old enemy, Dr. John Rolph, and bring him into his cabinet in 1851. Robert undoubtedly believed, as his friend J.H. Price did, that "Rolph is a black hearted rascal." That rascal was a minister of the Crown until 1854. Price, the loyal Baldwinite, was defeated along with his leader in the election of 1851. He tried again in 1854, still advocating Baldwin's policies. Alas, he was a husk of his former self, wasted by strong drink, and he once again lost. There might be moderates who pretended to be the Baldwin Party, but the personnel had changed altogether in a few years.[19]

Yet for Robert, past, present, and future all flowed into one reality. He sat, hour on hour, reading the love letters of the past, organizing the records of the present, and imagining a future, reunited with Eliza. The milestones were all there, to be revisited endlessly. He was still his father's favoured son, the boisterous little boy spoiled by doting relatives. He watched that boy grow into a young man, still open to the pleasures of the dance and the party, but heavily aware of the burdens of honour, morality, and duty. The young Robert was religious and had pretentions to be a poet. The two sides struggled in his uncertainty about his capacity to carry on the family work. It was great good fortune that they could fuse in his love for Eliza. She gave him reason to succeed in his career. She focused his morality and religion. In 1835 she was in New York, staying with relatives, the family of John J. Morgan, while she recuperated from the hard birth of Robert Junior. Robert reminded her of their agreement, the coincident readings that would conjure "simultaneous sympathies" between them, however far apart physically.

> I read this Morning the 61. 2. 3. 4 & 5 Psalms & the 9. 10. 11. & 12 chaps of Proverbs—On Monday I read the last chaps of Job in addition to the preceding ones which stood for that day because we never leave a Book unfinished unless there is enough to make at least another days reading. I mention this that we may not by any chance get into confusion—I like to know that we are reading the same part of Scripture the same day as we are unable to read it together—You know the simultaneous sympathies are favourites with me of old—[20]

The point about which his life pivoted was 11 January 1836 when Eliza died at the Front Street house. He would open the family Bible and read from the Memorandum that he and Eliza had begun to chronicle their wedding and the birth of their children, and that Robert completed on Eliza's death. There he remembered the anguish.

> She died of an attack of water on the brain, in which the general derangement of her system subsequent on the extensive hemorrhage attendant on her last confinement (to me at least most unexpectedly) terminated—During our short married life we were blessed with the most perfect and unbounded mutual confidence and affection—She was all a husbands love could wish her—The loss to her family and friends in general all who knew her can estimate—the loss—the sad—sad loss to me and her poor Children none can know but myself. . . . May the lord God Almighty look down upon me with mercy, and of his infinite Goodness, vouchsafe unto me the wisdom to bring up the dear pledged of my Elizas affection in the ways of his truth and after the words of the commandments, that both I and they in this life, steadfastly relying upon and looking to him as the giver of all our blessings and the kindest soother of all our afflictions, may in the life to come meet her whose loss we now deplore, and enjoy with her everlasting Glory and Felicity through our only Saviour and Redeemer, Jesus Christ our Lord.[21]

The remarkably complicated route of love and duty led him through the maze that was 1836 and 1837. His resignation from Bond Head's Executive was political as an attempt to force the question of responsibility to the forefront and make it the chief cause of the Reform Party. It was also personal; an opportunity to retreat into the wounded love of his bereavement. It was, as always, a reflection of his delicate understanding of honour and duty. He wrote in his resignation letter:

> [H]owever desirous I might be of giving my best support to His Excellency's Government, or of not hastily abandoning the important duties which had been most unwillingly assumed,

> I could not for a moment hesitate, when the alternative presented to me was the abandonment either of my principles or my place.[22]

Duty kept pulling him back into the present. It compelled him, with all his doubts, to return to politics. He was uncertain of his capacity for it and often resentful of the time spent from home. He was never uncertain about his ideas, however. They gave him the courage to confront Sydenham in 1840 and 1841, in the next step toward responsible government. They gave him the patience to wait through the Sydenham regime when friends such as Francis Hincks deserted him, and the stolid determination to win back Reformers, one by one, until the majority of 1842 was built. Duty propelled him to power in the LaFontaine–Baldwin ministry of 1842–1843. Then commitment to his ideas, and his ever-persistent need to retreat into family, caused him to give up power once more.

Looking back, he was struck by the dogged misunderstandings of his position and his ideas. Sydenham had considered him an "Ultra" because he would not take the knee. One-time liberal friends decried him as a radical for his opposition to Sir Charles Metcalfe's despotic rule, or saw him as a pawn of radicals. During the election campaign of 1844 Isaac Buchanan, the moderate Reformer and business leader in Hamilton, published a series of letters explaining his disapproval of Baldwin's political course. "My own opinion of Mr. Baldwin's personal *intention* is very high," Buchanan wrote, "but I now see clearly that, from a variety of causes, his character can never be sufficiently commanding, to enable him to call into existence, out of the elements in his power, *a party at once loyal and liberal*, and moulded to his views."[23]

He was denounced as ultra or radical throughout the 1840s and often belittled as an instrument of the French Party. Once responsibility was achieved in 1848 and he set to governing, the abuse came from the other side, from those who thought he was too Tory, too slow to bring reforms. Lord Elgin, viewing developments from above the partisan fray, knew better. Elgin, in 1850, was not certain that Baldwin had achieved the full splendour of the British constitution for Canada, as Robert seemed to believe. "I admire however the perseverance with which he proclaims

'Il faut jeter l'ancre de la constitution' in reply to proposals of organic change." Indeed, Robert had always and would always grasp firmly to the anchor of the constitution. His position was based on his understanding of what was best for Canada; the true transcript of British forms and the stability of an unchanging constitutional order. It was also his personal anchor. The Baldwins had struggled in Ireland to establish a responsible system that would do justice to the Irish people while assuring the maintenance of the British tie. Robert was brought up in the memory of that crusade and in the belief that the same solution would rescue Canada. His ancestors sought fair dealing for ordinary Irishmen and thought that their country was doomed without it. Robert brought the same sensitivity to the French Canadians and the same sympathy that the country could never be at peace without ethnic justice. His nature itself agreed with all this. He was shy and cautious, and found comfort in the certainty of the past. The rough jesting of Louis-Joseph Papineau captured a truth. Papineau wrote to his wife in 1854 of an encounter with Francis Hincks in Quebec City. Hincks broke off from a discussion to greet Papineau and jokingly remarked, "[W]e meet in an unusual manner—we were laughing just now, enquiring if Mr. Baldwin assented to it,—from want of a Precedent." Rather acidly, Papineau replied, "[W]e meet, that is good, we have to thank you to have made it easy: but it is admitted on all sides that you are far less scrupulous than was Mr. Baldwin . . . but in thruth [sic.] Mr. Baldwin was over scrupulous in point of precedents."[24]

Robert may have now realized that, with responsible government, he had set Canada asail on a voyage without precedents. Responsibility had always seemed to him the ideal solution. It was a truly conservative reform. It brought the virtues of the British constitution without demanding social or economic changes in the colony. Effective power would remain within the political class, only demanding that class pay heed to the general wishes of the rather narrow group of male voters, as expressed periodically in elections. This modest shift in emphasis would end despotic rule by unelected oligarchs and open government to a slightly larger constituency of men of education and sense of duty. Now he knew that the reform had, in truth, opened the floodgates. It raised expectations of reforms that went beyond the procedural.

Baldwin had seen his campaign as one for the British constitution, political ethics, and social stability. He had not understood how the society he hoped to govern was changing, changing at railway speed. He had not grasped that the tumult of the 1840s—with labour unrest on the canals, social conflict between immigrants cadres and with pre-existing groups, merchant anxiety and general anomie—was indicative of a vast and lasting revolution in Canada. The Reform Party was created, in large measure, on the firm base of his character. Its promise of fairness and justice was guaranteed by Baldwin's reputation. He recognized and was proud that duty and honour could bring about this great alliance. Yet the Reform alliance was both less and more than he realized at the time. He though of it as a union of Upper Canadian liberals with like-minded French Canadians. In fact, the French-Canadian Reformers were less in tune with Upper Canadian values and policies than he thought, and less committed to his party. They were prepared to entertain other offers, at any time, in the interest of their culture and language. The alliance was more because it brought together a broad spectrum of economic and social interests that coexisted uneasily in the common goal of seizing power away from the old oligarchy. Once that was achieved, in 1848, the bonds began to unravel.

He had not thought in terms of social class, and still did not. Class, nevertheless, was at the heart of the changes that ended his political career. Robert lived in memory, but he had forgotten Francis Hincks's defiant contention in 1843 that "We are now fighting the battle of the <u>Middle</u> <u>Class</u> against the aristocracy." Hincks was the champion of new capitalists, the railway promoters and the mining entrepreneurs. He found his allies across party lines, enlisting sympathetic businessmen whether Reform or Tory. Robert was wealthy enough to be one of them. He sold and rented land on a substantial scale. What he lacked was the instinct or the desire to turn the proceeds into working capital. His preference was always for stability rather than growth, the maintenance of landed property as the bedrock of the economy and society. Disagreement over how quickly land should become capital was at the root of the long debates over the usury laws and women's dower rights. In English Canadian politics, Robert was increasingly isolated. The main tendencies in liberalism were two: the business orientation that wanted to free individual enterprise while still using the state to advance economic growth and a laissez-faire radicalism that wished to pare the state down to a mere stub. Both regarded Baldwin as antediluvian.[25]

Robert did understand, at some subconscious level, that a Rubicon had been crossed between 1848 and 1851. He did not have the energy to fight for his social understanding, nor the confidence that a fight would succeed. So, to the puzzlement of those who felt less deeply than he did, he gave up office without even testing the confidence of the House. It was a peculiar but a consistent decision.

The burden of government removed, he could attempt to repair some of the damage it had done to family. He told his daughter Eliza that he regretted that he had not shown the children how much he loved them, and how proud he was of them. The renewed warmth was reciprocated, at least by Eliza. She was affectionate and open with her father, unconstrained by Victorian conventions. In 1854, after the birth of her son, she wrote to her father with happy frankness: "I do not think you would know I had been ill at all. I had a little trouble for a day with sore breasts but by great care and attention of my nurse, I am happy to say I have plenty of milk." When Eliza, John Ross, and baby Robert moved to their house on Davenport Hill, just west of Spadina, they joined a growing colony of Baldwins. Maria was at home with her father. Robert's uncle, Captain Augustus Warren Baldwin, and his wife, Melissa, were next door at Russell Hill. Augustus was an unreconstructed Tory, but family all the same. To the east was Mashquoteh, or "meadow" in Ojibwa, home of Robert's brother William Augustus and his second wife, Margaret. It would have been splendid indeed, as Robert told Eliza, if her mother were there to complete the family.[26]

The future would not be so kind for family. The children would all inherit substantial plots of land. The precise allocation of the properties was determined by the named trustees, William Augustus Baldwin, cousin Lawrence Heyden, and lawyer John Hector. Willcocks received the family home at Spadina immediately, while Bob got a direct inheritance of £5000. They did not harken to their grandfather's injunctions about preserving and increasing the family property. Despite studying agriculture at the University of Toronto, Willcocks could not make a go of farming. He peddled pieces of the Spadina land to keep his head above water, and finally sold what remained to a banker, James Austin. Willcocks subsisted on his father's memory, receiving a sinecure at Osgoode Hall as distributor of the stamps used to pay court charges. Bob had to give up his life at sea because of polio. He received both his inheritance and a divine message. Bob was born again in evangelical religion and was a familiar figure on Toronto street corners, preaching the gospel, until his death in 1885. Maria would die suddenly still unhappily a spinster, in the same year that Spadina was sold, 1866. Only Eliza fared well. Her husband, John Ross, was a successful businessman, politician, and senator until his death in 1871. Willcocks could not manage money and constantly found himself in distress. His desperation led to a bitter and embarrassing lawsuit in 1886, when he sued Eliza and Bob's estate in an attempt to gain sole possession of property that passed to them from Augustus Warren Baldwin. The unsuccessful action was a last betrayal of Robert Baldwin's understanding of the sanctity of family.[27]

There was one more strange twist in this future. Eliza and John Ross, to everyone's surprise, had another son in 1869. They named him, again, after his grandfather. This new Robert Baldwin would be a polar extreme from his namesake, except perhaps for his romanticism. He became a journalist and poet in England and, most famously, Oscar Wilde's lover.[28]

Robert spent the year of 1858 preparing. He organized his papers and copied the letters exchanged with his Eliza. Illness continued to distract him. That summer he was haunted by sleeplessness and, when he did sleep, by "dreams of a harassing and perplexing character." He was often confused. His work as treasurer of the Law Society was falling into disorder because he lost track of business and could not remember what had been done during previous terms. "I feel depressed and good for nothing," he told Eliza. Robert's health deteriorated further that autumn, and the house became a makeshift hospital. Bob, home from sea and suffering from polio, was chronically ill, and Maria was not well either. John Ross, at least, tried to maintain perspective. He was worried about the family invalids, and the family miscreants. Both William Willcocks and uncle William Augustus had defected from Ross' Liberal-Conservatives to support George Brown, while Willcocks strained relations by his financial profligacy. Still,

Ross did not want to criticize them openly. As he told Eliza, "[L]et it drop as I shall do because any words wd. only give pain to yr. father."[29]

It did pain Robert to see the family in disagreements. Still, they were all there as the winter set in. Robert was ready. He had made copies of his Eliza's letters and entrusted them to Maria. He had prepared his antemortem instructions and given a copy to her. They were poignant and explicit. In the document, he told the children how, after they had gone to bed, he would hold "sweet converse with my departed E." The letters he was now commending to Maria were filled with "mournfully happy recollections." He might have enshrined his wishes in his will, but he knew strangers would not understand, so they must remain privy to the family. Even though the requirements were not in his will, he wanted Maria to treat them as if they were legal obligations. He set down his needs for his astonished daughter to read.

First, before I am committed to my coffin let the following operation be performed on my body, being the same performed on that of your dear mother—let an incision be made into the cavity of the abdomen extending through the two upper thirds of the linea alba.

Secondly, let my little pearl brooch, a present from herself, be placed on my bosom, that as she rests with the nuptial ring upon her finger I may rest beside her with this token of her affection on my breast.

Thirdly, there will be found in my E.'s box the handkerchief that covered her face while she lay a corpse prior to her burial; let the same be used to cover mine.

Fourthly, the chairs on which rested her coffin previous to it being removed from our room will be found marked; let the same be used in like manner to support my coffin.

Fifthly, let the letters of which these are copies be deposited in my coffin . . . and let one of my E.'s handkerchiefs be spread over them.

Sixthly, let there be placed in my coffin a plain silver plate of the same dimensions and with a similar inscription to that which is my E.'s.

> Seventhly, let my coffin be placed by the side of my E.'s
> so that she will be on my left, that being the side she used to
> call her <u>own</u>, as nearest my heart, and let a small iron chain
> be passed around the two coffins and locked as to chain them
> together.[30]

He had made his pact with death. December began with an attack of
angina pectoris that sent him to his bed. Aware of how close he was
to the end by Saturday, 4 December, Robert asked Maria to bring him
pen and paper so he might revise his will. He was more ill on Sunday
and made little progress on the changes. That alarmed Willcocks who
harboured dark suspicions that Heyden was counselling his father
to reduce the eldest son's share of the estate—a fear that was false,
founded only on the son's insecurity. On Wednesday, 8 December
Robert's former law partner, Adam Wilson, came to the sick room
to assist Robert with his will. The next day, Robert consulted with
those he trusted most, Wilson and Ross, and dictated the changes.
He tried to reassure Willcocks, but the conversation was brief and
unsatisfying, for Robert was too exhausted and too emotional to
explain the situation to his anxious son. Everyone knew he was going.
The men of the family carried Bob to his father's bedside for a last
blessing. At five twenty on the afternoon of Thursday, 9 December
1858, Robert joined his Eliza.[31]

———◆———

St. Martin's Rood Cemetery at Spadina was a block of about
0.8 kilometres, abutting the Russell Hill estate on the east; the banks of
the stream that ran through Spadina on the south; and Aunt Maria's
Road, the "duck walk," to the north. A burial vault was set into the south
bank of the ravine, just behind the house. Baldwins had been laid to rest
there since 1829 when Robert's teenage brother, Quetton St. George, had
been interred. It was there, on Monday, 13 December, that the leaders of
Upper Canada gathered, more than a thousand strong, to honour Robert
Baldwin. The weather was bitterly cold and the city was eerily silent as
the stores closed in respect. There were friends and colleagues from the

legislature and the law. There were ancient enemies, the political and the ecclesiastical. Even Bishop John Strachan attended. The service was conducted, appropriately, by Anglican Rev. Henry James Grasett. Grasett was Robert's longtime colleague in the Bible Society, a tall, stooped, unassuming man, as uncomfortable speaking before this multitude as Robert himself would have been.[32]

Maria kept silent about her father's antemortem instructions, either out of resentment or embarrassment. It was by chance they were discovered. Willcocks had the task of sorting his father's things and found a worn, wrinkled copy of the instructions that Robert carried in a vest pocket, in case he died away from home. The senior men of the family gathered in the tomb in the January chill to fulfill those last requests.[33]

Robert rested with Eliza and the other deceased family members, but not forever as he had hoped. The new owners of Spadina were redeveloping the property, and the Baldwin tomb was an encumbrance. So there was one last journey. Robert and the others were removed from St. Martin's Rood and transported down Bloor Street to St. James's Cemetery in September 1874. There, in time, his headstone would fall and be overgrown by the inexorable grass. His memory would live, all the same, whenever Canadian parliamentarians tested the responsibility of their governments.

Note on Sources

The documentation on Robert Baldwin and his era is substantial. The notes indicate the wide variety of sources employed, primary and secondary.

There have been previous biographies,which include Stephen Leacock's joint biography, *Baldwin, LaFontaine, Hincks: Responsible Government* (Toronto: Morang, 1910). It is as vigorous and often entertaining as one might expect from Leacock, but more opinionated than well supported. George E. Wilson's *The Life of Robert Baldwin: A Study in the Struggle for Responsible Government* (Toronto: Ryerson Press, 1933) is as whiggish about political progress as the title would suggest. There is little about Baldwin the man. J.M.S. Careless contributed the sketch on Baldwin in J.M.S. Careless, ed., *The Pre-Confederation Premiers: Ontario Government Leaders, 1841–1867* (Toronto: University of Toronto Press, 1980), 89–147. It is an engaging and well-rounded account, but conventional in its liberal interpretation.

The book that best combines the political and the personal is R.M. and J. Baldwin's *The Baldwins and the Great Experiment* (Toronto: Longmans, 1969). It is a well-researched, if highly laudatory, study of the Baldwins from the Irish family through to Robert. The most recent contribution is John Ralston Saul's *Louis-Hippolyte LaFontaine and Robert Baldwin* (Toronto: Penguin, 2010). This is an excellent starting point, brief, engaging, and with a strong point of view. Saul sees LaFontaine and Baldwin as the architects of democracy and non-violent politics, a somewhat different emphasis than is found in my treatment.

The Baldwins' personal archives are extensive. Robert was obsessive about retaining and organizing his correspondence. His personally arranged archive is found in the Baldwin Room of the Toronto Reference Library as the Robert Baldwin Papers. Other collections have been gathered there, including his father's papers and, most recently, the research collection used for R.M. and J. Baldwin's book. There are smaller collections of Robert's papers in the Archives of Ontario and at Library and Archives Canada. Library and Archives Canada also house Louis LaFontaine's papers as well as those of governors and other political figures. The Mackenzie-Lindsey Collection in the Archives of Ontario is invaluable, since William Lyon Mackenzie corresponded with many of the chief actors as well as liberal rank and file. Louis-Joseph Papineau's correspondence at Library and Archives Canada is interesting both for the political commentary and Papineau's vivid, amusing, and often acidic assessments.

Somewhere between a primary and a secondary source is the historical writing of a newspaperman John Charles Dent, who was a confidante for many political leaders. He had unparalleled access to interviews and documents, giving his books an insider's knowledge of events. Dent was decidedly liberal and strongly supported the Clear Grit politician Dr. John Rolph. He was biased against William Lyon Mackenzie. Whatever the slant, however, Dent's histories are centrally important to understanding the period. Among his works are *The Story of the Upper Canadian Rebellion* (Toronto: C.B.Robinson, 1886) and, especially, *The Last Forty Years: Canada Since the Union of 1841*, volumes 1 and 2 (Toronto: G. Virtue, 1881).

Louis LaFontaine lacks a good full-length biography. Saul brings him alive in his brief assessment. Alfred D. De Celles, *LaFontaine et son temps* (Montreal: Librarie Beauchemin, 1907) is a rather bloodless political biography. Jacques Monet has described LaFontaine in *The Last Cannon Shot: A Study of French-Canadian Nationalism, 1837–1850* (Toronto: University of Toronto Press, 1969) and his sketch of the Lower Canadian leader in *Dictionary of Canadian Biography*, IX (Toronto/ Quebec: University of Toronto Press and Les Presses de l'université Laval, 1976), 440–51. Eric Bédard puts LaFontaine in the context of the Lower Canadian Reform movement in *Les Réformistes: Une génération canadienne-française au milieu du XIXe siècle* (Montreal: Boréal, 2009).

Quotations have been rendered with the original spelling and grammar so as to avoid littering the text with the scholarly *sic*. The exception is direct quotes from legislative debates. The newspaper reporters who recorded the debates in the era before an official Hansard rendered them in an awkward third person. I have corrected them to the first person.

Note Abbreviations

AO	Archives of Ontario
BFP	Toronto Reference Library, Baldwin Family Papers, uncatalogued
DCB	*Dictionary of Canadian Biography* (Toronto/Quebec)

V	1983
VII	1988
VIII	1985
IX	1976
X	1972

Debates	*Debates of the Legislative Assembly of the Province of Canada*, ed. Elizabeth Nish et al. (Montreal: Presses de l'école des hautes études commercialles, 1970–)
Journals	Province of Canada, *Journals of the Legislative Assembly*
LAC	Library and Archives Canada
MLC	Mackenzie-Lindsey Collection, Public Archives of Ontario
PL	LAC, MG24 B14, Papiers LaFontaine, Library and Archives Canada
RBP	Robert Baldwin Papers, Toronto Reference Library
TRL	Toronto Reference Library

Notes

Chapter 1

1. R.M. and J. Baldwin, *The Baldwins and the Great Experiment* (Don Mills, ON: Longmans, 1969), 244. Austin Seton Thompson, *Spadina: A Story of Old Toronto* (Toronto: Pagurian Press, 1976). LAC, MG24 K2, George Coventry, 13, 61.

2. RBP, II, Memorandum, Robert Baldwin, n.d.

3. The scene is described in an attachment to the above memorandum (note 2), written by Willcocks Baldwin.

4. Private, Memorandum, Robert and Elizabeth Baldwin, contained in the family bible.

Chapter 2

1. RBP, I, A86, Robert to William Warren Baldwin, 8 April 1843.

Chapter 3

1. Baldwin left office by resignation in 1836, 1841, and 1851. He tendered his resignation, but withdrew it in 1849 and 1851, and resigned a nomination in 1858. He described the agony of his 1841 decision in RBP, I, A86/1, Robert to William Warren Baldwin, 15 June 1841.

2. Ibid., 26 July 1841.

3. On the Irish background: Baldwin, *Baldwins and the Great Experiment*, 1–37.

4. *DCB*, VII, Robert L. Fraser, "William Warren Baldwin," 35–44. *DCB*, V, Edith G. Firth, "Peter Russell," 729–32. On elite society and the importance of family: Lawrence Stone and Jeanne C. Fawtier Stone, *An Open Elite? England, 1540–1880* (Oxford: Oxford University Press, 1984), esp. 9 and 421.

5. Baldwin, *Baldwins and the Great Experiment*, chs. 7 and 9.

6. AO, William Warren and Robert Baldwin Papers, William Warren Baldwin to Peter Russell, 27 July 1806. *Colonial Advocate*, York, 5 July 1828.

7. Private, Simon Scott, Toronto, Ross-Baldwin Family Papers, Robert Baldwin to Eliza Ross, 17 April 1854 (draft). TRL, Elizabeth Russell Papers, Diary, 10 January 1808.

8. Russell Diary, 9 February, 2 April 1806, 10 May 1807.

9. Russell Diary, 26–28 April 1806.

10. Russell Diary, 7 May 1807. TRL, William Warren Baldwin Papers, B108, William Warren Baldwin to John Large, 8 August 1834.

11. There are descriptions of the Grammar School in Edith G. Firth, ed., *The Town of York, 1815–1834* (Toronto: Champlain Society for Government of Ontario, University of Toronto Press, 1966). William Warren Baldwin's comments on Robert's schooling: TRL,

William Warren Baldwin Papers, II, William Warren to John Baldwin, 21 April 1818, 21 November 1820; ibid., William Warren Baldwin to Quetton St. George, 2 September 1818.

12. Baldwin, *Baldwins and the Great Experiment*, 86–7.

13. William Canniff, *The Medical Profession in Upper Canada, 1768–1850: An Historical Narrative* (Toronto: W. Briggs, 1894), 229–30. There is a very detailed account of the American attack on York: Robert Malcolmson, *Capital in Flames: The American Attack on York, 1813* (Montreal: R. Brass Studio, 2008).

14. Baldwin, *Baldwins and the Great Experiment*, 75–8. On Upper Canadian ambivalence toward the United States: Jane Errington, *The Lion, the Eagle, and Upper Canada: A Developing Colonial Ideology* (Montreal and Kingston: McGill-Queen's University Press, 1987).

15. A typical circuit, to the southwest with stops in Hamilton and Vittoria, is discussed in: RBP, I, A38/120, John S. Cartwright to Baldwin, 8 September 18.

16. *DCB*, VIII, Michael S. Cross and Robert Lochiel Fraser, "Robert Baldwin," 46. LAC, MG24 B11, William Warren and Robert Baldwin, Baldwin-Ross, Robert to Eliza, 22 October 1825.

17. On Maitland: *DCB*, VIII, Hartwell Bowsfield, "Sir Peregrine Maitland," 596–605. Aileen Dunham, *Political Unrest in Upper Canada, 1815–1836* (Toronto: Longmans Green, 1927). On Willis: *DCB*, X, Alan Wilson, "John Walpole Willis," 704–7.

18. LAC, RG11, CO42/390, William Warren Baldwin to the Duke of Wellington, 3 January 1829, enclosure, minutes of Constitutional Meeting, 15 August 1828, 94–6.

19. George E. Wilson, *The Life of Robert Baldwin: A Study in the Struggle for Responsible Government* (Toronto: Ryerson Press, 1933), 24–5. *Canadian Freeman*, York, 17 July 1828. RBP, I, A73/65, Sullivan to Baldwin, 1828.

20. Petition to the King's Most Excellent Majesty, n.d., in LAC, RG11, CO42/390, William Warren Baldwin to the Duke of Wellington, 3 January 1829, 98–103; the quote is at 91.

21. The most recent major study of responsible government is Phillip A. Buckner, *The Transition to Responsible Government: British Policy in British North America, 1815–1850* (Westport, CN: Greenwood Press, 1985).

22. LAC, RG11 CO42/384, Sir Peregrine Maitland to Sir George Murray, 18 September 1828, 148–62.

23. On responsible government in Britain: John Manning Ward, *Colonial Self-Government: The British Experience, 1759–1856* (Toronto: Macmillan, 1976), esp. 199–207. Buckner, *Transition to Responsible Government*, believes the principle was much clearer, much earlier, in Britain. The Upper Canadian Assembly petition of 1835 can be found, among other places, in LAC, MG24 B2, Papiers Papineau, 2, Address of the House of Assembly of Upper Canada to the King's Most Excellent Majesty, 15 April 1835, 1932–6. For Mackenzie's reservations: ibid., Mackenzie to Papineau, 18 February 1836, 1886. One Lower Canadian liberal felt that Upper Canadians had "forced . . . their peculiar hobby" of responsible government on the Patriotes, thus confusing and weakening the reform movement: ibid., E.B. O'Callaghan to Papineau, 17 July 1847, 3993.

24. Paul Romney, "From the Rule of Law to Responsible Government: Ontario Political Culture and the Origins of Canadian Statism," *Historical Papers* (1988), 111.

25. *Canadian Freeman*, York, 16, 30 October 1828.

26. Ibid., 17 July 1828. TRL, Broadside Collection, *The Reply of Robt. B*L*W*N, Esq. on being asked what could induce him to undertake the defence of the Editor of the C*d*n**F*ee*an.*

27. *Colonial Advocate*, 6 August, 3 December 1829, 4 February 1830.

28. *Canadian Freeman*, 21 October 1830.

29. LAC, MG24 I47, William Botsford Jarvis, letters to his family, 1832–1838, Jarvis to "My Dear Sister," 14 June 1834.

30. BFP, Box 1, Memories of My Youth and a Sketch of the Family History of the Ross-Baldwin Family by their Descendant Mary J. Ross, 1925. Ibid., R.B. Sullivan to "Dear Brother," Dublin, 7 January 1834. RBP, I, A32/37, W. Allan to Baldwin, 5 February 1835.

31. LAC, Baldwin-Ross, Robert to Eliza Baldwin, 31 May 1835. On Baldwin's health: Ibid., Robert Baldwin to Eliza Sullivan, 14 December 1825; Robert to Eliza Baldwin, 14, 21 August 1827; AO, Thomas Radenhurst Papers, Box 1, Envelope 13, Baldwin to Radenhurst, 16 November 1831. On Eliza's absence in New York: LAC, Baldwin-Ross, Robert to Eliza Baldwin, 27 May 1835; Phoebe to Robert Baldwin, 9 October 1835.

32. Private, Memorandum, Robert and Augusta Elizabeth Baldwin, contained in the family bible, n.d.

33. Among descriptions of his appearance: John Charles Dent, *The Last Forty Years: Canada Since the Union of 1841* (Toronto: George Virtue, 1881), I, 82; LAC, MG24 K2, George Coventry, 13, 61–2. The sleep episode: *Debates*, IV/2, 2514.

34. His speech in the House: *Gazette,* Montreal, 17 September 1841. Neil F. Morrison, ed., "Portraits of the Canadian Parliament of 1850," *Ontario History* XLII, 3 (1950), 157. His lapses: PL, 465-A, Baldwin to LaFontaine, 24 January 1848; LAC, RG5 C1, Provincial Secretary, 283/167, Baldwin to James Leslie, 1 February 1850. On hysteria: James Strachey, ed., "Fragments of an Analysis of a Case of Hysteria," in *The Standard Edition of the Complete Psychological Works of Sigmund Freud* (London: Hogarth Press, 1953), VII, 1–122, esp. 24; Carroll Smith-Rosenberg, "The Hysterical Woman: Sex Roles and Sex Conflict in 19th-Century America," *Social Research* 39, 4 (Winter 1972), 652–78.

Chapter 4

1. Robert described the agony of his 1841 decision in RBP, I, A86/1, Robert to William Warren Baldwin, 15 June 1841.

2. RBP, I, A54/62, John Joseph, Government House, to Baldwin, 8 February 1836. On Head: *DCB*, X, S.F. Wise, "Sir Francis Bond Head," 342–5. On the negotiations: MLC, Memorandum, William Lyon Mackenzie, 15 February 1836; LAC, MG11 CO42/49, F.B. Head to Lord Glenelg, 23 February 1836, 204–8; Legislative Assembly of Upper Canada *Journals* (1836), Appendix 106, Robert Baldwin to Peter Perry, 16 March 1836. One popular story had it that Head was influenced to appoint Robert Baldwin by the British consul in New York, James Buchanan, whose daughter was married to Robert's brother, William Augustus: Sir George Arthur to Lord Durham, 9 July 1838, in Public Archives of Canada, *Report* (1923), 104.

3. This analysis is informed by Sigmund Freud, *Civilization and Its Discontents*, trans. Joan Riviere, ed. James Strachey (London: Hogarth Press, 1972), 12, 62–76.

4. The executive council's representation of 4 March can be found in many places, including *Correspondent and Advocate*, York, 12 March 1836, and Colin Read and Ronald J. Stagg, eds., *The Rebellion of 1837 in Upper Canada: A Collection of Documents* (Don Mills, ON: Champlain Society in cooperation with the Ontario Heritage Foundation, 1985), 4. Head described his response in LAC, MG11 CO42/429, Head to Lord Glenelg, 21 March 1836, 295–6. *Journals* (1836), Appendix 106, Baldwin to Perry, 16 March 1836.

5. LAC, MG11 CO42/429, Head to Glenelg, 21 March 1836.

6. Arthur to Durham, 9 July 1838, in Public Archives of Canada *Report* (1923), 104. The ascribing of the key roles to Rolph and Bidwell is based on scattered evidence. The argument is made by Robert Fraser in Cross and Fraser, "Robert Baldwin," 48.

7. Gerald M. Craig, *Upper Canada: The Formative Years, 1784–1841* (Toronto: McClelland & Stewart, 1963), 236–40. LAC, MG11 CO42/430, Head to Glenelg, 27 July 1836, 424–5, with enclosure of a placard from the Constitutional Reform Society of Upper Canada, 428–9. TRL, William Warren Baldwin Papers, B105, Robert to William Warren Baldwin, 14 September 1836.

8. The British trip is described in RBP, II, Robert Baldwin, Memorandum of a visit to England, 1836. His comments on the ocean voyage: BFP, Box 5, Liverpool, Robert to Maria Baldwin, 5 June 1836 (copy).

9. RBP, Memorandum of a visit. LAC, RG 7 G1/77, Governor General's Office, Despatches from the Colonial Office, Glenelg to Head, 20 August 1836, 409.

10. John W. Cell, *British Colonial Administration in the Mid-Nineteenth Century: The Policy-Making Process* (New Haven: Yale University Press, 1970), 3–4. LAC, Governor General's Office, Despatches from the Colonial Office, Glenelg to Head, 20 August 1836, enclosure Baldwin to Glenelg, 20 June 1836, 402–8, enclosure Stephen to Baldwin, 20 June 1836, 411.

11. RBP, I, A73/57, Strachan to Campbell, 29 April 1836, A73/56, Strachan to Baldwin, 30 April 1836. Wilson, *Life of Robert Baldwin*, 56.

12. Wilson, *Life of Robert Baldwin*, 55–6. RBP, Memorandum of a visit. LAC, Governor General's Office, Despatches from the Colonial Office, Glenelg to Head, 20 August 1836, 836, enclosure Baldwin to Glenelg, 13 July 1836, 412–85.

13. LAC, CO42/431, Baldwin to Glenelg, 26 July 1836, 215. LAC, Governor General's Office, Despatches from the Colonial Office, Glenelg to Head, 20 August 1836, enclosures Baldwin to Glenelg, 12 August 1836, 501–2, Baldwin to Glenelg, 12 August 1836, 514–27. LAC, Governor General, Glenelg to Head, 25 July 1836. Baldwin, *Baldwins and the Great Experiment*, 148–9. TRL, William Warren Baldwin Papers, Robert to William Warren Baldwin, 29 August 1836.

14. BFP, Box 4, Dublin, Robert to Maria Baldwin, 30 November 1836, copy. Ibid., Box 1, Memorandum, Robert Baldwin, probably 1854.

15. Ibid., Box 5, Baldwin to Maria, 21 September 1836, copy. Ibid., Trunk 2, Box 2, Baldwin to Robert, St. Matthew's Day, 1836. RBP, I, A83/41, William Warren Baldwin to Robert Baldwin, 6 August 1836, enclosing letter from Maria.

16. Baldwin, *Baldwins and the Great Experiment*, 149–51. Wilson, *Life of Robert Baldwin*, 56–7.

17. Read and Stagg, *Rebellion of 1837*, 148–50. LAC, MG24 B24, John Rolph, deposition of William Ware, 20 December 1837, 96–8.

18. LAC, MG24 B11, William Warren and Robert Baldwin, 6, Bidwell to Baldwin, 9 December 1837. Kingston *Chronicle & Gazette*, 14 April 1838. *British Whig*, Toronto, 11 May 1838.

19. Chester New, *Lord Durham's Mission to Canada*, ed. H.W. McCready (Toronto: McClelland & Stewart, 1963), 85. Charles Buller, "Sketch of Lord Durham's Mission to Canada in 1838," in *Report of the Public Archives of Canada* (Ottawa: King's Printer, 1923), 353 f.f.

20. Public Archives of Canada *Report*, 1923 (Ottawa, 1924), William Warren Baldwin to Lord Durham, 1 August 1838, 184–6.

21. Ibid., Robert Baldwin to Lord Durham, 23 August 1838, 326–8.

22. LAC, MG11 CO42/429, Head to Glenelg, 27 April 1836, 453. Chester New is among those who credit Baldwin with giving Durham the idea: *Lord Durham's Mission*, 94–8. Janet Ajzenstat idolizes Durham and underplays the roles of others: *The Political Thought of Lord Durham* (Montreal and Kingston: McGill-Queen's University Press, 1988). Some revisionists simply discount the importance of Durham in bringing about responsible government: Ged Martin, *The Durham Report and British Policy: A Critical Essay* (Cambridge: Cambridge University Press, 1972).

23. On Hincks: William G. Ormsby, "Sir Francis Hincks," in *The Pre-Confederation Premiers: Ontario Government Leaders, 1841–1867*, ed. J.M.S. Careless (Toronto: University of Toronto Press, 1980), 148–96, and *DCB*, XI, William G. Ormsby, "Sir Francis Hincks," 406–16. RBP, I, A54/8, W.B. Jarvis to Baldwin, 15 November 1838.

24. *Examiner*, Toronto, 16, 23 October, 6 November 1839. MLC, W.T. Kennedy to Mackenzie, 22 October 1839, James Reid to Mackenzie, 22 October 1839. PL, Hincks to LaFontaine, 9 January 1840. *Journals*, 1841, report of special committee, 17 September 1841, 635–7. For a general account of the "Durham meeting" movement, see: Carol Wilton, "'A Firebrand amongst the People': The Durham Meetings and Popular Politics in Upper Canada," *Canadian Historical Review* LXXV 3 (September 1994), 346–75.

25. *DCB*, IX, Jacques Monet, "Sir Louis-Hippolyte La Fontaine (Menard dit La Fontaine)," 440–51. The comment about aristocratic style is from LAC, MG24 C3, Papiers Duvernay, 525, C. Dumesnil to Ludger Duvernay, 31 August 1841. Note that Monet believes the surname should be spelled "La Fontaine." The politician's signature, however, seems to read "LaFontaine."

26. For Neilson's dissent: Jacques Monet, "French-Canadian Nationalism and the Challenge of Ultramontanism," *Historical Papers* (1966), 41–2. William G. Ormsby, *The Emergence of the Federal Concept in Canada, 1839–1845* (Toronto: University of Toronto Press, 1969), 84.

27. Hincks's letters are in PL. On Baldwin's character: PL, 95, Hincks to LaFontaine, 22 February 1840; PL, 121, 15 December 1840; PL, 141, 29 May 1841. Charles R. Sanderson, ed., *The Arthur Papers: Being the Canadian Papers, Mainly Confidential, Private and Demi-Official of Sir George Arthur* (Toronto: Toronto Public Libraries, 1959), II, 373, copy of a letter from William Woodruff to Francis Hincks, 26 August 1839.

28. PL, 1092, Hincks to LaFontaine, 12 June 1840. Paul Knaplund, ed., *Letters from Lord Sydenham to Lord John Russell* (Clifton, NJ: A.M. Kelley, 1973), 13 February 1840, 48.

29. AO, Thomas Radenhurst Papers, Box 1, Envelope 13, Baldwin to Radenhurst, 17 February 1840. Hincks expanded on the reasons in PL, 95, Hincks to LaFontaine, 22 February 1840. On the attitudes of Reformers: PL, 120, Baldwin to Hincks (copy), 7 November 1840.

30. Neither the circular letter to Reformers nor any other document established what really happened at that meeting. The description here is a reconstruction that attempts to explain the otherwise inexplicable.

31. Knaplund, *Letters from Lord Sydenham*, Thomson to Russell, 13 February 1840, 48. The Russell dispatch has often been reprinted, including in: W.P.M. Kennedy, ed., *Statutes, Treaties and Documents of the Canadian Constitution, 1713–1929* (Oxford: Oxford University Press, 1930), 421–4.

32. For the second Russell dispatch: Kennedy, *Statutes*, 432. Most recent studies have contended that not even Durham was recommending responsible government as Baldwin understood it. For example: Buckner, *Transition to Responsible Government*, 257–9.

33. *Examiner*, 5, 12 August 1840. PL, 108, Hincks to LaFontaine, 23 August 1840. On the strains caused by Baldwin's retention of office: PL, 120, Baldwin to Hincks, 7 November 1840 (copy), Hincks to Baldwin, 25 November 1840 (copy); *Debates*, 1841, I, 99.

34. G. Poulett Scrope, ed., *Memoirs of the Life of the Right Honourable Charles Lord Sydenham, G.C.B., with a Narrative of His Administration in Canada* (London: John Murray, 1843), 185, 148. Charles C.F. Greville, *The Greville Memoirs: A Journal of the Reigns of King George IV, King William IV, and Queen Victoria*, ed. Henry Reeves (London: Longmans, Green, 1888) III, 330. Jacques Monet, "The Personal and Living Bond, 1839–1849," in *The Shield of Achilles: Aspects of Canada in the Victorian Age*, ed. W.L. Morton (Toronto: McClelland & Stewart, 1968), 67. Major Richardson, *Eight Years in Canada* (Montreal: H.H. Cunningham, 1847), 186. AO, John Rolph Papers, A7, Baldwin to Rolph, 28 March 1848.

35. Scrope, *Memoirs*, 149, citing a letter written by Sydenham on 20 November 1840. Knaplund, *Letters from Lord Sydenham*, Sydenham to Russell, 24 February 1841, 119. Sanderson, *Arthur Papers*, III, Sydenham to Arthur, 7 February 1841, 30.

Chapter 5

1. The act of Re-Union (3 & 4 Victoria, c.35) is reprinted in Kennedy, *Statutes*, 433–45.

2. AO, Macaulay Papers, J.W. Macaulay to Mrs. A. Macaulay, 7 March 1841. Knaplund, *Letters from Lord Sydenham*, 22 February 1841, 112.

3. LAC, Baldwin-Ross, William Warren to Maria Baldwin, 21 September 1841. *Chronicle & Gazette*, Kingston, 13 February 1841. Queen's University Archives, William Morris Papers, Box 1, Morris to F.A. Harper, 12 February 1841.

4. *British Colonist*, Toronto, 10 February 1841. *Chronicle & Gazette*, 13, 17 February 1841. Sanderson, *Arthur Papers*, III, Arthur to Sydenham, 10 February 1841, 311.

5. On the controversy over his retention of office: PL, 127, Hincks to LaFontaine, 16 February 1841; PL, 133, Hincks to LaFontaine, 6 April 1841; MLC, Hincks to T. Elliott,

16 April 1841; LAC, MG24 E1, Merritt Family, XV, Hincks to William Hamilton Merritt, 6 April 1841, 2230–3. On the law officers: J.E. Hodgetts, *Pioneer Public Service: An Administrative History of the United Canadas, 1841–1867* (Toronto: University of Toronto Press, 1955), 37–8; Paul Romney, *Mr. Attorney: The Attorney General for Ontario in Court, Cabinet, and Legislature, 1791–1899* (Toronto: Published for the Osgoode Society by University of Toronto Press, 1986). On patronage: LAC, RG7 G14, VII, Governor General's Office, Correspondence, Baldwin to Sydenham, 15 February 1841, 2796–9, 19 February 1841, 2812–15.

6. RBP, I, unbound correspondence with the Hon. R.B. Sullivan, Baldwin to Sydenham, 18 February 1841 (draft), Draper to Baldwin, 22 February 1841. The exchange of letters is reprinted in Sanderson, *Arthur Papers*, III, 339–40.

7. Ibid., Draper to Baldwin, 22 February 1841.

8. Ibid., Sydenham to Baldwin, 1 March 1841, Baldwin to Sydenham, 5 March 1841. Also in Sanderson, *Arthur Papers*, III, 339–40, 371–3.

9. TRL, Broadside 1840, Election City, To the Free and Independent Electors of the City of Toronto, Robert Baldwin, 25 February 1840. RBP, I, A43/7, James Durand to Baldwin, 20 February 1840. PL, 109, Hincks to LaFontaine, 28 August 1840. RBP, II, Letters to Lord Sydenham, 16 January 1841. TRL, Broadside 1841, Election Toronto, To the Electors of the City of Toronto, Robert Baldwin, 16 January 1841. AO, Toronto City Council Papers, motion of city council, 18 January 1841. Sanderson, *Arthur Papers*, III, Sydenham to Harrison, 20 January 1841, 255–6.

10. RBP, I, A37/17, E. Burnham to Baldwin, 10 February 1841. *Examiner*, Toronto, 10 February 1841. MLC, Baldwin to John McIntosh, 1 February 1841. RBP, I, A55/74, H. Lasker to Baldwin, 11 February 1841. PL, 128, Hincks to LaFontaine, 19 February 1841. RBP, I, A39/52, Thomas Coleman to Baldwin, 8 February 1841. *Examiner*, 10 March, 7 April 1841. *Chronicle & Gazette*, 2 June 1841.

11. There were probably deaths in other ridings as well but they cannot be confirmed. LAC, RG5 A1, Civil Secretary, Canada West, Miscellaneous Correspondence, Lieutenant Governor's Office, 261, Bristowe to S.B. Harrison, 9 March 1841. Sanderson, *Arthur Papers*, III, Sydenham to Arthur, 15 March 1841, 387. *Journals,* 1843, App. J.J., County of Montreal, testimony of Edward Martial Leprohon, n.d.; Terrebonne, testimony of Solomon Y. Chesley, 19 October 1843, Toronto, testimony of E.M. Leprohon, n.d. There is extensive material on election violence in: PL; LAC, RG8, British Military Records, C316, Military Aid at Riots; *British Colonist*; *Examiner*; Irving Martin Abella, "The Sydenham Election of 1841," *Canadian Historical Review* XLVII, 4 (1966), 326–43.

12. Scrope, *Memoirs*, 227. *Le Canadien*, Montreal, 2 April 1841, cited in Louis-P. Turcotte, *Le Canada sous l'union* (Quebec: L.J. Demers & Frère, 1882), première partie, 63. For details on the Terrebonne election: PL, 132, R. Adamson to LaFontaine, 31 March 1841; PL, 134, statement of William Turnbull. 3 April 1841; PL, divers 1841–3, 949, petition of the electors of the county of Terrebonne, n.d.

13. On Upper Canada: MLC, Hincks to T. Elliot, 16 April 1841; LAC, MG24 A30, Sydenham and Toronto, Isaac Buchanan to Sydenham, 8 June 1841. On Lower Canada: LAC, MG24 B68, Sir Francis Hincks, A.-N. Morin to Hincks, 8 May 1841; PL, 144, Thomas Aylwin to LaFontaine, 22 June 1841; PL, 146, Hincks to LaFontaine, 29 June 1841; PL, 159, John Neilson to LaFontaine, 27 August 1841.

14. Queen's University Archives, Cartwright Family Papers, J.S. Cartwright Correspondence, W.H. Draper to Cartwright, 22 March 1841, 12 April 1841.

15. RBP, I, A77/1, David Willson to Baldwin, 18 April 1841.

16. MLC, Mackenzie to George Lount, April 1841.

17. Sanderson, *Arthur Papers*, III, Sydenham to Arthur, 27 February 1841, 345.

18. RBP, I, A84/1, William Warren to Robert Baldwin, 13 May 1841.

19. Ibid., 8 May 1841. Wilson, *Life of Robert Baldwin*, 106. *Journals*, 1841, 186, App.L. AO, William Warren and Robert Baldwin Papers, Opinions and Decisions made by Robert Baldwin, 1840–1849, opinion of Solicitor General Day, 86. LAC, RG1 E2, Canada, Executive Council, Draft Minutes and Reports, 53, minutes of 17 May 1841. Knaplund, *Letters from Lord Sydenham*, Sydenham to Russell, 12 June 1841, 141. LAC, MG11 CO42/479, Original Correspondence, Secretary of State, Sydenham to Russell, 25 May 1841, 162–5.

20. RBP, I, A86/1, Robert to William Warren Baldwin, 13 May 1841. Wilson, *Life of Robert Baldwin*, 103.

21. There are graphic descriptions of the bad weather in: AO, Macaulay Papers, Ann Macaulay to Mrs. Macaulay, 26 March 1841, John to Ann Macaulay, 31 March and 12 April 1841, Robert Stanton to John Macaulay, 24 June 1841; *Chronicle & Gazette*, 5 May, 22 May 1841.

22. An excellent picture of Toronto at the time, by an unknown artist, is found in Henry Scadding, *Toronto of Old*, ed. F.H. Armstrong (Toronto: Oxford University Press, 1966), 158–9. On the Front Street house: *Evening Telegram*, Toronto, 1 December 1888. On the Grange: John Lownsbrough, *The Privileged Few: The Grange and Its People in Nineteenth-Century Toronto* (Toronto: Art Gallery of Ontario, 1980).

23. For maneuvering on the speakership: PL, 136, Hincks to LaFontaine, 19 April 1841; PL, 140, Hincks to LaFontaine, 26 May 1841; LAC, MG24 E1, Merritt Family, 15, Baldwin to Merritt, 4 May 1841, 2271. On the strategy meeting: PL, 140, Hincks to LaFontaine, 26 May 1841; PL, 141, Hincks to LaFontaine, 29 May 1841.

24. Knaplund, *Letters from Lord Sydenham*, Sydenham to Russell, 10 April 1841, 128. *Chronicle & Gazette*, 14 April, 15 May 1841. Sanderson, *Arthur Papers*, III, Sydenham to Arthur, 25 May 1841, 423.

25. Sydenham's arrival is described in the *Chronicle & Gazette*, 29 May 1841.

26. *Chronicle & Gazette*, 17 March 1841. Sanderson, *Arthur Papers*, III, Arthur to Sydenham, 17 March 1841, 390. Stephen Leacock, *Baldwin, LaFontaine, and Hincks: Responsible Government* (Toronto: Morang, 1910), 85. *Chronicle & Gazette*, 3 November 1841, 6 March 1841, 10 February 1841. Sanderson, *Arthur Papers*, III, Kingston Staff Memorial, T. Smith et al., 6 March 1841, 365–6. *Examiner*, 7 July 1841. AO, Macaulay Papers, Ann to John Macaulay, 12 March 1841.

27. RBP, I, unbound correspondence with the Hon. R.B. Sullivan, Baldwin to A.-N. Morin, 14 June 1841; Sydenham to Baldwin, 13 June 1841.

28. Baldwin repeated his version of their conversation in a two-part letter to Sydenham: Ibid., Baldwin to Sydenham, 11 and 12 June 1841.

29. Ibid., Sydenham to Baldwin, 13 June 1841.

30. Knaplund. *Letters from Lord Sydenham*, Sydenham to Russell, 27 June 1841, 145, 12 June 1841, 140–5. Sanderson, *Arthur Papers*, III, Sydenham to Arthur, 27 June 1841, 440–1. The summary of Sydenham's position is from MLC, John Smyles to Thomas Burrell [Mackenzie], 28 June 1841.

31. RBP, I, A84/10, William Warren to Robert Baldwin, 16 June 1841; A84/8, William Warren to Robert Baldwin, 11 June 1841; A85/52, William Warren to Robert Baldwin, 3 January 1843; A82/94, W.A. to Robert Baldwin, 7 March 1843. RBP, III, William Warren to Phoebe Baldwin, 26 August 1842.

32. RBP, III, draft of my will, Robert Baldwin, 17 March 1840.

Chapter 6

1. *Debates*, I, 1841, 1–4. Leacock, *Baldwin, LaFontaine, and Hincks*, 86–7.

2. *Debates*, I, 1841, 5–7. *British Colonist*, Toronto, 16 June 1841.

3. *Chronicle & Gazette*, 16 June 1841, 3 April 1841. AO, Macaulay Papers, John to Helen Macaulay, 15 June 1841.

4. Information on many of the members is available in the *Dictionary of Canadian Biography*. Among those whose careers are covered in volume IX are Daly, Harrison, Merritt, Ogden, Prince, Small, and Viger. Volume X includes Draper and Hopkins. Dent, *Last Forty Years*, I, profiles a number including Aylwin, Morin, and Viger. Robert Rumilly, *Papineau et son temps* (Montreal: Fides, 1977), II, discusses some parliamentarians including Neilson. There is a good description of Killaly in J.E. Hodgetts, *Pioneer Public Service: An Administrative History of the United Canadas, 1841–1867* (Toronto: University of Toronto Press, 1955), 176. Ormsby "Sir Francis Hincks," 148–96.

5. Dent, *Last Forty Years*, I, 122. *British Colonist*, 23 June, 26 June 1841. *Chronicle & Gazette*, 26 June, 19 June 1841.

6. *Journals*, 1841, 4–6, 112. *Debates*, I, 1841, 368–9. John Garner, *The Franchise and Politics in British North America, 1755–1867* (Toronto: University of Toronto Press, 1969), 204–5. LAC, Merritt, Hincks to Merritt, April 1841, 2231. *Examiner*, 7 July, 4 August, 6 September 1841. RBP, I, A68/9, John Ross to Baldwin, 27 August 1841. *Examiner*, 15 December 1841, RBP, I, A68/9, Ross to Baldwin, 27 August 1841.

7. Hincks's views were best expressed in the *Examiner*, 8 and 15 September 1841. Aylwin's comments: PL, 144, Aylwin to LaFontaine, 22 June 1841. The most recent study of responsible government also contends Sydenham "had conceded the essential principle": Buckner, *Transition to Responsible Government*, 263.

8. *Examiner*, 17 February 1841.

9. RBP, I, A84/8, William Warren to Robert Baldwin, 11 June 1841. Queen's University Archives, Cartwright Family, J.S. Cartwright Correspondence, Draper to Cartwright, 12 April 1841. For a more sympathetic treatment of Draper: George Metcalf, "William Henry Draper," in *Pre-Confederation Premiers*, 32–88.

10. *Debates*, I, 1841, 63–7. Leacock, *Baldwin, LaFontaine, and Hincks*, 91–5.

11. *Debates*, I, 1841, 881. There is a good discussion of Sydenham's modernizing and centralizing policies in Ian Radforth, "Sydenham and Utilitarian Reform," in *Colonial*

Leviathan: State Formation in Mid-Nineteenth-Century Canada, eds. Allan Greer and Ian Radforth (Toronto: University of Toronto Press, 1992), 64–102.

12. *Examiner,* 11 August 1841. *Gazette,* Montreal, 31 August 1841. *Debates,* I, 1841, 752.

13. *Debates,* I, 1841, 784.

14. PL, 249, Baldwin to LaFontaine, 14 August 1844.

15. *Debates,* I, 1841, 107, 117, 518.

16. Ibid., 682–6, 513–15.

17. LAC, Baldwin-Ross, Recollections of Mary Warren Breckenridge, written by her daughter Marie Murney from her mother's own words in 1859.

18. RBP, I, A69/24, Samson to Baldwin, 14 March 1819; A69/33, Samson to Baldwin, 20 July 1819; A69/25, Samson to Baldwin, 25 March 1819.

19. RBP, I, A69/30, Samson to Baldwin, 31 May 1819, A69/26, 11 April 1819.

20. RBP, I, A69/26, Samson to Baldwin, 11 April 1819; A69/23, 4 February 1819; A69/42, 10 May 1820. RBP, III, poems by Robert Baldwin and others.

21. RBP, I, A47/18, Givins to Baldwin, 10 November 1819.

22. LAC, Baldwin-Ross, Robert to Eliza, 2 June, 1 October 1825.

23. Ibid., 15 May 1825.

24. On Burney: Sir Paul Harvey, ed., *The Oxford Companion to English Literature* (Oxford: Oxford University Press, 1967); Albert C. Baugh, ed., *The Literary History of England* (New York: Appleton-Century-Crofts, 1967), 1032–4. Robert discussed *Camilla* in LAC, Baldwin-Ross, Robert to Eliza, 20 May 1826, and his dream in ibid., 20 May 1826.

25. LAC, Baldwin-Ross, Robert to Eliza, 15 May 1825, 12 May 1826, notation added 15 May.

26. RBP, I, A69/65, Samson to Baldwin, 14 March 1825. Private, Memorandum, Robert and Elizabeth Baldwin, n.d.

27. LAC, Baldwin-Ross, Eliza to Robert, 9 August 1827.

28. *Debates,* I, 1841, 494–9, 516–23, 532–6, 555, 619–25, 632–6. On local government: J.H. Aitchison, "The Municipal Corporation Act of 1849," *Canadian Historical Review* XXX, 2 (1949), 107–18. For contemporary assessment of the debate: *Chronicle & Gazette,* 7 August 1841; MLC, John Smyles to Thomas Burrell [Mackenzie], 14 August 1841.

29. *Debates,* I, 1841, 608, 624, 629–31. See Hincks's assessment of the issues in Sir Francis Hincks, *Reminiscences of His Public Life* (Montreal: William Drysdale & Co., 1884), 63–7, and the *Examiner,* 11 August 1841. The third reading of the bill is described in the *Examiner,* 1 September 1841.

30. LAC, CO42/479, Sydenham to Russell, confidential, 26 June 1841, 389; PL, 159, Neilson to LaFontaine, 27 August 1841.

31. *Chronicle & Gazette,* 3 July, 24 July, 4 August, 7 August 1841.

32. The importance of the legend is stressed by J.M.S. Careless, "Robert Baldwin," in *Pre-Confederation Premiers,* 120. Careless and George Metcalf ("William Henry Draper," ibid., 42–3) accept the traditional version of events. Other historians who essentially

accepted the Reform propaganda include: Leacock, *Baldwin, LaFontaine, and Hincks*, 109; Wilson, *Life of Robert Baldwin*, 138–9.

33. Harrison commented on the abortive agreement in *Debates*, I, 1841, 790.

34. The two sets of resolutions are found in: *Debates*, I, 1841, 790–2; *Journals*, 1841, 480–1; Leacock, *Baldwin, LaFontaine, and Hincks*, 109–10.

35. *Chronicle & Gazette*, 8 September 1841.

36. Legion [Robert Baldwin Sullivan], *Letters on Responsible Government* (Toronto: printed at the *Examiner* office, 1844), 21, 216.

37. Scrope, *Memoirs*, 260–5. *Chronicle & Gazette*, 8 September, 2 October, 6 October 1841.

38. For a description of the funeral: *Chronicle & Gazette*, 25 September 1841. The rationalization of Baldwin's position: *Examiner*, 15 September 1841.

39. *British Colonist*, 22 September 1841. Knaplund, *Letters from Lord Sydenham*, 27 June 1841, 145.

Chapter 7

1. PL, 147, Baldwin to LaFontaine, 15 August 1841, with enclosures of Robert to William Warren Baldwin, 12 August, 13 August.

2. RBP, I, A55/13, LaFontaine to Baldwin, 31 August 1841. Maria is quoted in Saul, *Louis-Hippolyte LaFontaine and Robert Baldwin*, 124. TRL, Broadside 1841, Election LaFontaine, notice of meetings. *Chronicle & Gazette*, Kingston, 25 August 1841. TRL, Broadside 1841, Election Freehold, A Freeholder, "To the Freeholders of the Fourth Riding of York". RBP, I, A77/3, Willson to Baldwin, 15 October 1841.

3. RBP, I, A77/3, Willson to Baldwin, 15 October 1841. C. Blackett Robinson, *History of Toronto and the County of York, Ontario* (Toronto: C. Blackett Robinson, 1885), I, 174–7. On Willson: *DCB*, IX, James Reaney, "David Willson," 841–3.

4. TRL, Toronto Papers, 1336, Resolutions to be proposed at a Meeting of the Committee of Vigilance, appointed for the Fourth Riding of the County of York, 4 August 1841, 36–7.

5. RBP, I, A77/7, Willson to Baldwin, 7 March 1844; A77/10, Willson to Baldwin, 5 October 1844; A77/6, Willson to Baldwin, 15 December 1843; A77/14, Willson to Baldwin, 4 February 1848.

6. RBP, I, A55/15, LaFontaine to Baldwin, 28 November 1841. LAC, Baldwin-Ross, Augusta Elizabeth Ross Correspondence, Baldwin to Eliza, 3 June 1843. RBP, I, A51/42, Hincks to Baldwin, 1 June 1844. Baldwin, *Baldwins and the Great Experiment*, 199–200.

7. PL, 390, Baldwin to LaFontaine, 19 July 1845. RBP, I, A51/42, Hincks to Baldwin, 1 June 1844; RBP, I, A50/79, Lawrence Heyden to Baldwin, 17 June 1846. LAC, MG24 B1, Neilson Collection, I, Baldwin to Neilson, 5 August 1843, 40–1.

8. PL, 349, Baldwin to LaFontaine, 14 August 1844. RBP, I, A55/38, LaFontaine to Baldwin, 2 December 1845. Baldwin's first statement on French-English equality was in a letter to LaFontaine on 26 November 1840: PL, 119. Baldwin's nationalism is discussed in later chapters.

9. RBP, II, Robert to Willcocks Baldwin, 17 April, 15 May 1843.

10. BFP, Box 1, Baldwin to Bob, 15 May, 13 February, 1 February 1845, 20 May 1846. BFP, Box 1, Maria to Master Robert Baldwin, n.d., 1845 or 1846.

11. Ibid., Mary J. Jones, "Memories of My Youth," 17 October 1925.

12. RBP, III, Robert to Willcocks Baldwin, 17 September 1842. LAC, Baldwin-Ross, Robert to Maria Baldwin, 27 February 1848. TRL, Robert Baldwin, Twenty Letters to John Ross, Robert Baldwin to Eliza Ross, 17 April 1854, 13. Sanderson, *Arthur Papers,* III, Sydenham to Arthur, 15 March 1841, 387. Peter Gay discusses the metaphor of the family in *The Bourgeois Experience: Victoria to Freud,* I, *Education of the Senses* (New York: Oxford University Press, 1984), 15.

13. RBP, II, Robert to Willcocks Baldwin, 17 September 1842. AO, York County, Surrogate Court, Probate and Administration, II, will of Robert Baldwin, 17 March 1840.

14. On the ideology of property: Stone and Stone, *An Open Elite?* 413–16. Macaulay's fears: AO, Macaulay Papers, Macaulay to John Kirby, 7 August 1841. Baldwin's initiative in the House: *Debates,* I, 1841, 608.

15. Romney, *Mr. Attorney,* 179–86. RBP, I, A77/20, Adam Wilson to Baldwin, 20 April 1841.

16. RBP, I, A32/2, Scott to Baldwin, 14 January 1848.

17. His cases are summarized in Thomas Taylor, *Reports of Cases Argued and Determined in the Court of King's Bench in York, Upper Canada, Commencing in Trinity Term, in the Fourth Year of the Reign of George IV, and Ending in the Trinity Term, in the Eighth Year of George IV* (York: printed by J. Carey, n.d.), and William Henry Draper, *Report of Cases Decided in the Court of King's Bench of Upper Canada,* 2nd ed. (Toronto: H. Rowsell, 1861). The case against the Montreal firm of Forsyth and Richardson is found in Draper, *Report of Cases,* 291–4, 317, and the Canada Company case in ibid., 189–90, 413.

18. Ibid., 664–8.

19. LAC, RG5 C1, Provincial Secretary, Canada West, 141/9655, Baldwin to Daly, 12 February 1845.

20. There is no simple or comprehensive record of their properties. Information has been gathered from: TRL, Baldwin Family Land Record, 1838–1855; AO, Court of Probate, Estate Files, Toronto, 1793–1859, will of William Warren Baldwin, 25 August 1842, deposition of Robert Baldwin, sworn 29 January 1844; AO, York County, Surrogate Court, Probate and Administration Books, IX, 1844–1859, deed of partition, 28 July 1848, 32251W; AO, Abstract Index to Deeds.

21. The estimates can only be rough ones. Sources include: TRL, Baldwin Family Land Record; AO, York County, Surrogate Court, Probate and Administration Books, II, will of Robert Baldwin, 9 December 1858; AO, Toronto Assessment Records; AO, York Township, Abstract Index to Deeds, 1796-1898; AO, City of Toronto, Abstract Index to Plans; TRL, Robert Baldwin Junior Papers, II, Property, Mortgages, et., Robert Baldwin 1859 & prior to 1859. Land sales outside Toronto have been assumed at an average of £1 per acre and interest at 6 percent. On land sales and interest rates: David P. Gagan, "The Security of Land: Mortgaging in Toronto·Gore Township, 1835–95," in *Aspects of Nineteenth-Century Ontario: Essays Presented to James J. Talman,* ed. F.H. Armstrong (Toronto: University of Toronto Press in association with the University of Western Ontario, 1974), and David Paul Gagan, *Hopeful Travellers: Families, Land, and Social Change in Peel*

County, Canada West (Toronto: University of Toronto Press, 1981). The comparisons are from: Brian Young, *George-Etienne Cartier: Montreal Bourgeois* (Montreal and Kingston: McGill-Queen's University Press, 1981), 18, and Mary Larratt Smith, *Young Mr. Smith in Upper Canada* (Toronto: University of Toronto Press, 1980), 169.

22. RBP, IV/3, Plan of the subdivision of southerly part of lot no.23 concession 2 from Bay in the Township of York. Thompson, *Spadina*, 98, 111. There is an account of his holdings at death in BFP, Box 1, Schedule of Property of the Late Honorable Robert Baldwin.

23. AO, York County, Surrogate Court, Probate and Administration Books, II, will of Robert Baldwin, 17 March 1840. AO, William Warren and Robert Baldwin Papers, Baldwin to Quetton St. George, 14 November 1845. RBP, I, A50/91, Heyden to Baldwin, 14 August 1848; A50/92, 7 September 1848; A50/95, 11 December 1848; A50/93, 22 September 1848; A35/29, H.J. Boulton to Baldwin, 15 October 1849.

24. AO, J.M. Snyder Papers, Baldwin to W. Lawson, 26 February 1846. RBP, III, Baldwin to Heyden, 21 April 1847 (misspelling in the original).

25. RBP, I, A35/92, Brennon to Baldwin, 26 December 1849; A67/72, Louisa Rolph to Baldwin, 3 July 1845; A67/73, Rolph to Baldwin, 28 May 1846, Baldwin to Rolph, 28 May 1846. A similar case is that of George Ward, found in RBP, I, A75/75, A75/76, A75/77.

26. AO, John Rolph Papers, A-7, Baldwin to Rolph, 19 January 1847.

27. TRL, William Warren Baldwin Papers, B105, Robert to William Warren Baldwin, 27 November 1836. RBP, II, 2.

28. BFP, Box 1, Baldwin to Bob, 17 April 1846.

29. RBP, I, A51/9, Hincks to Baldwin, 5 December 1840, Baldwin to Hincks, draft.

30. Francis Lewis, ed., *Toronto Directory and Street Guide for 1843* (Toronto: H. & W. Rowsell, 1843), 112–3. George Brown, ed., *Brown's Toronto City and Home District Directory, 1846–7* (Toronto: G. Brown, 1846), 33. RBP, II, 2.

31. *Debates*, 1843, 101. Sir Arthur Doughty, ed., *The Elgin-Grey Papers* (Ottawa: J.O. Patenaude, 1937), IV, excerpts from the *Church*, Toronto, 16, 23 April 1847, 1309–11. Smith, *Young Mr. Smith*, 109. AO, Thorburn Papers, circular from the Irish Relief Committee Room, Toronto, signed by Robert Baldwin and John Duggan, 27 February 1847. Nicholas Flood Davin, *The Irishman in Canada* (Toronto: Maclear and Co., 1877), 541–2. AO, Toronto City Council Papers, Baldwin and John Duggan to the Corporation, 1 March 1847.

32. J.G. Hodgins, ed., *Documentary History of Education in Upper Canada, 1792–1876* (Toronto: L.K. Cameron, 1893), V, 271. Thompson, *Spadina*, 96. He also filled some purely honorific posts such as that of honorary vice-president of the African Institution, a British-based association for the suppression of the slave trade: LAC, Baldwin-Ross, William Warren to Maria Baldwin, 23 May 1843; David Brion Davis, *The Problem of Slavery in the Age of Revolution, 1770–1823* (Ithaca, NY: Cornell University Press, 1975), 32, 247.

33. Thompson, *Spadina*, 85. AO, Toronto Assessment Rolls, 1845. *Evening Telegram*, Toronto, 1 December 1888. BFP, Box 6, William Warren to Maria Baldwin, 29 September 1840, copy.

34. AO, Court of Probate, Estate Files, Toronto, 1793–1859, will of William Warren Baldwin, 25 August 1842. Thompson, *Spadina*, 80. Scadding, *Toronto of Old*, 34.

35. LAC, Baldwin-Ross, Robert Baldwin to Eliza Sullivan, 1 February 1826.

36. Hodgins, *Documentary History,* VII, 230. RBP, I, A51/25, Hincks to Baldwin, 15 June 1843. William Cobbett, *The Political Register,* 14 April 1821, cited in Asa Briggs, "The Language of 'Class' in Early Nineteenth-Century England," in *Essays in Labour History in Memory of G.D.H. Cole,* ed. Briggs and John Saville (London: Macmillan, 1960), I, 45. Some revisionist historians have challenged this concept of differing values: Alan Macfarlane, *The Origins of British Individualism: The Family, Property and Social Transition* (Oxford: Blackwell, 1978). On the ball: BFP, Box 4, Baldwin to John Ross, 27 February 1851, copy.

37. LAC, Baldwin-Ross, Robert to Eliza, 22 October 1825.

38. PL, 157, Baldwin to LaFontaine, 28 June 1842. RBP, II, Robert to Willcocks Baldwin, 17 September 1842 (emphasis in the original).

39. Paul Knaplund, "Some Letters of Peel and Stanley on Canadian Problems," *Canadian Historical Review* XII, 1 (1931), Peel to Stanley, 5 October 1841, 47.

40. Ibid., Peel to Charles Buller, 10 September 1841, 46. LAC, CO42/481, Stanley to Bagot, 8 October 1841, 545–7.

41. *Chronicle & Gazette,* Kingston, 13 October 1841. *Examiner,* Toronto, 13 October 1841. LAC, CO42/489, Bagot to Stanley, 23 February 1842, 384–92. Queen's University Archives, Cartwright Family, J.S. Cartwright Correspondence, MacNab to Cartwright, 17 December 1841. PL, 157, Baldwin to LaFontaine, 28 June 1842.

42. *British Colonist,* 13, 20, 27 April 1842. Smith, *Young Mr. Smith,* 76–7.

Chapter 8

1. TRL, John Hillyard Cameron Papers, Cameron to Elizabeth Boulton, 22 September 1842.

2. *British Colonist,* 1, 15 December 1841, 5 January 1842. *Quebec Gazette,* 12, 14, 15 January 1842. LAC, CO42/489, Bagot to Grenville, 27 March 1842, 385, 391. LAC, MG24 A32, Thomas Grenville, 1842, Bagot to Grenville, 27 March 1842. LAC, CO42/489, Bagot to Stanley, 23 February 1842, 388. Rumilly, *Papineau et son temps,* II, 243–4. LAC, CO42/490, Bagot to Stanley, 16 March 1842, 230–48, 26 March 1842, 378–82, 27 May 1842, 251–61.

3. PL, 157, Baldwin to LaFontaine, 28 June 1842.

4. LAC, MG24 A13, Sir Charles Bagot, 2, John S. Cartwright to Bagot, 16 May 1842, 312; 12, Stanley to Bagot, 17 May 1842, 50–1; 7, Bagot to Stanley, 28 April 1842, 146; 12, Stanley to Bagot, 17 May 1842, 62; 7, Bagot to Stanley, 8 February 1842, 59–60; 3, Draper to Bagot, 16 June 1842, 374–6.

5. LAC, Bagot, 3, Harrison to Bagot, 11 July 1842, 412–27; Draper to Bagot, 16 July 1842, 447.

6. LAC, Bagot, 8, Bagot to Stanley, 28 August 1842, 150; Stanley to Bagot, 1 September 1842, 153.

7. LAC, RG1, Executive Council, Canada, Executive Council Minute Books, State Book A, 16 September 1842, 447.

8. LAC, CO537/140, Bagot to Stanley, 13 September 1842, 17, 18, Memorandum, Secretary's Office–East, 12 September 1842, 108–10, Memorandum of explanation, 111–18. AO, John George Hodgins Papers, Draper to Dr. Ryerson, 16 September 1842.

9. Bagot's letter to LaFontaine is found in several places, including: LAC, Bagot, 3, 13 September 1842, 587–92; PL, 167; *Gazette*, Montreal, 19 September 1842. Bagot's description of the negotiations: LAC, CO537/140, Bagot to Stanley, 26 September 1842, 98–9.

10. *Debates*, 1842, 29–30, 32. For examples of conflicting views among Reformers: PL, 168, Thomas Falconer to LaFontaine, 14 September 1842; RBP, I, A43/67, Hugh Eccles to Baldwin, 17 September 1842.

11. *Debates*, 1842, 32, 33.

12. Ibid., 33–8.

13. LAC, Bagot, 3, LaFontaine to Bagot, 16 September 1842, 593–4 (also PL, 173); Bagot to LaFontaine, 16 September 1842, 595–6.

14. LAC, Bagot, 8, Bagot to Ogden, 19 September 1842, 125–30; Bagot to Sherwood, 16 September 1842, 107.

15. Wakefield to Girouard, 20 August 1842, cited in Elizabeth Nish, "LaFontaine and the Double Majority," *Revue du Centre d'Etude du Québec*, I (1967), 9. On Wakefield: Paul Bloomfield, *Edward Gibbon Wakefield: Builder of the British Commonwealth* (London: Longmans, 1961); *DCB*, IX, H.J.M. Johnston, "Edward Gibbon Wakefield," 817–9. On Girouard: *DCB*, VIII, Beatrice Chass, "Jean-Joseph Girouard," 330–4.

16. Archives nationales du Québec, Jean-Jacques Girouard, 1, Wakefield to Girouard, 17 September 1842; Berthelot to Girouard, 29 September 1842; 2, pétition . . . Girouard, September 1842. TRL, John Hillyard Cameron Papers, Cameron to Elizabeth Boulton, 22 September 1842. LAC, Bagot, 12, Stanley to Bagot, 3 November 1842, 189.

17. LAC, Executive Council, State Book A, 463.

18. RBP, I, A36/110, Buell to Baldwin, 16 September 1842; RBP, I, A64/41, Price to Baldwin, 28 November 1842. See also RBP, I, A66/5, George Ridout to Baldwin, 17 September 1842.

19. Dent, *Last Forty Years*, I, 244. RBP, I, A85/52, William Warren to Robert Baldwin, 3 January 1843.

20. Greville, *Greville Memoirs*, V, 119. Leacock, *Baldwin, LaFontaine, and Hincks*, 151. LAC, Bagot, 12, Stanley to Bagot, 3, November 1842, 191. LAC, CO537/140, Stanley to Bagot, November 1842, 85.

21. Leacock, *Baldwin, LaFontaine, and Hincks*, 131.

22. *Examiner*, 28 September 1842. *Debates*, 1842, 99–103.

23. John Garner, *The Franchise and Politics in British North America, 1755–1867* (Toronto: University of Toronto Press, 1969), 100–6, 232.

24. PL, 200, Baldwin to LaFontaine, 6 October 1842, 7 October 1842. Charges and countercharges are found in: *Chronicle & Gazette*, 24 December 1842; TRL, Broadside 1842, Hastings Election, Cato, "A Few Facts for the Electors of Hastings to Ponder Over"; AO, James and Ogle Gowan Papers, Thomas Lloyd to James Gowan, 26 September 1842, postscript 5 October 1842; RBP, I, A68/30, John Ross to Baldwin, 23 October 1842.

25. RBP, I, A68/30, John Ross to Baldwin, 23 October 1842. TRL, Broadside 1842, Election Meeting, C.J. Baldwin to his constituents in Second York, 5 November 1842. RBP, I, A38/86, John Carey to Baldwin, 22 November 1842; A38/87, Carey to Baldwin, 5 December 1842; A34/20, James Durand to Baldwin, 25 December 1842.

26. RBP, I, A34/48, Borne to Baldwin, 20 January 1843. J.M.S. Careless, *The Union of the Canadas: The Growth of Canadian Institutions, 1841–1867* (Toronto: McClelland & Stewart, 1967), 75.

27. LAC, Baldwin-Ross, Robert to Eliza, 24 June, 14 October 1825. RBP, I, A86/85, Robert to William Warren Baldwin, 16 May 1843, repetition of "others" in the original.

28. LAC, Baldwin-Ross, Robert to Eliza, 2 June 1825, 1 March 1826.

29. RBP, II, Memorandum, Robert Baldwin, n.d.

30. LAC, RG7 G20, Governor General, Civil Secretary's Correspondence, 18, Baldwin to R.W. Rawson, 3 November 1842, 1886, 7 November 1842, 2192. AO, Attorney General, A-1, 4, Letterbook, 1843–1851, Baldwin to Etienne Parent, 24 November 1843, 30–4. AO, A.N. Buell Papers, Baldwin to Buell, 21 April 1843.

31. RBP, I, A51/21, Hincks to Baldwin, 12 January 1843.

32. LAC, Bagot, 8, Bagot to Stanley, 28 October 1842, 167–8.

33. RBP, I, A55/20, LaFontaine to Baldwin, 26 November 1842.

34. TRL, Samuel Peters Jarvis Papers, Mary Boyles Jarvis to S.P. Jarvis, 28 November 1842. LAC, Bagot, 8, Bagot to Aylwin, 29 March 1843. *Examiner*, 24 May 1843. TRL, William Warren Baldwin Papers, Robert to William Warren Baldwin, 19 May 1843.

Chapter 9

1. The words are from a summary of Metcalfe's views by his faithful biographer, John William Kaye: *The Life and Correspondence of Charles, Lord Metcalfe* (London: Richard Bentley, 1858), II, 343.

2. On Metcalfe's arrival: *British Colonist*, 5 April 1843. LAC, MG24 A15, Derby Papers, IV, Cabinet Memoranda, 1843, Prince Albert to Stanley, 22 May 1843. See also Albert's letters of 31 May and 2 June 1843. Kaye, *Metcalfe*, II, 315–17, 336–8.

3. Private, Ross-Baldwin Family Papers, Robert to Eliza Baldwin, 17 April, 3 June 1843.

4. PL, 798, Aylwin to LaFontaine, 17 April 1843. Kaye, *Metcalfe*, II, 359–60. Hodgetts, *Pioneer Public Service*, 76. LAC, RG1 E1, Canada, Executive Council Minute Books, State Book C.

5. RBP, I, A51/25, Hincks to Baldwin, 16 June 1843.

6. AO, Justice Department, Attorney General, Series A-14, Letterbook 1843–51, Baldwin to unknown, 2 February 1843, 24–4. RBP, I, A71/33, Small to Baldwin, 14 June 1843; RBP, I, A64/63, Price to Baldwin, 6 February 1843.

7. RBP, I, A36/82, Buell to Baldwin, 4 August 1843. AO, Justice Department, 796, Attorney General, Fiats, Petitions and General Correspondence, 1843, William McVity to Baldwin, 6 April 1843. LAC, MG27 I E17, Sir James Robert Gowan, petition of the loyal inhabitants of Adjala and vicinity to Hon. Robert Baldwin, n.d. RBP, I, A83/42, William Warren to Robert Baldwin, 2 February 1843.

8. Hincks, *Reminiscences of His Public Life*, 107–8. RBP, I, A35/9, H.J. Boulton to Baldwin, 5 May 1843.

9. Egerton Ryerson, *The Story of My Life*, ed. J. George Hodgins (Toronto: William Briggs, 1883), Baldwin to Ryerson, 25 May 1843, 308–9, Baldwin to Bidwell, 2 June 1843, 308. LAC, CO537/141, Stanley to Metcalfe, 29 May 1843, 5–19. PL, Divers, 1843–4, 1006, Notes "Relatives de mes entrevues avec Chs. Metcalfe au sujet du nolle prosequi log, sur l'Indictment contre M. Papineau," L.-H. LaFontaine, July 1843. Dent, *Last Forty Years*, I, 299.

10. Dent, *Last Forty Years*, I, 296–8. PL. 282, Ogle Gowan to [William Harris], 11 July 1843 (copy); PL, 339, Baldwin to LaFontaine, 22 May 1844.

11. *Examiner*, 25 October 1843. Hodgins, *Documentary History*, IV, 233–62. Hincks, *Reminiscences of His Public Life*, 177, 241–2.

12. Explanations of the bill were offered by Hincks in AO, David Thorburn Papers, Hincks to Thorburn, 6 November 1843, and *Debates*, 1843, 836. For opposition: *British Colonist*, Toronto, 9 November 1843; RBP, I, A33/17, Charles Baker to Baldwin, 8 November 1843; *Debates*, 1843, 838.

13. *Debates*, 1843, 415–17.

14. *British Colonist*, 13 October 1843. RBP, I, A36/89, Andrew Buell to Baldwin, 14 November 1843. *Debates*, 1843, 556–61, 658.

15. *Journals*, 1841, 97, 260. LAC, MG27 I, E17, Sir James Robert Gowan, A1, General Correspondence, Baldwin, Baldwin to Gowan, 3 April, 13 July 1843. *Chronicle & Gazette*, Kingston, 15 July 1843. W. Allan Fisher, ed., "The Tale of a Trunk," *Ontario History*, LXX, 2 (1978), 137–43. LAC, British Military Records, C316, R. Armstrong, report, 13 July, 239.

16. *Debates*, 1843, 210, 453, 749–50. LAC, RG7 G18, Governor General, Miscellaneous Records, 82, Lord Metcalfe's Reports on the Acts of 1843.

17. Hincks, *Reminiscences of His Public Life*, 122.

18. The vote on third reading was 55 to 13: *Debates*, 1843, 497–511, 546–8, 662–3. There is a good account in Wilson, *Life of Robert Baldwin*, 179–81.

19. Wilson, *Life of Robert Baldwin*, 181. *Journals*, 1844–5, 1 December 1844, dispatch from Lord Stanley dated 27 March 1844.

20. Cecil J. Houston and William J. Smyth, *The Sash Canada Wore: A Historical Geography of the Orange Order in Canada* (Toronto: University of Toronto Press, 1980), 28. RBP, I, A32/5, "Justice," Cavan Township, to Baldwin, 25 November 1843. Peter Neary, ed., "'Neither Radical Nor Tory Nor Whig': Letters by Oliver Mowat to John Mowat, 1843–1846," *Ontario History* LXXI, 2 (1979), Oliver to John Mowat, 7 November 1843, 99. RBP, I, A33/17, Charles Baker to Baldwin, 8 November 1843.

21. RBP, I, A80/42, Eliza to Robert Baldwin, 9 November 1843. PL, 341, Baldwin to LaFontaine, 15 June 1844.

22. RBP, II, Prayers, 19, 21.

23. TRL, William Warren Baldwin Papers, B105, Robert to William Warren Baldwin, 27 November 1836.

24. Hincks, *Reminiscences of His Public Life*, 177, 241–2. Hodgins, *Documentary History*, IV, 251–62.

25. John Moir, "Methodism and Higher Education, 1843–1849: A Qualification," *Ontario History* XLIV, 3 (1952), 102. LAC, Bagot, 7, Bagot to Stanley, 8 February 1842, Bagot to the Bishop of Oxford, 10 May 1842.

26. LAC, RG7 G14, King's College, 58, part 1, Memorandum relative to the University of Toronto, Robert Baldwin, 5 May 1843.

27. Hodgins, *Documentary History*, V, 2–13. John S. Moir, *Church and State in Canada West: Three Studies of Denominationalism and Nationalism, 1841–1867* (Toronto: University of Toronto Press, 1959), 87. Hodgins, *Documentary History*, V, 18. William John Alexander, ed., *The University of Toronto and Its Colleges, 1827–1906* (Toronto: The University Library, 1906), 26.

28. Hodgins, *Documentary History*, V, 2–13. Moir, *Church and State in Canada West*, 87. Hodgins, *Documentary History*, V, 18. Alexander, *University of Toronto and Its Colleges*, 26. TRL, Robert Baldwin, University Bill (U.C.), 1843. Hodgins, *Documentary History*, V, 61–87.

29. *Debates*, 1843, 979–85. Hodgins, *Documentary History*, V, 27. RBP, I, Your fellow churchman to Baldwin, 23 November 1843.

30. *Debates*, 1843, 89, 97–8.

31. *Debates*, 1843, 742–3, 1162.

32. PL, Divers, 1843–4, 1015, C, Metcalfe to Lord Stanley, 10 October 1843.

33. Paul G. Cornell, "The Genesis of Ontario Politics in the Province of Canada (1838–1971)," in *Profiles of a Province: Studies in the History of Ontario,* ed. Edith G. Firth (Toronto: Ontario Historical Society, 1967), 62.

34. RBP, I, A38/89, Carey to Price, 3 January 1843.

35. LAC, Derby, Metcalfe Transcripts, Stanley to Metcalfe, 1 November 1843.

36. Hincks, *Reminiscences of His Public Life*, 123–4. Dent, *Last Forty Years*, I, 319.

37. LAC, Civil Secretary, 25, 2972, LaFontaine to Metcalfe, 29 November 1843. Thomas Chapais, *Cours d'histoire du Canada* (Montreal: J.-P. Garneau, 1932:1972), V, 165. Ryerson, *Story of My Life*, 314.

38. LAC, Civil Secretary, 25, 2972, LaFontaine to Mr. Baldwin, 29 November 1843.

39. There is a colourful account of the events in Dent, *Last Forty Years*, I, 320–4. *Debates*, 1843, 1034–7.

40. *Debates*, 1843, 1037.

41. Ibid., 1043.

42. Ibid.

43. Ibid., 1077.

44. The best version of Wakefield's speech is in Dent, *Last Forty Years*, I, 348–9.

45. LAC, MG24 Bagot 158, Joseph-Amable Berthelot, LaFontaine to Berthelot, 63–4. LAC, RG7 G14, Governor General, Governor General's Correspondence, 15, W.C. Hanson to Capt. Higginson, 20 September 1844, 8071.

Chapter 10

1. RBP, III, anonymous to Baldwin, 23 April 1844.

2. PL, 289, Baldwin to LaFontaine, 20 January 1844. *Examiner*, Toronto, 10 January 1844. RBP, I, A81/21, Maria to Robert Baldwin, 18 January 1844. R.-É. Caron delivered the news of William Warren Baldwin's death to Maria.

3. RBP, I, A84/23, William Warren to Robert Baldwin, 25 and 26 June 1841.

4. Baldwin, *Baldwins and the Great Experiment*, 123.

5. PL, 289, Baldwin to LaFontaine, 20 January 1844.

6. *Examiner*, 3 January 1844. Eric Jackson, "The Organization of Upper Canadian Reformers, 1818–1867," *Ontario History*, LIII, 2 (1961), 107–8. TRL, Toronto Papers, Bagot 35/11–4, meeting of the Friends of Responsible Government, 6 February 1844. AO, Thorburn Papers, Constitution of the Reform Association of Canada, 6 February 1844; ibid., circular letter, Joseph Curran and Skeffington Connor, corresponding secretaries, 26 February 1844. PL, 329, Baldwin to LaFontaine, 24 February 1844.

7. *Pilot*, Montreal, 5 April 1844. *Examiner*, Toronto, 3 April 1844. Careless, *Brown of the Globe*, I, *The Voice of Upper Canada* (Toronto: Macmillan, 1959), 50. *Globe*, Toronto, 21 May 1844. Jackson, "Organization of Upper Canadian Reformers," 108.

8. LAC, MG24 A15, Derby, Metcalfe Transcripts, Metcalfe to Stanley, 26 November 1843. PL, 3, D.-B. Papineau to L.-J. Papineau, 16 October 1843, 3875.

9. *Examiner*, 31 January 1844.

10. *Examiner*, 3 January 1844. The comment was from Baldwin's speech to a Reform dinner on 28 December 1843. RBP, I, A53/117, Peter Brown to Baldwin, 28 July 1845. Careless, *Brown of the Globe*, I, 41. PL, 320, Baldwin to LaFontaine, 20 January 1844.

11. Edward Gibbon Wakefield, *A View of Sir Charles Metcalfe's Government in Canada* (London: Smith, Edler & Co., 1844). Hincks's letter was reprinted in the *Examiner*, 14 February 1844. LAC, MG24 B6, Papiers Denis-Benjamin Viger, 5, J. Wickstead to Viger, 10 February 1844, 2537–40, D. Daly to Viger, 10 February 1844, 2541–4, Christopher Dunkin to Viger, 10 February 1844, 2545–8. A Reformer of 1836, *The Ministerial Crisis: Mr. D.B. Viger, and His Position* (Kingston: s.n., 1844). Legion, *Letters on Responsible Government*, 216.

12. PL, 322, Hincks to LaFontaine, 24 January 1844. LAC, MG24 B2, Papiers Papineau, 3, E.B. O'Callaghan to Papineau, 17 July 1844, 3994. RBP, I, A43/24, James Durand to Baldwin, 29 July 1844. *Pilot*, 10 July 1844. *Examiner*, 25 September 1844.

13. Jacques Monet, *The Last Cannon Shot: A Study of French-Canadian Nationalism, 1837–1850* (Toronto: University of Toronto Press, 1969), 174–5. *La Minerve*, 28 March 1844, cited in ibid., 175.

14. The documentation on the riots is very extensive. See, for example: depositions from citizens and soldiers in LAC, RG8 C316, British Military Records, Military Aid at Riots; LAC, RG7 G14, Governor General's Correspondence, 15, Capt. Brook Taylor to Capt. Higginson, 20 April 1844, 7659–62, J. Baily Turner to Higginson, 20 April 1844, 7655–8; Elinor Senior, "The British Garrison in Montreal in the 1840s," *Journal of the Society of Army Historical Research* 52, 201 (1974), 113–15; Monet, *Last Cannon Shot*, 177.

15. RBP, I, A55/27, LaFontaine to Baldwin, 19 April 1844; A51/39, Hincks to Baldwin, 17 April 1844; A68/53, Ross to Baldwin, 8 May 1844; A41/83, Derbishire to Baldwin, 18 April 1844; A45/40, Hincks to Baldwin, 8 May 1844.

16. PL, 339, Baldwin to LaFontaine, 22 May 1844.

17. Buchanan announced his support of Metcalfe and attacked the Reformers in a series of letters published in the Toronto *British Colonist*, beginning on 5 January 1844. On Merritt's defection: LAC, MG24 E1, Merritt Family, Merritt to Baldwin, 7 November 1843, 2601–2, 28 November 1843, 2728–31, 18 December 1843, 2747–8; ibid., 18, Draper to Merritt, 5 January 1844, 2759–62; Ryerson, *The Story of My Life*, 314–15.

18. On Ryerson: C.B. Sissons, *Egerton Ryerson: His Life and Letters* (Toronto: Clarke, Irwin, 1937); Neil McDonald and Alf Chaiton, eds., *Egerton Ryerson and His Times* (Toronto: Macmillan, 1978).

19. Egerton Ryerson, *Sir Charles Metcalfe Defended Against the Attacks of His Late Counsellors* (Toronto: s.n., 1844), 5, 11.

20. Metcalfe quoted in Chester Martin, *Foundations of Canadian Nationhood* (Toronto: University of Toronto Press, 1955), 183. *Pilot*, Montreal, 2 September 1844.

21. *Pilot*, 9 September 1844. LAC, RG5 C1, Provincial Secretary, Canada West, 136, 8429, Baldwin and Small to Dominick Daly, 10 September 1844. PL, 354–A, Baldwin to LaFontaine, 10 September 1844. T.C. Aylwin argued cogently against the action: PL, 352, Aylwin to LaFontaine, 9 September 1844.

22. RBP, III, Baldwin to Mrs. Sullivan, 31 May 1845.

23. LAC, MG24 B1, John Neilson, ii, Baldwin to Neilson, 23 January 1844, 152. On constancy and pleasure: Sigmund Freud, "Beyond the Pleasure Principle (1920)," in *The Standard Edition of the Complete Psychological Works of Sigmund Freud*, ed. James Strachey et al. (London: Hogarth Press, 1955), XVIII, 7–10.

24. RBP, I, A49/1, Isaac Campbell to Baldwin, 9 July 1844, A49/15, R.S. Hall to Baldwin, 1 October 1844. *Globe*, 10 September 1844. RBP, I, A52/28, Hopkins to Baldwin, 6 October 1844. *Globe*, 15 October 1844.

25. RBP, I, A35/103, Brown to Baldwin, 13 October 1844; A35/104, Baldwin to Hopkins, 18 October 1844 (draft).

26. R.S. Hall was one Reformer who warned how damaging the affair was for the party: RBP, I, A49/15, Hall to Baldwin, 1 October 1844.

27. RBP, I, A51/57, Hincks to Baldwin, 14 July 1844. Dent, *Last Forty Years*, I, 361.

28. *Pilot*, 14 June 1844. PL, 341, Baldwin to LaFontaine, 15 June 1844.

29. LAC, British Military Records, C316, James West to Lt. Col. Plumer Young, 25 October 1844. *Examiner*, 23 October 1844.

30. LAC, Governor General's Correspondence, 15, W.H. Yello to Capt. Higginson, 20 October 1844, 8148. Major Richardson, *Eight Years in Canada* (Montreal: S.R. Publishers, 1847), 222. AO, Miscellaneous Collection 1850, file 9, reminiscences of William Kingsford, Montreal *Witness*, 7 March 1896. *Journals*, 1844–5, Col. G.A. Wetherall to Metcalfe, 26 October 1844, 212–13. Elinor Senior, "The Provincial Cavalry in Lower Canada, 1837–1850," *Canadian Historical Review*, LVII, 1 (1976), 16–17.

31. Paul Cornell, *The Alignment of Political Groups in Canada, 1841–1867* (Toronto: University of Toronto Press, 1962), 15–16, 98.

32. MLC, General Correspondence, O'Callaghan to Mackenzie, 27 August 1844.

33. Kaye, *Metcalfe*, II, 400–10.

34. LAC, MG24, C5, N. Wallick, Metcalfe to Wallick, 26 February 145.

35. *Globe*, 2 December 1845. RBP, I, A55/38, LaFontaine to Baldwin, 2 December 1845.

Chapter 11

1. *Debates*, 1846, 1946.

2. Kingston *Herald*, 10 September 1844, cited in David Mills, *The Idea of Loyalty in Upper Canada, 1784–1850* (Montreal and Kingston: McGill-Queen's University Press, 1988), 594. *Debates*, 1846, 594, 24.

3. *Debates*, 1844–5, 207. Dent, *Last Forty Years*, 37. William G. Ormsby, "The Civil List Question' in the Province of Canada," *Canadian Historical Review* XXXV, 2 (1954), 114–15. *Debates*, 1846, 232, 313–14, *Debates*, 1844–5, 1035.

4. RBP, III, Baldwin to Mrs. Sullivan, 31 May 1845. Baldwin, *Baldwins and the Great Experiment*, 203. AO, Andrew Norton Buell Papers, S. Richards Jr. to Buell, 9 March 1846. *Pilot*, Montreal, 17 March 1846. RBP, I, A80/37, A.M. Baldwin to Robert Baldwin, 3 April 1846.

5. RBP, I, A50/79, Lawrence Heyden to Baldwin, 17 June 1846. Private, Ross-Baldwin Family Papers, Baldwin to Eliza Baldwin, Xmas Eve, 1845.

6. Columbia University, New York, Butler Library, Special Collections, Dix Collection, Morgan Dix to Anne Maria Baldwin, 7 January 1846, 1 May 1847. BFP, Trunk 2, Box 2, Maria to Robert Baldwin, 3 March 1846, copy.

7. RBP, II, Baldwin to Sir William Betham, Dublin, 22 May 1845. On parental sovereignty: John Demos, "The Changing Faces of Fatherhood," in *Past, Present, and Personal: The Family and the Life Course in American History*, ed. Demos (New York: Oxford University Press, 1986), 41–67; David Roberts, "The Paterfamilias of the Victorian Governing Classes," in *The Victorian Family: Structure and Stresses*, ed. Anthony S. Wohl (London: Croom Helm, 1978), 59–81; Freud, "New Introductory Lectures on Psycho-Analysis (1933) [1932]," in *Standard Edition* XXII, 66–7.

8. RBP, III, Baldwin to Heyden and W.A. Baldwin, 14 February 1845. TRL, Broadside 1845, Baldwin, notice by Robert Baldwin and W.A. Baldwin, 31 December 1845.

9. RBP, I, A51/46, Hincks to Baldwin, 14 February 1845. Ronald Stewart Longley, *Sir Francis Hincks: A Study in Canadian Politics, Railways and Finance in the Nineteenth Century* (Toronto: Ayer Publishing, 1943), 150. Careless, *Brown of the Globe*, 62–3. RBP, I, A51/53, Hincks to Baldwin, 18 September 1845. *Pilot*, 9 March 1847. *Globe*, Toronto, 13 March, 7 July 1847. RBP, I, A51/65, Hincks to Baldwin, 25 March 1847.

10. The quote is found in Edward Porritt, *Sixty Years of Protection in Canada, 1846–1907* (London: Macmillan, 1908), 55. There is no more modern comprehensive account to replace G.N. Tucker, *Canadian Commercial Revolution, 1845–1871* (New Haven, CN: Yale University Press, 1936).

11. *Pilot*, 31 August 1847. Donald MacKay, *Flight from Famine: The Coming of the Irish to Canada* (Toronto: Dundurn, 2009).

12. On Monklands: Robert Rumilly, *Histoire de Montréal*, II (Montreal: Fides, 1970), 321. On the party: *Hamilton Spectator*, 31 July 1847.

13. Brown, *Brown's Toronto and Home District Directory*, 34. *Debates*, 1843, 101. *Examiner*, Toronto, 14 April 1847. *Globe*, 17 February, 6 March, 1 September 1847. *Debates*, 1844–1845, 1504–19.

14. *Examiner*, 10 September 1845. *Pilot*, 3 March 1846. *Gazette*, Montreal, 4 March 1846. *Journals*, 1846, App.E.E.E.E. *Pilot*, 2 March 1847.

15. *Debates*, 1845, 2, 2425. *Globe*, 1 April 1845.

16. *Pilot*, 16 January 1846. *Gazette*, Montreal, 16 January 1846.

17. On Cathcart: Dent, *Last Forty Years*, II, 33; Jacques Monet, "The Personal and Living Bond, 1839–1849," in *Shield of Achilles*, 86–7. *Gazette*, Montreal, 4 May 1847.

18. LAC, CO537/143, Metcalfe to Lord Stanley, 4 April 1845. Metcalf, "William Henry Draper," 54–6, 69–74. *Debates*, 1844–5, I, 1191–3. *Pilot*, 31 January 1845, 30 May 1845. *Gazette*, Montreal, 1 June 1846. *Examiner*, 31 March 1847.

19. *Debates*, 1844–5, I, 511–12, 937–8; ibid., II, 2330–1.

20. Ibid., II, 2514. *Gazette*, Montreal, 7 May 1846.

21. *Globe*, 1 September 1847.

22. Porritt, *Sixty Years of Protection*. LAC, MG24 D16, Buchanan, 117, Isaac Buchanan to the Editor, *Liverpool Standard*, 24 March 1846, 76119. Robert Baldwin Sullivan, *Lecture Before the Mechanics' Institute on the 17th November, 1847* (Hamilton: s.n., 1848).

23. *Debates*, 1844–5, II, 1915–16; ibid., 1846, 24, 119, 679. *Journals*, 1846, 45–6, 222, 229.

24. TRL, Broadside 1846, Baldwin R., "Public Dinner to the Hon. Robert Baldwin"; *Speech Delivered by the Hon. Robert Baldwin at a Public Dinner Given to Him by the Reform Electors of East Halton, on Wednesday, Nov.11, 1846* (Dundas: s.n., 1846), 6.

25. *Debates*, 1844–5, II, 1225–39. *Globe*, 16 December 1846. RBP, I, A51/64, Hincks to Baldwin, 25 March 1847.

26. *Debates*, 1847, 669. On the law of master and servant see Paul Craven, "The Law of Master and Servant in Mid-Nineteenth Century Ontario," in *Essays in the History of Canadian Law*, ed. David H. Flaherty (Toronto: University of Toronto Press, 1981), I, 175–211. On usury: *Debates*, 1847, 487, 966–7; the *Globe* continued to support repeal of usury laws, e.g., 13 March 1847. On dower: *Debates*, 1847, 361–5; W.G. Draper, *A Handy-Book of the Law of Dower* (Toronto: W.C. Chewette & Co., 1863).

27. Gay, *Bourgeois Experience*, I, 60. AO, Macaulay Papers, Macaulay to Ann Macaulay, 4 September 1847

28. Robert Brenner, "Bourgeois revolution and transition to capitalism," in *The First Modern Society: Essays in English History in Honour of Lawrence Stone*, ed. A.L. Beier et al. (Cambridge: Cambridge University Press, 1989), 285–88. Karl Marx, *Capital: A Critique of Political Economy* (London, 1974), 146–9. Peter J. Smith, "The Dream of Political Union: Loyalism, Toryism and the Federal Idea in Pre-Confederation Canada," in *The Causes of Canadian Confederation*, ed. Ged Martin (Fredericton: Acadiensis Press, 1990), 149.

29. J.L.H. Henderson, ed., *John Strachan: Documents and Opinions* (Toronto: McClelland & Stewart, 1969), 176. *Gazette*, Montreal, 18 March 1845. *Debates*, 1844–5, II, 2065.

30. *Debates*, 1844–5, 2331–49.

31. *Gazette*, Montreal, 1 April 1845. Hincks, *Reminiscences of His Public Life*, 174–5.

32. *Examiner*, 11 February 1846. RBP, Miscellaneous Unbound, subscription to the University Reformation Committee, 20 March 1846. *Debates*, 1846, II, 1713–29.

33. W. Stewart Wallace, *A History of the University of Toronto, 1827–1927* (Toronto: University of Toronto Press, 1927), 32–3. Macdonald's explanation of the bill, in a speech after dissolution of Parliament, is in Hodgins, *Documentary History*, VII, 36–8.

34. Hodgins, *Documentary History*, VII, 33–5, 42–65. *Debates*, 1847, 809–11, 1110–11.

35. *Debates*, 1844–5, I, 273.

36. *Gazette*, Montreal, 15 February 1845. LAC, CO42/531, Stephen to Gladstone, 12 January 1846. Kennedy, *Statutes*, Grey to Harvey, 3 November 1846, 494–6.

37. *Gazette*, Montreal, 17 September 1846, 8 January 1847. *Debates*, 1847, 65.

Chapter 12

1. PL, Robert Baldwin to L.-H. LaFontaine, 26 November 1840, 119.

2. Ibid., 24 February 1844, 329.

3. *Debates*, V, part 1, 24 April 1846, 924.

4. The Parliament is described in Edgar Andrew Collard, *Montreal Yesterdays* (Toronto: Longmans, 1962), 211, and LAC, MG29 D21, Alfred Perry, "A Reminiscence of '49: Who Burnt the Parliament Building?" extract from the Montreal *Daily Star*, 5 February 1887.

5. *Gazette*, Montreal, 28 November 1844.

6. *Examiner*, Toronto, 11 December 1844. *Gazette*, Montreal, 3 December, 5 December 1844.

7. Rumilly, *Histoire de Montréal*, II, 273–4, 316.

8. Robert S. Mackay, *The Montreal Directory for 1845–6* (Montreal: s.n., 1845). Léon Trépanier, *Les rues de vieux Montréal au fil de temps* (Montreal: Fides, 1968). Charles de Volpi and P.S. Winkworth, *Montréal: A Pictorial Record*, I, 1535–1885 (Montreal: Dev-Sco Publications, 1963).

9. Rumilly, *Histoire de Montréal*, II, 296, 302. The newest analysis of French-Canadian nationalism in the period is Éric Bédard, *Les Réformistes: Une generation canadienne-française au milieu du XIXe siècle* (Montreal: Boréal, 2009).

10. Elizabeth Nish, "LaFontaine and the Double Majority," *Revue du Centre d'Étude du Québec*, I (1967), 13.

11. LAC, MG24 A15, Derby Papers, Metcalfe Transcripts, IV, cabinet memoranda, Memorandum, Lord Stanley, 10 August 1843, attached cabinet memorandum initialed by cabinet ministers. LAC, MG11, Colonial Office, CO 537/143, Metcalfe to Stanley, 13 March 1845. *Debates*, IV/1, 1250, IV/2, 1783. Dent, *Last Forty Years*, II, 12–13. William G. Ormsby, "Sir Charles Metcalfe and the Canadian Union," Canadian Historical

Association *Report* (1961), 44. LAC, CO42/549, Jan.–Mar. Despatches, Memorandum, Use of the French Language in Public Proceedings in Canada, 15 April 1848, 213–7.

12. *Debates*, IV/2, 1558–60, 511–2, 937–8, 1338–52.

13. J.-Yvon Thériault, "Étienne Parent: les deux nations et la fin d'histoire," *Les nationalisms au Québec du XIXe au XXIe siècle*, dir. Michel Sarra-Bournet (Quebec: Presses de l'Université Laval, 2001), 37–56. On Parent, also see: Gérard Bergeron, *Lire Étienne Parent: Notre premier intellectual (1802–1874)*, (Sainte-Foy, QC: Presses de l'Université du Québec, 1994). On the new Catholicism: Jacques Monet, "French–Canadian Nationalism and the Challenge of Ultramontanism," *Historical Papers* (1966), 41–55.

14. Philippe Sylvain, "Libéralisme et ultramontanisme au Canada français: affrontement idéologique et doctrinal (1840–1865)," in *Shield of Achilles*, 116–8. *Pilot*, Montreal, 3 September 1846.

15. Rumilly, *Histoire de Montréal*, II, 290. *Pilot*, 30 December 1844.

16. *Examiner*, 20 November, 18 December 1844, 25 June 1845. *Pilot*, 29 January, 20 May 1845. *British Colonist*, Toronto, 5 January 1844.

17. *Debates*, IV/2, 1338–52.

18. LAC, MG11 Colonial Office, CO537/143, Metcalfe to Stanley, 26 January 1844.

19. PL, Divers, 1845–1847, Mesures concernant le Bas Canada, vote par des Majorités du Haut Canada, en 1845–6 & 7. *Debates*, IV/2, 2282, V, 1349.

20. *DCB*, X, J.-C. Bonenfant, "René-Édouard Caron," 131–6. Archives nationale du Québec, Papiers Caron, D.-B. Viger to Caron, 10 March 1844. *Pilot*, 3 September 1846. *La Minerve*, 8 May, 23 May 1845.

21. RBP, I, A55/37, LaFontaine to Baldwin, 23 September 1845.

22. PL, LaFontaine to Caron, 10 September 1845. RBP, I, A55/37, LaFontaine to Baldwin, 23 September 1845; A55/38, LaFontaine to Baldwin, 2 December 1845; A55/39, Draper to Caron, 19 November 1845 (copy); A51/54, Hincks to Baldwin, 23 September 1845. *Pilot*, 27 September 1845. PL, 408, Baldwin to LaFontaine, 16 October 1845.

23. RBP, I, A55/56, LaFontaine to Baldwin, 16 August 1845. PL, 404, Dr. Thomas Bouthillier to LaFontaine, 3 October 1845. PL, 419, LaFontaine to Papineau, 6 December 1845.

24. RBP, I, A55/38, LaFontaine to Baldwin, 2 December 1845; A55/37, LaFontaine to Baldwin, 23 September 1845; A51/54, Hincks to Baldwin, 23 September 1845. *Pilot*, 27 September, 28 October 1845.

25. PL, 408, Baldwin to LaFontaine, 16 October 1845.

26. PL, 425, Caron to LaFontaine, 10 March 1846; 430, Caron to LaFontaine, 23 March 1846.

27. *Debates*, 1846, 428–35.

28. RBP, I, A51/58, Hincks to Baldwin, 16 August 1846. LAC, MG24 B54, Pierre-Joseph-Olivier Chauveau, 2, LaFontaine to Cauchon, 2 April 1847, 123.

29. RBP, I, A73/77, Sullivan to Baldwin, 29 August 1846.

30. RBP, I, A55/42, Baldwin to LaFontaine, 10 August 1846. PL, 119, Baldwin to LaFontaine, 26 November 1840.

31. The Elgin memorandum is found in LAC, Chauveau, 2, Elgin to Morin, 23 February 1847, 2–3, and Sir Arthur G. Doughty, ed., *The Elgin-Grey Papers, 1846–1852* (Ottawa: J.O. Patenaude, 1937), I, 19. Morin's reply: LAC, Chauveau, 2, Morin to Elgin, 27 February 1847, 7–13 and Doughty, *Elgin-Grey,* I, 21–2. For further negotiations: Doughty, *Elgin-Grey*, I, Elgin to Grey, 27 March 1847, 23–4; LAC, Chauveau, 2, Resumé de ce que qui s'est passé entre M.M. Papineau et Caron depuis le 12 mars au 6 avril 1847, 135–9; ibid., Chauveau to Morin, 17 March 1847, 28–9, 18 March 1847, 35–6; *Examiner*, 16 June 1847; *Globe*, 20 March 1847. For Caron and LaFontaine: LAC, Chauveau, 2, Caron to LaFontaine, 16 May [April] 1847, [copy], 160–1, LaFontaine to Caron, 19 May [April] 1847, [copy], 165–7; and in PL, 444.

32. Doughty, *Elgin-Grey*, I, Elgin to Grey 26 April 1847, 33. PL, 448, Baldwin to LaFontaine, 8 May 1847. *Debates*, 1847, 47.

33. *Examiner*, 11 August 1847.

34. Read and Stagg, *Rebellion of 1837*, 148–50. LAC, MG24 B24, John Rolph, deposition of William Ware, 20 December 1837, 96–8.

35. On Sullivan: *DCB*, VIII, Victor Loring Russell, Robert Lochiel Fraser, and Michael S. Cross, "Robert Baldwin Sullivan," 845–50; Victor Loring Russell, *Mayors of Toronto* (Erin, ON: Boston Mills Press, 1982), I, 17–19; Davin, *Irishman in Canada*, 410. TRL, William Warren Baldwin Papers, B105, Robert to William Warren Baldwin, 24 September 1836.

36. AO, Macaulay Papers, John to Helen Macaulay, 29 November 1843.

37. Barbara C. Murison, "Enlightened Government: Sir George Arthur and the Upper Canadian Administration," *Journal of Imperial and Commonwealth History*, VIII, 3 (May 1980), 172–3. RBP, I, A73/62, Sullivan to Baldwin, 6 March 1843; A55/22, LaFontaine to Baldwin, 23 December 1843; A51/35, Hincks to Baldwin, 28 January 1844. Peter Neary, ed., "'Neither Radical Nor Tory Nor Whig': Letters by Oliver Mowat to John Mowat, 1843–1846," *Ontario History* LXXI, 2 (1979), 101. RBP, I, A50/86, Lawrence Heyden to Baldwin, 11 May 1848.

38. RBP, I, A87/64, Robert to William Warren Baldwin, 28 November 1843.

Chapter 13

1. D.R. Beer, "Sir Allan MacNab and the Adjutant Generalship of Militia, 1846–1847," *Ontario History* LXI, 1 (1969), 20. Sir Allan MacNab to Dominick Daly, 25 June 1846, in *Debates*, 1847, 20; Daly to MacNab, 3 July, 4 July 1846; MacNab to Daly, 7 July 1846. *Debates*, 1847, 21.

2. *Pilot*, Montreal, 10 September 1846. PL, 438, Baldwin to LaFontaine, 11 December 1846. Spelling in the original.

3. PL, 439, Baldwin to LaFontaine, 21 December 1846, 440, Baldwin to LaFontaine, 22 December 1846. Beer, "Sir Allan MacNab and the Adjutant Generalship," 29.

4. *Debates*, 1847, 3–10.

5. Ibid., 24–34.

6. RBP, I, A51/57, Hincks to Baldwin, 14 July 1846. *Gazette*, Montreal, 1 February 1847. The constitutional change was signalled in a dispatch from Colonial Secretary Grey to Lieutenant-Governor Harvey of Nova Scotia on 3 November 1846, reprinted in Doughty,

Elgin-Grey, III, dispatch to Harvey in draft chapter of Lord Grey, *The Colonial Policy of Lord John Russell's Administration*, 1022–3. Wilson, *Life of Robert Baldwin*, 230.

7. The best biography of Elgin remains J.L. Morison, *The Eighth Earl of Elgin: A Chapter in Nineteenth-Century Imperial History* (London: Hodder and Stoughton, 1928). Elgin's correspondence has been mostly printed, in the four volumes of *The Elgin-Grey Papers* and in Theodore Walrond, ed., *Letters and Journals of James, Eighth Earl of Elgin* (London: John Murray, 1872). There are good portraits of Elgin in Morison, *Elgin*, frontispiece and opposite p. 102, and an effective verbal description in *Gazette*, Montreal, 1 February 1847.

8. PL, 440, Baldwin to LaFontaine, 22 December 1846.

9. *Globe*, 23 December 1846, commenting on the Brockville *Statesman*.

10. *Speech Delivered by the Hon. Robert Baldwin . . . Nov.11, 1846*, 2.

11. Ibid., 2–3, 6, 7–8.

12. PL, 448, Baldwin to LaFontaine, 8 May 1847.

13. Longley, *Sir Francis Hincks,* 150. RBP, I, A35/106, Brown to Baldwin, 10 July 1845.

14. PL, 447, Baldwin to LaFontaine, 7 May 1847. RBP, I, A34/21, Blake to Baldwin, 12 May 1848.

15. RBP, I, unbound, file 4, Baldwin to Durand, 30 April 1847.

16. LAC, MG24 B24, John Rolph, I, Baldwin to Dr. Park, 31 March 1847, 234–6.

17. RBP, I, A43/41, Durand to Baldwin, 7 March 1847, A43/42, 20 April 1847.

18. PL, 448, Baldwin to LaFontaine, 8 May 1847.

19. Frederick H. Armstrong, ed., "The Macdonald-Gowan Letters, 1847," *Ontario History* LXIII, 1 (1971), Macdonald to Gowan, 30 April 1847, 6–7.

20. PL, 448, Baldwin to LaFontaine, 8 May 1847. Doughty, *Elgin-Grey*, I, Elgin to Grey, 24 February 1847.

21. Armstrong, "Macdonald-Gowan Letters," Macdonald to Gowan, 8 March 1847. Wilson, *Life of Robert Baldwin*, 229. PL, 440, Baldwin to LaFontaine, 22 December 1846, 448, 8 May 1847.

22. LAC, MG24 B1, Neilson, Correspondence with James Allison re Immigration, 1846–1849, George Nellis Douglas, M.D., Medical Superintendent, Quebec, to Hon. D. Daly, 27 December 1847, 978–1003. *Pilot*, 15, 17 June 1847.

23. *Debates*, VI, 1847, 67, 70–2, 78.

24. Ibid., 85–6, 88–91, 227, 411–61, 717–35, 809–11, 1110.

25. Ibid., 474–6, 524. Dent, *Last Forty Years*, II, 37.

26. *Debates*, 1847, 307–9.

27. Ibid., 729, 59, 65.

28. RBP, I, A73/66, R.B. Sullivan to Baldwin, 2 August 1824; A80/112, J.S. Baldwin to Robert Baldwin, 9 September 1839.

Chapter 14

1. *Globe*, Toronto, 26 February 1848.

2. Karl Marx, *The Eighteenth Brumaire of Louis Bonaparte* (1852), Ch.I.

3. RBP, Section 1, file 4, Baldwin to Durand, 16 April 1847.

4. *Examiner*, Toronto, 8 December 1847.

5. *Gazette*, Montreal, 8 December 1847, 28 January 1848.

6. PL, 465–A, Baldwin to LaFontaine, 24 & 25 January 1848. RBP, I, A47/54, Gorham to Baldwin, 6 December 1847; A50/135, William Hall, East Gwillimbury, to Baldwin, 8 December 1847. TRL, Broadsides, 1847 Election Willson, D. Willson, Sharon, "Brothers in the Cause of our Country and Constitution," 8 December 1847; Broadsides, 1847 Election, Baldwin, 8 December 1847.

7. *Examiner*, 12 January 1848. *Globe*, 8 January 1848. *Gazette,* Montreal, 3 March 1848; *Journals*, 1848, 13 March, 29–30. *Hamilton Spectator*, 15 January 1848. PL, Mémoire, n.d., Divers 1847, 1072. *Pilot*, Montreal, 14 January 1848. *Gazette,* Montreal, 12 ,14 January 1848. McCord Museum, Montreal, McCord Papers, Queen's Light Dragoons, Military Papers of Capt. Thos. Walter Jones, Box 1, G.S. Wetherall, General Order, 17 January 1848. LAC, British Military Records, C317, 135–142.

8. PL, 465–A, Baldwin to LaFontaine, 25 January 1848. LAC, MG24 B30, John Sandfield Macdonald, I, Baldwin to Macdonald, 1 February 1848, 83–4. *Gazette,* Montreal, 17 January 1848.

9. *Journals*, 1848, 17.

10. Ibid., 18. Doughty, *Elgin-Grey*, I, Elgin to Grey, 17 March 1848, 135–6. LAC, CO325/41, Responsible Govt., Mr. Hawes, 28 June 1848, 40–4.

11. Doughty, *Elgin-Grey*, I, Elgin to Grey, 17 March 1848, 135. *Gazette,* Montreal, 15 March 1848. *Globe*, Toronto, 5 April 1848.

12. *Debates*, 338. Doughty, *Elgin-Grey*, I, Grey to Elgin, 14 April 1848, 138. Longley, *Sir Francis Hincks*, 163–71. LAC, RG19 E1 (a), 3365, Department of Finance, Minister's Office Correspondence, L.M. Viger to F. Hincks, 28 August 1848; ibid., J. Harvey to Earl Grey, 19 June 1848. Doughty, *Elgin-Grey*, I, Elgin to Grey, 4 May 1848, 150. LAC, CO42/550, Memorandum, Inspector General, n.d., 9–11, transmitted by Elgin to Grey, 8 April 1848. LAC, RG1, E1, Executive Council, State Book I, 71, Inspector General, "Memorandum on Immigration and on Public Works as connected therewith," 20 December 1848, 400–15.

13. J.F. Merritt, *Biography of the Hon. W.H. Merritt, M.P.* (St. Catharines, ON: E.S. Leavenworth, 1875), 325–6. *Examiner*, 15, 22 August 1849. RBP, Merritt to Baldwin, 14 March 1848. There is a useful discussion of the transition from a "bipolar" division between the gentry and the masses, to a more complicated view of social classes in: Nancy Christie, "The 'Plague of Servants': Female Household Labour and the Making of Classes in Upper Canada," in *Transatlantic Subjects: Ideas, Institutions, and Social Experience in Post-Revolutionary British North America,* ed. Nancy Christie (Montreal and Kingston: McGill-Queen's University, 2008), 83–132.

14. Bruce W. Hodgins, *John Sandfield Macdonald, 1812–1872* (Toronto: University of Toronto Press, 1971), 17. AO, Attorney General, Legal Books, Baldwin to C. Small, 15 August 1848, 71. RBP, I, A77/86, Adam Wilson to Baldwin, 19 May 1848. *Pilot*, 21 January 1848. *Globe*, 29 April, 6 May 1848. RBP, I, A73/32, John Steele to Baldwin, 15 May 1848; A56/100, George Lount to Baldwin, 29 February 1848. Private, Ross-Baldwin Papers, W.B. Richards to John Ross, 9 September 1848. RBP, I, A66/50, Charles Robinson to Baldwin, 13 November 1848.

15. LAC, MG24 B11, Baldwin-Ross Family Papers, Baldwin to Miss Baldwin, 27 February 1848.

16. For theoretical discussion of merchant capitalism see: Robert Brenner, "Bourgeois Revolution and Transition to Capitalism," in *The First Modern Society: Essays in English History in Honour of Lawrence Stone*, ed. A.L. Beier et al. (Cambridge: Cambridge University Press, 1989), 271–304, and Karl Marx, *Pre-Capitalist Economic Formations*, ed. E.J. Hobsbawm (New York, 1969). AO, Jarvis-Powell Papers, S.P. Jarvis to S.P. Jarvis Jr., 11 April 1848.

17. RBP, I, A43/1, J.H. Dunn to Baldwin, 1 September 1848. Queen's University Archives, John Young, 1811–1878, Box 1, Correspondence 1847–1860, Young to William Hamilton Merritt, 27 July 1848. LAC, RG7 G18, 20, Navigation Acts, Elgin to Grey, 15 June 1848, 44–8; ibid., Statement on the Subject of the Amelioration of the Navigation Laws, Executive Council, Province of Canada, 8 May 1848, 2–39. LAC, MG24 A16, Elgin Papers, 397/3, Private Letters from the Colonial Secretary, Grey to Elgin, 10 August 1848. Hodgetts, *Pioneer Public Service*, 249–50.

18. LAC, RG1, Executive Council, "Memorandum on Immigration and on Public Works," 20 December 1848. Private, Ross-Baldwin Papers, W.B. Richard to John Ross, 4 September 1848. LAC, RG1 E1, Executive Council, State Books, 1848. RBP, I, A76/70, Widmer to Baldwin, 9 October 1848; A34/29, W. Hume Blake to Baldwin, 10 October 1848.

19. Christopher Moore, *The Law Society of Upper Canada and Ontario's Lawyers, 1797–1997* (Toronto: University of Toronto Press, 1997), 67–8. The quote is from *Journals of the Advocate Society*, IX (March, 1823), 67–74, cited in G. Blaine Baker, "The Juvenile Advocate Society, 1821–1826: Self-Proclaimed Schoolroom for Upper Canada's Governing Class," *Historical Papers* (1985), 78.

20. Moore, *Law Society*, 69–70.

21. Ibid., 91–2. William Renwick Riddell, *The Legal Profession in Upper Canada in Its Early Periods* (Toronto: Law Society of Upper Canada, 1916), 87–8, 95.

22. Moore, *Law Society*, 71–2. John Honsberger, *Osgoode Hall: An Illustrated History* (Toronto: Dundurn Press, 2004), 95–122, 135–7, 143. Riddell, *Legal Profession*, 125–6.

23. Hodgetts, *Pioneer Public Service*, 36.

24. LAC, RG5 C1, Provincial Secretary, 290, 676, Stayner to Leslie, 8 April 1850; Leslie to Stayner, 15 April 1850.

25. LAC, State Book J, 25 October 1849, 464–5.

26. Jos. O. Coté, *Analytical Index to the State Books of the Province of Canada from 10th February 1841 to 30th July 1867*, letterbook, LAC, 434–58.

27. LAC, State Book J, 26 September 1849, 417–18.

28. Ibid., 26 September 1849, 420–1. An appeal from the Aboriginals in August was rejected, but an appeal from a white person, Robert Symes, was accepted: State Book J, 31 August 1849, 366, 4 September 1849, 374–5.

29. LAC, RG7 G20, Civil Secretary, 48, 5267, Baldwin to R. Bruce, Secretary to the Governor, 31 December 1849; ibid., Lt. W.R. Davis, MS *Cherokee*, to L. Parker, Secretary of the Admiralty, 11 December 1849; ibid., Baldwin to Bruce, 31 December 1849.

30. Ibid., 50, 549, petition of the inhabitants of the Magdalen Islands to the queen, 14 October 1850.

31. RBP, I, A73/50, John Stewart to Baldwin, 10 September 1850, and Baldwin's draft reply.

32. RBP, I, A62/36, Notman to Baldwin, 18 February 1851; A62/37, Notman to Baldwin, 10 March 1851; Baldwin to Notman, 12 March 151.

33. AO, Justice Department, Attorney General, Legal Books, circular letter, Robert Baldwin, 23 August 1848. RBP, I, A34/29, W. Hume Blake to Baldwin, 10 October 1848.

34. *Debates*, X/1, 387–92, 599–500. *Journals*, 1851, App.MMM.

35. A good summary of the legislation is found in John David Blackwell, "William Hume Blake and Judicial Reform in the United Province of Canada" (unpublished MA thesis, Queen's University, 1980), 7. Historians have tended to argue that the legislation was Blake's work, as did Wilson in *Life of Robert Baldwin*, 263, and John David Blackwell; Donald Swainson went further, claiming Blake had to overcome Baldwin's "profound reservations": *DCB*, IX, Donald Swainson, "William Hume Blake," 58. Francis Hincks, who was in the Executive, would disagree since he said Baldwin laid out the basics of the legislation while Blake helped with the drafting: Elizabeth Nish, "How History is Written: The Hincks-Dent Letters," *Revue du Centre d Étude du Québec*, 2 (1968), Hincks to Dent, 26 January 1882, 70. Baldwin himself, in 1851, credited Blake for the Chancery reform and said they worked together on the rest: *Debates*, X/1, 605.

36. *Debates*, VIII/2, 1296, 2323, 2378–80, 2394–5. AO, Blake Papers, W.H. Blake Papers, Correspondence, Baldwin to Blake, 10 September 1849, notice Blake's name has been submitted to the Governor General. MLC, Lesslie to Mackenzie, 23 January 1850. There is a good account of the Chancery issue in John D. Blackwell, "William Hume Blake and the Judicature Act of 1849: The Process of Legal Reform at Mid-Century in Upper Canada," in *Essays in the History of Canadian Law*, I, 132–74.

37. LAC, RG5 C1, Civil Secretary, 292, Baldwin to Leslie, 8 May 1850; Leslie to Blake, 8 May 1850.

38. *Debates*, VIII/3, 1915–21.

39. Ibid., VIII/2, 1670–2.

40. Ibid., 1733–7.

41. Ibid., IX/1, 545, VIII/2, 1320.

42. RBPI, A66/56, John Bruce to Baldwin, 22 October 1849; A66/56, Charles Robinson to Baldwin, 22 October 1849; A66/57, note by Baldwin, 25 October 1849.

43. PL, 478, Baldwin to Small, 9 March 1849, copy.

44. For the charges, see *Journals*, 1849, Appendix BBBBB, Report of the commissioners appointed to inquire into and report upon the conduct, economy, discipline and

management of the Provincial Penitentiary. The first report looked at evidence while the second contained recommendations. Accounts of the penitentiary affair are found in Careless, *Brown of the Globe*, 78–85, and Richard B. Splane, *Social Welfare in Ontario, 1791–1893: A Study of Public Welfare Administration* (Toronto: University of Toronto Press, 1965), 137–45.

45. For an overview of the prison question: Peter Oliver, *"Terror to evil doers": Prisons and Punishment in Nineteenth-Century Ontario* (Toronto: University of Toronto Press, 1998).

46. Doughty, *Elgin-Grey*, I, Elgin to Grey, 24 August 1848. AO, Baldwin Papers, Opinions and decisions by Robert Baldwin, 1840–9, Memorandum respecting the position of the parties connected with the Troubles in Upper Canada, 5 August 1848. *Debates*, VIII/1, 362.

47. RBP, I, A47/65, Gourlay to Baldwin, 6 July 1848, A47/66, Baldwin to Gourlay, 24 October 1848, Gourlay to Baldwin, 11 January 1849.

48. LAC, MG24 B40, George Brown, I, Price to Brown, 28 December 1848, 28–9. AO, Hodgins, John George, Papers, Baldwin to Egerton Ryerson, 20 December 1849.

49. LAC, Brown, I, Price to Brown, 28 December 1848, 27. RBP, I, A64/63, Price to Bidwell, 29 December 1848. AO, Hodgins, Baldwin to Ryerson, 20 September 1849. AO, Buell, Andrew Norton, Papers, A.N. Buell to Bidwell, 21 December 1849. For an example of Bidwell's suspicion and self-pity: AO, Rolph, John, Papers, Bidwell to Mrs. Rolph, 21 December 1849.

50. Albert Schrauwers, *"Union is Strength": W.L. Mackenzie, The Children of Peace, and the Emergence of Joint Stock Democracy in Upper Canada* (Toronto: University of Toronto Press, 2009), 177.

51. MLC, Mackenzie to Baldwin, 14 February 1847, Mackenzie to Dr. Wolfred Nelson, 2 April 1848, Lesslie to Mackenzie, 9 August 1848.

52. RBP, I, A61/63, Mackenzie to Baldwin, 4 September 1850; A61/63, Baldwin to Mackenzie, n.d., draft.

53. For Mackenzie's changed views, see his letter to Colonial Secretary Grey in February 1849, quoted in Charles Lindsey, *The Life and Times of Wm. Lyon Mackenzie* (Toronto: P.R. Randall, 1862), II, 291–2.

Chapter 15

1. Perhaps an omen, the weather turned severely cold on 2 January: *Gazette*, Montreal, 3 January 1849. *Debates*, 1849, VIII/1, 8. *Journals*, 1849, 26. The complacent view of Canadian peace was shared by liberal newspapers such as the *Globe*: 3 January 1849.

2. On the "Montreal way": RBP, I, A57/42, D. Maguire, Quebec, to Robert Baldwin, 21 January 1850. The general unrest of the decade is treated in Michael S. Cross, "'The laws are like cobwebs': Popular Resistance to Authority in Mid-Nineteenth Century British North America," in *Law in a Colonial Society: The Nova Scotia Experience*, ed. Peter Waite et al. (Toronto: Carswell, 1984), 103–23.

3. Miles Taylor, "The 1848 Revolutions and the British Empire," *Past and Present*, 166 (2000), 146–80.

4. Donald G. Paterson and Ronald A. Shearer, "A History of Prices in Canada, 1840–1871: A New Wholesale Price Index," *Canadian Journal of Economics* 36/1 (March 2003), 224–53. On Orange-Green and other unrest: Cross, "'The laws are like cobwebs.'"

5. Michael McCulloch, "The Death of Whiggery: Lower Canadian British Consti-tutionalism and the *tentation de l'histoire parallèle*," *Journal of the Canadian Historical Association* (1991), 199–213.

6. AO, Ms. 78, r.4, Macaulay Papers, J.B. Robinson to John Macaulay, 23 March 1843.

7. *Debates*, VIII/1, 10 January 1849, 8–10. Hincks, *Reminiscences of His Public Life*, 189–90. Doughty, *Elgin-Grey*, I, Elgin to Grey, printed letter from Francis Hincks, 10 February 1849, 302–5.

8. *Gazette*, Montreal, 14 February 1849. *Globe*, Toronto, 28 February 1849. Wilson, *Life of Robert Baldwin*, 267–8.

9. Doughty, *Elgin-Grey*, I, Elgin to Grey, 1 February 1849, 300. *Journals*, 1849, 108–9.

10. *Debates*, VIII/1, 770, 776. Donald Creighton, *John A. Macdonald: The Young Politician* (Toronto: Macmillan, 1952/1998), 136–8. *Globe*, Toronto, 17 March 1849. Doughty, *Elgin-Grey*, I, Elgin to Grey, 11 April 1849, enclosing clippings from the New York *Commercial Advertiser* with excerpts from Canadian newspapers.

11. MLC, Series A-1-1, General Correspondence, William Lyon Mackenzie to James Mackenzie, 2 April 1849; A card from William Lyon Mackenzie, 28 March 1849; WIK, Sec., to Mackenzie, 24 March 1849. RBP, I, A71/43, J.E. Small to Baldwin, 23 March 1849; A66/11, George Ridout to Baldwin, 28 March 1849. Accounts of Mackenzie's travails: Lindsey, *Life and Times of Wm. Lyon Mackenzie*, II, 292–5; Lillian F. Gates, *After the Rebellion: The Later Years of William Lyon Mackenzie* (Toronto: Dundurn Press, 1988), 157–8. BFP, Mary Jones, Memories of My Youth and a Sketch of the Family History of the Ross-Baldwin Families, 1925.

12. *Journals*, 1849, 259–62. *Debates*, VIII/33, 2046. Doughty, *Elgin-Grey*, IV, Elgin to Grey, 30 April 1849. *Globe*, Toronto, 2 May 1849.

13. The quote is from LAC, MG24 B56, William Manson, 1849, Henry Rose to Manson, 7 May 1849. *Debates*, VIII/3, 2049. Doughty, *Elgin-Grey*, IV, Elgin to Grey, 30 April 1849, 1458.

14. LAC, MG29 D21, Alfred Perry, "A Reminiscence of '49: Who Burnt the Parliament Building?," extract from the Montreal *Daily Star*, 5 February 1887. Doughty, *Elgin-Grey*, IV, Elgin to Grey, 30 April 1849, 1461. LAC, MG24 A53, John Grant Letters, 1849, F.A. Grant to John Grant, 1 May 1849.

15. Lists of speakers are found in: Perry, "A Reminiscence"; *Globe*, 30 April 1849. On the meeting: LAC, John Grant Papers, F.A. Grant to John Grant, 1 May 1849; LAC, MG24 B56, William Manson, Rose to Manson, 7 May 1849.

16. Sir James Alexander, *Passages in the Life of a Soldier, or, Military Service in East and West* (London: Hurst and Blackett, 1857), I, 9–11. Perry, "A Reminiscence". LAC, Manson, Rose to Manson, 7 May 1849. AO, Justice, RG4 A-1-1, General Correspondence, 1844–1850, Box 3, George K. Chisholm to J.S. Macdonald, 16 March 1850 [Chisholm was the sergeant-at-arms]. *Montreal Herald*, 28 April 1849. Journals, 1849, 262.

17. Doughty, *Elgin-Grey*, IV, Elgin to Grey, 30 April 1849. McCord Museum, Library Files, Elgin, James Bruce, clipping from *Gazette*, Montreal, 25 December 1916, interview with Captain Samuel Filgate. LAC, John Grant Letters, F.A. Grant to John Grant, 1 May 1849. Doughty, *Elgin-Grey*, I, Grey to Elgin, 14 June 1849, 360. Gore defended his actions, pointing out the troops had helped prevent the fire from spreading: LAC, RG8

C Series, 616, Political Disturbances, 1849–50, Gore to Captain Kirkland, 26 April 1849. Other commanders also tried to justify themselves: McCord Museum, Queen's Light Dragoons, Ledger and Letterbook, 1844–1850, Colonel G.A. Wetherall to Captain G.R. Clermont, n.d.; McCord Museum, Queen's Light Dragoons, Military Papers of Captain Thomas Walter Jones, Box 1, Petitions, Requisitions, Jones to Lieutenant General George Wetherall, 31 January 1859. A strong defence of the police actions: LAC, RG5 B33, Records of the Provincial and Civil Secretaries, W. Ermatinger, Inspector Superintendent of Police to James Leslie, Provincial Secretary, 10 May 1849.

18. Perry, "Reminiscence." William Weir, *Sixty Years in Canada* (Montreal: J. Lovell & Son, 1903), 28–9. Alexander, *Passages*, 13.

19. Perry, "Reminiscence." Alexander, *Passages*, 14. *Montreal Herald*, 28 April 1849.

20. Letter from "E.E." in *Gazette*, Montreal, 7 May 1849. *Montreal Herald*, 28 April 1849. Alexander, *Passages*, 14. Jacques Monet, *The Last Cannon Shot: A Study of French-Canadian Nationalism, 1837–1850* (Toronto: University of Toronto Press, 1969), 339. PL, John G. Dinning to LaFontaine, 26 April 1849, 532. *Debates*, VIII/3, 2070.

21. LAC, RG1, Executive Council, E1 Canada, Executive Council Minute Books, State Book J, 27 April 1849, 66–8, 28 April 1849, 70. LAC, MG24 B2, Papiers Papineau, Gustave Papineau to Amédée Papineau, 28 April 1849, 4462–3. Alexander, *Passages*, 16. Perry, "Reminiscence." Elinor Kyte Senior, "The Influence of the British Garrison on the Development of the Montreal Police, 1832 to 1853," *Military Affairs* 42/2 (April 1979), 66. *Gazette*, Montreal, 30 April 1849. John Ralston Saul gives a more favourable interpretation of the actions of LaFontaine and Baldwin, insisting theirs was a considered decision to avoid violence by refusing to confront the Tories with armed forces: John Ralston Saul, *Louis-Hippolyte LaFontaine and Robert Baldwin* (Toronto: Penguin, 2010), 17–19.

22. *Journals*, 1849, 263–4. *Debates*, 1849, VIII, 3, 2079–97, 2113–15. Francis Hincks provided a good, if highly partisan, account of the manoeuvres over the address: LAC, MG24 A16, Elgin, reel 398, 4A: Private Official Correspondence with Canadian Officials, Francis Hincks, Memorandum, 27 April 1849. For the attacks on Elgin: Perry, "A Reminiscence"; Alexander, *Passages*, 18–19; *Globe*, 2 May 1849; LAC, Manson, Rose to Manson, 7 May 1849; *Gazette*, Montreal, 2 May 1849. Doughty, *Elgin-Grey*, IV, Elgin to Grey, 30 May, 2 June 1849. John Ralston Saul has an evocative account of events in Chapter 1 of *LaFontaine and Baldwin*.

23. *Gazette*, Montreal, 14 May 1849. *Examiner*, Toronto, 16 May 1849. Careless, *Brown of the Globe*, 90. Swainson, "William Hume Blake," 57.

24. Toronto *Examiner*, 9 May 1849. LAC, RG8, British Military Records, C616, Political Disturbances, 1849–1850, George Gurnett to Lieutenant Colonel Egerton, 1 May, 2 May 1849; Egerton to the Military Secretary, 4 May 1849, 24–5. Careless, *Brown of the Globe*, I, 89. Effigy burnings are described in various letters to Robert Baldwin: RBP, I, A47/57, A63/48, A66/96, A75/21. On the Sherbrooke affair: Jack E. Little, "The Short Life of a Local Protest Movement: The Annexation Crisis of 1849–50 in the Eastern Townships," *Journal of the Canadian Historical Association* (1992), 53. Orange and other threats: RBP, I, A72/41, James Smith, Port Hope, to Baldwin, 20 June 1849; A47/57, Eli Gorham, Newmarket, to Baldwin, 11 May 1849; A43/70, Godley Eckard to Baldwin, 12 May 1849; A54/52, William Johnson, Georgina, to Baldwin, 7 May 1849. AO, Jarvis-Powell Papers, Samuel Jarvis, junior, to Mary B. Jarvis, 25 May 1849. On Henry Sherwood: Doughty, Elgin-Grey, I, Elgin to Grey, 3 June 1849, 362–3. PL, John G. Dinning to LaFontaine, 27 June 1849, 541.

25. On the British American League: Gerald A. Hallowell, "The Reaction of the Upper Canadian Tories to the Adversity of 1849: Annexation and the British American League," *Ontario History* LXII/1 (March, 1970), 41–56; *Gazette*, Montreal, 20 April 1849; *Globe*, 2 August 1849. On organizing support for the ministry: RBP I, A54/52, William Johnson, Georgina, to Baldwin, 7 May 1849; A87/5, Baldwin to Joseph Thompson et al., 30 April 1849. Lobbying: Doughty, *Elgin-Grey*, I, Elgin to Grey, 13 May 1849, 354, Grey to Elgin, 1 June 1849, 355–6, 14 June 1849, 360, 22 June 1849, 372, 29 June 1849, 377. On cholera: Geoffrey Bilson, *A Darkened House: Cholera in Nineteenth Century Canada* (Toronto: University of Toronto Press, 1980), 118–28; *Globe*, 7 July 1849; Smith, *Young Mr. Smith*, 132–3.

26. Doughty, *Elgin-Grey*, I, Grey to Elgin, 1 June 1848, 355. *Globe*, 16, 30 June 1849, 14, 21 July 1849.

27. *Gazette*, Montreal, 20 July 1849. *Globe*, 9 August 1849. Monet, *Last Cannon Shot*, 342. Archives nationales du Québec, Taché, famille, 1730–1912, Article 1, Correspondance, É.-P. Taché, 1848–1865, Taché to Madame Taché, 1 August 1849.

28. *Gazette*, Montreal, 15, 16 August 1849. *Papers Relating to the Removal of the Seat of Government and to the Annexation Movement. Presented to Both Houses of Parliament by Command of Her Majesty, 15 April 1850* (London, 1850), C. Wetherall to J. Leslie, 20 August 1849, 3, 6. *Pilot*, Montreal, 18 August 1849. LAC, RG8 British Military Records, C616, Political Disturbances, 1849–50, W. McCord, J.P. et al. to Lt. Col. Hay, 14 August 1849, 239, Capt. A. Christie to Town Major, 16 August 1849, 241; Lt. Col. Charles Hay to the Military Secretary, 16 August 1849, 250–3. Doughty, *Elgin-Grey*, II, Elgin to Grey, 20 August 1849, 449–50. PL, Personnel, Testimony before inquest by L.-H. LaFontaine, 1849, 1402. The events of that night are described in the testimony at the inquest into the death of William Mason, which was reported in detail in all the major newspapers. LaFontaine admitted he had fired at the attackers.

29. *Globe*, 21, 25 August 1849. Alexander, *Passages*, 20.

30. Doughty, *Elgin-Grey*, I, Elgin to Grey, 27 August 1849, 453–5. *Pilot*, 23 August 1849. Doughty, *Elgin-Grey*, II, Proclamation! Britons of the City of Toronto!, August 1849, 463. Brockville *Statesman*, 19 September 1849. Doughty, *Elgin-Grey*, II, Elgin to Grey, 23 September 1849, enclosing poster from "The Watcher," Toronto 10 September 1849. Michael S. Cross, "Stony Monday, 1849: The Rebellion Losses Riots in Bytown," *Ontario History* LXIII/3 (September 1971), 177–90. LAC, MG24 A16, Elgin Papers, R.401, 8: Private Letters of the Earl of Elgin to the Countess Elgin, 26 September 1849. The troubles in Upper Canada are well treated in: Ian Radforth, "Political Demonstrations and Spectacles during the Rebellion Losses Controversy in Upper Canada," *Canadian Historical Review*, 92/1 (March 2011), 1–41.

31. Letter from Baldwin to a friend, 8 September 1849, reprinted in Dent, *Last Forty Years*, II, 177–8, footnote.

32. Doughty, *Elgin-Grey*, II, Elgin to Grey, 27 August 1849, 452–4, 3 September 1849, 463–6, 19 October 1849, 523. Smith, *Young Mr. Smith*, 134.

33. The State Books document scores of dismissals of officials who spoke out for annexation. On the Reform Party discipline, see RBP, Section III, Baldwin to Lawrence Heyden, 5 October 1849.

34. *British Colonist*, Toronto, 1 July 1851.

35. LAC, Elgin Papers, 4A, Elgin to Sir Edmund Head, 14 April 1849.

36. Carol Wilton, "'Lawless Law': Conservative Political Violence in Upper Canada, 1818–41," *Law and History Review*, 13 (1995), 11–36. Blaine Baker, "'So elegant a Web': Providential Order and the Rule of Secular Law in Early Nineteenth Century Upper Canada," *University of Toronto Law Journal*, 38 (1988), 184–205. There is a good discussion of "lawless law" in the American setting in Lawrence M. Friedman, *Crime and Punishment in American History* (New York: Basic Books, 1993), 172–92.

37. AO, RG4 A-1, Justice, Crown Prosecution Case Files, 1843–1849, Box 7, Baldwin to S.B. Harrison, 14 August 1843. Cross, "'The laws are like cobwebs.'"

38. LAC, British Military Records, C317, Major G. Egerton to the Town Major, 11 January 1848, 137–43. *Gazette*, Montreal, 14 January 1848. Doughty, *Elgin-Grey*, II, Elgin to Grey, 3 September 1849, 464.

39. *Gazette*, Montreal, 2 May 1849. LAC, RG4, Civil and Provincial Secretaries' Offices, Canada East, 2489, Wetherall to J. Leslie, 18 August 1849.

40. LAC, Perry, "A Reminiscence," *Gazette*, Montreal, 2 March, 30 April, 14 May 1849.

41. On Upper Canada: S.F. Wise, *God's Peculiar People: Essays on Political Culture in Nineteenth-Century Canada*, eds. A.B. McKillop and Paul Romney (Ottawa: Carleton University Press, 1993); David Mills, *The Idea of Loyalty in Upper Canada, 1784–1850* (Montreal and Kingston: McGill-Queen's University Press, 1988); and the best discussion of providentialism, Robert L. Fraser, *"Like Eden in Her Summer Dress": Gentry, Economy and Society; Upper Canada, 1812–1840*, Ph.D. Thesis, University of Toronto, 1979. On Lower Canada: Donald Creighton, *The Commercial Empire of the St. Lawrence, 1760–1850* (Toronto: Ryerson Press, 1937); Alan Greer, *Peasant, Lord and Merchant: Rural Society in Three Quebec Parishes, 1740–1840* (Toronto: University of Toronto Press, 1985); McCulloch, "The Death of Whiggery."

42. Camillus [Adam Thom], *Anti-Gallic Letters: Addressed to His Excellency, the Earl of Gosford, Governor in Chief of the Canadas* (Montreal: s.n.,1836). Creighton, *Commercial Empire*, 296–8.

43. Grey's dispatch was reprinted in, among others, Rosa M. Langstone, *Responsible Government in Canada* (London: J.M. Dent and Sons, 1931), 158–9. Queen's University Archives, William Morris Papers, Box 2, Correspondence, 1842–1853, John A. Macdonald to William Morris, 31 May 1847. *British Colonist*, Toronto, 7 May 1850, quoted in Jeffrey L. McNairn, "Publius of the North: Tory Republicanism and the American Constitution in Upper Canada, 1848–54," *Canadian Historical Review* 77, 4 (December 1996), 510.

44. *Debates*, VIII/3, 2128. *Gazette*, Montreal, 7 July 1849.

45. *Debates*, IX/1, 290, 370–1, 789–94.

46. Elgin noted Baldwin's innate conservatism: Doughty, *Elgin-Grey*, II, Elgin to Grey, 28 June, 5 July 1851, 832–4. On Tories and French: Elgin to Grey, 2 August 1850, in Morison, *Eighth Earl of Elgin*, 115–6.

47. RBP, I, A50/105, Lawrence Heyden to Baldwin, 27 August 1849; A50/106, Heyden to Baldwin, 4 September 1849.

Chapter 16

1. J.M.S. Careless, *The Union of the Canadas: The Growth of Canadian Institutions, 1841–1857* (Toronto: McClelland and Stewart, 1967), 133.

2. Examples of patronage: LAC, RG5 C1, Civil Secretary, Canada West, 279, 2220, Baldwin to James Leslie, 15 December 1849, 331, 1082, Baldwin to Leslie, 23 June 1851, 304, 1678, List of new Coms. Of Trustees for Carleton Grammar Schools, "Recommended, Robt. Baldwin 15 Augt.50," 305, 1703, Baldwin to Leslie, 20 Sept 1850. LAC, MG24 B2, Papiers Papineau, 4, Papineau to John Friel, 13 June 1861, 6073–4.

3. Doughty, *Elgin-Grey*, I, Elgin to Grey, 4 January 1849, 279; ibid., IV, 1431–4.

4. J.H. Aitchison, "The Municipal Corporation Act of 1849," *Canadian Historical Review* XXX, 2 (1949), 107–22. C.F.J. Whebell, "Robert Baldwin and Decentralization, 1841–9," in *Aspects of Nineteenth-Century Ontario*, 60–2. TRL, Martin Donald Macleod Letterbooks, Macleod to [Baldwin], 24 January 1850. LAC, RG13 B1/797, Justice, Attorney General, Canada West, Official and Semi-Official Correspondence, 1849.

5. *Debates*, IX/2, 1277–93. Spelling in the original.

6. Hodgins, *Documentary History*, VII, 230–9. LAC, RG7 G14, King's College, 59, Minutes of the proceedings of the Council of King's College, 18 March 1848.

7. *Debates*, VIII/2, 1685. Doughty, *Elgin-Grey*, II, Elgin to Grey, 25 October 1850, 726–8. John Moir, "Methodism and Higher Education, 1843–1849: A Qualification," *Ontario History* XLIV, 3 (1953), 126. Hodgins, *Documentary History*, VIII, 125. Beavan is quoted in Curtis Fahey, *In His Name: The Anglican Experience in Upper Canada, 1791–1954* (Montreal and Kingston: McGill-Queen's University Press, 1991), 185. The text of the bill can be found in Hodgins, *Documentary History*, VIII, 147–66.

8. Hodgins, *Documentary History*, IX, 53, 146–7, 152–3. Doughty, *Elgin-Grey*, II, Elgin to Grey, 25 October 1850, 727.

9. Hodgins, *Documentary History*, VIII, 69–74. Peter N. Ross, "The Free School Controversy in Toronto, 1848–1852," in *Education and Social Change: Themes from Ontario's Past*, eds. Michael B. Katz and Paul H. Mattingley (New York: New York University Press, 1975), 57–80. *DCB*, X, Margaret Coleman, "Malcolm Cameron," 124–9.

10. *Debates*, VIII/3, 1872, 2460, 2479. Hodgins, *Documentary History*, VIII, 167–85. AO, Hodgins, John George, Papers, An Act for the better establishment and maintenance of Public Schools in Upper Canada. Dent, *Last Forty Years*, II, 424–7. Ryerson, *Story of My Life*, 370–1. Hodgins, *Documentary History*, VIII, Ryerson to Baldwin, 232–43.

11. LAC, RG13 B1/797, Department of Justice, Attorney General, Canada West, Official and Semi-official Correspondence, 1850, John G. Buchanan to Baldwin, 4 February 1850. RBP, I, A77/15, David Willson to Baldwin, 18 May 1849. LAC, RG7 G20, Governor General's Office, Civil Secretary's Correspondence, 48, Cameron to Lord Elgin, 1 December 1849, 5209. Coleman, "Malcolm Cameron," 125. PL, Joseph Cauchon to LaFontaine, 2 December 1849, 569. *Debates*, IX/1, 103–4. MLC, James Lesslie to Mackenzie, 23 January 1850, 7353–6. RBP, I, A58/94, Hannibal Mulkins to Baldwin, 18 February 1850. PL, Lewis Drummond to LaFontaine, 8 December 1849, 572.

12. *Debates*, VIII/3,2345–93. LAC, RG7 G20, Civil Secretary, 48, L.-M. Viger to Lord Elgin, 24 October 1849, 5252, R.-É. Caron to Lord Elgin, 20 December 1849, 5274. PL, Joseph Cauchon to LaFontaine, 24 October 1849, 550. Elgin described the tense negotiations in the cabinet: Doughty, *Elgin-Grey*, II, Elgin to Grey, 27 August 1849, 452–4, Elgin to Grey, 3 September 1849, 463–6.

13. Dent, *Last Forty Years*, II, 183. LAC, MG24 B158, Joseph-Amable Berthelot, LaFontaine to Berthelot, 16 November 1849, 67–70. RBP, III, R. Baldwin to Lawrence Heyden, 1835–1848, Baldwin to Heyden, 5 September 1849, 18. Peter Way, "The Canadian Tory Rebellion of 1849 and the Demise of Street Politics in Toronto," *British Journal of Canadian Studies* 10/1 (1995), 23–4.

14. *Examiner*, 10 January 1849. Sullivan reported on the uproar in Toronto over the matter: RBP, I, A73/77, Sullivan to Baldwin, 18 January 1849.

15. MLC, Lesslie to Mackenzie, 15 November 1849.

16. RBP, I, A32/1, anonymous to Baldwin, 15 August 1849; A35/22, Boulton to Baldwin, 2 January 1850; A35/23, Boulton to Baldwin, 21 January 1850; A58/78, Morley to Baldwin, 14 April 1849. TRL, Petitions Presented to Robert Baldwin Protesting the new Medical Bill, 1850. *Debates*, X/2, 937–9, 1653.

17. LAC, MG24 B40, I, George Brown, Hincks to Brown, 13 February 1849, 32. RBP, I, A51/74, Hincks to Baldwin, 21 November 1849. LAC, MG24 B11, William Warren and Robert Baldwin, Ross–Baldwin, John Ross to Hincks, 6 December 1849, Hincks to Ross, 7 December 1849, Ross to Hincks, 13 December 1849. PL, Cauchon to LaFontaine, 9 December 1849, 573.

18. *DCB*, VIII, H.E. Turner, "Peter Perry," 694–9. Geo. M. Jones, "The Peter Perry Election and the Rise of the Clear Grit Party," Ontario Historical Society *Papers and Records*, XII (1914), 164–75. Doughty, *Elgin-Grey*, II, Baldwin to Perry, 4 October 1849, 520–1. RBP, I, A51/71, Hincks to Baldwin, 22 October 1849.

19. *Examiner*, 12 December 1849, 19 December 1849. AO, Ms.516, William Lyon Mackenzie Correspondence, 10, James A. Davidson to Mackenzie, 21 December 1849; ibid., James Lesslie to Mackenzie, 30 January 1850.

20. Careless, *Brown of the Globe*, 112–13. Charles Clarke, *Sixty Years in Upper Canada* (Toronto: Briggs, 1908), 78–9.

21. Careless, *Brown of the Globe*, I, 109.

22. Ibid., 108–9. Kenneth Dewar, "Charles Clarke's '*Reformator*': Early Victorian Radicalism in Upper Canada," *Ontario History* LXXVIII/3 (1986), 233–52. For an interpretation of the development of liberalism see Ian McKay, "The Liberal Order Framework: A Prospectus for a Reconnaissance of Canadian History," *Canadian Historical Review* 81/4 (December 2000), 617–45.

23. *Examiner*, 20 March 1850.

24. RBP, I, A68/83, John Ross to Baldwin, 28 January 1850. MLC, James Lesslie to Mackenzie, 23 January 1850, 7354. LAC, MG24 B158, Joseph-Amable Berthelot, LaFontaine to Berthelot, 6 March 1850, 124–9. PL, W.N. to LaFontaine, 26 February 1850, 602.

25. John Charles Dent, *The Story of the Upper Canadian Rebellion* (Toronto: C.B. Robinson, 1885), I, 220, 267–8. Dent's account of the rebellion, and the politics leading to it, remains the most compelling study of the time, since he was able to consult many of the actors in the events. It is marred, however, by his attempts to make a hero out of John Rolph and villain out of Mackenzie.

26. A. Gérin-Lajoie, *Dix ans au Canada, de 1840 à 1850: Histoire de l'établissement du gouvernement responsable* (Quebec: Typ. de L.J. Demers & frère, 1891), 46. Dent, *Story of the Rebellion*, 296–7. On the Executive Council: CIHM/ICMH, Microfiche Series, 07973, Hon. Robert Baldwin's Letter Read by Mr. Perry on Thursday last, in the House of Assembly, March 16, 1836; Sir Francis Bond Head, *A Narrative* (London: John Murray, 1839), 53–68.

27. Baldwin, *Baldwins and the Great Experiment*, 149 and 150, quoting P. Baldwin to Robert Baldwin, 2 September 1836.

28. Dent, *Story of the Rebellion*, II, 60–1, 63–75. William Lyon Mackenzie, "Head's Flag of Truce, Or a defence of the memory of the late Colonel Samuel Lount," *Mackenzie's Weekly Message Extra* (1852).

29. On the trials: Dent, *Story of the Rebellion*, II, 250–2; Paul Romney and Barry Wright, "The Toronto Treason Trials, March–May 1838," in *Canadian State Trials*, II, *Rebellion and Invasion in the Canadas, 1837–1839*, eds. F. Murray Greenwood and Barry Wright (Toronto: University of Toronto Press, 2002), 72–83; *British Colonist*, Toronto, 5 April 1838.

30. Governor General Elgin reported on the demonstrations in Doughty, *Elgin-Grey*, I, Elgin to Grey, 10 May 1848, 163–4, Elgin to Grey, 18 May 1848, 166–76 and on continuing threats, Elgin to Grey, 4 January 1849, 280–1, Elgin to Grey, 16 July 1849. Warnings from the military are in LAC, RG8, British Military Records, C317, Col. Spark to Col. Pritchard, 12 April 1848, General Benjamin D'Urbain to Captain Thomas Jones, 8 January 1849. Panicky civilian reports include that of a "Toronto lawyer" in Elgin's report to Grey of 16 July 1849 and LAC, MG24 B76, William Matheson 1848, Rhoda Ann Rose to "Dear Uncle," 7 December 1848.

31. RBP, I, A61/66, A.A. McLauchlin to Baldwin, 8 April 1850; A72/41, James Smith to Baldwin, 20 June 1849. LAC, RG1 E1, Canada, Executive Council, Canada State Book J, 10 September 1849, 385, offering £25 reward for a cattle maimer. LAC, RG7 G14, 48, Inspector General, Public Business conducted by the Honourable Robert Baldwin Atty Genl for Upper Canada as Counsel for the Crown at the Sittings of Oyer & Terminer and General Gaol Delivery for the County of York . . . Monday 13 to Wednesday 29 October 1851.

32. LAC, British Military Records, C318, petition of the Inhabitants of the City of Hamilton, 12 February 1851, 190–6. Report of a Committee of the Executive Council, 17 February 1851, 188–9. John R. Holden, Mayor of Hamilton, to Hon. J. Leslie, 12 April 1851, 221–3, Major General Gore to Lieutenant Colonel D'Urbain, 6 May 1851, 215–35, Holden to Leslie, 21 June 1851, 243–4.

33. The warnings are found in LAC, State Book J, 19 November 1849, 491. The dispatch of troops: LAC, RG7 G20, Civil Secretary, 48, 5248, George Talbot to R. Bruce, 28 November 1849. The executive council lecture: State Book J, 11 January 1850,

590–1. The settlement of the cases: LAC, RG7 G14, Inspector General, Public Business conducted by the Honourable Robert Baldwin . . . October 1851.

34. On sailors: Province of Canada, *Journals*, 1849, Appendix RRRR; *Debates*, VIII/3, 2462–4. The school revolt has had diverse interpretations: Wendie Nelson, "'Rage Against the Dying of the Light': Interpreting the Guerre des Éteignoirs," *Canadian Historical Review* LXXXI, 4 (December 2000), 551–81; Cross, "'The laws are like cobwebs.'" The documentation on the crisis is large and found in such sources as the PL, LAC, RG7 G14, Governor General's Correspondence, 19, LAC, RG1 E1, Canada, Executive Council, Minute Books, and LAC, RG4 B61, Provincial Secretary, Canada East, St. Grégoire Riot Papers, 1850–51.

35. *Globe*, 2 October 1849.

36. BFP, Box 3, Bonnet Box Letters; Eliza Baldwin to Eliza MacDougall, 3 November 1850.

Chapter 17

1. LAC, MG24 B11, William Warren and Robert Baldwin, Baldwin-Ross Papers, Robert to Eliza, 16 August 1827.

2. *Globe*, Toronto, 16, 21, 30 May 1850.

3. Ibid., 16 May 1850.

4. Ibid., 9 May, 8 June 1850.

5. *Debates*, IX/1, 51–2, 87, 124–32, 262.

6. LAC, MG24 B158, Joseph-Amable Berthelot, LaFontaine to Berthelot, 15 April 1850, 143–4.

7. *Globe*, 9, 23 May 1850. *Debates*, IX/1, 616–20. *DCB*, XI, Lillian F. Gates, "James Hervey Price," 712–4.

8. This account of the speech has been compiled from *Debates*, IX/1, 658–62, and the *Globe*, 20 June 1850.

9. *Debates*, IX/1, 668, 733.

10. *Debates*, IX/1, 684–88. Doughty, *Elgin-Grey*, II, Elgin to Grey, 28 June 1850, 689. *Globe*, 22 June 1850.

11. *Globe*, 20 February 1851.

12. On "papal aggression" and Brown's anti-Catholic campaign: Careless, *Brown of the Globe*, 125–8. LAC, Joseph-Amable Berthelot, LaFontaine to Berthelot, 3 January 1851, 276–7.

13. MLC, James Lesslie to William Lyon Mackenzie, 23 January 1850, 7355. LAC, RG5, Civil Secretary, Canada West, C1, 292, Baldwin to James Leslie, Leslie to Blake, 8 May 1850. *Globe*, 23 May 1850. James Leslie was provincial secretary in the LaFontaine–Baldwin ministry.

14. TRL, William Warren Baldwin Papers, B102, William B. McVity to Robert Baldwin, 26 December 1850.

15. *Debates*, IX/1, 9, 351–5.

16. Ibid., IX/2, 1450–3, 1515–6, 1545–76.

17. Ibid., IX/1, 291–2; IX/2, 1578.

18. CIHM/ICMH Microfiche Series, 40810, Printed Ephemera and Broadsides from the Metropolitan Toronto Library, Robert Baldwin, *To the Free and Independent Electors of the County of York* (1828).

19. The best source on Upper Canadian politicians before the Union is J.K. Johnson, *Becoming Prominent: Regional Leadership in Upper Canada, 1791–1841* (Montreal and Kingston: McGill-Queen's University Press, 1989).

20. There is no source comparable to Johnson for the Union period. There are accurate lists of members in Paul G. Cornell, *The Alignment of Political Groups in Canada, 1841–1867* (Toronto: University of Toronto Press, 1962). Biographies of many House members are found in the *DCB*, VIII–XI. Wikipedia has entries on some.

21. RBP, I, A87/5, Baldwin to Lord Elgin, 10 April 1850. *Globe*, 20 July 1850.

22. Ibid., 20 July 1850.

23. Ibid., 23 March 1850. *Debates*, IX/1, 20 June 1850, 700.

24. RBP, I, A51/25, Hincks to Baldwin, 15 June 1851. *Debates*, VIII/2, 1319–20. *Journals*, 1849, App.A, 1852–3, App.B.

25. *Debates*, VI, 578; VIII/3, 1823, 1902; IX/1, 509–18.

26. Ibid., VI, 361–2, 364–5; VIII/1, 618. On the law of dower: Draper, *A Handy-Book of the Law of Dower*, and Malcolm Graeme Cameron, *A Treatise on the Law of Dower* (Toronto: Carswell & Co., 1882).

27. *Debates*, IV/2, 1237, in a debate on primogeniture. In 1822 William Warren Baldwin had bitterly opposed an attempt by Reformers to abolish primogeniture: Wilson, *Life of Robert Baldwin*, 9. *Debates*, IV/2, 1225–39.

28. Ibid., VI, 65.

29. LAC, MG24 B68, Sir Francis Hincks, Hincks to MacNab, 8 June 1849. LAC, MG24 D16, Buchanan Papers, 31, Robert W. Harris to Hincks, 4 August 1849, 25776–8. RBP, I, unbound, File 4, Hincks to Baldwin, 24 April 1849. LAC, MG24 A16, Elgin Papers, 4A, private official correspondence with Canadian officials, Hincks to LaFontaine, 30 April 1851, Baldwin to LaFontaine, 2 May 1851.

30. TRL, Petitions presented to Robert Baldwin protesting the new medical bill, petition of residents of the Fourth Riding of York, 25 July 1850. RBP, I, A58/78, F.B. Morley to Baldwin, 14 April 1849. *Debates*, VII/1, petition from John H. Assens and 2000 others, 22 February 1849, 875; VIII/2, 1558–9; X/2, 1651–3. *British Colonist*, Toronto, 2 September 1851.

31. *Debates*, IX/1, 325. MLC, J. Reed to Mackenzie, 20 May 1851

32. G.W.F. Hegel, *Philosophy of Mind*, trans. by William Wallace and A.V. Miller (Oxford: Oxford University Press, 1971), 263, quoted in David McGregor, *Hegel, Marx, and the English State* (Toronto: University of Toronto Press, 1996), 12.

33. The *Globe* provided coverage of the election every day in lively, if biased, fashion. There are accounts of the by-election in John Young, *Public Men and Public Life in Canada* (Toronto: s.n., 1882), 52, and Careless, *Brown of the Globe*, I, 129–32.

34. Francisco Panizza. ed., *Populism and the Mirror of Democracy* (New York: Verso, 2005), especially Panizza, "Introduction," 5–13, and Benjamin Ardit, "Populism as an Internal Periphery of Democratic Politics," 76.

35. The phenomenon of institutionalized populist movements is discussed by Ernesto Lacau in his essay, "Populism: What's in a Name?" in Panizza, *Populism*, 46.

36. *Globe*, 6 July 1859. *Debates*, IX/2, 1620–22.

37. *North American*, 8 November 1850. *Examiner*, 26 June 1850. Letter by Peter Perry to the *Globe*, 14 November 1850. The most recent study of the Clear Grits overemphasizes the middle class element of the movement: Michael E. Vance and Mark D. Stephen, "Grits, Rebels and Radicals: Anti-Privilege Politics and the Pre-History of 1849" in Canada West," in *Canada 1849*, eds. Derek Pollard and Ged Martin (Edinburgh: University of Edinburgh, Centre of Canadian Studies, 2001), 181–208.

38. *Debates*, IX/1, 365–6, 370–1, 372–3, 376.

39. Jeffrey L. McNairn, "Publius of the North: Tory Republicanism and the American Constitution in Upper Canada, 1848–54," *Canadian Historical Review* 77/4 (December 1996), 504–37. McNairn cites the *Independent* of 25 October and 12 December 1849 at 519.

40. Eric Bédard, the most recent chronicler of Lower Canadian Reform, and the earlier historian, Jacques Monet, differ on the relative centrality of religion. Bédard sees Catholicism primarily as an aspect of French-Canadian nationalism, while Monet argued that an ultramontane version of the religion had eclipsed other political concerns: Bédard, *Les Réformistes*, 214–25; Jacques Monet, "French-Canadian Nationalism and the Challenge of Ultramontanism," *Historical Papers* (1966), 41–55.

41. Dent, *Last Forty Years*, I, 95–6. Bédard, *Les Réformistes*, 305, 93.

42. Bédard, *Les Réformistes*, 98, 133–4. *Globe*, 11 July 1850.

43. Donald Cuccioletta, "The Montreal Annexation Manifesto of 1849: An Appeal for Liberal Democracy in the Canadas and the Rise of French Canadian Liberalism," in *Canada 1849*, 75. Bédard, *Les Réformistes*, 106, 163. *Globe*, 17 December 1850. *Debates*, X/1, 678–9.

44. LAC, Berthelot, LaFontaine to Berthelot, 23 December 1850, 269.

45. RBP, I, A80/40, Eliza Baldwin to Robert Baldwin, 29 May 1847; A65/1, Robert Ramsay to Baldwin, 5 July 1849; A65/3, Ramsay to Baldwin, 14 December 1849. Baldwin, *Baldwins and the Great Experiment*, 213–4.

46. BFP, Box 1, Glasgow, Robert to Eliza, 30 December 1850. Baldwin, *Baldwins and the Great Experiment*, 242–3.

47. Ibid., 243. John Charles Dent, *The Canadian Portrait Gallery* (Toronto: J.B. Magurn, 1880), I, 45.

48. D.C. Masters, *The Rise of Toronto, 1850–1890* (Toronto: University of Toronto Press, 1947), 11. Eric Arthur, *Toronto, No Mean City* (Toronto: University of Toronto Press, 1986), 84–5, 117–24.

49. John Ross Robertson., *Old Toronto: A Selection of Excerpts from Landmarks of Toronto*, ed. E.C. Kyte (Toronto: Macmillan, 1954), 64. Masters, *Rise of Toronto*, 33, quoting Broomhall Scotland, Elgin, Private Papers, Elgin to Cumming Bruce, 12 July 1850.

50. RBP, I, A48/71, Gurnett to Baldwin, 30 August 1850.

51. BFP, Box 1, Memories of My Youth . . . Mary J. Jones, 17 October 1925, 19–21 (copy). Ibid., Box 3, Maria to John Ross, 21 March 1853, copy.

52. *DCB*, X, Paul Cornell, "John Ross," 631–3. Ross-Baldwin, Ross to Baldwin, 14 November 1850; Baldwin to Ross, 18 November 1850. LAC, MG24 B11, William Warren Baldwin and Robert Baldwin, Baldwin-Ross Papers, clipping from the *Long Point Advocate & Norfolk County Advertiser*, 20 October 1851.

53. BFP, Box 1, Memories of My Youth . . . , 22. LAC, Baldwin-Ross, Draft notice of wedding announcement, Robert Baldwin, 4 February 1851. *Examiner*, Toronto, 5 February 1851. TRL, Robert Baldwin, Twenty Letters to John Ross, 27 February 1851, 2–2 (a).

Chapter 18

1. There are many descriptions of the scene, including: *Debates*, X/1, 603–7; *British Colonist*, Toronto, 1 July 1851; *Examiner*, Toronto, 2 July 1851. A politician's perspective is found in Archives nationale du Québec, Taché, famille, Article 1, Correspondence, Ser. É.-P. Taché, 1848–1865, A15, Taché to Ma chère Adéle, 1 July 1851. The same letter is found in: AO, National Archives of Quebec Collection, Taché Family Papers, K-1. I have relied on Baldwin's own draft of the resignation speech, which he included in a letter to his son-in-law: TRL, Robert Baldwin, Twenty Letters to John Ross, 28 June 1851.

2. The best representation of Baldwin's demeanour is from Taché's letter cited above. A less sympathetic Lower Canadian view was that of Louis-Joseph Papineau: LAC, MG24 B2, Papiers Papineau, 3, Papineau to Madame Papineau, 30 June 1851, 4647–50.

3. *Debates*, X/1, 607–15.

4. LAC, MG24 B11, William Warren and Robert Baldwin, Baldwin-Ross Papers, Robert to Eliza, 2 June 1825. The spelling and other errors are in the original.

5. On the Merritt resignation: *Globe*, Toronto, 24 December 1850; LAC, MG24 E1, Merritt Family Papers, 28, Speech of the Hon. Wm. Hamilton Merritt, explaining the grounds of his resignation, 5113. On prosecutions: *Examiner*, Toronto, 29 January 1851; LAC, RG13, B1, Department of Justice, Attorney General, Canada West, 797, Official and Semi-Official Correspondence, 1851, Baldwin to Clark Gamble, 3 February 1851.

6. *Globe*, 25 February 1851.

7. On the dispute with Hincks, see Chapter 14 and LAC, MG24 A16, Elgin Papers, R.398, 4A, Private Official Correspondence with Canadian Officials, Hincks to L.-H. LaFontaine, 30 April 1851; Baldwin to LaFontaine, 2 May 1851. The negotiations around the Quebec-Halifax line are discussed in: *Debates*, X/2, Appendix AAA, 1307–11. RBP, III, R. Baldwin to L. Heyden, 1835–1848 [sic.], 21; Baldwin to Heyden, 4 April 1851.

8. On the reserves: LAC, RG1 G1, Governor General's Office, Despatches from the Colonial Office, 126/551, Grey to Elgin, 27 January 1851, and the publication of the dispatch, *Globe*, 8 March 1851. On the post office: John Willis, "The Canadian Colonial Posts: Epistolary Continuity, Postal Transformation," in *Canada 1849*, 247, and Louis-P. Turcotte, *Le Canada sous l'union*, deuxième partie, 1857–53 (Quebec: Des presses mécaniques du Canadien, 1882), 144–5.

9. There is a good discussion of the cabinet changes of 1851 in Dent, *Last Forty Years*, II, 493. *Examiner*, 5 March 1851.

10. Wilson, *Life of Robert Baldwin*, 280–1. RBP, II, Acts of the Province of Canada, Fourth Session, Third Parliament, 1851.

11. TRL, Robert Baldwin, Twenty Letters to John Ross, Baldwin to Mrs. John Ross, 17 April 1854, 13. On Robert's illness: RBP, I, 53/47, Abner Hurd to Baldwin, 10 May 1851; Robert Nelson to LaFontaine, 17 May 1851, quoted in Wilson, *Life of Robert Baldwin*, 281; Baldwin, *Baldwins and the Great Experiment*, 226.

12. *Globe*, 24 December 1850.

13. *Debates*, X/1, 493–509.

14. Ibid., 547–50.

15. Ibid., 641–53.

16. The quote about the law aristocracy is from Dr. James Grant to Mackenzie, in MLC, 10 May 1851. There is a discussion of Mackenzie's proposed legal reforms in Gates, *After the Rebellion*, 181–2. *Debates*, X/1, 308. *Globe*, 12 June 1851.

17. *Debates*, X/1, 562.

18. Ibid., 564–6.

19. Ibid., 569–70.

20. *Globe*, 5 June, 21 June 1851.

21. Doughty, *Elgin-Grey*, II, Elgin to Grey, 28 June 1851, 833.

22. *Globe*, 1 July 1851.

23. MLC, Benjamin Davies to Mackenzie, 1 July 1851, quoted in Gates, *After the Rebellion*, 188. *Examiner*, 9 July 1851. LAC, Papiers Papineau, 3, Papineau to Madame Papineau, 30 June 1851, 4648.

24. TRL, Robert Baldwin, Twenty Letters to John Ross, 28 June 1851.

25. TRL, Thomas Strahan Shenston Papers, Hincks to T.S. Shenston, 7 July 1851. RBP, I, A64/98, J. Radenhurst to Baldwin, 9 July 1851. LAC, MG24 A16, Elgin Papers, R.397, 3, Private Letters from the Colonial Secretary, Grey to Elgin, 1 August 1851. Doughty, *Elgin-Grey*, II, Elgin to Grey, 22 August 1851, 891.

26. PL, testimonial to L.H. LaFontaine, J.H. Price et al., August 1851, 707. AO, Colonel Charles Clarke Papers, W. McDougall to Clarke, 26 July 1851. RBP, I, A55/56, LaFontaine to Baldwin, 6 November 1851.

27. TRL, Robert Baldwin, Twenty Letters to John Ross, 20 September 1851. RBP, I, A68/96, John Ross to Baldwin, 7 September 1851. *North American*, Toronto, 4 November 1851.

28. RBP, I, A58/30, William Miller and Henry Rose to Baldwin, 12 August 1851; A74/105, Joseph Rich to Baldwin, 18 August 1851; A61/74, Arthur McMaster to Baldwin, 23 October 1851; A75/88, John B. Warren to Baldwin, 24 November 1851. *North American*, 11 November 1851. RBP, I, A50/111, Lawrence Heyden to Baldwin, 14 December 1851. On Mackenzie's influence: MLC, J.S. Macdonald to Mackenzie, 9 February 1852, 8454–5.

29. *North American*, 26 December 1851.

30. RBP, IV, John Ross to Baldwin, 20 December 1851.

31. RBP, II, LaFontaine to Baldwin, 22 December 1851.

Chapter 19

1. *Globe*, Toronto, 1, 29 January 1852.

2. Thompson, *Spadina*, 95.

3. RBP, II, References of Press to myself, my positions Conduct and opinions, 1851 & 2. TRL, Robert Baldwin, Cash & Day Book, 6A, Spadina, 1 January 1856–27 November 1858. RBP, II, LaFontaine to Baldwin, 2 March 1852. LAC, MG24 B11, William Warren and Robert Baldwin, Ross-Baldwin, Eliza Ross to Baldwin, 4 February 1852.

4. RBP, John Ross Correspondence, Eliza to John Ross, 7 July 1855.

5. On the law office: James Cleland Hamilton, *Osgoode Hall: Reminiscences of the Bench and the Bar* (Toronto: Carswell, 1904), 148–9. On Trinity: AO, MS 525, John Simcoe Macaulay Papers, 1835–1857, John Strachan to Colonel John Simcoe Macaulay, 19 November 1851; William Westfall, *The Founding Moment: Church, Society, and the Construction of Trinity College* (Montreal and Kingston: McGill-Queen's University Press, 2002), esp. Ch.2.

6. Hodgins, *Documentary History*, X, 229. RBP, II, Baldwin to Professor Henry Croft, 30 November 1852, Baldwin to Professor Croft and the gentlemen of the Committee of Convocation of the University of Toronto, 8 December 1852. The university debate in 1852–1853 is discussed in Moir, *Church and State in Canada West*, 82–115.

7. Hodgins, *Documentary History*, XI, 137–43. TRL, Robert Baldwin, Twenty Letters to John Ross, Baldwin to Ross, 18 January 1855.

8. LAC, MG24 C42, Moore A. Higgins, Baldwin to Higgins, 18 November 1855. TRL, Robert Baldwin, Twenty Letters to John Ross, 18 January 1855.

9. G.P. de T. Glazebrook, *The Story of Toronto* (Toronto: University of Toronto Press, 1971), 123. PL, 748, W.B. Richards to Baldwin, 23 April 1853, Baldwin to Richards, 30 April 1853. TRL, Robert Baldwin, Twenty Letters to John Ross, 15 February 1854. Thompson, *Spadina*, 95. TRL, Robert Baldwin, Twenty Letters to John Ross, 17 August 1854.

10. TRL, Robert Baldwin, Twenty Letters to John Ross, 21 December 1853, 15 February 1854. W.R. Brown, *Brown's Toronto General Directory* (Toronto: printed and published for W.R. Brown by Maclear, 1856), xlvi. Thompson, *Spadina*, 96. There is a discussion of Jenny Lind in Toronto, and the Orphans' Home, in Frank N. Walker, *Sketches of Old Toronto* (Don Mills: Longmans, 1965), 323–41. BFP, Box 1, Invoice, Cathedral Church of St. James, Toronto, 18 June 1852; receipt, T.D. Harris, St. James Church, 7 November 1852.

11. AO, John Rolph Papers, A-9, Lesslie to Rolph, 1 January 1852. *Globe*, 26 February 1852. AO, John Rolph Papers, A-1, Workman to Rolph, 1 March 1852.

12. AO, Andrew Norton Buell Papers, John O'Hare to Buell, 7 March 1853. RBP, I, A78/20, John Wilson to Baldwin, 28 July 1854. There is a good analysis of the situation in 1854 in

New York Daily Times, 12 July 1854. W.A. Langton, *Early Days in Upper Canada: Letters of John Langton from the Backwoods of Upper Canada* (Toronto: Macmillan, 1926), John Langton to William Langton, 17 April 1856, 256–7.

13. TRL, Twenty Letters to John Ross, 29 September, 2 November 1853, as examples of patronage requests. LAC, MG24 A16, Elgin Papers, R.398, 4A, Private Official Correspondence with Canadian Officials, Baldwin to Lord Elgin, 13 July 1854. LAC, MG24 D16, Isaac Buchanan, 2, undated newspaper clipping quoting a letter from Baldwin to "a Reform friend," 1005.

14. W.H. Higgins, *The Life and Times of Joseph Gould* (Toronto: C.B. Robinson, 1887:1972), 286. LAC, MG24 B11, William Warren and Robert Baldwin, Ross-Baldwin, Fred Jones to Baldwin, 16 August 1858. TRL, RBP, II, Baldwin to S. Richardson Jr., 12 August 1858; Baldwin to My Dear Child, 25 August 1858; Baldwin to My Dear Sir, 3 September 1858; Abstract of Minutes of an adjourned Meeting of the General Committee for conducting the Election of the Hon. Robert Baldwin, 3 September 1858. *Daily Colonist*, Toronto, 4 September 1858.

15. RBP, John Ross Correspondence, Eliza to John Ross, 20 May, 10 June 1853. PL, 748, Baldwin to LaFontaine, 21 September 1853.

16. PL, 748, Baldwin to LaFontaine, 21 September 1853.

17. RBP, John Ross Correspondence, Eliza to John Ross, 14 October 1855.

18. Robertson, *Old Toronto*, 254–5, 298.

19. Lucy Booth Martyn, *Toronto: 100 Years of Grandeur* (Toronto: Pagurian Press, 1978), 33–7. LAC, MG24 B40, George Brown, Price to Brown, 28 December 1848, 29. RBP, A78/20, John Wilson to Baldwin, 28 July 1854.

20. LAC, MG24 B11, Baldwin, Baldwin Ross, Baldwin to Eliza, c/o J.J. Morgan, Bond St., New York, 4 June 1835, spelling and punctuation as in the original.

21. Private, Memorandum, Robert Baldwin and Elizabeth Baldwin, n.d., spelling and punctuation in the original.

22. The whole affair is laid out at length in *Appendix to the Journal of the House of Assembly of Upper Canada, 1836–1837*, II, Appendix 106. The quote is from Baldwin's resignation letter of 16 March 1836, 42.

23. Isaac Buchanan, *First Series of Five Letters, Against the Baldwin Faction, by an Advocate of Responsible Government and the New College Bill* (Toronto: s.n., 1844).

24. Doughty, *Elgin-Grey* , II, Elgin to Grey, 23 March 1850, 613. LAC, MG24 B2, Papiers Papineau, Papineau to Madame Papineau, 15 June 1854, 5132.

25. RBP, I, A51/25, Hincks to Baldwin, 15 June 1843. The literature on class and nineteenth-century capitalism is vast. For those, like this author, who are not inclined to heavy theorizing, there are some useful shortcuts to understand the class question. See: Peter Osborne, *How to Read Marx* (New York: W. W. Norton & Co., 2006), especially ch. 7, "Capitalism as Modernity"; and a brief and lucid discussion of social class on the blog *Lenin's Tomb,* http://www.leninology.blogspot.com/2011/03/class-and-capitalism-mentioning-c-words.html.

26. Private, Ross-Baldwin Family Papers, Robert Baldwin Correspondence, Baldwin to Eliza Ross, 3 November 1854, Eliza to Baldwin, 1 June 1854. The family homes are situated by Thompson, *Spadina*, 95–6.

27. Thompson, *Spadina*. Hamilton, *Osgoode Hall*, 65. BFP, Box 1, Mary Jones, "Memories of My Youth. High Court of Justice for Ontario," *Ontario Reports*, ed. James F. Smith (Toronto: Rowsell & Hutchison, 1889), XVI, 341–64.

28. Jonathan Fryer, *Robbie Ross* (London: Constable, 2000).

29. RBP, II, Baldwin to My Dear Child, 25 August 1858. LAC, Baldwin, Baldwin-Ross, John Ross to Eliza, 26 October 1858, 28 September 1858.

30. RBP, II, Memorandum, Robert Baldwin, n.d. The spacing has been adjusted for readability. Spelling in the original.

31. The revised will is at RBP, IV, 8. The troubles over the will are discussed in Private, Ross-Baldwin, Phoebe Maria Baldwin Correspondence, Maria to Lawrence Heyden, draft, n.d. See also: LAC, MG24 K2, George Coventry, transcripts, 13, Robert Baldwin, 39 and *Globe*, 10 December 1858.

32. St. Martin's Rood is described in AO, G.S. 5933, Old York County Deeds, 30, Memorial of C.J. Baldwin to the Registrar, 5 November 1842, instrument number 20336, and Thompson, *Spadina*, 82. *Globe*, 14 December 1858. *DCB*, XI, H.E. Turner, "Henry James Grasett," 367–9.

33. Willcock's note is attached to the memorandum in RBP, II.

Index